07 08 09 10 11 12

I MISS MY PENCIL

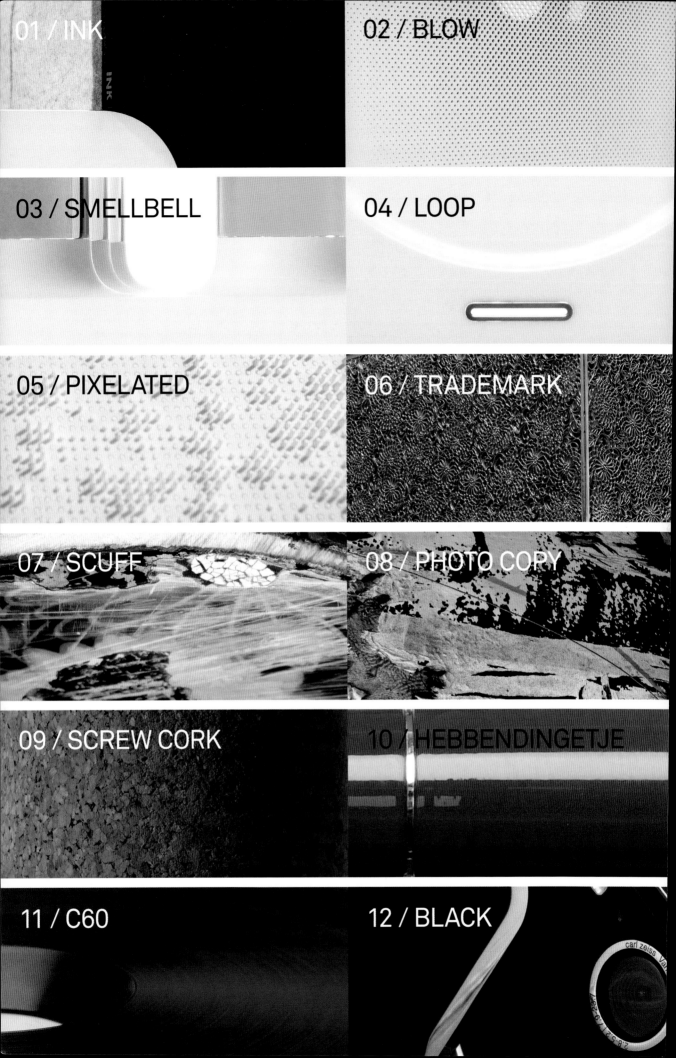

01 / INK

02 / BLOW

03 / SMELLBELL

04 / LOOP

05 / PIXELATED

06 / TRADEMARK

07 / SCUFF

08 / PHOTO COPY

09 / SCREW CORK

10 / HEBBENDINGETJE

11 / C60

12 / BLACK

MISS MY PENCIL

A design exploration

Martin Bone
Kara Johnson

CHRONICLE BOOKS

SAN FRANCISCO

Text copyright © 2009 by Martin Bone and Kara Johnson.
Images copyright © 2009 by IDEO, except where otherwise noted.
Image on page 106 copyright © Performance Structures.

Library of Congress Cataloging-in-Publication Data available.
ISBN: 978-0-8118-6075-8

Manufactured in China.

Designed by IDEO.

10 9 8 7 6 5 4 3 2 1

Chronicle Books LLC
680 Second Street
San Francisco, California 94107
www.chroniclebooks.com

INTRODUCTION

martin	kj
	Oops. My IM broke.
	I sent an image that was too big or something.
	Sorry...
	Are you there?
Are you there?	
You broke it.	
You killed it.	
:-o	
:-|	
:-(	
:-[	
This is what a person talking to himself in a chat room looks like . . .	

martini

Think about the first few minutes of your day. You wake up, turn off your alarm, perhaps turn on a light. You roll out of bed, lift the lid, or cop a squat on the loo. You tear off a few sheets of your preferred brand of TP. You pull back the shower curtain, turn on the faucet, set the temperature and step in. Even before the water hits you, you've touched a dozen or so designed and branded products. If your eyes were open you've seen countless others. And that was just the beginning. Imagine what the rest of your day holds: your newspaper, your hair pomade, your laptop, cell phone, and those socks on your feet.

This is the stuff that surrounds us, stuff that most people don't give a second thought to. Why should they? They see it every day. There are more important things to think about—family, work . . . life.

All this stuff represents thousands of hours, billions of dollars, tons of raw materials, and multiple global corporations, and somewhere in that mix sits the designer. The person who woke up that morning the same way you did, went to work, and decided that next season your sleeves would be two inches shorter, your phone would be pink metal and that coffee-shop experience you just had would be slightly different tomorrow.

That's me; that's what I do. Well, not the sleeve thing. But I am obsessed by those things that many people overlook, those meticulously, obsessively crafted objects that represent our personalities, memories and environments. Design can elevate and neutralize; it can shout and it can whisper.

And that brings us to what this book is about: an insight into the obsessive nature of designers. What inspires us to create, why we make certain decisions, and why going to a focus group is like attending a funeral.

Top 5 things I wish I'd done but I didn't:
1. Directed *Seven* or *Fight Club* or *Alien* or *Goodfellas*—oh, fuck, this list would be too long if I kept going.
2. Painted the Screaming Pope series—the paintings that made me want to go to art school.
3. Written and illustrated *Arkham Asylum*—it's Batman and it's beautiful.
4. Played James Bond—basically because I'm a bloke and I'm a Brit.
5. Played for England at Wembley.

kj:

I'm sitting on a plane from San Francisco to New York, and I just read a line from Cory Doctorow's book *Down and Out in the Magic Kingdom*: "Ten thousand years ago, the state of the art was a goat..." It makes me wonder what the state of the art is today. Is it really the iPhone or the next product that Apple decides to sell? Maybe it's automatic windshield wipers that know when it's raining, or lasagna noodles you don't have to pre-cook, or text messaging from a remote beach in Thailand.

As designers, our main point of influence is the products we create. But as our world moves quickly from analog to digital, from physical to virtual, what will be our legacy? What will we leave behind? (Which would you rather play: Wii tennis or "real" tennis?) I don't want us to let go of our love of artifacts or the experiences that accompany them, because products tell our stories.

Archaeologists understand human culture by digging in the dirt, looking for the artifacts, piecing together what was left behind. If archaeologists in the future examined our culture of products today, what would they say about us? What stories would these objects hold? What could they tell about us?

Like, what if they dug up my dented VW Golf? Could they know that I loved this car from the moment I bought it? The blue lights on the dashboard, the simple power of the wind-shield wipers and washer fluid, its overall cuteness when outfitted with a rack for my mountain bike and surfboard. I'll admit that I had a car-crush as soon as I drove it out of the dealer's parking lot. This past winter, however, its perfection was disrupted. I was in Tahoe for a snowboarding weekend, and my friend Farnell asked me to move my car into the garage. Although I was careful in my approach, I managed to hit a stealthy layer of ice and slide directly into a wall. My previously flawless car now registered a dent above the back rear wheel. But my love did not waver. In fact, perhaps surprisingly, it grew: I love my car even more now with this little dent, this thing that reminds me of Farnell.

For me, this book is about experimenting with those human connections to objects. I want to explore the connection and conflicts between people and materials, people and products, people and process. The artifacts we will create and leave behind are our story.

Top 5 reasons to be cheerful:
1. The ocean is always moving
2. Your friends usually laugh at your jokes (even if they aren't funny)
3. Everyone looks better in black and white photographs
4. A marathon is only 26.2 miles
5. The color cobalt blue

martin

When I was a young kid, maybe around six years old, my dad used to take my brother and me every now and again to the factory where he worked as a machine toolmaker. There he taught me that there is no substitute for sharp tools, that there is no reason to use emery cloth on a machined part, and when you face off a part it should be done in one clean pass. My dad was a craftsman. When he turned a piece of aluminum, the swarf would spiral off the machine in one long continuous ribbon. My brother and I used to carefully uncoil and straighten the swarf to see which was the longest, and then play gunfights with the air hoses.

When he came home from work, my father smelled of metal and coolant. He would wash up for dinner with great gobs of Swarfega, which had the vivid green look of liquid kryptonite and a unique smell (lemon zest, disinfectant, with a hint of gasoline). When we sat down to eat, I would look at the swarf that stuck to his hair. He looked like a human disco ball, only without the Bee Gees soundtrack.

The combination of all of these things—the smells, the machines, the shiny metal—I was hooked. In those moments, watching how something beautiful was carved from these lumps of raw material, I saw how design could transform the amorphous and manipulate its meaning. One moment, a block of steel, the next, a fork or a chair or a door handle.

Materials are both the connection to an object and a connection to history, and more importantly, the connection to personal memories. They also represent the common ground between Kara and me. She studies materials from the inside out, and I look at them from the outside in. As a material scientist, she understands their structure, and as a designer, I know how to explore their qualities and enhance their beauty.

So how do these first loves of material, form and manufacturing stay relevant in a profession now more focused with the latest freakonomic, longtailed, tipping pointed business strategy than the texture of stainless steel? I started as an industrial designer and now I find myself working as something that could be more appropriately termed a marketing designer. The balance has swung from trying to solve problems in manufacturing to finding new opportunities for business innovation. This often feels like trying to climb Everest in a pair of stilettos. Not the easiest of journeys for someone educated in sawing stuff. I find solace in thinking about broader connections, about different ways for companies to talk to consumers, weaving compelling stories that engage and provide context for our ideas. Products I used to create with a singular vision are now part of the larger brand vocabulary. Nowadays the hero is often the supporting cast. No more Stallones and Schwarzeneggers but many more *Ocean's 11s* and *Gosford Parks*.

This evolution has caused me to use my brain more, and my pencil less. The act of thinking is quickly replacing the act of doing. What this book represents is the desire to reconnect with that six-year-old me, to revisit those things that I'm passionate about, to look for the magic that happens when pencil touches paper.

But how do we talk about the intuitive and the abstract without sounding like a *tosser*? How do we demystify something that we as designers have spent decades trying to keep to ourselves? How do we peek behind the curtain to see what the wizard is doing? The only way we know how: by *doing* something, creating something tangible, playing around with some ideas, and trying a bunch of experiments. The only way to really learn about design is to do it.

I took away a lot from those early days with my dad: if you're going to do one thing, do it well; don't make it overly complex; just get it right. If you have beautiful material, let it speak for itself. The form should accentuate, not fight; the details should be natural and not forced. I learned that when the material is the story, the exercise is in keeping design out.

Top 5 people you shouldn't take aesthetic criticism from:
1. People with tassels on their shoes. Actually, anyone who can't pick good shoes. How do you know if you have the right shoes? Ask a designer.
2. People with MBAs.
3. Tenured professors or lecturers who haven't worked in the real world.
4. Any CEO—unless you're Steve Jobs.
5. Anyone who calls him- or herself a design critic.

kj

Materiality is about more than just materials. Materiality is how we begin to build connections to products and develop an awareness of their meanings. The stuff that things are made of is more important than we realize, and for designers this connection is a point of inspiration. Materials matter. And nowadays it seems that people are more aware of what the stuff is. Each of us knows something about materials that can be recycled, materials that enable a specific experience, materials that represent a particular brand. Materials are the ingredients. They are the starting point for product design.

We name periods in history by the materials that were available to us: iron, bronze, plastic, silicon, "green." These material technologies enable us to create new experiences. But there are some limitations. We expect things to be what we know them to be. A cork is made of cork, a glass is made of glass, an iron is made of iron—or it was. Each of these materials has inherent meaning. But the essential meaning of a material can be manipulated. Out of context, or in unexpected combination, materials can surprise us.

The materiality of fashion is evident on the runways and on the street. Last year Jack Spade and Louis Vuitton each introduced products inspired by the woven plastic bags commonly used by Chinese migrant workers living and working in the city. A simple sheet of woven red, white, and blue plastic can be cut and sewn in any shape, but the meaning

of the material changes when the designer introduces small variations in the details of the product. You can buy a plaid bag for one dollar or a hundred or a thousand. They are each derived from the same material, but they are very different objects and tell very different stories. For one dollar, it's a cheap plastic bag with a plastic zipper. For one hundred dollars, it's a well-constructed tote with thick handles and metal details from Jack Spade. For one thousand dollars, the surface is woven from thin strips of red, white, and blue leather and a Louis Vuitton logo is applied.

There is materiality in the movies, even though they have no physical form. In The *Usual Suspects*, the entire plot is based on how the main character observes and inter-

prets the objects he sees in the detective's office. In *Stranger than Fiction*, the hero's watch is trying to tell him something, but he's not listening.

And there is materiality in my living room. My grandfather's trunk (a military foot locker) is my coffee table. I never knew him (he died in WWII) and this was his trunk for carrying stuff around. I like the personal history of this trunk: it's a product with a story, a connection beyond just the thing itself. Advertising tries to attach stories to products before you even buy them, before you have that connection. But I want to find a way to let the objects we create tell their own story.

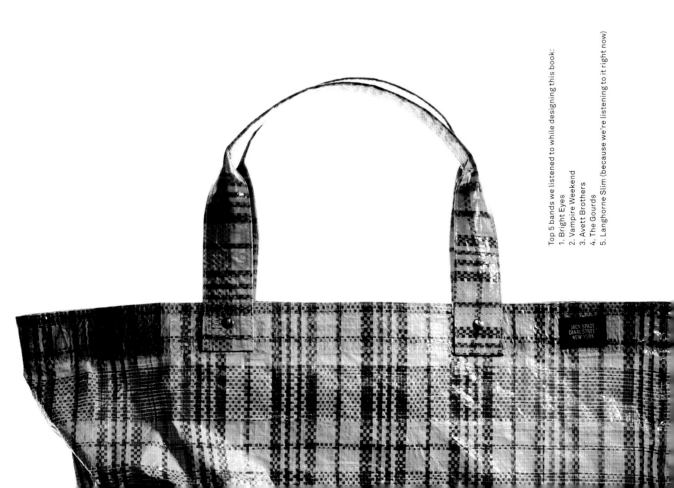

Top 5 bands we listened to while designing this book:
1. Bright Eyes
2. Vampire Weekend
3. Avett Brothers
4. The Gourds
5. Langhorne Slim (because we're listening to it right now)

martin

Designers need constant love and attention, kinda like puppies. We like people telling us what's good or bad. I like the bad but that's because I have an oddly perverse personality. Ultimately design is a dialogue. Without this kind of discussion and critique, it's impossible to see the value of an idea. The same goes for creating this book. It would not have happened without the major contributions of the following people:

Michael Chung—Industrial Designer. A master of CAD and camera, Michael contributed to the concepts, building and rebuilding design databases. Because I've known him for so long, our process consists of: me frantically waving my arms around, carving out imaginary forms in the air; Michael building them; me saying they're shit, then apologizing for gesturing the wrong shapes; and then repeating the whole thing again until we get it right.

Gregory Germe—Industrial Designer. Greg offered opinions on our concepts and generated a few of his own. With a flair for the visual, he was a key partner in the design discussions (if you could pry the headphones from his ears).

Ian Groulx—Graphic Designer. A cool bloke for two reasons: one, because he has an X in his name, and two, because designers make the worst clients. He's been patient and committed, providing layout after layout despite Kara and I never hitting a content deadline.

Sarah Lidgus—Writer. When I first met Sarah she was angry and I liked her instantly. We bonded over lesbian porn scripts, Adidas sneakers, and Joe 90 glasses. She helped us with the words, stopped me writing in tantrums, and was a deliciously brutal critic.

Andre Yousefi—Master Prototyper. No challenge is too great and seemingly nothing is impossible for Andre and the guys in the workshop. If it can be machined, etched, grown, or molded, Andre's the man. The weirder the idea, the happier he is. It's now my life's goal to design something he and the guys can't build.

Nicolas Zurcher—Photographer. Whether documenting a model being built or dunking a teddy bear in liquid latex, Nicolas captured the majority of the images in the book. At the time of writing this, we are trying to shoot a skateboard in a morgue. The more absurd the situation, the more inspired he is.

Michael Chung

Gregory Germe

Ian Groulx

Sarah Lidgus

Andre Yousefi

Nicolas Zurcher

This book is a risk. It's a series of experiments based on a few things that we've been thinking about over the last few years.

The process of design always includes experimentation. In the context of design, experimentation is about taking a small step into the unknown, building a tangible outcome, and telling the story. In this book, each experiment starts with a question or a statement—a twisted hypothesis. Design is about constraints, and these hypotheses serve as such. Constraints guide innovation. We aspire to the ideal, but trade-offs are what make things real.

Our experiments have been inspired by conversations between Martin and me, with our colleagues, our friends and family, and experts we know. The objects that we will create in this book are a reflection of the world we live in, what we see, the questions we ask, whom we talk to, and how we think. We intend to use these objects to tell a story about how things are today and how they might be in the future. And as we go, to share the process of design with others, illuminating our own particular brand of experimentation. In each experiment, the failures as well as the successes will be documented for the reader. Not in retrospect. In real time. Over the past two years, we have spent our days, nights, and weekends trying to create objects or explore ideas that we believe matter. This book is an expression of that process. At times, it's been frustrating. Other times, it's been fascinating.

As we've written this book, we have used almost every form of communication and documentation available to us: a blog, e-mail, stopping in the street outside the office, shouting across our desks, long-distance phone calls, dictated voice recordings, text messages, and IM. These conversations are important and we've used them to tell the story of our design process. Not everything we said was important, and it has been difficult for Martin and I to stay in touch, to stay connected, and to stay on schedule. I live in San Francisco, and Martin lives in New York. This made everything take a bit longer but led us to the best form of communication: instant messaging. We were able to chat at any time of the day about anything in particular in an unconstrained and comfortable context.

There are three chapters: Aisthetika, Punk Manufacturing, Love and Fetish. We will start with Aisthetika, an exploration of the senses.

Top 5 movies for foodies:
1. *Eat, Drink, Man, Woman*
2. *Tampopo*
3. *The Cook, The Thief, His Wife and Her Lover*
4. *Big Night*
5. *Like Water For Chocolate*

What does a
laptop taste like?

THIS IS THE CHAPTER ABOUT
AISTHE

kj

Aisthetika is the Greek word for "things that we perceive through the senses."

It's easy for designers to pay attention to visual details, but here we want to think about design a little bit differently. This means going back to the source and looking at how our perceptions are created. We aren't talking about how beautiful things can be— that's a totally different kind of aesthetics. We are interested in ideas that manipulate our aesthetic expectations, focus our attention on one sense or another, or explore unique combinations of the senses. We are interested in the idea that aisthetika is about more

than sight, sound, taste, smell, and touch. There are also senses that are a bit less specific—a sense of time, a sense of humor, a sense of style, a sense of balance, a sense of rhythm, etc.

In product design, taste is the sense that is most often forgotten. But that makes sense, right? We don't lick our laptops or our surfboards. However, even if it's indirect or improbable, taste matters. Taste is intimate; you can only taste with your tongue. Another forgotten sense is the sense of smell. Like taste, it is not used very often when we design products. Your sense of smell is

martin

I love Mark Morford. Well, his writing and subject matter at least, because I've never met him, although I'm sure he's a very lovable bloke. He's a columnist for the *SF Chronicle*, an astute political, social, and cultural observer. Occasionally, when presidents aren't doing something particularly stupid, he writes about brands and products. In a sea of dull, overly complicated, and difficult-to-understand commentaries on design, his are refreshingly delightful, funny, and, er, moist. After reading one of his articles you feel like you should light up a Lucky cigarette and grab a shower. It's product porn at its finest. What's the relevance? We actually used one of his articles as inspiration for this chapter:

"I have right here in my hot little hands that actually aren't all that little and are only slightly warm at the moment a brand new lick-ready smooth-as-love Apple MacBook Pro Core 2 Duo Super Orgasm Deluxe Ultrahard Modern Computing Device Designed by God Herself Somewhere in the Deep Moist Vulva of Cupertino Yes Yes Don't Stop Oh My God Yes . . . "

Morford talks about the sensual nature of products, the sometimes lusty, sexual connection we have with objects and the global, culture-shifting impact they can have. I only wish that I could design an object that would elicit the preceding paragraph; to provoke such a passionate, somewhat smutty review.

ГIKA

unfiltered; it's direct. It is probably the basis of most attraction. That's why perfume exists. Of course, the way things sound matters too. Should a car door sound like it is well-made? Most automotive manufacturers think so—or, at least, they should. Should a bag of potato chips sound crunchy, like the chips themselves? Maybe. How something looks and how something feels are more obvious elements of product design, but they are equally capable of surprising us.

One of the more interesting books I have read recently is called *The Man Who Tasted Shapes*.

This is a book about people who have a disorder called synesthesia. If anesthesia is about an absence of sense, synesthesia is about the combination of senses. For some people who have this disorder, when they eat chicken, they feel prickles on their skin. It's not imagined, it's an actual physical sensation. Most people can clearly separate taste and touch. This aspect of synesthesia makes the phrase "it tastes like chicken" mean something more like "ouch."

When our sensory attributes are isolated or crossed it's weird, and inspiring.

So how could we look at what we do in another way? Challenge our preconceived notions of the right way to start projects? Could we use sense perceptions to build stronger connections between people and objects? We know that people empathize with objects and relish experiences. How many times do you hear "I love my car" as a part of everyday conversation? The senses are the conduit through which these emotional connections are made. If we play around in this space for a while, maybe some fresh ideas will begin to surface. Instead of asking what should this product look like, can we ask what should it smell like? Feel like? Or even taste like? If we started there and let those questions influence the way

it looked, would we get something unconventional, something that is not self-referential? Why should a cell phone smell like plastic and electronics? It's as close to your nose as it is to your ear. What if Nokia's brand identity was the smell of freshly cut grass?

Top 5 comfort foods:
1. Artichokes (with lemon butter)
2. Mac 'n cheese
3. Fried egg and a cup of tea
4. Super veggie burritos
5. Really good cherry pie

martin

One of the great things about this job is the opportunity to collaborate with people you admire in professions that have no direct relation to your own. I've always enjoyed eating the chocolates created by Michael Recchiuti, a San Franciscan chocolatier. He balances and refines really interesting flavors. So when we needed to come up with a way to increase the sensory impact of an invitation for people to participate in a project to explore the senses, I thought of him. We gave him a call and he was interested, so a custom mold was made and batch of chocolates was cooked up. This edible invitation became our first step in reaching out to a broader group of designers.

kj

Our exploration of chocolate was one of the best things about this invitation. The idea of playing with chocolate to create various drug scenarios seemed to get people's attention. And the Recchiuti chocolates that spelled A-I-S-T-H-E-T-I-K-A-0-3 were tasty. It was easy to get people to eat the chocolates, but it was a little harder to get people motivated to design based on our hypothesis that the senses can inspire design (because we had no client and no deadline, just an idea). Publishing this book became our motivation. We started to explore the senses with an experiment based on the aesthetic qualities of a printer—a ubiquitous object that is often ignored. And rarely loved.

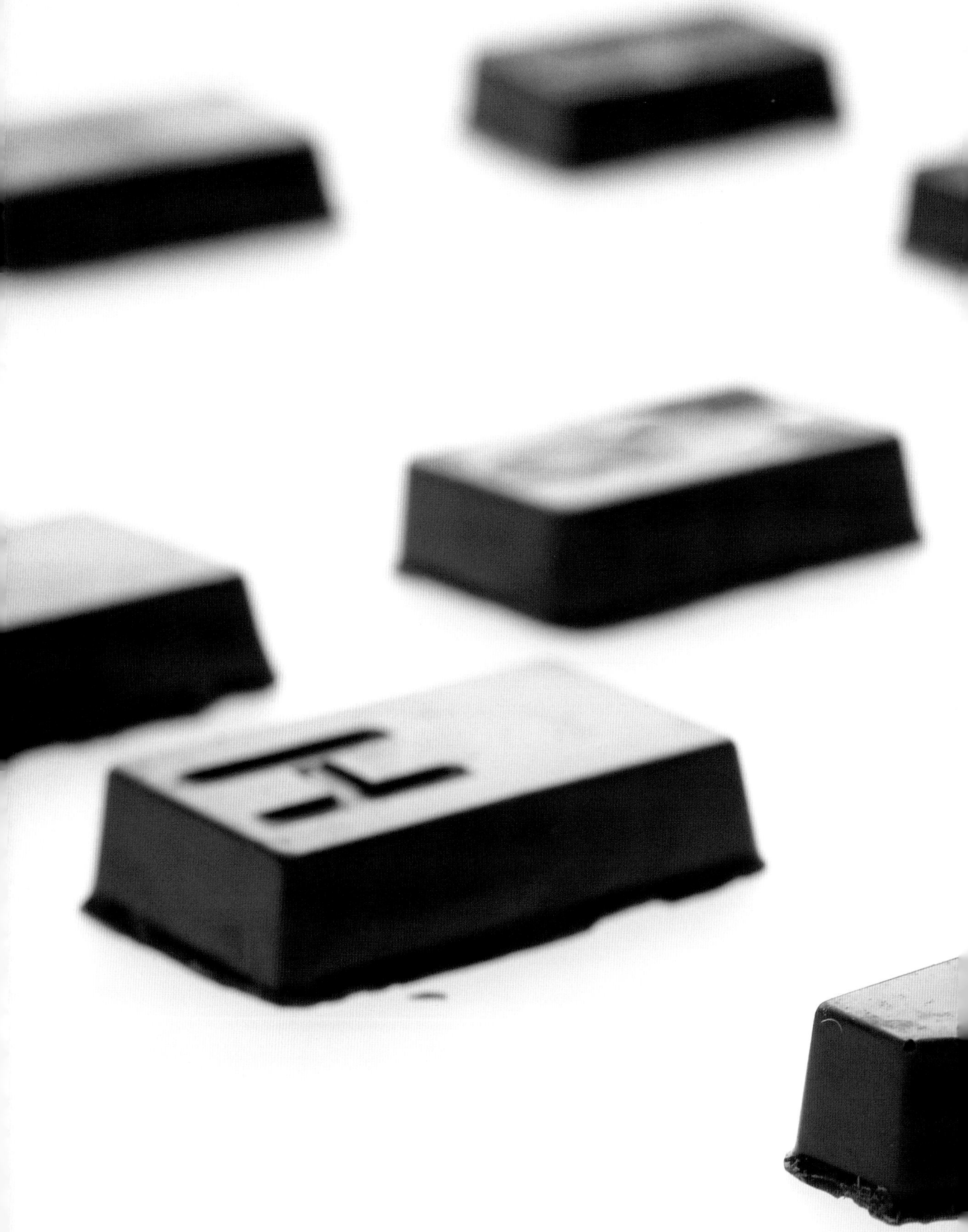

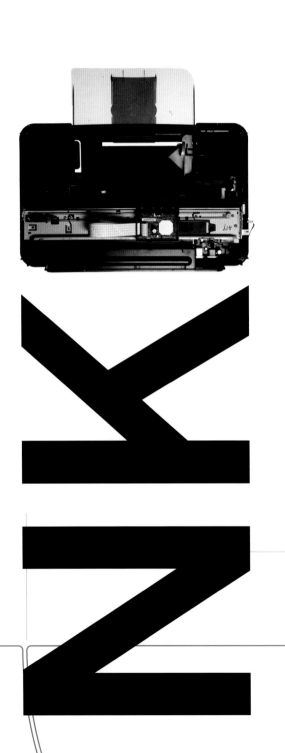

69

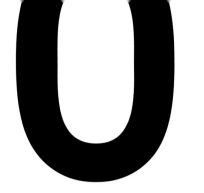

Do sheep dream of electric printers?

6

martin

Printers just flat out suck. I hurl obscenities at this lifeless lump of plastic that chews up my paper and whose LEDs, I swear, blink "FUCK YOU" in Morse code. Wouldn't it be cool if, when a printer jams, it actually dispenses jam to counter this bitter taste of failure? The HP/Smuckers retail partnership blossoms as we snap in our raspberry cartridges alongside magenta and cyan. Could we really hate something as much when it proffers tasty treats by way of an apology? I'm sorry for your loss; here's a little something for your toast.

Realizing the futility of a jam-based printing future we challenged ourselves with this question: What should the sound of printing be? In some ways the printer is a catchall for all of those products that are created without any thought given to the way they sound. Some products are aural delights, like a Mercedes car door, a bike chain on cog, or a camera shutter, but are these the result of intricate engineering or happy coincidence? What can the designer do? What can we pull from our bag of tricks to ease this squeaking, whining, and stuttering white noise nightmare?

I see something fluffy in this experiment. Baa . . .

kj

A printer is based on highly engineered ink technology that is embedded in a complicated mechanism. The internal engineering is sort of beautiful, in its own way, but the plastic that wraps around it isn't. And when the ink cartridges move back and forth or when you open and close the paper tray, the flimsiness of its construction is revealed as the plastic parts move against each other.

There are an overwhelming number of parts and many individuals who contribute to a printer's design and construction. There is an internal substructure that holds the printing mechanism, and gray, white or black plastic is molded as the external surface. The outside surface is rarely considered with the same level of detail as the internal mechanism; it is not elegant...and sometimes it is just plain ugly.

27

martin	kj

Let's buy a printer and get some foam and duct tape and wrap it.

Maybe we sandwich it between two pillows.

Then we do a neutral form in foam around the outside of the printer and the paper is pushed and pulled from inside the foam through an open slot. The outside foam works as acoustic insulation and as protection for shipping.

Yeah, that's great. Then the product is made ready to ship. The printer is its own shipping crate.

We'll have to get a decibel meter or whatever it's called to measure the sound, make the pillow prototype, and then measure it. Or we could just do a qualitative thing.

OK, I'll buy a
cheap printer.

And then we should get
the pillows and tie it
with string.

A little bit
of bondage.

We can try pillows and if
it doesn't work then we'll
do the printer wrapped
in foam—a white foam
block—in a cardboard
box; it's a sort of tea
cozy analogy.

You really think
about tea a lot.

Inspired by bondage
techniques, we
wrapped a standard
printer (the kind you
get for free when
you buy a laptop; the
cheaper the printer
the louder it is)
between two pillows
and some twine.

The decibel level dropped from 75 to 55 dB when we added the pillows and twine. Five dB is noticeable by the human ear, so this seemed like enough of a change to encourage us to continue this experiment (but truthfully, I'm not sure we really cared; we were going to continue no matter what).

It's not often that the process is as beautiful or picturesque as shown here. The prototype survived long enough to be photographed but soon the printer was needed (to print something, I guess) and at that point it was unwrapped and returned to its former life—printing, loudly. Later we had to wrap another printer in pillows and twine. I think the people we work with started to think we were a little bit crazy.

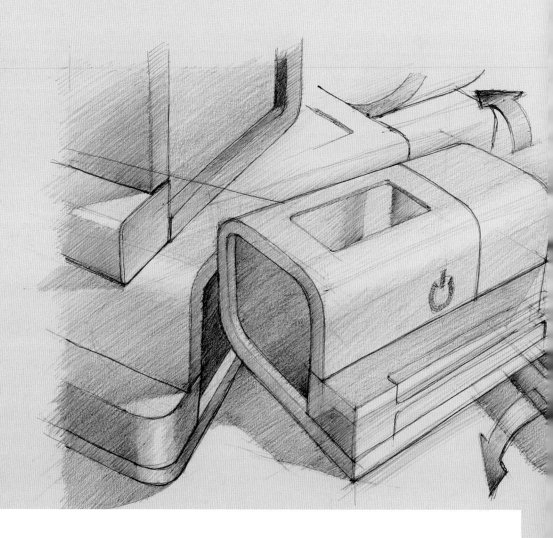

So here's a thing I realized about my work which I hadn't noticed until now: I draw corners. Lots of corners. They become shorthand for the entire shape. Get the corner right and I can create the rest of the shape in my head. Most designers have the ability to see and create 3-D forms in their head. If you've ever seen a 3-D CAD model, that's a pretty accurate representation of the inside of a designer's head.

The first drawing on the page is the Big Idea; everything else is a variation of this sketch. I drew inspiration from furniture, using thick felt wrapped over a sheet-metal core. The felt wrap also represents the paper-flow as it travels through the printer. The right side of the felt can be lifted and uncurled to access the ink.

The designs evolve a little to consider paper-tray access. The felt wraps over the front edge to hide doors and to complete the shape.

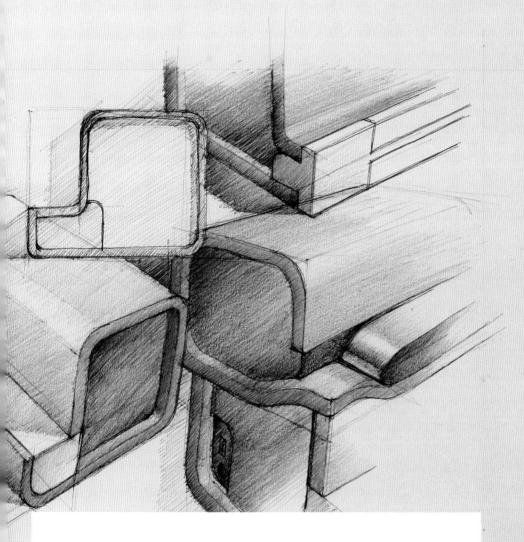

The arrow indicates that access is gained by pulling down the front edge.

But by the end of this sketching exploration I realize that the designs have gone too far and I've tried too hard. Things start to feel forced. Some contouring to the lead edge leaves awkward corners and a strangely shaped paper tray. Often when concepts end up over-designed it muddies the overall story. The idea of sound as a starting point leading to felt as a material choice is enough of an interesting idea. An overly designed shape rather than a naturally evolving one detracts from, rather than enhances, the concept.

We need to build a foam model to get from a lump of pillows to a usable, viable design and to see how it might actually work in context. This will give us a good sense of overall proportions and allow us to balance all the elements. It should be pretty easy to build something quickly. We can use cheap foam and quickly machine a bit of plastic to simulate the paper tray, slap on a coat of paint, and we're done.

martin	kj

kj: Something is not quite right about the scale of the first model we built. It seems a bit too tall and a bit too wide.

martin: We can make it shorter. And I'll check the width again. But that dimension is fixed by the ink cartridges that have to travel back and forth across the width of a piece of paper.

kj: We might also look at reducing the thickness of the felt on the edges.

martin: We can make that edge thinner.

kj: Let's put a zipper in for ink cartridge access.

martin: Oh, I didn't think of it that way. That's better than I had it. And I want to put a tag on the printer with the brand, like you'd see in clothing.

kj: Or you could put the tag on the zipper pull.

martin: Hmmm.

What about the functional controls? Could we use a touch screen?

It would be set into a pressed area of felt. We could attach the screen with rivets at each corner that fix the screen to a structure under the felt. I think we might need two layers of felt.

That might work better for production too.

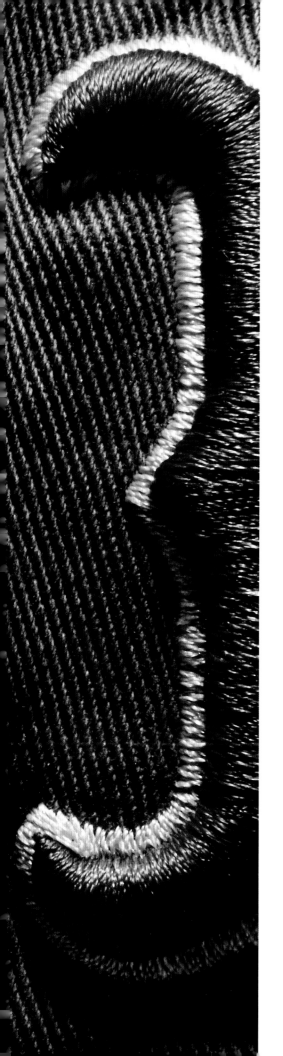

And then I was think-
ing that the idea of the
zipper could also allow
you to unwrap the entire
surface so that you
could service the
internal mechanisms,
when they break.

Of course. But what
about the basic
components, like
a power button?

It can be stitched, like
a baseball hat.

With metallic thread?

Yeah. I also like the idea
of stitching, the classic
wool felt stitching.

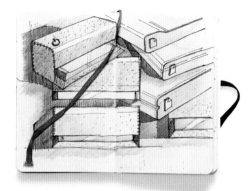
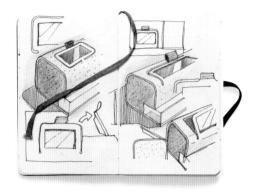
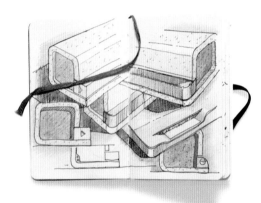
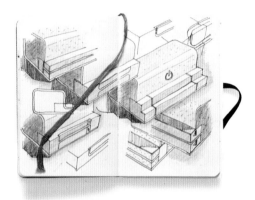

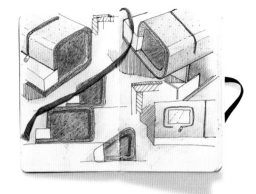

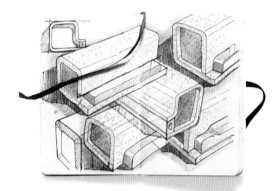

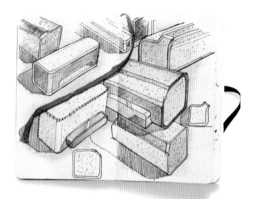

martin	kj

How will these
parts be assembled?

Maybe you could put
studs on the inside
surfaces. The sub-
structure is metal and
then the felt attaches
to that frame.

As if it is
upholstered
furniture...?

I like the printer.

Yeah.

Me too. Did you notice
there are some die-
cut details for cable
management in the felt?
The flap gets peeled
back and the cables get
plugged in and then fed
through the slits. The
flap then gets put back
and the cables are
all nice and tidy. This
execution really plays
up the material,
because you could not
do this kind of solution
in plastic.

Sweet. It's like a
felt cable turtle.

You pull one of the tabs
to lift the screen and
to gain access to the
ink. There's no tab on
the cable area because
that's not a "high traf-
fic" area. You do it once
and you're set.

How do the flaps stay
flat when they are
closed? Is the felt
heavy enough that
it sits flat on its
own or is there a
little bit of Velcro
or something more
elegant than that?

Maybe stitched magnets.
Something with a little
"snap" to it.

That would be nice.

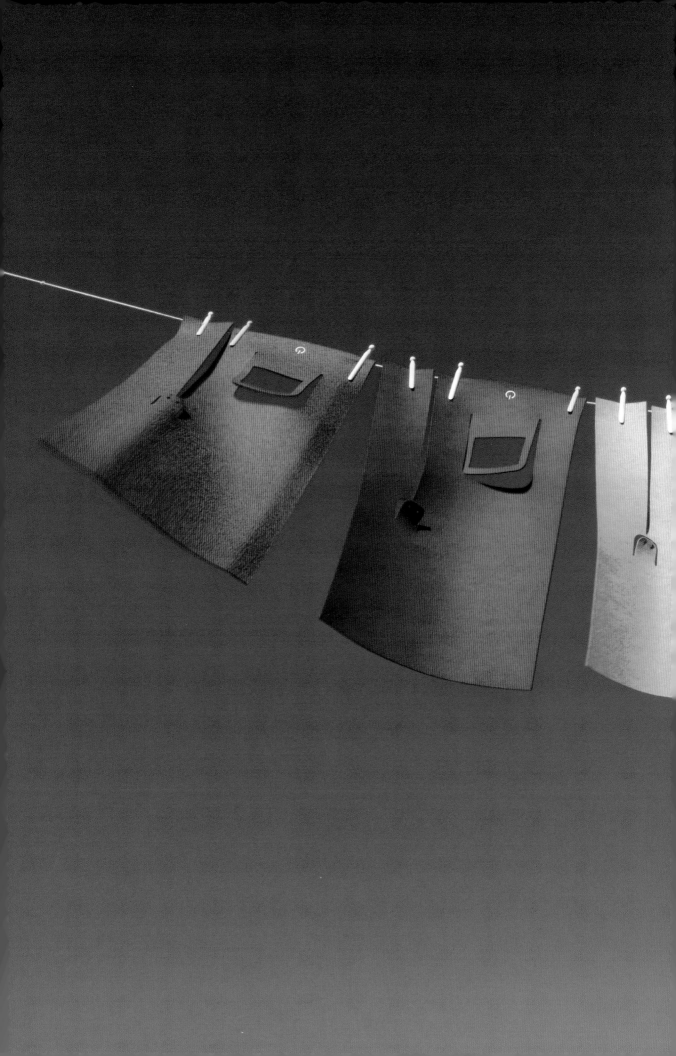

Some days just start off bizarrely. I find myself Googling "sheep-farts-New-Zealand." Not something that I normally wake up with a desire to do. I have to write about felt and why we chose it for this printer, and so one of the rationales is that it's a beautiful, natural, and somewhat, environmentally friendly material. Then I have this nagging sense that I read something about the flatulence problem with sheep causing excess amounts of methane. Not wanting to be wrong, I find myself researching sheep farts. Turns out sheep burps are the bigger problem. Any-way, it's just another reminder of how this profession can take you to some strange places.

So why felt? The reality is that sometimes design ideas come quickly and then you find yourself faced with having to explain them. So I could post-rationalize it, give the choice of felt a little more depth by saying that as a material it represents nature or man's connection to our four-legged friends. But the truth is that on some unconscious level I was just looking for a reason to use felt, to use it in a way that I hadn't really seen before.

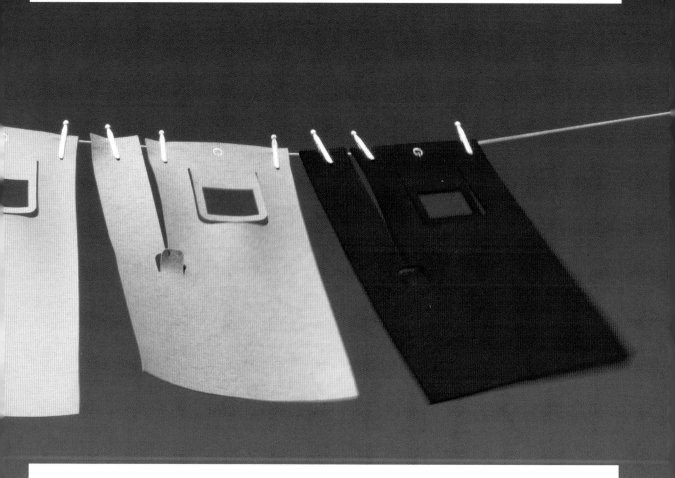

I'd always wanted to use it on consumer electronics, and then the quiet printer came along and the lightbulb went off. Seemed like a perfect combination of material properties and my desire to make an inkjet you would want to pet. I have no idea why anyone would want to pet a printer, but for some reason I think it's a fun idea. Perfect for a book at least; not sure how I'd pitch it to a client. "Hey you know when you're printing your holiday snaps, wouldn't it be cool while you're wait-ing to be able to stroke your printer?" But that's what felt does—it's this great tactile material; you want to touch it; it cries out for a quick grope. I'd love to say I used it for altruistic reasons, like doing my bit for the environment, but that would be a lie. I did it for the stroke factor, and it's not often I get to say that.

martin

This design was a long time in the making. The basic idea happened pretty quickly: a quiet printer, with some felt used for sound deadening, form dictated by material, and so on. But the proportions, scale, and paper tray caused us no end of problems. Three days to design a zipper pull seems like a ridiculous amount of time but as things progress in a design the risk of screwing things up with the final detail increases. It's like that one bad song on an otherwise stunning album or picking the wrong way to end a film.

I like that it's called INK and that a clothing tag is used to access the ink. I was happy that we kept all the features and usability of a printer that you would find in a store now. But above all I like that it's an unconventional idea: a printer with a wool overcoat.

In the end it doesn't feel like such a crazy concept. Is this something that you're likely to see in a store anytime soon? Probably not. This is undoubtedly a more expensive printer, and in a market where companies make no profit on printers, only on ink, this is a proposition that's unlikely to make it past the first review in a real project for a real client. Unfortunately, designing a printer has become an exercise in reducing cost. A printer made from a material that costs more than plastic to start with is a difficult argument to win.

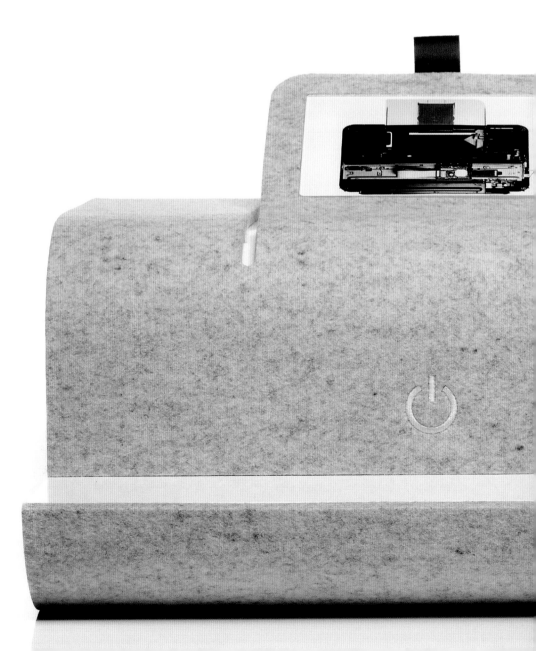

kj

The thing I like most about this design is
that it looks so simple. And that it's made of
felt. Everybody loves felt, right? I like that
we've made the surface more lovable (really,
anything is better than plastic). The cable
turtle is incredibly cute, and the zipper too.
I'll admit, I'm a little worried that the felt
will collect dust, get dirty, and be difficult
to clean. But that happens to every consumer
electronics product in my house no matter what
material it is made of.

I also love the idea that the product tag
focuses our attention on the business model
behind the printing industry—the ink itself.
The felt has aesthetic and insulating qualities. I wonder how quiet this printer will
be. And what if the printer is too quiet? That
would be an interesting problem. Sometimes
the only way you know the printer is working
is that you can hear it from across the office
floor as it starts feeding paper. I guess some
noises have some unintended benefits.

One idea we didn't have time to realize is the
design of the ink cartridges themselves. This
printer would certainly have really beautiful
ink cartridges. The inside should aspire to be
as lovely as the outside.

AN EXPLORATION OF THE SENSES:

---

martin

How can you devise a project that creates passion amongst eighty designers across the globe? You can't. Or should I say we couldn't. We tried; we even made chocolates. But the group was too big and the task abstract. Ideas flowed in but execution died out. Of the invited participants only five made it to the end. Our first contribution was the printer. What follows are the ideas from other designers.

---

kj

Aisthetika is the designer's first connection to emotion. It's about looking beyond what we see.

When asked to explore the senses as a starting point for design, the participants created objects that manipulate and redefine time, light, color, and nature. None of these strictly correspond to the traditional five senses, but each is part of how we perceive the world. The senses are discrete, but designers cross boundaries.

Inspired by these four concepts, Martin and I continued our exploration of the senses with a focus on touch, smell, and taste.

SATURDAY

(Peter Riering-Czekalla)

A sense of time is human. Imagine a watch that reflects the extremes of our perception of time. Two modes: one shows the hundreds flickering on our wrist, reflecting modes in our life where time is very present and dominating our mood; the other is where time is absolutely absent in our mind.

Imagine a Saturday in the park where time doesn't matter. You just don't care about hours at all. You might be asked by someone what time it is, and after checking your watch you just say, "It's Saturday."

I really liked Peter's watch. Probably this is mostly because I really want to live this way. Fast and slow. On Saturday, time moves slowly. On any other day, time is accelerated. When our sense of time is manipulated, our emotions easily follow.

You could imagine all kinds of extensions: "lunch" instead of noon, "happy hour" after 5 p.m., and "football" on Monday nights.

PEEK-A-BOO

(Graeme Findlay + Mikkel Kosser)

As children we are often aware of the hallway light shining through the edges and bottom of the bedroom door. It was comforting in the middle of the night, but it is also fascinating as your eyes grow accustomed to the dark room. The edges of the door seemed to magically come alive.

This door has a pattern within its structure that can be seen only when light shines from one side of the door into a darkened room.

During the day the door hides its pattern and keeps its design secret. Only at night or in darkness will the door come to life and display its pattern.

This would have made my childhood easier. I never liked the dark or being home alone. When you're a kid, the sliver of light coming from under the bedroom door is your only connection to the safety of your parents, who are somewhere in the house, probably watching TV. And the door itself, when closed, creates an uncomfortable barrier. But with a micro pattern of holes, that door can instead become a connection between two spaces.

PINK

(Thomas Overthun)

I am interested in objects that we desire because of their color more than anything else. Imagine someone saying, "I woke up this morning and I just needed a lot of blue." I wanted to create something made of color.

So here's an idea: A "color puddle" in a vaguely creature-like shape is lifted off the ground into the third dimension, transforming into two more familiar objects— a chair and a table.

I was skeptical that Thomas would be able to play with color and create something whose sensory impact went beyond the purely visual. What he managed to achieve with this idea is something simple but powerful. The temporal nature of the casting process is where the transformation takes place. The color pink suddenly can be manipulated; it has form, texture, and function. To someone witnessing the final result, it is a chair that is pink. To the creator, it is some pink that is a chair.

BLOOM

(Gregory Germe)

While in Milan for the furniture fair I was asked during one of those evening parties to contribute to a half-hour design exercise. To be honest I was quite drunk, and the first idea that came to my mind is the one you can see on this page. I think the topic had to do with "small spaces," and we had to design something from it. Living in New York, where you learn to deal with shrunken spaces,

I just thought that it would be nice to have a way to "escape" and bring a feeling of bigger space. Scents, flowers, nature are to me one answer to the question, What if you had the scent of flowers in front of you while working? Out of your pen? The power of scents, flowers and nature can take you back in time or transport you somewhere else instantly; at least, it does for me.

The best thing about this "vase" is that it's based on a very ordinary but potentially iconic object: the pen. For me, Gregory's vase/pen makes me want to look in more detail at other ubiquitous objects that are often forgotten or ignored.

Well, clearly, interesting ideas can come from a drunken stupor.

martin	kj
	Did you just send me an angry face?
I think so. I'm fucking around now.	
	Sometimes you go crazy with the emoticons...
Yeah, I know, they are so lame but I can't stop myself. It's like watching *American Idol*. I know it's bad for me, I just can't stop.	

AISTHETIKA

0.25

0.5

DIN MITTELSCRIFT

BLOW

1

SECTION A-A

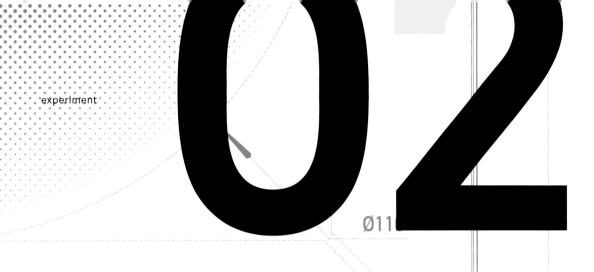

02

Ø11

R1

I'll huff and I'll puff and I'll cool your house down!

45°

martin

This idea came from a discussion with a colleague, Joanne Oliver, who had been thinking about creating objects that somehow reflect or react to natural human behaviors. As part of a workshop she had the idea of a thermostat that references the way people blow on their hands to cool or warm themselves. Even though the concept did not progress beyond the workshop, I wanted to explore that notion further, to take Joanne's idea and make it tangible. I loved the idea: you blow on your house and your house blows back.

kj

It should be easy to design objects that reflect people's behaviors—if we can be inspired by direct observation of how people live and act. The hypothesis that it may be possible to build a product that is directly linked to one very specific human behavior is an intriguing challenge.

Martin was intrigued by the details of how we breathe, and I was ready to go along for the ride. We'd have to find some way to physically represent this behavior...

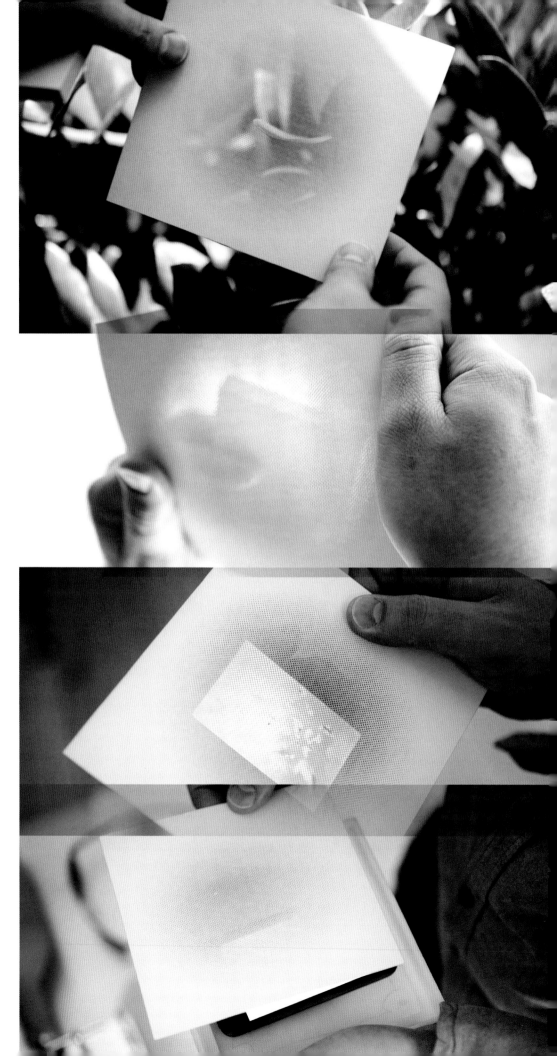

martin	kj

kj: My favorite thing about this design is the functional use of a perf pattern. It's really surprising.

martin: I've been obsessing over halftone patterns lately. They really represent breath to me.

kj: How nauseatingly poetic. Is that a word?

kj: I like that the holes are so small, they're hard to see.

kj: Why are you obsessed with halftone patterns?

martin: That's what gives it a delicate quality, like a breeze.

kj: I don't know. I think because they are a challenge to physically model and because they blur lines. I started to use them around LCDs so that you couldn't tell where the screen ended and the plastic began.

kj: It does make you think of breath, not just air.

martin: Like when you mist a window on a cold day.

kj: Right...

kj: That's a good trick... the perf seems to make it harder to build, but the harder it is to build, the better it will be when we can figure out how to do it.

kj: Yes, and it will be more original. Ultimately, if it's harder to do, there are probably fewer examples out there, because it's more risky.

kj: I appreciate the ambition.

kj: Chemically etching this small halftone pattern is already causing us a number of headaches. Andre's been having trouble getting it right; there are always some dots missing.

Once we get the
pattern made,
how does it work—
behind the dots?

There's a temperature
sensor and a small color
LCD display directly
behind the perf. Then a
bunch of clever circuitry
that I couldn't possibly
understand.

And the sensor reacts
to how you breathe?
How does it knows
whether to turn on
the heat or the AC?

But we have to make it
easy for people to do.

Yep.

OK. Does it adjust
one degree for each
breath?

With this much breathing
on the device, we may
have created the first
product with bad breath.
Maybe we need to design
mints too . . .

Not sure. It could be
single breaths or you
could just breathe until
the display reaches the
correct temperature.

I was thinking it's
sort of weird to
imagine someone
standing so close
to the wall, to
activate the sensor...
I wonder if there
could be some kind
of remote control
that is activated by
the same behaviors?

It seems easier to
do single breaths.
Blowing or huffing
for an extended
period of time
could be difficult.

You could be right.
Huffing. I like that. It's
like warming your hands
on a cold day.

Nah. I hate that idea.
I like people behaving
weirdly. It's no different
from standing and turn-
ing a dial. Well, a bit
stranger perhaps. The
world has too many re-
mote controls anyway.

I'm OK with the
weirdness. I just
wanted to say, it's
weird. Also, it's
nice there are no
buttons on the out-
side surface. Not
even one, right?

Nope.

Cool...and I think
we should definitely
design some mints.

61

When you wish to cool a room, blow onto the thermostat (like you're blowing bubbles) and wait until the desired temperature is displayed. The thermostat can sense that this is cool air, and this ambient temperature is displayed in white.

After the blowing ceases, the thermostat reverts to displaying the original temperature, only now it slowly pulses a blue light. When the desired temperature is reached, the display color returns to white.

For heating it's almost the same, except that when you want to heat a room you huff air, like warming your hands on a cold day, onto the thermostat until the desired temperature is displayed. The thermostat can sense that this is hot air. After the huffing ceases, the thermostat reverts to displaying the original temperature, and again it slowly pulses a red light. When the desired temperature is reached, the display color returns to white.

martin

I wish I had thought of the original idea for this
concept, but I'm happy that Jo let me play around
with it and come up with this design. It's one of
those simple but compelling observations of human
behaviour that leads to a product that delights.
It makes me smile, in part because of the bizarre
notion of people blowing on their houses, but also
because we had fun telling the story.

kj

While writing this book I bought a small
apartment in San Francisco, and my dad came
to visit me for a few weeks to help with some
fix-it projects. While he was here we were in
the middle of finalizing the design of this
thermostat. The thermostat had started in a
sort of weird place—where we were thinking
of the subtle distinction between how you
blow on soup to cool it off and into cupped
hands if you're cold—and it wasn't really
clear to me if that idea would translate
and make sense to anyone, especially my dad.
But as I tried to explain the idea to him,
I was impressed by how much he was able to
really get it—not because he usually doesn't,
of course, but because the idea really did
resonate with him. I was surprised. But it
made sense, so he just got it.

And although my new apartment doesn't have
a thermostat that is anything more than a
light brown Honeywell box, I think that
there is something really interesting here,
an object with intriguing surfaces and
surprising behaviors. Some of the details
of this experiment are specifically created
to make the idea even a little more weird.
Perhaps now it has become too weird for my
dad, but that's OK.

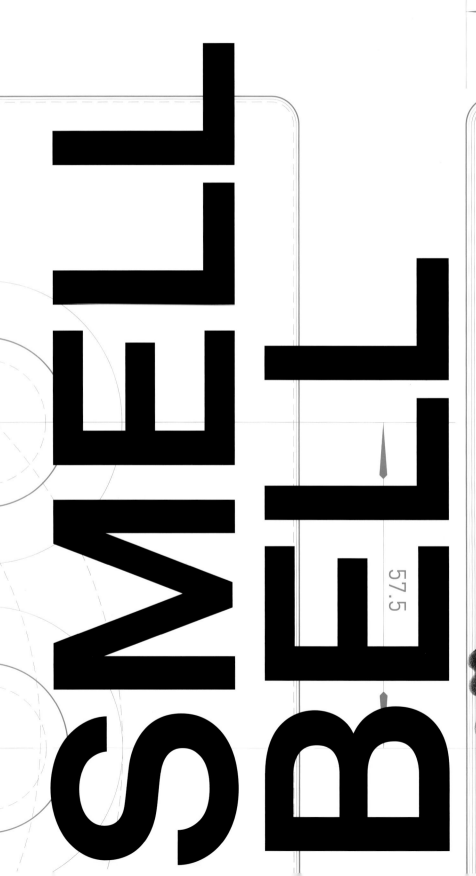

SMELL BELL

57.5

CAR-FRESHNER

®

Royal Pine

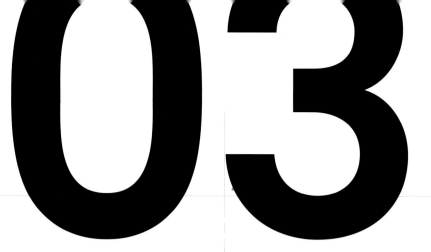

I'm getting a hint of postman and lavender...

martin

Our sense of smell has the strongest link to memory. With the smell of disinfectant, I'm transported back to 1972 and a stay in the hospital. So from a design perspective, I was really intrigued by the notion that we could create connections for ourselves to friends, referencing positive memories and tying them to time and place. The idea that at any point a smell would remind you of someone and transport you back to a dinner party or time with family seemed more compelling than your house smelling like a tropical mist for no good reason at all. What the hell does a tropical mist smell like, anyway? I think it would be more interesting to have the smells in your house be somehow relevant to your life. Like everyone who rings the doorbell is automatically assigned a unique fragrance signature. Over time, your house begins to reflect your life and the people who visit you.

kj

When we first starting exploring the senses I wasn't sure how we were going to build products that related to the sense of smell. It seems very removed from the attributes of products that we work with every day. The perfume industry has of course captured scent for its own purposes, but it's very difficult for anyone else to build scent into their products without it seeming a bit too cheesy. So for this experiment, we had to find a much more compelling role for scent; something with purpose, not just decoration. With this experiment we're trying to build on the connection between scent and memory.

martin	kj	

martin: Why do companies think that people want their houses to smell like scented pine or pumpkin spice or a wooded glen?

kj: I guess it's just easy to create a manufactured reality with scent.

martin: It's bullshit.

kj: Wow—I didn't know you felt so strongly.

martin: No one aspires to live in a faux wooded glen do they?

kj: I really don't like air fresheners.

kj (col 3): What would your scent be?

martin: All these products that exist to bring a piece of the outdoors into your living room through your nose, they have no soul. What does pine bark say about me? We know that smell is the strongest sense, tied to memory. We are suddenly transported back to another time and place by the faintest whiff of a recognizable smell.

kj: Earl Grey. ;-)

kj (col 3): Of course.

kj: It's like an air freshener, but it links the scent of your house to your guests. What's cool is that your house would start to smell like the people who visit you over time. In a good way.

kj (col 3): Yeah, that is cool.

kj: What do you want to do about it?

kj: And the doorbell is triggered by your fingerprints.

martin: I want to design a doorbell that tells a story about the people who visit your house. Every person would have his or her own scent.

kj (col 3): It's an evolution of the peephole, where you smell someone first before you look at them through a tiny hole in the door.

kj: Smell you later.

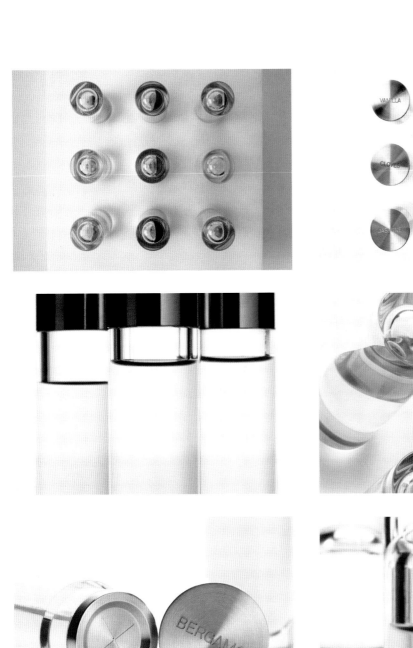

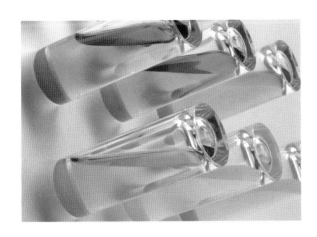

martin

kj

And the stuff just keeps getting weirder. I'm not completely sure why the stranger the idea the more I like it. Maybe it's because I've seen so many products that to find something original in my work I have to go outside the bounds of what might be considered normal. My loathing of plug-in air fresheners, which in itself is an odd thing to be bothered by, made me look for an alternative to give an emotional value to scent or at least make it relevant to a person's life. I like that we exploited the decorative nature of the scents themselves, displaying them, celebrating how they might combine together. I like that sound, smell, and then finally sight combine to create evocative memories as people enter a house. The house, in essence, becomes a scent bank for all those Christmas parties and 4th of Julys. A sensory tag for those moments in time. Cousin Jane is jasmine and rose, Uncle Pete is bergamot and vanilla, and the postman is lavender citrus. I told you it was weird.

Do I care that it's far from being marketable? Or slightly absurd? Nah. Although it could be manufactured, this is far from an exercise in reality. This is about what happens when you start out by skewing your perspective on design, when you look for a new way into an idea, when you create something that attempts to represent the emotional value of scent. In this case it's memory.

I like the fact that this doorbell is really just the story of a glorified air freshener. An air freshener with a purpose. We have made scent functional, not just aesthetic.

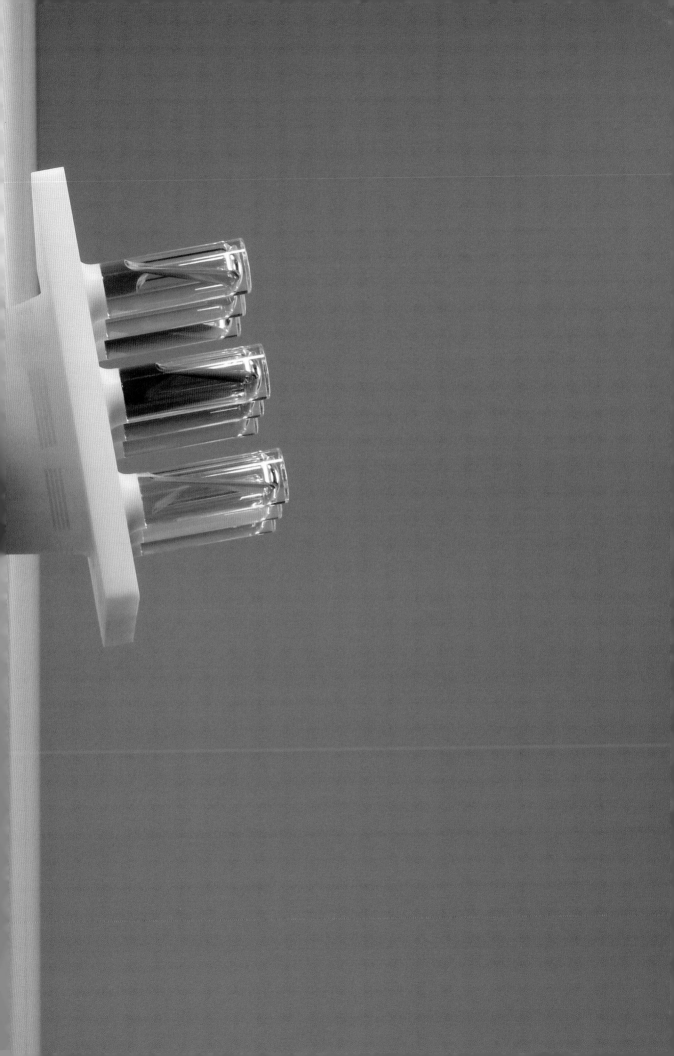

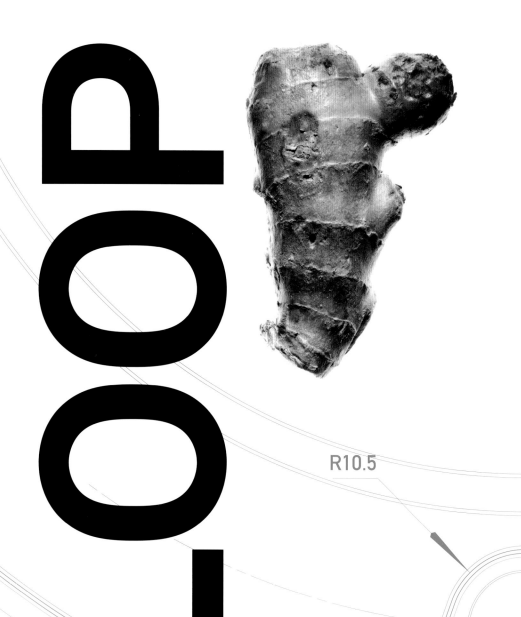

LOOP

R10.5

experiment

Knife, Fork,
Spoon, Nose

martin

I've always thought there were a lot of parallels
between a chef and a designer. Like all creative
endeavors, being an excellent chef requires a lot
of commitment and passion: long days and nights,
experimenting to get things just right. The thing
I've always envied about chefs, though, was that mistakes like miscalculations of flavor or seasoning
are consumed and ultimately forgotten about. Errors
in judgment can be digested and, ultimately, flushed
away. It's not the same for bad products; they hang
around and torture you for decades.

I've always wanted to design something that involved
food, that reflected my love of cooking, and this
particular idea came after a discussion we had about
two restaurants, Craft and WD50, here in New York.
Kara had the idea of trying to interview Daniel
Patterson, the chef at Coi in San Francisco. Coi
is inspiring because of Daniel's use of scents and
essential oils.

kj

For the last twelve months, my kitchen counter
has been unfinished, a deconstructed surface.
I moved into this apartment and removed the
tiles from the counter within days. It hasn't
been ideal. I love being in the kitchen and
I love cooking. I love sitting on the counter
watching other people cook. But I don't know
much about food or restaurants or cooking,
really. Martin does, though, and I'm equally
excited about the idea of pushing design into
the culinary experience. There are already
strong aspects of design in the character of
today's most popular restaurants, on reality
TV, and with celebrity chefs. Ferran Adria's
team at the famed El Bulli restaurant includes
a chemist and an industrial designer who help
him explore the boundaries of food. I wanted
to see what happens when we look more closely
at the objects that surround us when we eat.

martin

kj

I'm phobic of restaurants.
I'm particularly uncom-
fortable in high-end
restaurants. But I find
the interior and the
staff and the presenta-
tion at WD50 is very
good. Did you go to WD50
the last time you were in
New York?

Yeah, I went. It was
OK. I didn't love it.
But I think that I
might have just been
a little confused.

The deconstructed
coffee cake.

What did you have?

Right.

I had corned duck
on little crackers
and that was pretty
OK. We had this funny
thing that was a
mixture of oysters
and rabbit sausage.
It was weird. But
good. A really
strange mix of
flavors. The desserts
were great, but it
was as if someone
had said, I dare
you: make a dessert
out of chocolate and
avocado. My friend
got this chocolate
thing with avocado
puree and mint jelly
and lime sorbet for
dessert. And I got
some coffee cake.

There are molecular
reasons why those
ingredients are put
together even though
it's unexpected. But
what's interesting is
that if you put it in
your mouth and it
doesn't taste good,
then it doesn't matter.

I don't like the
fact that it takes
so much away from
the food to do it
that way. It depends
why you think that
eating food or going
to a restaurant is
a good idea. And I
think there is an
experience part for
sure, but if you're
so confused by what
you're being served
and you're not
enjoying eating it,
then that's not good.
You don't walk out
and say, "Mmmm,
yummy." You say,
"That was weird."

See, I like it. I have a great experience when I eat there. It's like modern art vs. the Renaissance.

No really. You could go somewhere like Kraft, which is in New York City, is very comfort-food based, and you'd probably like it; it would be easy. But we're in the midst of a culinary move-ment that is sort of like the Renaissance, where there is a rebirth of learning. And, like modern art painters, I think that what molecular guys are doing is basically deconstructing cooking and then reinventing it.

Um, sure...

Hmm...sounds com-plicated. But I do like comfort food.

The molecular guys use things that you know but they introduce them and display them and cook them (or even don't cook them) in ways that you're not used to. Much like if you look at Picasso's earlier drawings, they look like figure work from the Renaissance. But in his later work he decon-structed everything and re-assembled it in a way that is more thought-provoking.

I wish I could think of something that was deconstructed and weird that I really like, because it's not that I don't like the idea inherently. I just think it's hard to eat at a molecular restaurant and think it's such a designed experience—too foofy and silly.

You just don't get it.

I get it and I actually like the focus on ingredients part of it. I like the fact that it's about red grapefruit meets porcini mushrooms, and that's cool. But I don't know what to do with it. The menu was overwhelming and unfamiliar.

They really know about the ingredients. I feel very comfortable there. You feel comfortable but you eat things that are uncomfortable. That dichotomy or whatever you want to call it—the juxtaposition—makes it an interesting experience.

Also, I noticed that all the fanciness is in the food. WD50 didn't have a fancy interior.

Right. And that's certainly true, but I don't know if, when we design, we want people to know they're having an experience. It should be more subtle than that.

Yeah, so that's part of the reason that I wanted you to go there. Because it is so similar to what we do in a lot of ways. It is the fine art of food. But it's done in a way that the atmosphere is very convivial. It's food as theater. So the experience that you leave with is that you've had an experience, not just that you've eaten.

It is interesting to think that you can't set up an experience by telling people the experience they're going to have. It never works. It's like saying you're going to love this joke. As soon as you preface it, inevitably, they're not going to laugh. You have to let people have the experience themselves.

A few years ago I went to a fancy five-star restaurant outside of Yosemite and the food was great, but the thing I remember most is that the waiter was wearing a Mickey Mouse watch under his fancy black suit. We asked him about it because it seemed out of place. And that made us laugh—all of us. The observation made our experience of eating there more natural and relaxed.

Yeah. I hate when you go into a restaurant and there are things listed in a foreign language or they're using ingredients that you've never heard of. So you have to say, What is X? They make you feel stupid. Some molecular restaurants do this but I like their intention to experiment.

I'm going to deconstruct the PB & J sandwich and cookies & milk, as an experiment. I'll document it.

Next time I go to WD50, I'll get the fish.

OK. I can't wait to see the results.

AN INTERVIEW WITH
DANIEL PATTERSON

Daniel is the chef/owner of Coi, a restaurant in San Francisco that is famous for focusing on a sense of smell, cooking with essential oils, and concentrating on specific ingredients. We wanted to talk to him about cooking and ingredients and other things relating food to design.

KJ: A few nights ago, I ate here with a friend.

Daniel: Did you like it? What did you eat?

It was great. And we had a very funny wine experience. Your sommelier is really cool. He did an awesome impersonation of a lion to describe one of your wines. He suggested a red wine that was a bit like this: "Raarrgh."

But I walked away feeling like I might not have understood some of the details. So I'd like to hear more about what you intend people to experience.

I want them to enjoy their meal! It's really that simple— I make things that I think will make people happy. The problem is that food is highly subjective, like art. But I'm not making a food-to-art comparison, because I think that's bullshit. Food is more primal—when you eat, your sense of taste, your sense of smell is so closely and physiologically connected to your emotional center and your sense of memory that it generates very strong reactions. Everything we know about what we eat is learned, so that by the time we get old enough to eat out at nice restaurants, we're pretty hard-wired.

If someone doesn't like beets, it's very difficult to make them love beets. I have a friend who thinks that beets taste like a swimming pool because they contain trace amounts of chlorine. She uses this information to explain how her reaction is logical. But there's nothing logical about food.

In a dining experience, like in an art museum, someone who comes to it with a sense of history or cultural context is going to see the hidden layers that for some people won't be evident. But the difference is that, because of the way our sense of smell works, we react much more emotionally to food. At the restaurant we try and use these connections to trigger strong emotional responses in diners.

This is one reason why we were interested in talking to you. We have the same feeling about design: you can't create an experience, but you can enable one.

Exactly. People are not always self-aware. They are very influenced by all kinds of things: environment, life events, and, especially in restaurants, media. They come in with a certain set of expectations. And so one of the things we've done is to deliberately try to undo some of those things that people expect in this kind of meal. Things like using handmade ceramics and not fine china, or being really warm and friendly instead of having a traditional stiff, formal fine dining attitude.

Yeah, I think in your restaurant there is not as much attitude as you expect. The sommelier's lion impersonation helped...

This kind of dining experience can be a little daunting for some people, so we try extra hard to engage people on a very human level. Paul's great at that—his goofiness helps to diffuse the anxiety that some diners have around encountering something new or different. When I was looking for a partner I knew I wanted someone who could put people at ease.

What is unique about the way that you cook?

Unique . . . that's hard for me to say. Right now we're very concerned with the idea of finding a sense of place in the food, while still retaining space for individual expression. It's not that easy! Part of it is local ingredients—cultured plants from heirloom seeds, wild plants, pastured meats and poultry. To me these are the flavors of place.

But then there's this other dimension, of cultural and conceptual. Flavor by itself has no objective meaning. The way that certain smells and tastes connect to memory—of childhood, of place, whatever—dictates

how we feel about those smells or flavors, and that's what gives food its emotional value. Intellectual ideas are all well and good, but if food has no emotional component then, on a basic level, it fails. It's like trying to evolve a new language in a way. In any event, we're still learning.

Can you give me an example...?

Well, I live right near the water, so I think a lot about the balance between earth and sea flavors. We did a dish recently that had tiny potatoes sitting in squid ink-cucumber vinaigrette—which looked black, like dirt—with borage, sea beans, which is a coastal grass, and ice plant flowers, a wild plant which grows along the coast. It's a dish that to me evokes a specific place.

And I grew up near the ocean, so the smell of seaweed is very transporting. I found someone in Monterey Bay who harvests fresh seaweed that we use in a dish with abalone. It's like abalone in its natural habitat, but for me it also has this extra layer of childhood memories.

What do you think about the idea of molecular cooking? Were you at all inspired by it?

I think it's a label that is useless, for me. I cook food. I don't conduct science experiments. I want direct flavor and something that isn't modulated in any way. The science part is about understanding more about the way things work. I recently wrote an article about a new way of cooking scrambled eggs. It was something that was not in any cooking books.

What was the process for the eggs?

It's basically just cooking eggs by dropping them

into water. You beat them first and then you pour them into boiling water. They take about twenty seconds to cook.

Like poaching eggs?

Kind of. It's at a higher temperature. The intense heat expands all the cells and the protein fixes it, and so you get these incredibly light, delicate eggs that you can't get any other way. It's not about getting to the same place by different means. It's about getting to a different place. To me, that's innovation. There's no reason to go to the same place with a different path.

Or you've wasted that journey.

There would be something incomplete about it. You haven't really discovered anything. It's the same with any kind of manufacturing process. If you're curious and you're constantly trying new things and you try a lot of things and you find lots of dead ends and go nowhere. But then later you're like, "Ah-ha," that thing that I did earlier that didn't go anywhere, now I know where that fits, where it will work. So all these things kind of stack up and bring you to something new.

How did you get to that scrambled eggs idea? Did you imagine it and then try it or was it the result of a failed experiment that didn't work?

It was deliberate. I was making poached eggs and I thought, What if I beat them first? It was just one of those moments where I thought, What if I do this?

That's very much like the attitude that we are trying to adopt for this book, because we feel like design is sort of stuck on a known path to an expected result.

One of the interesting things to come out of writing a book about aroma and cooking with essential oils was that I was forced to reconsider something that cooks mostly take for granted, our sense of smell. It really changed how I think about cooking.

Smell is the sense most connected to memories. And taste is the most intimate sense. You have access to the perfect tools to connect with people.

Yes, our sense of smell is amazing. It's a survival mechanism that evolved to bring us closer to things that sustain us and move us away from danger—like the expression "smelling danger". Our sense of smell is connected in an ancient part of the brain to our center of memory and emotion. It defines everything we know about the world; it's infinitely fascinating.

I should probably go. I have to finish the flowers for today's lunch.

OK. Let me give you something to think about. We have been thinking about trying to design some servingware—plates, forks, etc.—something that would fit in your context of food.

That I would love. I kind of have a fetish about pottery and how you get the same feeling of craft in something that isn't handmade . . .

Cool—that would be fun for us to explore too. We'll see what we can do and then share it with you.

martin	kj

OK. Here's my idea for Coi. It's a plate in two parts, the bottom being porous and the top glazed. The bottom gets immersed in essential oils. You leave with your hands smelling of the experience. The chef picks scents that match the food, similar to a sommelier picking wine. The experience lingers.

I'm trying to imagine how you would use this plate...

I always smell my food in a restaurant. I stick my nose right in there, but most people don't.

I don't think that I smell my food very often. But I do smell wine. I know you're supposed to do that.

Think of the bottom of the plate as a tray; that's how you carry the food and touch the scent. And then your fingers carry the scent to your nose.

It seems like the waitress would touch the plate, not you...am I missing something?

The bottom part of the plate comes through the top at the edge.

If the porous material was at the edge of the plate, then you might touch it.

The bottom could lip around the side and move the scent closer to the center of the plate.

I should talk to Daniel about this design.

OK.

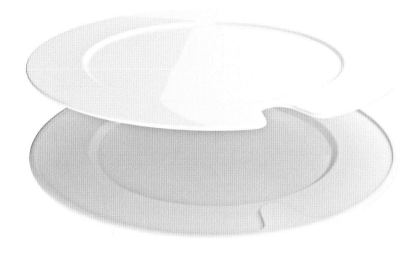

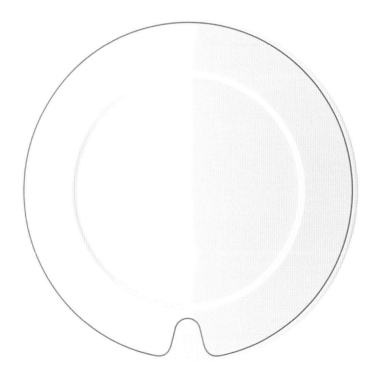

I invited Daniel to our San Francisco office for a lunch meeting to review our first design of a plate. I asked him how he would use this plate to serve his customers. Immediately, he started to recite a recipe for plain, peeled, roasted eggplant, with curry spices hidden underneath the top plate. You would think you were eating curried eggplant, but you wouldn't be. You're smelling curry and eating eggplant.

Daniel said it is very difficult to wash essential oils from a porous surface, even in a strong industrial dishwasher. He imagined the plate would be better if there was a small gap between the two surfaces that allowed the chef to apply oils, spices, or other forms of scent that could be presented to or hidden from the customer, and then the oil wouldn't get stuck in the surface of the plate.

We talked about the intersection of taste, smell, and sight. I asked Daniel, Do you want customers to smell something and think that they taste it, but taste something else? Do you want customers to smell something but not see it? How confused do you want your customers to be? Daniel said he likes to play with sensory sleight-of-hand.

martin	kj

martin

I want to make a variation with three strips. Touch me, taste me, smell me.

"Taste me" is about mixing strange combinations—maybe the licorice dissolves on your tongue while you eat a piece of roast beef. I thought about putting licorice oil on some kind of edible paper.

kj

We could use edible rice paper for "taste me."

"Touch me" puts the smell on your fingers so the experience lingers. And "smell me" is easy to understand: you smell the essential oils as you eat. And they either complement or enhance or contrast whatever it is you are eating at the time.

Maybe we could use a really thick textured or perforated paper.

What about the other variations?

Do you know Heston Blumenthal? The MP3 dude?

No.

I need to make a couple
changes and look at the
insert, but we're ready.

OK.

He's the biggest chef
in the UK right now.
He served food accom-
panied by an iPod.
The sound of the music
affected the taste of
the food.

The other thing that
could be interesting
is to create a digital
plate (made of an LCD
screen) that changes as
you eat to see if color
and pattern change how
something tastes.

He sounds smart.
And he seems to be
making science cool.

Wow—that's a little
crazy. Another day,
my friend.

He also did this
thing where he captured
the smell of roasted
chestnuts for a dessert.
Bloody brilliant.

All righty. I'm
inspired. Do you
think we can
start prototyping
the plate?

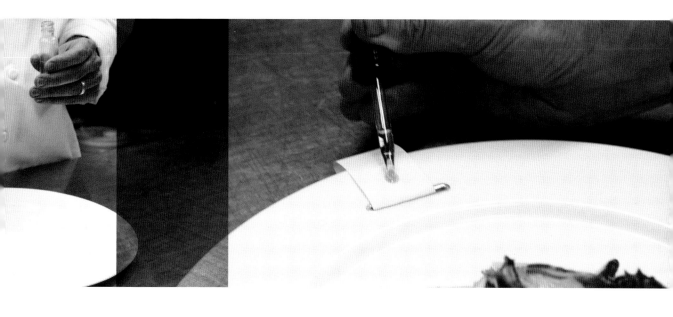

martin

Of all the experiments, this was the most fun from a process perspective. The normal design tools of the trade are a pencil and piece of paper, so exchanging those for a knife and whisk in order to play around in the headspace of a chef was a real blast. Deconstructing and reconstructing food and then applying those ideas to a product is definitely not a conventional approach to the task of designing a plate. Aside from its functional role, the plate is the platform on which ideas are presented; they frame the creation. What we've attempted to do here is deconstruct its role and reconstruct it with an additional olfactory element. The plate now has the ability to create a context for the food beyond the restaurant, to transport the diner to a day at the beach, to the first rains after a long summer, or the heady aroma of a spice bazaar. It's become a multisensory overture to a meal.

kj

I've always felt like the kitchen is an important part of life; it's where some of the best conversations happen when I go home for Christmas with my brother to visit my parents. But I've never spent much time in the professional culinary space. And designing plates is not something that we get the opportunity to do very often in our day jobs. The slot cut into this plate is such a simple modification of the basic form of a plate that it seems like something that could address both the gourmet market and the mass market. People are already interested in ingredients and process of cooking, but not many amateur cooks are playing with scent.

Where do we go from here? I think it would be interesting to ask a craft-based company like Heath Ceramics to merge their traditional pottery techniques with modern culinary elements. Or maybe we should talk to Target about taking this plate into production, introducing molecular cooking to the masses.

How knitting
became cool . . .

THIS IS THE CHAPTER ABOUT

PUN K MA NUF AC TURIN G

Craft is suddenly more popular than it has been in a long time. People who work at their computers all day long can't wait to get home and knit. Knitting is cool.

Punk manufacturing is an extension of the idea of craft. It's the idea that people want, to some extent, to create the stuff that they buy or use, even if it is mass-produced. But it's about more than just personalization or customization; it's about actual participation. People want to play a part in the process of creation, in the evolution of a product. It's building connections to products as they are made and as we use them. It's the human imprint registered on products through personal experiences. It's the dent on the bumper of your car, not the bumper sticker. It's the scar from when you tripped running down the street, not your tattoo. It's your oldest and best pair of jeans, not the two-hundred-dollar pair you bought with rips and tears by that trendy designer living in New York or Paris or Tokyo. It's the surface of my surfboard; shaped by hand, with a unique patina of sand, waves, and rocks. As consumers, we want our products to reflect ourselves, from the moment they are assembled to the end of their life. We want the stuff we own to wear in, not out.

Manufacturing doesn't end when the product is shipped from the factory.

I love craft; I just can't do it. At least not the conventional version—the one that takes manual aptitude, years of practice, and the constant honing of skills. I don't have the patience. So rather than the act of homemade, I'm in love with the idea of homemade, with those custom, personal, intimate experiences. I love the collaboration between designer and artisan.

One of the best design experiences I ever had was having a custom suit made by Timothy Everest. The fittings, the discussions, the fabric selections . . . every moment was a carefully choreographed bespoke experience. Hand cut and hand stitched with one client and one suit at a time. That's the very essence of what makes craft different from mass: the evidence of the maker. But still, more often than not, the notion of craft fills your head with thoughts of knitting and shells stuck on lamps, local market stalls, and the faux-antique store. Craft doesn't really feel contemporary; we need a new description, something that seems to truly reflect us today, as we are now.

Punk manufacturing . . . I think we read it somewhere or maybe someone told us about it. Anyway, I thought it was an intriguing phrase. We can design one-offs and low production runs but make them on big, fuck-off machines that are packed to the gills with technology. This is twenty-first-century lasers and resins and artisans colliding with eighteenth century techniques. After hundreds of years of technical evolution, we still hit stuff with hammers. This isn't a quilting circle after all.

Punk manufacturing is a hybrid, modern craft, a place where the maker does in fact meet mass. It's an idea that lets me celebrate machines and technology and mix them with the artistry of the craftsman. It's Andre, our master prototyper, wielding a mouse and running a milling machine like his vintage brethren used a chisel and scribe. It's the web site where I can create custom T-shirts and make only six, self-publish just a hundred books, or if I had the talent, give an album of my songs away free. I can say "up yours" to conventional practices and do whatever I want. That's punk.

kj

I love the idea of altering the materiality of an object at the touch of a button. Maybe we can start with a simple white chair. Chairs seem to be one of the most immediately personal objects, where designers can experiment with materiality in human scale. There are so many chairs already that manipulate almost every kind of material.

The idea of mixing low-tech and high-tech processes, craft and mass production, made me think about projecting an image of various materials onto the surface of a white object, to create an almost real experience without actually building it. I learned this technique from Arvind Gupta, one of the designers we work with. But here we're thinking that the form doesn't change, the material does. We can quickly project a plaid chair, a concrete chair, an aluminum chair, a cork chair. And then we can let people experience it, in context and to scale. We can digitally alter the surface of an object, its material, and then we can see how the materiality of an object changes how people think about it. It's performance art with macro-photography and digital projection.

martin

We do a lot of CAD modeling in the course of our work and produce some very convincing renderings, and that's fine. Exciting, even. But on a computer screen, you lose the sense of physicality, being able to walk into a space and see something in three dimensions. So we stole, or should I say, evolved this from another idea of Arvind's. We wanted to create a chair that acted as a simple canvas. We could project materials on the canvas and experience them, at least visually, at actual scale. Then we could create virtual versions of the same materials and compare the experience of the projected chair with its virtual counterpart.

Often we relegate the choice of material to the end of the process and because of time constraints are forced to take a leap of faith that we're making the right selection. Virtual prototyping at least allows us to minimize the risk.

Top 5 movies with stunning production design:
1. *Blade Runner*, 1982
2. *Gattaca*, 1997
3. *The Day the Earth Stood Still*, 1951
4. *Mon Oncle*, 1958
5. *Brazil*, 1985

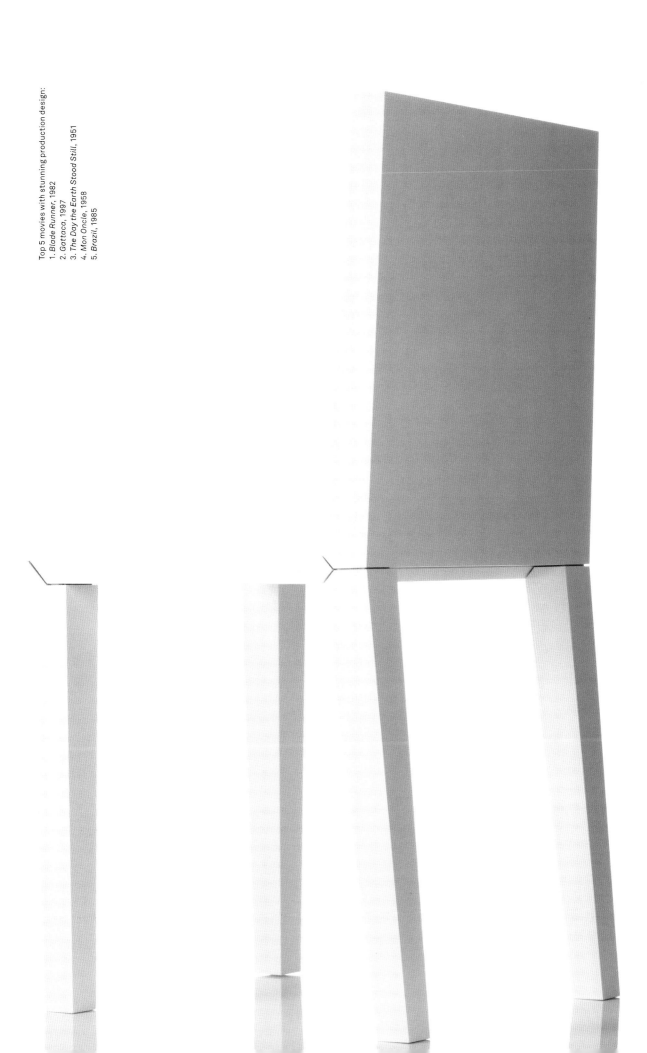

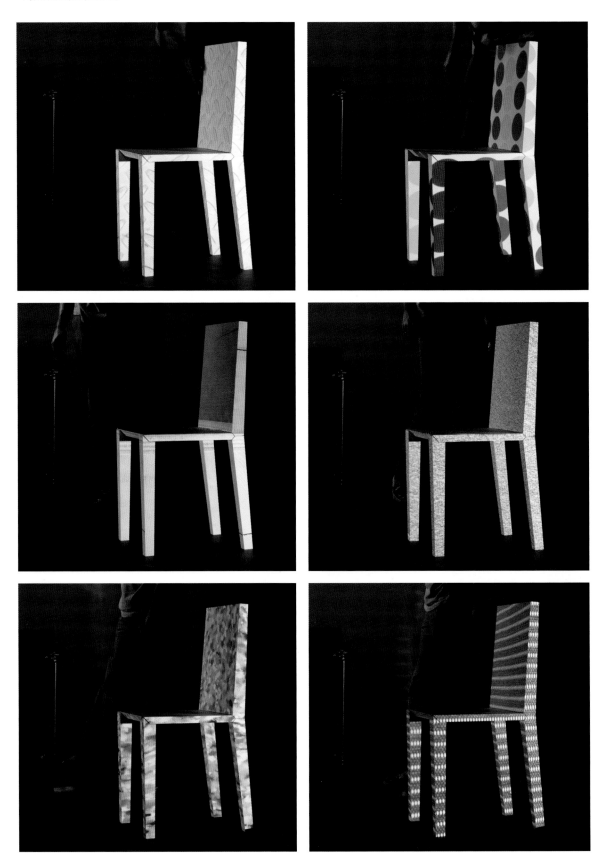

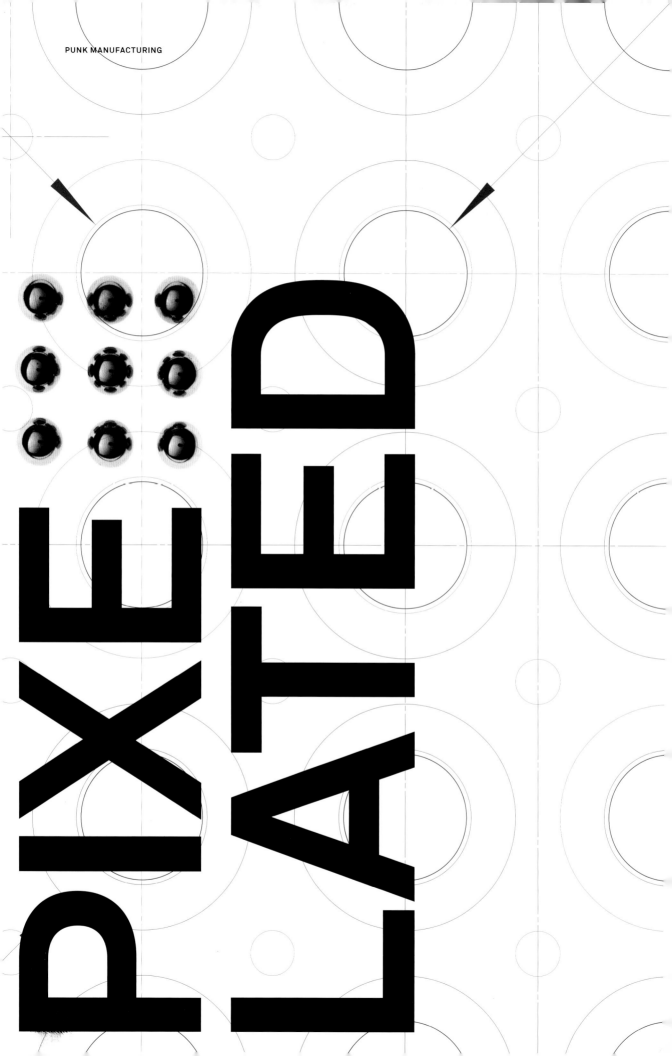

PUNK MANUFACTURING

PIXE LATED

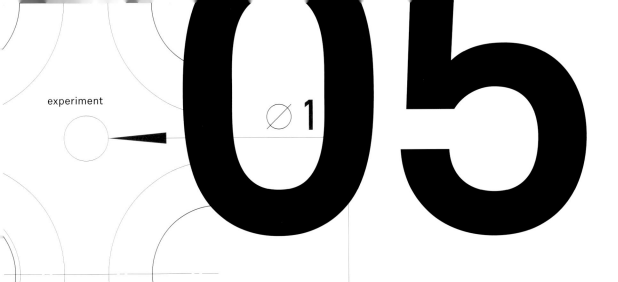

experiment

∅1

05

Saint Peter wished he had this one.

100

I just want to do something big and architectural.

kj

Someday soon there will be little difference between production technologies and proto-typing technologies. If we can connect these two extremes then the manufacturing options available to designers are suddenly almost limitless. Rapid prototyping techniques can be applied to a wider range of materials, and mass-production manufacturing facilities are getting better at doing low-volume production. Maybe we can consider this technology overlap in the design of a space for our New York office. We could create a large-scale design element in our office space that would let us express our process and ourselves.

Before we start to design something so big, maybe we should talk to the guys at Perfor-mance Structures. They build large metal structures for architects. They are truly large-scale crafters.

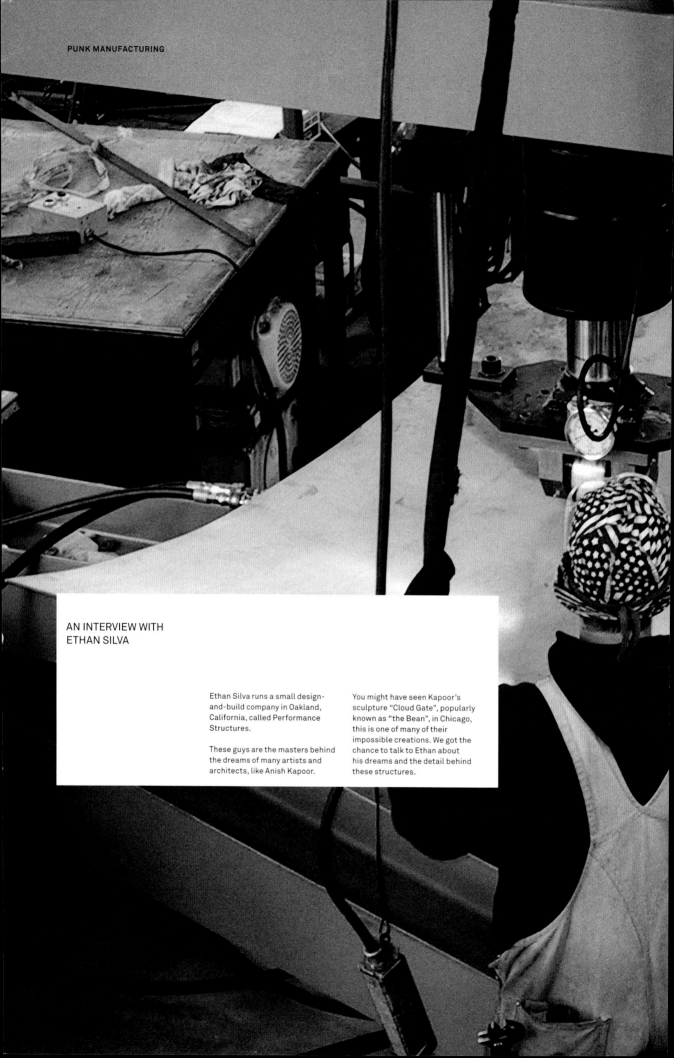

AN INTERVIEW WITH
ETHAN SILVA

Ethan Silva runs a small design-and-build company in Oakland, California, called Performance Structures.

These guys are the masters behind the dreams of many artists and architects, like Anish Kapoor.

You might have seen Kapoor's sculpture "Cloud Gate", popularly known as "the Bean", in Chicago, this is one of many of their impossible creations. We got the chance to talk to Ethan about his dreams and the detail behind these structures.

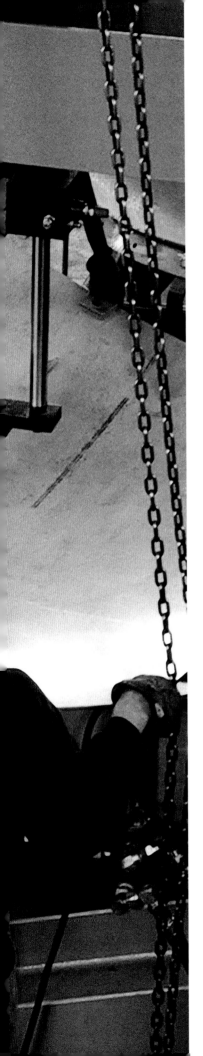

KJ: In your studio, I feel like we're surrounded by metal.

Ethan: Thirty-five years ago, I had this dream to build
a boat. I wanted to build a large boat, an expedition
boat. It had to be big enough so that I could actually
have some interesting adventures on it. So my choice
for materials was pretty limited but in the end I decided to use steel. So I learned about steel and I was
lucky enough to run into somebody who became my
boat-building mentor and who showed me the art of
steel boat-building.

Did you finish your boat?

Yes, I use it for marine mammal acoustic research and
other projects, doing my part to help the planet. It
also took a lot longer to complete than I ever thought
it would, mainly because it cost a lot more than I
anticipated. I would make some money and I would
make some progress on my boat. I have had several
businesses that I have run out of this place. I started
out building steel boats. The one that endured the
longest was actually in the theatrical effects industry.
It started when I stumbled into a friend of mine who
knew some people who needed help building lighting
trusses for stage performances. I ended up doing
mechanical and structural stuff for the Rolling Stones,
Pink Floyd and U2. Then I did some theme park work, I
started doing some stuff with Universal Studios and
Disney World and that was OK, I kinda liked doing that.
I also did a big project with Fox Studios in Australia.

So you go from boats to stage effects to art,
like "the Bean" in Chicago.

I got into this "Cloud Gate" thing thru a friend of mine,
an engineer who I worked with on a Pink Floyd project.
And I went to visit him in England in 1999 to see the
eclipse in Cornwall, and then I went to visit my friend
in Brighton. Near the end of our visit he said, Oh,
you might be interested in this. And he gave me the
prospectus for this sculpture.

Cloud Gate was the first sculpture you did?
The first piece of art?

Well . . . I had studied art as my minor at UC Berkeley.
Physics was my major. And my minor was art.

People who study physics and art always end-
up with really interesting lives and they ask
interesting questions.

Well, the subjects are kind of related in way. I'm not
sure how. I decided I didn't want to pursue physics
because it mostly seemed to be only about high-energy
particle physics. That wasn't interesting to me.

Was it more the physical or mechanical stuff
that was interesting to you?

Actually, I was, and in a way I still am, interested in the
more esoteric aspects of our universe. The bigger world

that we live in. The classic physics—Newtonian physics is pretty straight laced—the apple falling, Newton watching it, calculus, and then, you know, relativity and four-dimensional space. And then high-energy particle physics as an outgrowth of that, and the atomic age, which really got intense in the twentieth century, Max Planck and all the rest, Einstein of course. But what about the bizarre phenomena that we notice from time to time, that you might be aware of, that are dismissed but sometimes not completely dismissable.

What do you mean?

For instance, everybody's had this experience, I'm sure. You're looking at the back of somebody's head and you're just staring at them, then suddenly they turn around and stare right back at you. Or maybe you are the one who suddenly without thinking turns your head to look back at someone staring at you. Once is an incident, twice is interesting, but after that it gets to be a pattern. What's that pattern about? Is it electromagnetic? I don't think so. Which of the physical theories that we studied is it? Well I don't think it's any of them. So now where are we at? There are parallels to these esoteric phenomena in measurable physics. These are the kinds of things that were interesting to me in my twenties, and they're interesting to me now. But Physics with a capital P wasn't about that when I went to school. Maybe it will be in the future.

Before we get too far into physics...when did you start working on the "Cloud Gate" project?

I remember looking at the prospectus in Brighton and saying, Oh, shit. Two thoughts. Number one, this would be really fantastic if somebody could figure out how to do this. Number two, I have no idea how to make this. My boat-building experience did not prepare me for this. I didn't really want to do it. But over a period of several months I was seduced. They needed someone, they were stuck, I thought I could maybe figure out how to do it. And I needed a job.

Where did you start?

Originally, I explored composite materials, and then I had this idea to make it out of ferro-cement and then coat it with metal.

But that didn't work?

The theory was that you could fabricate the whole surface and then sand it perfectly smooth and then plate it. And you'd have something that would be smooth and shiny, so I made a sample piece and sent it to the artist and he got really enthusiastic and he said, Great, let's make a presentation. So I flew to Chicago; I had never met Anish Kapoor, but I met him there, in Chicago. And we made a presentation, and to make a long story short, we were shot down. They were determined that it had to be stainless steel.

The city didn't like the concrete idea?

It was not plain old concrete; this material has a tremendous amount of steel-reinforcement in it.

But they didn't like it?

No, they didn't think it was going to be able to withstand extreme weather conditions. So as I left Chicago, I went to O'Hare airport, and there was a blizzard coming in. And it was one of those things, just standing there looking at the snowflakes I got this new idea. Maybe I could make individual metal plates so that each and every one had the perfect shape and then they could be joined together and then all I'd have to worry about is the distortion when you weld it.

So, let's go back a minute, and I'll tell you why when I looked at the concept initially I had no idea how to build it. The boats I'd built had three-dimensional shape in them but the way you do that is you stretch metal sheets around a framework and then weld the seams, but in so doing, you end up with a lot of stress points. And if you wanted to grind the surface smooth and polish it so it has a perfectly mirrored finish, when grinding the surface you wouldn't know how it would react because of all the stress in the metal from the fabricating. Not an acceptable proposition. But . . . if you could get each part perfectly shaped and perfectly smooth in advance, and made to fit together tightly, then you could control the welding stress, and you could actually do this near-impossible project.

Ahh, because you only have to deal with the seams instead of the surface now.

Right. So I took one of the sharper curved areas from the model of the sculpture and I produced a piece made out of four carefully smoothed pieces welded together. And when it was done we air-freighted it to London. Fifteen hundred pounds of stainless steel. Two days later I got a call from a very excited artist saying, You did it! I've been looking for two years, you're the only one who succeeded, I want you to build my sculpture. And so that was the beginning.

That must have been amazing. How do you think of yourself in this process? Artist or physicist or craftsman or engineer?

None of those. I'm an entrepreneur; that's some fundamental part of this. And I'm an adventurer. And I'm a builder. And I'm a dreamer and something of a schemer. I have a technical background which has been really useful and I have an appreciation for fine lines.

Have you done any sculptures yourself?

Not recently. At one point I thought about pursuing art, but in the end I didn't want to primarily because I didn't have any burning visions that were just desperate to come out into the world, that I couldn't live without getting out. I didn't have that. And plus, I didn't know how I could make a living at it. On the other hand,

I have found that I can build art for others. One of the things that some sculptors do, not all of them, depending on the nature of their work, is to get really into the subtleties of the material, to make it exude its presence, and it means working with the material in very refined ways, not a cavalier or careless way, but in a very careful way.

When you say sculptors, does that mean you or your team, or do you mean the artist that you work with?

Well, sometimes both ultimately. The artists that we work with depend on us to have that sensitivity to the material and to notice the small details and to subordinate all the parts into a whole that feels right. And anything you build is the sum of all its little details. So you might be working on lots of little details and in and of themselves, nobody notices them. But in the aggregate, it's all there, and you feel it.

What about the subtleties of a material, what does that mean to you? Is it mechanical?

Every process you do to the material changes it. I'm talking about metal because that's what I work in. But on some level I assume that's true with every material. When you weld it, it changes it. When you grind it, when you polish it, when you bend it, all those things affect it in some way. Some ways that are really obvious and some ways that are really subtle.

The material itself that you're working with is pretty much the workhorse of stainless steels; it's very ordinary.

Yeah, it is.

So the unique attributes that you try to leverage are more from the process.

The process and, of course, the technologies. When I came into "Cloud Gate", our first job was to evaluate suitable software for a precision fabricating process. It was suddenly going to the next level where you could spend a lot less and get much more. The software technology was becoming more accessible and you had the power of being able to do this sophisticated 3-D modeling for peanuts.

As product designers, we've been really excited from a technology point of view about rapid prototyping and 3-D printing techniques—like SLS, SLA, or FDM, lots of letters. Those processes will make a step change at some point.

Yeah, it's just the same for us with software today (like CAD).

I wanted to ask why you're focused on stainless steel or have you worked with other materials?

Well, I've worked with aluminum and I've worked with fiberglass a bit, and I've done different things, but people keep wanting stainless steel.

Is it because the sculptures are outside? Or do they like the reflectivity of it? Or the weight of it?

All of that. It seems like the inquiries we get are people who want the reflectivity and the durability of stainless. That seems to be the recurring theme. But it's expensive.

What if someone came in and they wanted to make a big sculpture out of cork? Or something like that...but it was still a problem of craft and scale?

I'd be interested. I looked at this one project, it was a Frank Gehry design, that had these glue-lams; imagine a whole network of them. It was just about metrology, and gluing up a bunch of wood. I talked to them and they said, You don't do glue-lams, so why are you here? And I said, Well, I think this is a difficult project and I'm interested in the challenges but if you have a regular glue-lam guy who will do it, that's fine, but if they can't do it, call me. That's sort of what we do; we do things that other people can't do. That's sort of what we exist for, it turns out.

A few weeks ago we started an experiment around one of our favorite rapid prototyping technologies. It's a tile for a gate, part of a modular system. The gate is built out of steel and these tiles fit within the gate. You know those metal pins where you push against your face or your hand and the pins take the shape of your face or hands. We did one just like that, but in plastic. So then we could basically draw letters onto the surface of these tiles. Maybe we can show it to you and ask you the same question that the artists ask you: How would you do this in stainless steel?

Yeah, one of my jobs is to figure out how to convert ideas into structures made out of stainless steel for people who want it. I find I can make a living doing it, so that's what I'm doing now. It's not exactly what I thought I'd be doing when I was in school.

I didn't think I'd be making little plastic tiles for a giant steel gate when I was studying material science. Somehow, by accident, we seem to have built a giant game of Boggle.

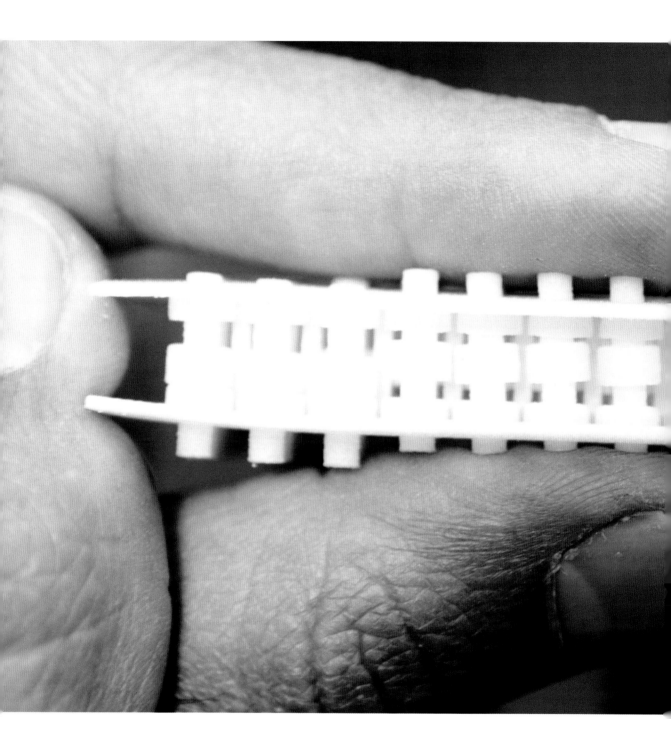

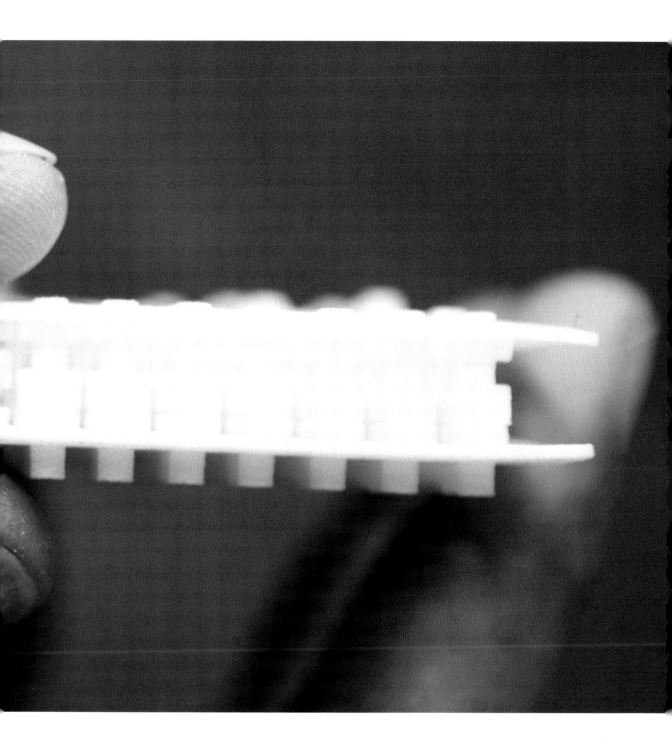

martin	kj

I thought the prototype
was actually pretty good,
but I think the pins are
too small and the walls
are too thin.

It seems delicate?

Yeah. A side wall will
help, but we can beef
it up. I was hoping the
thin walls would make
it more translucent,
but they don't.

I didn't know
you were going
for translucency.

I wanted people to be
able to see through the
gate—otherwise it will
feel oppressive. Some
SLA materials can be
more transparent, but
I think the resolution
gets dodgy.

Got it. So our
next step is to
make everything
a bit bigger: the
pins, the walls,
the tile itself.

What does that mean?

Yeah, and we'll try a
more open front wall
idea. It will feel like
a decorative grille.

The area between the
pins is open. The front
wall is gone.

Is it still an
"impossible structure"
if you open the
front wall? I don't
want us to let the
shape become less
complicated.

It feels kinda
Moroccan, and yes,
still "impossible."

All right then. Let's
make the tile full-
size and see how it
works in the gate.

martin

The more I see this design, the more I hate it. A giant missed opportunity. I had such high hopes for this gate. Working with the architects was great, the scale was perfect, a huge canvas on which to play. I wanted a complex, intricate series of panels that were inter-active and dynamically changing, that represented the essence of the design activities inside the building. What we ended up with was a derivative idea that never really managed to get off the ground. It did photograph beautifully though; Nicolas rescued this experiment for me.

Most of the time my work never quite manages to rise to the level of the idea that's in my head when I first begin a project. I imagine it's the same for most designers, but that's what drives us, this quest for the unattainable. "Next time," I say to myself, "I'll get it right." I never do. I might get closer, I may even love the outcome, and like much of this book, I might even be surprised by how stuff turned out. But there's always something, some obscene little detail that fucks with your head. That nagging disappoint-ment that remains because it's too late, it's too tricky, and the machines are running. Time to move on.

kj

We started this book project in San Francisco and then Martin moved to New York. As he worked with the team to define the space that would be our office, it seemed that we would be able to build a massive gate between the elevator and the main reception desk. This gate needed a story and Martin was ready to give it one. But we ran out of money and we were never able to finish the build. We could only afford to make one tile and we needed sixty-six.

A

152

TRADE MARK

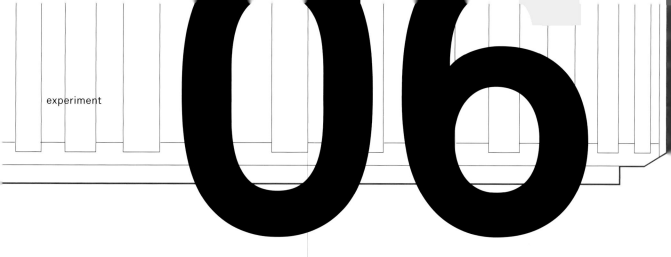

What if manufacturing's steel toe met craft's soft underbelly in a dark alley?

130

martin

Craft and Manufacturing together form a strange kind of alliance: Manufacturing, which deals with perfect reproducible copies and Craft, the definition of hand-made. This clash of perspectives makes for a really intriguing experiment. After Kara returned from her research tour of a number of craft houses in China, she brought some samples of filigree that I found really appealing. They were highly decorative twisted-wire pill boxes which I thought we could use as an alternative to mesh in speakers. I want to see if we can take this organic technique and constrain it to fit within very specific geometry, to use the simplicity of form to showcase the intricacy of the decoration. The question is, will they balance or will one element, form, or decoration dominate.

kj

Recently I've started to pay attention to the "Made-in-China" mark that appears on many products, and I've been frustrated by the fact that it has no connection to the traditional craft of China, but only to inexpensive industrial manufacturing. This "logo" is not perceived as a mark of good quality, just the opposite. After talking to Andy Switky, who works with our design teams as a manufacturing engineer, we were inspired to find connections between traditional craft processes with funny names like "wire filigree" and modern product design. Wire filigree is used to create intricate patterns that are usually only decorative, but we wanted to find a way to make them functional. We decided to focus on designing a set of speakers. Speakers require an open pattern to let sound out, of course, so it seemed like a good place to start.

martin	kj

I want to talk about the idea of looking at things from the inside out. When I was in China, I was thinking about how this idea is related to craft. The craft movement is about getting people to think about how things are made, to make things themselves. For designers, craft is about getting inside the factory—to be directly inspired by manufacturing.

True. So we should try to act more corporate? That's a surprising thing to say.

It's beyond our control. As consultants, our clients determine how things play out. When I led a more corporate life, the money was never a determining factor of my involvement in a project.

I wonder if craft is less about thinking and more about experiencing and doing.

That is possible. Or it's about getting as close as you can to the people who are *doing*. It's about being inspired by their craft.

Yeah, did I ever tell you that to get designers inside products, we've been doing these product forensics where you carefully cut a product in half to see how it's made? A very cool object of its own results.

Designers observe processes, and craftspeople are the process.

Interesting. But do designers really observe manufacturing? The good ones do, but many are stuck at their desks, or computers, or in their office, or at client meetings.

It's like those X-ray product photographs that were all the rage a few years back.

Yes, similar...looking from the inside out... and it's also sort of why micro-structures are inspiring.

I think that's more a reflection of corporations vs. consultancies. Corporate designers are linked directly to the factories and have a greater responsibility to the final outcome. Consultant designers are often forced by fiscal constraints to give up control.

Yeah, they're cool.

There were two
filigree factories
that we visited in
China, in Beijing
and Chengdu. I was
traveling with Eddie
Wu, a mechanical
engineer that we
work with, who could
translate for me.

The process of
creating filigree
starts with silver
wires that are drawn
and twisted until
they are ready to be
bent into shape. The
shapes are soldered
together and then
plated. It's amazingly
intricate work, like
most craft, but there
is this odd mass-
production quality
to it. It's not an
art form, necessar-
ily; there are some
efficiencies. The
filigree is built,
wherever possible,
in sub-assemblies of
repeating, modular
components.

We had to wait what seemed like months for the first filigree box prototype to be made by the factory in China. When it arrived it was presented to us in the most incredible packaging. On the cardboard box itself was a layer of clear tape affixed in so many directions that it was almost impossible to penetrate. Inside the box, a layer of protection had been created with crumpled bits of pink and purple Chinese newspaper.

The prototype itself was tucked inside an ornate fabric box, seeming overly decorated when you thought about its purpose as a container. The lining of the box was bright golden yellow, and the filigree box sat safely inside, with an inner layer of red cardboard printed with Chinese characters to protect the filigree's surface.

Although slightly crooked, the filigree was gorgeous. The craftsmanship was a little imperfect in places, but that really did make it better. And there was one mistake, where the structure of the box was on the outside instead of the inside—but that made the structure look more like architecture. We became slightly worried that it might be hard to get these guys to hold tight tolerances that we would need to build the final prototype, but there was something really interesting here.

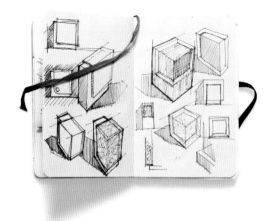

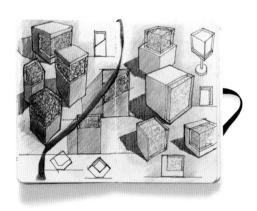

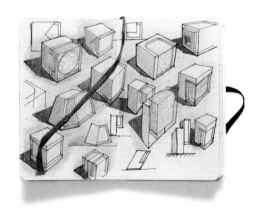

martin

kj

I saw the new design you sent...why did you change the format? Not leaning forward but two blocks on top of each other? Is this more balanced? Half filigree, half support structure? And easier to orient/spin the speaker so it's directional?

I don't think it has any real functional element to it, like changing speaker angle, swiveling, etc. The reality was that the first version wasn't very good. There was no real reason for that form. There was nothing about it tied to filigree. When I saw the first prototype from the factory in China, their interpretation of our idea, I noticed that they had built a frame into which they wove the filigree. I thought that it had a real architectural feel to it, and so I started to play around with that notion. And because of doing the renovation I had a bunch of books around the house, and I was intrigued by the idea of cantilevered buildings. It seemed really appropriate to separate out the bass and treble and give them their own "rooms."

And are you now thinking that we do show the "structure" of the box, like they did on the China prototype? I remember that was a mistake from our original drawings/intentions... they put the frame on the outside.

I think they have to frame it even if the frame is internal. But even an internal frame will be visible.

Yes, OK. It's probably up to us, inside or outside, for the frame.

Perhaps they will do what they want, not what we ask. But I think we should do it on the outside.

True, it may be hard to get these guys to follow all our rules, but I like that we've adapted the design to fit what we saw in the first proto.

So the bass is in the bottom and the treble in the top?

Exactly. Perhaps that's the truest definition of co-creation: adapting another person's perspective to work for you.

Yes.

OK...so...is the bottom block still wood? Or something else? It looks very glossy.

I like the idea of using two of the techniques of the craftsmen you found on your trip to China. The blocks could be lacquer. But I think for our sanity we may have to make it simpler for now.

Simple is good; this one is going to take a while to build.

I think I'd like to make an anodized aluminum version too, so that we can control tolerances. Also I like the notion of craft meeting industrial processes. If we do both in a "craft" way it may not be as cool. What I'd really like is a palette of options that we can put together like cooking ingredients. I'd like an aluminum box and lacquer box with filigree and etched stainless or aluminum "mesh."

I like how "neutral" the form of the design is now, like building blocks... so it's easy to do this kind of mix and match.

Bollocks. I like your term better: "neutral," like a canvas. It's better than simple.

I wasn't sure if I would offend you by saying the form was neutral...

Ah, I see...so there's a craft version and an industrial version for both the top and the bottom? Mix and match, craft and industry. Cool.

I use that all the time, right? Canvas . . . I sound like a broken record.

But you're a painter at heart...it's perfectly natural. We all have vocabulary that we fall back on when we're stuck.

We combine etching with lacquer and anodizing with filigree. Not sure if that was clear.

I got that part.

Hey, you're onto something. I realize that I use a lot of painting references. Neutral is definitely not offensive to a designer, I think, or at least this designer . . . neutral forms are very important.

Exactly. The forms are simple so that it becomes about juxtaposition of these two things.

Good. Another
question: do these
speakers have
a power cord? An
on/off button?

Yes, they have cables.
Not sure yet whether
they have a power and
volume switch.

One other idea is to make
everything to do with
power linked to the cable
and put the volume on
the cable. Then it doesn't
matter so much and we
just design a really cool
cable, later.

One thing I was
thinking is that
these details could
be related to the
"lacquer" process.
So the power button
could be some cool
lacquer decoration/
detail. Maybe the
power button is
made of a pattern
of broken eggshells
or pieces of foil.

I like this design.
I think it's about
taking something
simple and often ugly
(like speakers) and
making them more
challenging (in terms
of the production/
prototyping process),
and more beautiful.
I also like the idea
of craft + industry.
Of course. :)

Yep I remember. How would
we make that "actuate?"
Eggshells are not
conductive, or is it that
other electrical term I
keep forgetting?

For the power
button, I was
just thinking
that those details
were decoration,
not conductive
or anything fancy
like that. Just
better than a
painted button.

martin

This experiment was like the final beatdown at the
end of a Rocky movie. Manufacturing, the grizzled
veteran; Craft, the young upstart, together in the
ring, circling and jabbing, each trying to gain the
upper hand. In the end, I'm not sure if we created
speakers that produced a balance between the two or
if one dominated. We forced the decorative filigree
to be constrained by the geometry of a block. At
the same time the machine-made elements had to be
persuaded by hand to accommodate the organic, not-
quite-straight, twisted wire cage. So I guess it's a
tie, more *Rocky* than *Rocky III.* (I clearly watch too
many movies while I work.)

kj

Budget is always something we have to consider
as designers, and cost is what makes a lot of
ideas and products not happen. These speakers
were really expensive to make; just the filigree box itself cost a thousand dollars, and
for speakers you need two of them. Maybe there
is some market for high-end luxury speakers,
but if there isn't that's OK, too.

It's not always cheap to make something in
China—and maybe it shouldn't be. We should
respect craft for what it is, and we should
be willing to pay for it.

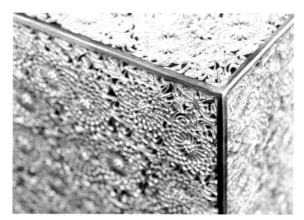

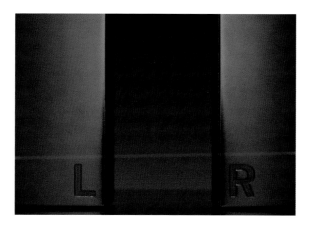

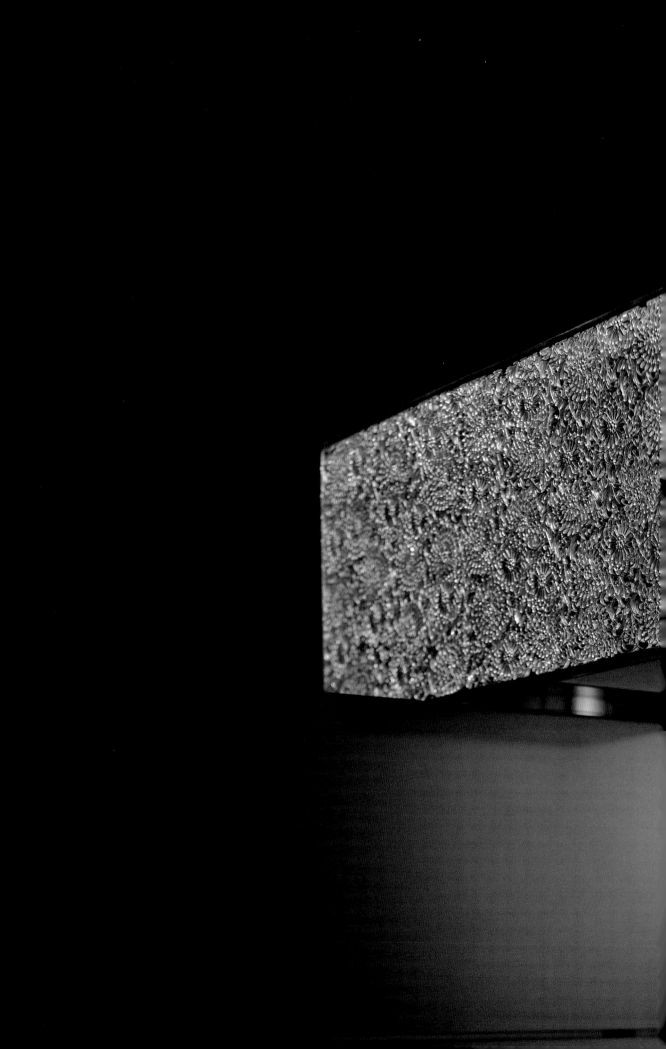

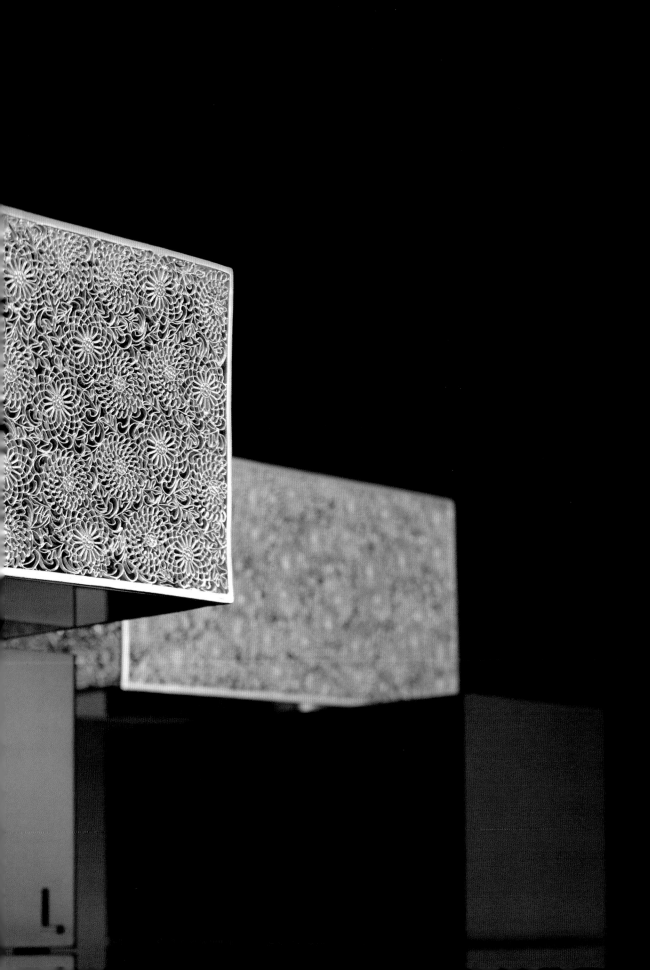

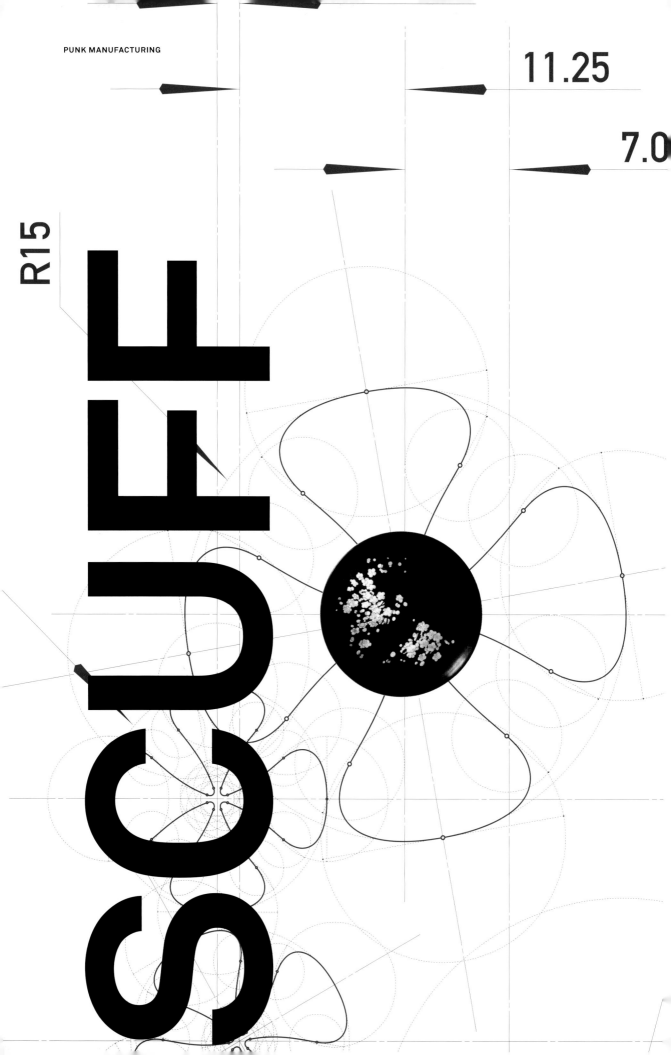

PUNK MANUFACTURING

11.25

7.0

R15

SCUFF

A composition in rail slides, eggshells, and empty pools.

12.22

16

martin

I enjoy skateboarding as much as I do a trip to the dentist. I'm not meant to have wheels attached to me. So for me the way into this project was the idea that no product is ever the same once you remove it from its packaging and begin to use it. This sense of manufactured perfection that we strive for is really an illusion. Scuffs, scratches, rust, dents, and all the other signs of wear and tear are the realities of ownership and should be embraced. I've always been interested in the idea of products aging with dignity, that as designers we can think beyond that moment of the shiny product on the store shelf. What about year one, two, and three? How do we want the patina of use to affect our designs? Most of these effects are slow in their evolution; with the skateboard, these effects are immediate.

kj

My trip to China had me thinking about how to apply decorative surface processes to the products we design, but I wasn't interested in just decoration: I wanted to create conflict. At some point we realized that the contrast between material traditions in skateboarding and Chinese lacquer would be an interesting juxtaposition. I worked on this experiment a bit with two designers, Meike Toepfer and Soren DeOrlow. Meike and I talked about how skateboarding is the perfect combination of decoration and destruction, and that the graphic design of these objects can be as important as the way you ride them. Then we asked Soren, an avid skateboarder and graphic designer, for help with the design details. He applied his own knowledge of skateboarding and connected the graphic design with specific skateboarding moments—a bird for harmony, a mountain for obstacles.

Chinese lacquer is focused on intricate details of decoration and simple combinations of red and black. These colors are the most common in Chinese lacquer products. The black is very deep and the red is incredibly vibrant. The decoration has its own elements of craft: broken eggshells, crumbled pieces of lacquer, thin lines of silver or gold foil. Lacquer is usually applied to a wood, plastic, or papier-mâché surface. The amazing parts of this process are the time required for the lacquer to dry and the amount of polishing that is required on each layer. The lacquer has to dry in a dark room, with high humidity, and it takes five days. To create a final surface with the qualities that are expected, four layers of lacquer are required. So that's twenty days! And in between each layer, and every few days, the lacquer is polished, usually by hand, for what seems like hours.

martin	kj

martin

I was shit at
skateboarding.

Yeah. I kept hitting
the paving stones
and falling off. Not
my cup of tea.

Yeah. It took a little
longer to hit Europe.

kj

When you were a kid?

The craze started in
the U.S., in L.A.,
Venice Beach, right?
With Dogtown and
Z-Boys and all that,
right?

What did you think
of the skateboard
prototype we got back
from China? I noticed
that we made a few
mistakes, because we
were working quickly,
early in the process.

You can't get every-
thing right.

I really like the notion
of worn products, and
this is definitely worn.

Yeah, the notion of
something very delicate,
very precious being
applied to an object
destined for some kind
of abuse was interesting.
The question is, do we
think it looks better
scratched up, or worse?

The pattern looks
Japanese, not Chinese.
And we put layers
of red/black/red/
black on the top
surface, but Gary
(the skateboarder)
covered the top
surface with grip
tape. Oops.

I think it's cool that
we transferred one
element of craft in
China to a "low-tech"
product...and later we
will do the same with
a "high-tech" product.

It's interesting that he didn't feel comfortable riding it without some convincing. I love that it wears so quickly and that it's not faked; it's genuine damage.

And I liked it because I only had to design a logo.

It definitely looks better scratched. But whenever anyone saw the skateboard when it was new, they were intrigued. I think it really confused people, in a good way. And when Gary first saw it he said: "Really? You want me to ride this? It will get scratched, I want to hang it on my wall, not destroy it..."

Cool. Glad you liked it.

I can't say that I've ever been inspired by a sense of obstacle.

Nice. Maybe we should design a few more variations. And we could pick a Chinese pattern, too.

I don't know if we ever talked about it before, but we were thinking that different patterns or images would represent different elements of the skateboarding experience. This one was about harmony. There was another one about obstacles.

If you look closely at the prototype you can see the Chinese character for harmony.

It also would be cool to establish a brief for this idea and let people contribute their own designs online, after the book is published.

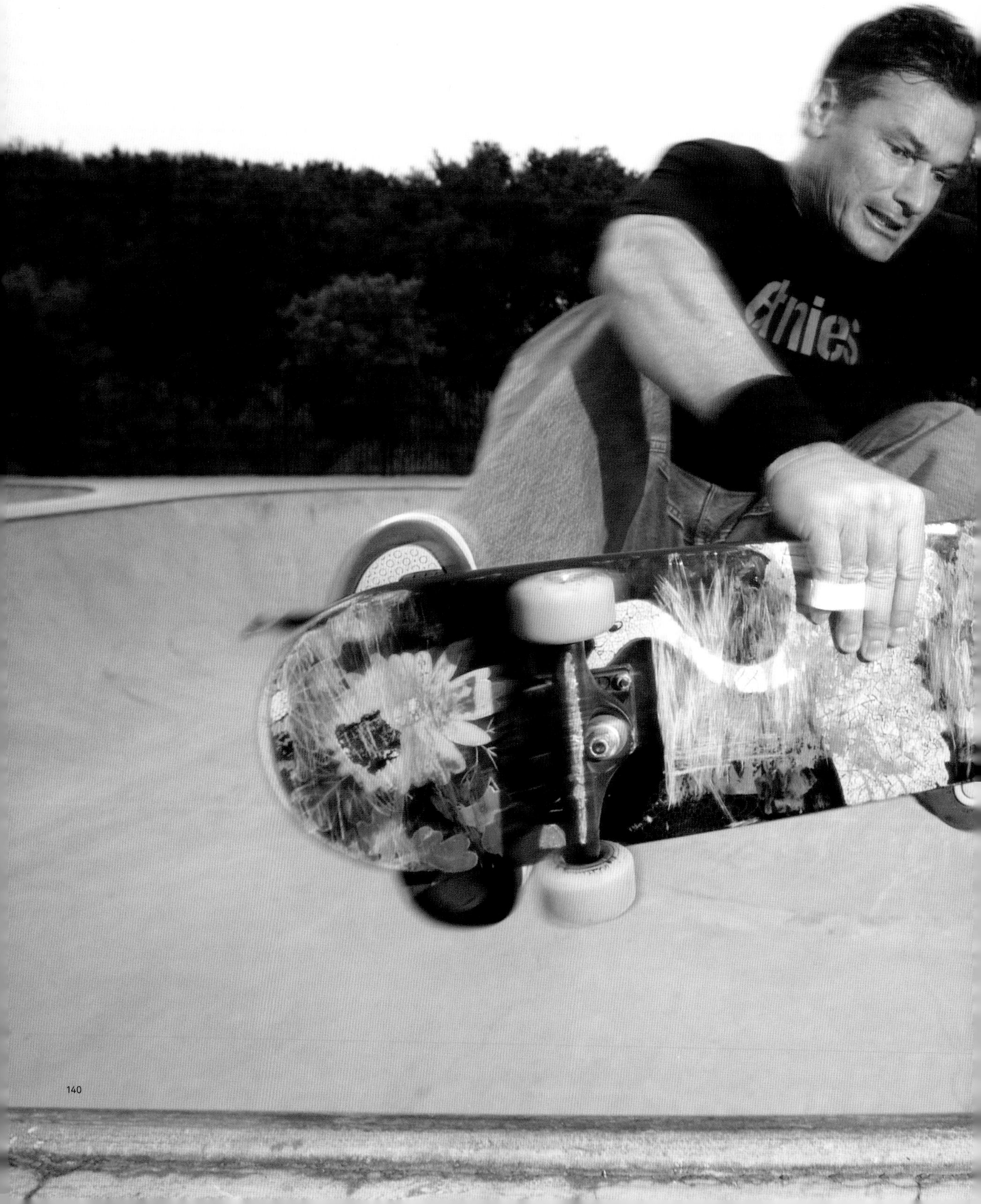
etnies

The skateboard was designed quickly, and then a file was sent to China to start the painting process. It took forever to make because of the layers of lacquer and the layers of decoration—metal foil and broken eggshells—and then eight layers of lacquer on the top surface, alternating red and black. The production of this prototype was important, and finding someone to ride it was necessary to finish the experiment.

Each person who looks at this board is overwhelmed by the beauty of it and doesn't want to ride it. But that's not the point. The thing we're trying to do is create a sense of surprise, tension, and in the end (hopefully) we will create a sense of beauty in the destroyed decoration after weeks of use and abuse.

A friend of mine introduced me to Gary Holl, a professional skateboarder, who lives nearby. We asked him to ride this board so that it could be scratched by a professional. He accepted our request to ride the prototype.

---

martin

Yep. We killed it.

---

kj

In this experiment we attempted to create a layer of decorative narrative on this simple object. The connections we were trying to make, between traditional craft and extreme sports, did not go unnoticed by Gary (our rider). The board communicates a weird combination of artistic detail and purposeful destruction. I wish we had created original graphics, but this one was applied quickly, as we were exploring how easy it would be to work with the Chinese craft "factories." Anyway, I like it better when it's scratched, and at that point the original art doesn't matter. The final graphic design is created as you ride.

If we do this again I think we'll have to limit the number of layers of lacquer because Gary said the board was really heavy when he rode it, but he loved the details and beauty of the lacquer. I loved how people were confused by a skateboard that is intended to be both intricately decorated and massively worn.

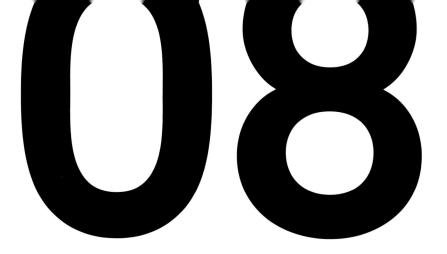

Brought to you by the letters C, A, and D.

martin

We're interested in the idea that fiction, the art of storytelling, can inspire reality, the art of mass production. Using a story as the starting point for the creation of an object is something I've never done before. Narratives create images in our heads; translating those images into tangible things is a very engaging proposition. There's more potential for this change in process to give us a different perspective on how we inspire ourselves, something more akin to movie production design than industrial design.

kj

The industries of design and advertising both use words and images in their process, but in this experiment we tried to reverse that process. We wanted to start with a story of a product that doesn't exist and then build it. If it's true that fiction is a reflection of our own reality, then the object that we design will fit into our own world. And at the end of the experiment, we can ask ourselves: If a writer sees a need for a product in a fictional world or narrative that they create, then does that need really exist in reality? Is the writer's imagination an untapped source of market research data?

BUNKER SPRECKELS

SURFING'S DIVINE PRINCE OF DECADENCE 1949–1977

DESIGNING

DESIGN

[Arthur Plotnik]

Chicken's Laundry SPIKE M

OBBINS Skinny Legs And All

DOWN and OUT in the Magic Kingdom

Cory DOCTOROW

HOW TO BREW

AN INTERVIEW WITH
CORY DOCTOROW

Cory Doctorow is a man who writes about the future, blogs like crazy, and fights for digital media rights and against copyright.

As an award-winning science fiction writer, he imagines futures where we might live and tells a compelling story about what life might be like. He is coeditor at one of the most popular blogs today: BoingBoing.net. He posts his own writings on Craphound.com. He is obsessed with Disney.

Basic Functional Japanese

Pegasus Language Services

The Japan

ON THE ROAD Jack Kerouac

SIGNET NOVEL AE 8562

THE ALPHABET FROM A TO Y WITH BONUS LETTER, Z! by Steve Martin and Roz Chast

KJ: You seem a little bit obsessed with Disneyland. Just out of curiosity: did you write *Down and Out in the Magic Kingdom* while sitting with your laptop on a bench somewhere within the gates of Disneyland? That's the image I have in my head—I imagine that it would be inspiring just to sit there and watch people walk by and pretend that it was more reality than fantasy.

Cory: I wish. I finished it at Walt Disney World, doing a thousand words a day on my balcony at the Polynesian Resort, but I mostly wrote it while traveling the world, raising money for a start-up and speaking at conferences. Most of that book was composed on an airplane's cramped seat-back trays . . .

Maybe since I already admitted to not being a techno-geek, can you tell me about your web sites, BoingBoing.net and Craphound.com? How did you get started?

I've always been a collector of interesting bits, physically and intellectually (even before I started writing fiction), but it's sort of how I write fiction. It's sort of like bricolage—finding little bits and pieces and putting them together.

What did you call it?

Bricolage . . . a collage of physical things. It's a French word. If only there was a web site that listed the meaning of words and perhaps one that is collectively editable by lots of people . . . maybe we could call it Wikipedia?

So...are you obsessed with anything else besides the Disneyland stuff?

Oh yeah . . . tikis, garbage, recycling, thrift sales, constructive reuse, Art Deco, science fiction, watches, revolutionary movements and their history, many writers, copyright, technology, cryptography. Comics, kitsch, haunted houses, Asia in general, and certain things in Asia in particular . . .

Clearly you're inspired by and interested in many things, but the detail that you know about Disney seems to be on a different level. Do you feel the same about all your obsessions?

Yup, all those things I just mentioned. Absolutely. It's popular culture, which is fun.

This is a question that I would ask with a bias, I think, but would you say it is easier to be obsessed with objects or with ideas? Some of the things you describe are physical artifacts.

At this point, because I move so much, physical objects are a real albatross for me. It's not trivial to figure out what to do with all that stuff. I have a hard time throwing away T-shirts. I get really sentimental about them. I came here with ten T-shirts, and now I must have a hundred T-shirts.

Is it harder to deal with those things once you've collected them—objects vs. ideas?

I don't believe in feng shui in terms of all the strength that that word has, but I do think that living in clutter is reflected in your life, and that your life is reflected in your environment. And for me, I have a hard time clearing my thoughts when I can't clear my desk. And so . . . physical objects have an overhead. A management overhead that is much higher than the overhead of ideas.

So it's harder to manage the physical objects. Yeah, I mean I guess that's because they're real, they're physical, you knock them, you kick them.

Or you just have to know where to put them, you have to store them, you have to dust them.

And like you said before, that's why you have a blog; it's a better place to keep things; it's sort of like a digital sketchbook for your thoughts and ideas?

Yeah. But, you know, all this stuff in my apartment is ephemera. I do like it. I like to collect stuff. Like these comic books on the table. Do you know who Will Eisner was? He was the first person to really make comics into art, and he, during World War II, did piecework for the military, doing extended maintenance guides.

I don't know him.

This one is from the year I was born. It is great. I found it at a yard sale. These are particularly unlovely objects; these are not intended to endure.

But they are beautiful, in their own way.

Yeah, they are. And it's because they're ephemera.

Recently I've heard some designers say that we are in a pluralistic world of design. It's all out there; we've seen it all before. And a lot of it is crap, not worth keeping or something that won't last very long. Everything's been done already. And the output is short-lived.

I would say that what we've done is we've abandoned progress in favor of change. So I don't think that there's a sense that we've run out of things to do, but I think that we've run out of narrative that says that *this* is the logical outgrowth of *that*. And we're moving toward (and

I always get this word wrong) apotheosis, somewhere down the road.

That makes sense. That we're moving toward things that are new and different, but with no meaning, no connections.

Yeah. And without that narrative of things getting better, of progress. In my next novella there's a character who is hell-bent on preserving the last junkyard full of steel-belted radials, because it's the last one. There's someone else who wants to get rid of it and turn it into arable land; they have nano-disassemblers that can turn anything into arable land. It's the details of lives of average people that really expose the guts of the society. The graffiti in Pompei is more interesting than the murals in Pompei; so this stuff, in a sense, this ephemera has that value.

So I understand that these things have that ephemeral quality to them, in the same way that all this semi-disposable IKEA furniture that we bought when we moved here (because you don't buy permanent furniture if you're only here for a year). But all this stuff has that character and in fifty years we'll look back and we'll go, "That's a mint-condition unlovely IKEA sofa . . . how wonderful."

Right, so it's true only because we're looking back at it.

Right.

Do you think that the things that you surround yourself with say something about you?

Oh, absolutely. It's communicative and it's also self-reinforcement. It tells you who you are, and it tells other people who you are.

And the idea is not quite linked, but it's like pluralism, it's abundance of information. And we have to deal with it and we have to filter it and we sort of love it and we're annoyed by it.

Abundance is a real theme in everything that I work on. So we have an abundance of ephemera. That's one of the differences between now and years gone by, that we have a lot more ephemera than we ever had. It's much cheaper to make ephemera than it's ever been, and it's much cheaper to distribute it.

What exactly do you mean by ephemera?

Anything that is not intended to endure.

So, including the iPod?

Yes, absolutely.

Cars?

Yes, absolutely, most cars are ephemera. But sports cars aren't ephemera. Coffee cups are ephemera. I think that what's characteristic of ephemera is that one of the ways that it's often distributed is as a giveaway. So I think that's a marker of a Happy Meal toy, or win a free iPod, or win a free car.

Based on how you feel connected to objects and what they mean to you, or could mean to us...would you consider writing a bit of text for us? About a product of your choice? Something really familiar to people. And then we'll use that text as our starting point for a design...

Make It a Verb
by Cory Doctorow

"Make it a verb," my daughter Tara said to me, looking over my shoulder as I worked at the kitchen table with my cardboard and knives, designing my next camera.

"Where'd you learn about verbs?" I said, holding the cardboard between my finger and thumb, pinching it while the glue dried. I'd scored the card and bent it around my finger, gluing twist ties in rows along its length so it would stay in whatever curve I bent it to.

"School," she said, picking up the round pieces I'd made to represent the lenses in my prototype. I could have used CAD modeling and the rapid prototyping printer, but handling the physical pieces engaged a different part of my brain, made the whole thing seem alive, changeable in a way that the wire frames on screen could never be. "Mr Denchasi's class. Verbs and nouns and adverbs and adjectives. Why no ad-nouns?"

"I don't know," I said, watching her dirty little fingers rub over the round edges of the disc, softening it. She smelled of orange juice, some of it still sticky at the corners of her mouth.

"Me neither. Everything you make is a noun, Pa. I have your camera. I want to *do* camera."

"What does that mean?" Every day, one of these little surprises. What went on behind those big brown eyes, so like Hilda's that it sometimes seemed I was talking to my wife in miniature, not my daughter?

"Everything you make is *too smooth*," she said. She brought me her backpack, a cheap thing made of Chinese ripstop nylon in forest green. "This too. Can't color on it. Can't make anything stick to it. But look at this." She brought out her binder, which had been covered in matching green vinyl. She'd neatly cut away the vinyl skin, leaving behind the heavy cardboard beneath. It was covered in dense hieroglyphs, doodles and games, sketches and words repeated endlessly until they lost all meaning. The ink flowed in rivers through the banks of stickers, endless stickers, oval banana stickers that said CHIQUITA and cut-up letters, characters pasted in layers. I put my finger out and traced them, feeling their furry, worn surfaces, the dimensionality where she'd built them up in layers, like a painter applying thick blobs of oil.

"You want to be able to put stickers on your camera?"

"I want to be able to *attach* things to it. Stickers, tape, anything. To draw on it."

"Won't it get full? Covered, I mean?"

She laughed. "Of course. So you take a picture of what it looks like when it's all covered over, scrape it off and start again. Silly."

She'd bent the "lens" around her finger, curling it into a cylinder. I got out my compass and drew another one on a fresh piece of cardboard. My models—they all had the evidence of my hands on them. I made my mark on them—fingerprints and fat lumps of glue and all manner of errata, hesitation marks and strokes of inspiration. Why should I be the only one?

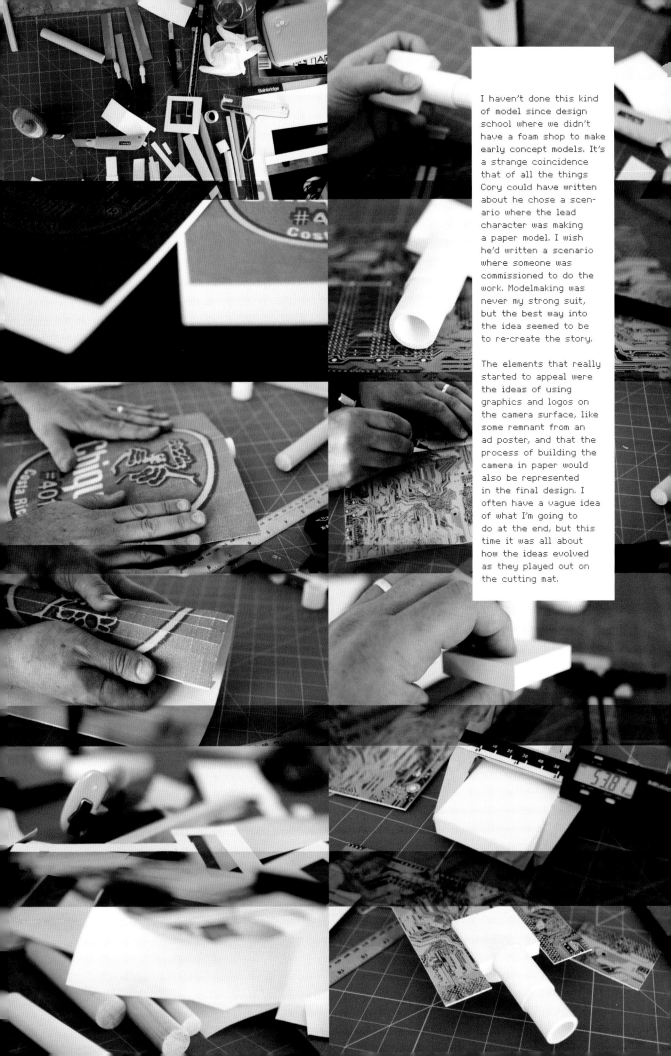

I haven't done this kind of model since design school where we didn't have a foam shop to make early concept models. It's a strange coincidence that of all the things Cory could have written about he chose a scenario where the lead character was making a paper model. I wish he'd written a scenario where someone was commissioned to do the work. Modelmaking was never my strong suit, but the best way into the idea seemed to be to re-create the story.

The elements that really started to appeal were the ideas of using graphics and logos on the camera surface, like some remnant from an ad poster, and that the process of building the camera in paper would also be represented in the final design. I often have a vague idea of what I'm going to do at the end, but this time it was all about how the ideas evolved as they played out on the cutting mat.

martin	kj

When I first read Cory's story I thought I would just do a consumer camera. But then I read more about him and some of the things he talks about on his blog and thought it would be cool to do a surveillance camera: CCTV.

I like that twist, it's a nice sci-fi reference.

I think that any design exercise requires additional research, not taking the brief at face value. His motivations play into it as much as any client's would if this were a conventional project.

Yeah, I agree, it's just interesting to watch how we have to "add" to the inspiration... totally good.

He's seems, er, a little preoccupied with governments and freedoms, etc.

Yes, and digital rights management (DRM) and all that... he's definitely an obsessive character, but that's what makes him interesting and he always has something to say. Lots of opinions.

Yep. The words will only get you so far. What's interesting for me about this experiment is understanding the right place for literal interpretation and where to take artistic license. It really highlights the act of making something tangible. "Words to object" is, in a sense, the foundation of design consultancies. Our clients give us words and we reply with a thing.

That's more useful for us. I'm curious about his reaction when he sees the thing.

I think it's interesting that this exercise in design from a narrative is as much about him (the author) as it is about what he writes...

Speaking of words (his)...what do you think of the first sentence? "Make it a verb." It's an interesting twist on design to say that we usually design "nouns" and the girl wants a "verb."

In what way? You know him better than me.

I only say that because you connected with the idea that he is into surveillance and government regulation and such... and that's not so much what he wrote about here.

I think it may mean, make it dynamic, give it action. Or maybe that's how I would like to interpret it. But I like how he puts it across. That's the great thing about writers; designers would never have written that or received a brief using that language.

How does a camera have action? or be dynamic? beyond the normal stuff—like taking pictures? It would be cool if the folds of the cardboard somehow opened and closed; not sure why but they could be part of a mechanism.

It's interesting to let the material of the model dictate the final material. The constraints of paper and board reflected in the final piece.

I'm not sure how to manifest it yet. I think the decision to go to a surveillance camera in some ways plays into it. Always present always watching. In a sense always active.

Yeah, I kinda like the idea...although I don't like vinyl much. Maybe we can use a different kind of paint and get a similar effect.

Maybe the little blinking red light that says it's tracking you can be something to play with...

I'm less interested in the green and the vinyl and more interested in the stickers.

I wanted to ask you about the reference to Chiquita banana stickers...do you know that reference? Or is it just a US thing? Those stickers really make me think of being a kid...

Yeah or we could shroud the lens and have it appear when working.

A little eye that pops out to see you...

I know it but I can't remember if I had them in the UK. My mum just said no on Chiquita in the UK.

There could be something in eyes and eyelids as long we don't end up on the cheesy end. Something in the organic nature of seeing.

I definitely remember seeing the banana stickers in random places. For some reason people feel it's OK to stick them anywhere. I never eat bananas anymore...

I agree, no cheese. I was also thinking about the idea of working with green vinyl...you can buy pre-coated metal (painted green) and then bend it to the form of the camera body...just like you would the cardboard. It might be cool if we do something like this, and even get a little tearing of the paint at the corners.

Stickers as camouflage and personalization.

I like the idea... it's very urban.

155

martin

I never thought we'd have anything. This was another experiment destined for the cutting room floor. This was the hardest experiment and the last one we finished. Even though we convert words into images every time we read, converting those images into tangible objects is tricky. I'd never really worked this way before, creating something based on someone else's narrative.

What's provocative about this idea is that commercial consultant design work doesn't always have to begin with user research; it's a default practice. I like the idea that forms of inspiration can come from many sources and that people can be represented in a number of ways. That creating something specifically for a fictitious character and situation can find relevance in the real world with real people.

kj

When you read a book, what you "see" is your interpretation of the words on the page. It isn't possible to know what the author actually intended you to visualize, and in some ways it doesn't really matter. The same is true of products. What the designer intended doesn't really matter, but what people think does.

When we shared this concept with Cory, he said it was different than what he had imagined: "The thing I'd visualized was a LOT more 'decorer'—something layered with the traces of many different trips, mementos, etc.—like a steamer trunk covered in beautiful luggage labels from the great hotels of the world, but for kids. Like a bone-cast that has been elaborated by a million felt-tip pens. Something that doesn't feel *designed*, but grown by its user." He liked it, but our design process had corrupted his original intention.

Julie Andrews
made me do it.

160

THIS IS THE CHAPTER ABOUT

LOVE + FETISH

kj

A few years ago I learned a business term called "net promoter." It's a calculation of the number of people who *love* a product (or would strongly recommend it) minus the number of people who *hate* the same product (or would tell people not to buy it). It's a quantitative measure of extreme emotional connection between people and products. This term is used to predict the possibility for viral marketing. We don't want to measure emotion, but we want to explore the extremes of love and fetish.

One product that we love and fetishize more than any other is the automobile. We live in a car culture. Not just because we drive them too much and we ignore the possibilities of public transportation, but because we love them. The automobile is a fully sensorial experience, where function and style are easily connected in your garage and on the open road. And to the truly obsessed, they are objects of fetish. And almost everyone

has a favorite. Your car says a lot about you. My favorite car is the BMW 2002; my dad's is the Pontiac Fiero. My mom's favorite car is an old yellow Volkswagen Rabbit. These cars don't become favorites without some other level of connection. They have stories, reasons they mean something to each of us. I had a crush on a guy in college who drove a BMW. My dad's midlife crisis was based on the idea that he could buy and drive a two-seat sports car, without my mom's approval and the kids would love it. And in the 1970s my mom was all about the color yellow because it reminded her of the state flag of New Mexico, where she grew up. And for her, that color paired nicely with a VW, which she always saw as a practical choice.

I am interested in the idea that you can build products that represent love or fetish. You can make ordinary objects sexy, and everyday tasks can be filled with ecstasy.

martin

Designers have our quirks, our compunctions, our obsessions that drive us to create. We tend to lead a bipolar existence, a devil and an angel on our shoulders, making little deals with ourselves to design our way through the day. Like I really love minimalism, but at the same time I also fetishize decoration. I realize that my desire for decoration is a temporary one, but my love for all things minimal is enduring. I'd sleep with William Morris wallpaper but marry a John Pawson interior. I don't want to live with the wallpaper—doing so may leave me constantly nauseated—but every now and again I crave it like someone may desire a good spanking or perhaps thigh-high patent leather boots. Maybe it's my secret shame? A designer in the modern age admitting to a love of ornament. Maybe that's what makes a fetish different from love: we admit our loves in public, write sonnets and poetry, but our fetishes lay buried in the darkest recesses of our minds. I fetishize

objects for a living. I have to; I have to find a way to connect to them. We revere the soda bottle, the toothbrush, and the automatic battery-operated thingamajig that cleans floors and steams vegetables. But ultimately I want to create objects that people love. We don't casually discard things that we love. We may still be fetishizing them, but we use a language of love.

Objects have the ability to delight and move us in the same way as a great painting, song, or movie. A trip to the local electronics emporium can be as vital and compelling as an afternoon in the Louvre. Er, not quite the same, but you know what I mean. In the spirit of the song so rousingly sung by Julie Andrews: when you've been bitten or stung, or feel bad or sad, you can think about your favorite things and, well, feel better.

kj

At some point, sitting in an apartment in Boston, we thought it would be important to ask someone else about these ideas. It seemed as though we were on some weird tangent about the love and fetish value of things, and that these ideas wouldn't make sense to anyone else. We thought it would be fun to ask a Brit about the hypothesis that Julie Andrews sings about: that people have favorite (or, favourite) things.

The Brit we decided to ask was Tony Hawks, a comedian/actor/singer who also writes books about slightly off-center things like hitchhiking around Ireland with a fridge (www.tony-hawks.com). Tony seemed as good an audience as any for this conversation. (I knew him because he's my friend's stepbrother, but the funny coincidence is that Martin actually recognized Tony from an episode of *Red Dwarf* about a talking toaster, and from a popular song called "Stutter Rap" that mocked the Beastie Boys, something that only someone who grew up in England in the '80s would know anything about.) We asked Tony by e-mail what he thinks about what I am now calling "The Julie Andrews Factor;" we tagged particular things or specific experiences as favorites so that when we need to feel better we can recall them more easily. A mental Post-it note, if you will. Is this a cultural obsession or human nature?

Tony replied to our e-mail with the following comment: "Hi. I think it is both human nature and cultural obsession. There's nothing wrong with us having a favourite thing unless suddenly being without it would make us unhappy. We tend to 'attach' to things and imagine that they are hugely important to us. It would pay us to remember that there are millions of wonderful, lovely things out there and that there really is no need to have a 'favourite.' Julie Andrews' character listed as one of her favourite things: 'Brown Paper Packages tied up with string.' Poor thing.

If 'we need to recall memories to feel better,' then it's a recipe for feeling a bit miserable or maudlin. Those moments are gone—we'll never get them back—and they'll never be the same anyway, however hard we try to re-create them. We can remember and enjoy the memory, yes, but if we do it in order to feel better I believe that we're deluding ourselves. Our responsibility, at least if we want to remain vibrant and contented, is to create new moments all the time. Like now—the moment you're reading this. Pretty goddam fantastic, eh?"

I was actually sort of surprised by Tony's opinion. As designers, we work in a world where we strive to create things and engaging experiences that people can love. We believe that people have favorite things and we believe that we can design them.

martin

Handcuffs and wedding rings, both objects that represent very different emotional states; rings for love, cuffs for fetish. Both essentially circles of metal, one encloses finger the other wrist yet worlds apart when it comes to our perception. Here we sculpt, tweak, colour and select our way through these experiments, manipulating materials in an attempt to elicit these empathic responses.

Top 5 guilty pleasures:
1. Watching an episode of *Seinfeld* or *Frasier* that you've already seen more than once
2. Neil Diamond
3. A vanilla milkshake and fries, with ketchup
4. *Columbo*, on a rainy day
5. Long, hot showers

THE SECRET LIFE OF OBJECTS:

martin

This is a small group project that explores the secret life of objects and the notion that a product tells more than one story from more than one owner. Whether private or public, intimate or shared, our interaction with products inevitably leaves a mark. From chance encounters on a train or the isolation of an iPod, these are moments that, as designers, we can use to explore ideas around the passage of time, memories, and community.

kj

I've been thinking about the secret lives of objects since I read Tom Robbins' novel *Skinny Legs and All* in which one of the main characters is a can of beans. The idea that the products we create might be trying to tell us something should not be just an interesting concept for fiction. As designers, it's a compelling opportunity to send messages and tell stories through the creation of products. The stuff we create is an enabler for our message, or for a company's message; it's a new way to look at and understand an object's identity or its "brand".

Inspired by the four concepts that we have included here, Martin and I step further into the world of love and fetish, where secrets are only part of our emotional connection to objects.

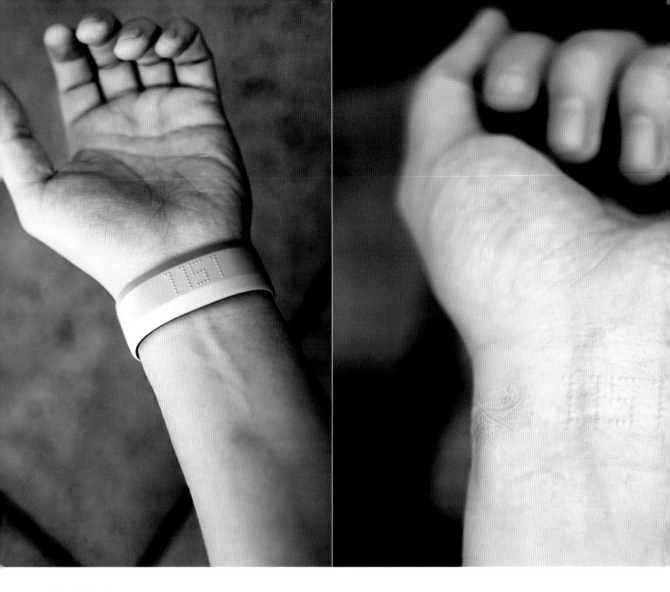

TATTOO

(Gregory Germe)

Objects change over time.
Like us, they evolve and
age. They leave marks on
us as we leave marks on
them. Temporarily or for
life, they are the wit-
nesses of the intimacy
we share with products.

What's really interesting about this idea is that it
plays with the temporal nature of a watch. When you
take the watch off, the very moment you do so is
recorded on your skin as small indentations. As your
skin slowly recovers, that moment in time is gone,
but the representation lasts longer than normal. One
minute lasts several; time is still moving on, your
skin is responding, but at that moment the manifestation of time is changing from numeric to physical.

This watch takes the concept of tactile
branding to a new level. It's a product that
can tattoo you. By wearing it, you adopt
its logo as part of your skin. And in this
case, the watch speaks to you, even when
you're not wearing it. I think this idea
connects nicely with the notion that even
when you're not wearing a watch, you tend
to look at your wrist to see what time it
is. And this is where my dad would usually
make a not-so-funny joke: "What time is
it?" "A hair past a freckle."

OASIS

(Jeewon Jung)

How can a public place offer a more intimate experience to an individual? By adding a solar-powered reading lamp, a street bench is transformed into a comforting private space.

At the bus stop and in the park, benches are everywhere, but they are often not designed for use; in fact, they often discourage use. Sometimes they are built so that people cannot sleep on them; sometimes they are built to separate people from each other. In this concept, we are looking at the idea that the city's furniture can be as comfortable and inviting as the things you keep in your own home.

An interesting way to deal with public space: The transforming of a park bench to essentially give it a second life at night and the capturing of space for privacy.

SQUAT

(Jeewon Jung)

The mirror-coated space makes privacy available in public areas, which traditionally a public phone booth would have offered.

I like the idea that the void is shiny to reflect its environment, rendering it "invisible" and further reinforcing the notion of secret. I also really like that you can see people's feet and imagine their conversations based on how they are standing.

With the introduction of cell phone technology, the phone booth has lost most of its purpose, but people still need a quiet place to have a conversation.

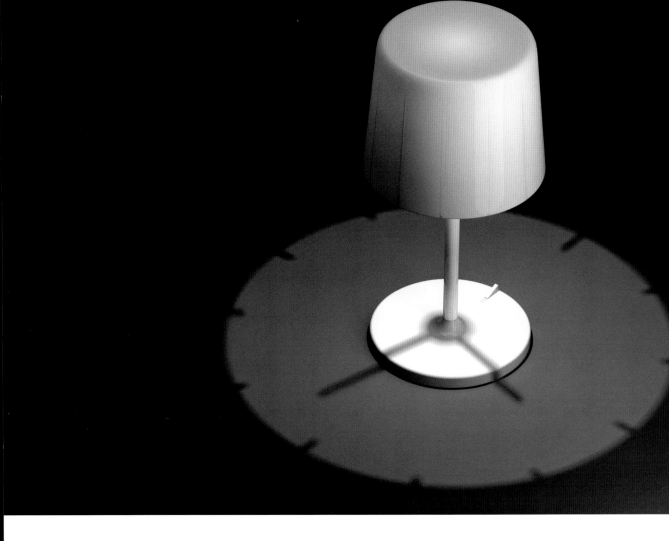

SHADOW

(Angie Kim)

Shadows are alive. I often look at shadows and see something different from the object projecting it. They embody different forms that capture all the moods of the day. Shadows are a reflection of time.

This is an object that really has a secret life. The clock is hidden and is revealed only in shadow when the lamp is turned on. Off, a solitary existence. On, a marriage of objects.

The table light reminds me of a simple white lamp I just bought at IKEA (a wonder of packaging as the stand for the light was packed in the light shade itself). But the coolness factor of this table light is so much greater. Using light for two purposes is really intriguing. The edges of a useless and perhaps annoying shadow that is cast by a light are given function here in a way that is amazingly simple. It also seems easy to sell clock-adapters for any lamp. It's an easy way to create secrets in an ordinary object.

martin	kj
Hmmm, smoked cheese . . . I'm eating smoked cheese.	
	That's funny, I was just eating some brie. And I was going to IM you to say that really good brie is, like, really good... :)
Mmmmmmmmmm, brie.	
	What I really need right now is some wine, to go with the brie, but I'm all out...
Mmmmmmmmmmmmmm, wine . . . now I'm doing three things: eating lunch, typing with one hand, and watching *The Sopranos*.	
	How very "girlie" of you—multi-tasking... I guess that would make more sense if you were watching *Sex and the City*.
Yes, the difference is though that girls can do all three well, I can only manage the eating part.	
	Too bad...

SCREW

CORK

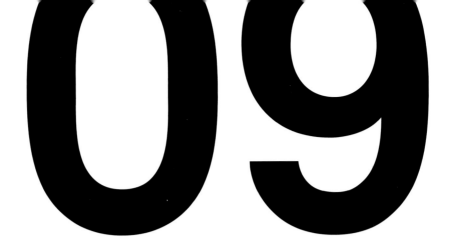

Shall I compare thee
to a Bordeaux's cork?

martin

Kara is obsessed with this crappy fake cork stuff.
It's weird. Really weird. I mean how can you spend this
much time thinking about what sits in a wine bottle
and have those thoughts not be about the grape?
But that's the nature of our loves and fetishes: they
defy logic. One person's "bit of strange" is another
person's vanilla ice cream.

Personally I don't like synthetic cork. It's boring;
it hasn't got the character of real cork. It may be
better for the wine but so is a screw cap. Unless we
run out of real cork, this is a material that could
be doomed to extinction before anyone knew it existed. After all, it doesn't even have its own name. But
despite all of this, Kara has made me interested in
seeing what we could do with this material: one to
overcome my lack of interest, and two, to see if we
can do something to help some manufacturers that
Kara has a connection to.

kj

I have been a little bit obsessed with synthetic cork for years. Not because I like wine,
but because I find it an intriguing imitation.
Real cork is cool too. I want to use design
to manipulate this mostly ignored material
and make people think about it in different
ways. Cork is one of those materials that has
been sort of stereotyped. A cork is made of
cork. That's just the way it is. And why can't
cork be furniture, not just the stopper on a
bottle of wine? There are more possiblities
than we expect.

martin	kj	

You want to talk about cork?

First I want to talk about materiality.

Like what?

Oh, yes—I remember from my Craft, Design, and Technology A-level.

Plaid.

Really?

You're so smart.

Plaid is awesome; plastic isn't. Agree or disagree?

Yeah, but it clearly stopped there when I was seventeen. Wait— isn't that a Frank Sinatra song? Just heard it on The Sopranos . . . "A Very Good Year," or something. I'm gonna look it up on the internet.

Plaid is wank.

Why?

I don't have to justify my remarks. :-0

Ah, of course, the Internet. What a god- send that thing is.

What do you think people would say if I asked them: "Cork or Polymethyl- methacrylate?"

Can you imagine if we didn't have it? Stop the chat and run to the library to get a book . . .

Ah . . . my old friend PMMA.

Glad you recognized her, but most people wouldn't...I guess the more common question is: "Paper or plastic?"

That would not be good. I'd have to run to the library to get a book that could convince you about how cool plaid is...

I have no idea why people like plaid, do you?

I like that it has history. I like that it makes me think of L.L.Bean pajamas that every- one used to have when I was in high school. I like that it only exists as a pattern. But I don't own any plaid— except that Jack Spade bag I bought because it looks like the Chinese migrant worker bag. That's a sort of a modern plaid.

I guess.

Do you like argyle
socks?

Are you reading the big
book of medieval fabrics?

No. Just being silly.

I think we've lost our
focus here. Didn't you
want to talk about cork?

Yeah. I want to
make something out
of cork.

Why do you love cork
so much?

Real cork is just
cool because it comes
from the bark of old
trees in Portugal.
I think synthetic
cork can be beau-
tiful, but it's
something no one
notices.

Maybe we should try
to reverse the idea of
cork in a wine bottle.
Make a glass cork and
a cork bottle.

Awesome. Let's do
it. I'm going to
ask the guys in
the shop to build
us a cork bottle.

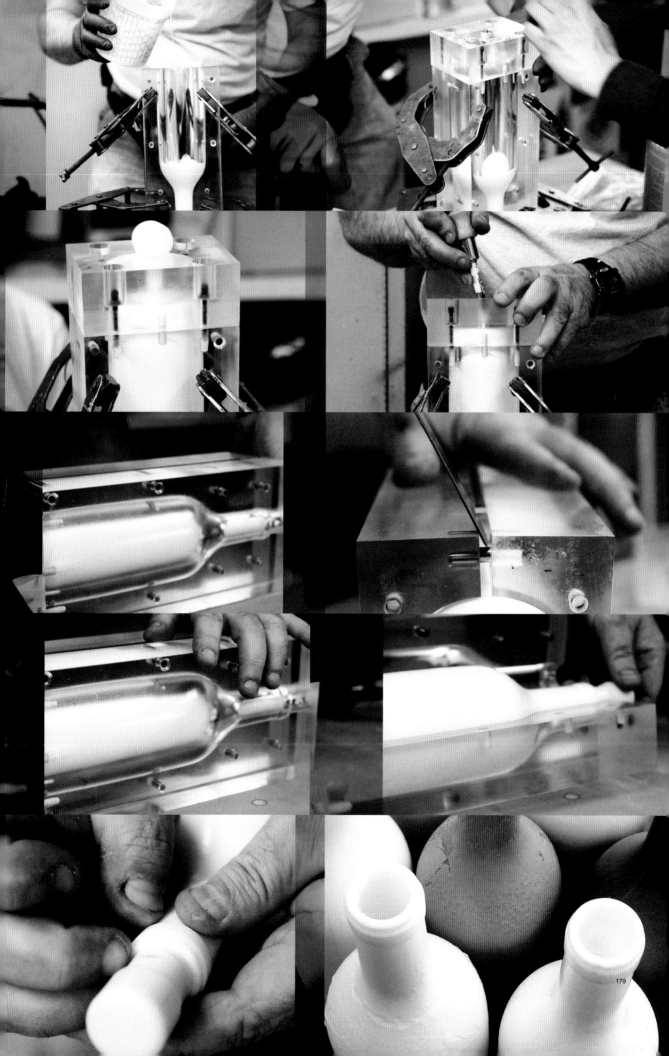

martin	kj	
	What do you think of the cork bottle stuff so far?	
This is one of those three-second ideas that suddenly got a life of its own. "Hey—what if we did a bottle made from cork? That would be a laugh." Then suddenly we're machining lumps of cork and the thing snowballs.		
	Yeah, funny how that happened. It was also a little trick to create momentum.	
Remember how crazy the faux-cork people thought we were?		
	Oh yeah-I remember. Maybe I should send an e-mail back to that guy with the results of our experiment. Just to say something like, "I told you so."	
	I thought it was a cool promotional idea for their material—sending people faux-cork bottles as a way to talk about the properties of the material. I just thought of a tagline for them: "This wine is corked!" Über cheesy. Wine and cheesy, in fact.	
		Yes. Funny (almost). ;)
	Wine and cheesy? Kidding . . .	

martin

Some ideas are like a long torrid love affair that lasts forever, and some are like a quick shag with someone you met in a bar whose name you don't know. This is the latter. Quick and dirty: you either get it or you don't.

kj

I don't know exactly how this experiment got started, but I think that I've finally had a chance to express how I feel about cork— real and synthetic. It's not a material that we often get the chance to work with, but I believe it has the ability to mean some-

thing to people. If we look closely, we can find design opportunities to manipulate that meaning. Cork is a material that people recognize. To play with the idea of mater- iality, we reversed the materials in a wine bottle and we fell in love. Everyone who saw these bottles was intrigued and wondered what we were doing. It was a perfect, although accidental, viral marketing campaign for our process of experimentation and this book in general.

HEBBE
BBE
NDIN
DIN
GETJE
TJE
GE

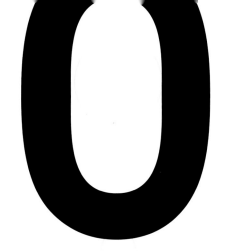

I gave her my heart and she gave me a pen.

---

martin

An obsession for me over the years has been collecting stories about why people love stuff. I'm happy to film anyone who's enthusiastic about one of their possessions, because that goes to the heart of why I do what I do. I want to understand why things exist that make no sense to me: bad ceramic figurines, hell even good ceramic figurines, those lamps that have oil droplets running down wires, decorative thimbles, plastic flowers, bumper stickers, pet clothes. We are a culture of collectors. Some of us are good at it, some bad, and some are experts in the field of commemorative spoons and plates. It's fascinating to see the motivations behind some of these things and to hear the language these people use. It's really a language of love.

---

kj

These days it is common for designers to talk about the emotional connections that people have with products. But I don't think we truly understand details of how this connection works. We know it exists, but we haven't really tried to manipulate it.

We should ask people to tell us why they love something, an object. And then we can transfer the details and experience of each object to another object. I wonder if we can design for love in this way.

I met a guy named Ivan at my friend Perry's party. Ivan is a restoration car mechanic. It would be great to interview him for this love experiment. I want to find out why he loves cars so much. When I was talking with him at the party, he said something about how he builds people's impossible dreams. That sounded intriguing. Maybe we can transfer his love of vintage racing cars into a more ordinary and humble object...like a pen?

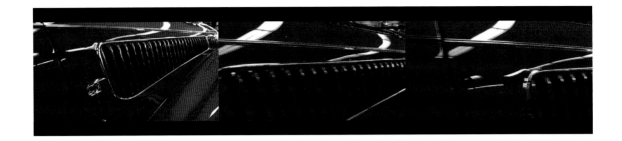

Ivan Zaremba
Car Maestro

I was seven in 1950. I went from comic books to car magazines, which were on the next rack in the store. I went to the car magazines, I just gravitated to them. I had no family influence; there was nobody else around. But gee, it's cars—little boys, cars, you know. And I started reading about hot rods, and cars and cars and cars and more cars. And that's never left me.

There's gratification involved in doing something with your own hands, as opposed to being some-one who is a deal-maker, who shuffles papers or whatever. This car just

happens to be here now; this happens to be one of my favorites. This is an Alfa Romeo. And it's called an 8C2900B Millemille Spider. This car has had a 9,700-hour restoration. I'm really looking forward to fixing this car for two reasons. Number one, I love it—on paper, in the books. And number two, I'm proud of the fact that it was sent here for this kind of job. It has an artful appearance, it has a mechanical fun-ction, it is everything that is not natural. It's artificial in the sense that it's man-made and you have actually had a hand in this.

The idea of infecting other people with the love of this stuff, in the same way that I've received it from others, that's the deal. And if you can then breed in the next generation a love of this stuff, all this stuff will be as wonderful to my grandkid as it was to me when I first saw it and heard it. And passing on the stories and all the rest of that, the lure of it, that sense of the camaraderie of the road, and these adventures that you had, I think for all of us we relive our youth in some of this. Don't we?

martin	kj	

kj: I guess we should start by talking about what caught your eye in the video of Ivan and his cars.

kj: The exterior. I got a sense from the video you sent that was what resonated with Ivan.

kj: Interesting...the next step is to design a pen based on the interior. ;)

martin: I think I just reacted to the stuff that he liked. I'm not that interested in cars. The Alpha doesn't appeal to me. But it's not really about what I like.

kj: It's such a red car! And the view looking down the car from the front is awe-inspiring...

kj: Oh God, no.

kj: Just kidding...do you think the red paint and the swooping lines and the metal details on our pen make too obvious of a connection?

martin: It's not my cup of tea.

kj: It seems to me that even if it's not your style, it's sort of universally amazing, but maybe not.

kj: Nah. He says he loves the car but he doesn't say why. We have to give form to the pen and so we should draw from those elements of the car that can be translated. It's not like we can be inspired by the engine block.

martin: I didn't see it in person so it may have something that I'm not seeing.

kj: Maybe. Is there anything you did like about it?

kj: That's true...and I think that Ivan probably really likes those details. Those details are something that he spends all his time restoring, as well as the engine block.

martin: I liked the interior details. It's not that I dislike it or can't appreciate its build quality, I just don't share Ivan's passion. But that's the point: This stuff is very personal.

kj: Did you pull any of the interior details to the pen...or was it more about the exterior?

kj: I think the video provides a filter that makes it interesting. You are seeing something that's been edited. It's not raw so you end up reacting to it on a surface level, visually. But the tone and language of our heroes adds a layer of depth.

I got off a plane from Seoul, this morning and drove across the Golden Gate Bridge to meet Ivan for lunch near his garage. I wanted to ask him to evaluate the prototype of a pen that we built for him based on his love of cars. Our prototype was a "looks-like" model, which means it didn't actually work.

The lack of mechanical function was the first thing we talked about. I wondered if it would be possible for Ivan to fall in love with this pen if he can't "drive" it. But I think that to Ivan it was really interesting that it didn't work. He said it makes the pen more of a memento of our meetings, a symbol (like so many other things in our world), a symbol of our relationship and this experiment.

Ivan also reminded me that the color of the car that inspired this pen is controversial—there are people who think it was a darker red more like red wine, more like the Alfa that I helped push into his garage today when I parked outside for lunch. But Ivan believes these cars were a bright red and that the pigments used to create this red are almost pure, just a single pigment creates the color; there is no mixing. I think it's the purity that is interesting to Ivan.

Pens are one of these things that you hold in your hand like a tool. Like a Snap-on wrench, it has to have a good feel. And I think that the shape of the pen here is well-matched with the shape of the car. Our pen looked comfortable in his hands. I think I'd like to build a "works-like" model and leave it with him for a few months. I think this pen would look better with age.

Nicolas Zurcher
Photographer

My work is not trendy; even doing commercial work I'm creating art, so I'm looking for a time-lessness. This shell container that my grand-mother gave to me, when you realize what it actually is, it becomes even more of a cherished item, sort of a lover's keepsake.

This is Cesar—he feels really sturdy (see suitcase on opposite page). It's the weight that makes it feel comforting, the patina on this leather, and I can sort of get lost in these sorts of details for hours. It ended up being the perfect size for my four-by-five camera. I love the fact that I was the only kid in college who didn't have a sort of a cloth case, perfectly constructed, bought from the same store and everything. I like to express some of my character.

A lot of it is history: where does it come from, not who made it or the pres-tige of it, but where's it been, what's its potential? I love morphing something into a new role.

Eric Stangarone
Former Sous-chef

After high school I went to Johnson Wales Academy, which is a culinary school. I began my first internship at a restaurant called Galileo, in Washington, D.C., for a chef named Roberto Donna. He was a big-name Italian chef, a big chef in general, kind of known for his temper. I worked for him for a year, cooking fish and meat on the grill. And I had great times: it was the time of my life; I was twenty years old, and working for a superstar chef. It was unbelievable.

This is called an "abattre." It's a French knife (see knife on opposite page). This is the kind of knife that you'll probably sit on your entire life. It's basically a cross between a cleaver, which would end here, but it continues on and it has this long edge here. So when you're taking apart an animal, like a duck or a chicken or a goat, you cannot only hack bones, but you can push through. This is probably my favorite of the bunch.

When it all clicks, it feels like an extension of your arm; it feels like it's a piece of you. I think it's more gaining trust with that knife, rather than going out and say-ing I want that one or that one based on looks or whatever.

martin

I'm not sure how I feel about this one. To me it feels like one of those shirts that read "My friends went to Ibiza and all I got was this lousy T-shirt." Here people poured out their feelings and we designed, well, a pen.

In many ways this whole book can be summed up in this one experiment: How do you connect objects to people emotionally? It's the very essence of trying to create stuff that has value and the foundation of what it means to be an industrial designer. So what's the problem? I'm not sure a pen can capture all of that. On one hand it's a simple product that's easy to understand, personal, and something we all use. On the other it's hard to know if it's the kind of object that would elicit strong passionate responses from people. It's not exactly an Aston Martin DB4 Zagato. I'm not a car guy, but even my heart rate increases when I look at it. That's why men have the same glassy-eyed, goofy look on their faces at a car show that they have at a porn convention. We're hard-wired to have emotional reactions to certain things and experiences. A vintage Parker 51 pen or a cruise down Route 66 in a 1957 Porsche speedster—either one can elicit the same endorphin response if they happen to be your personal obsession. I prefer pens to cars (there's nothing more arousing than a 0.1mm Rotring Rapidograph) but that probably puts me in the minority.

kj

At Ivan's garage, it's easy to see how he can love his job and his life and his cars. It seemed impossible to re-create these emotions in a pen. This pen doesn't even write—it's just a model. But still he loved it. And I think more than anything he was touched by the fact that we tried to capture his love in a physical object. Meeting Ivan (or Ivanski, as his car friends call him) was one of the most delightful and inspiring experiences of my life. His casual and yet intense person-ality is a joy. He is a man who is exactly who he is, and that's beautiful.

I want to open this experiment up to a broader audience. It would be cool if people were encouraged to submit their own videos describing their love of an object and then designers can access those videos to inspire the design of a pen. Perhaps in the end we could create an entire product line based on how people love what they love.

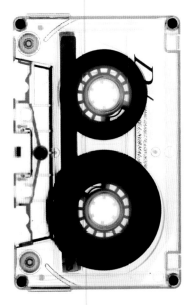

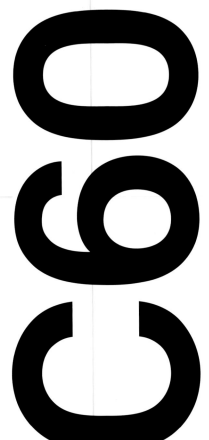

experiment

The "10cc's of Vinyl" Mix, Summer '09

martin

I recently sold my record collection, my musical youth. Gone forever is my 1979 pink vinyl single of "Cool for Cats," by Squeeze. Why? Because I hadn't listened to it, or any of the others, for eighteen years. It had been left dormant in a box somewhere as I had gone on a quest to find the perfect turntable—an object so beautiful that to purchase one on a whim seemed like an inexcusable act. No, this was something that required thought, discussion, and as it turned out, a considerable amount of time. The ones I loved I couldn't afford, and by the time I could, the love affair had ended.

Meanwhile, behind the scenes, like some insidious audio virus, my CD collection had started to take over. With its "oh-so-convenient" compact format, and its "oh-so-infuriating" clear plastic case, it had killed my beloved vinyl. Rest in peace, 2 Tone records. I loved you once. Gone are my dreams of a perfect turntable, replaced by the nightmare of the CD player, which sticks out its tongue and swallows my music whole, taking it to a dark place to scorch it with lasers like some kind of techno torture chamber. Boxy and bland, it has no soul, no ritualistic tendencies, and, above all, no love, for me or my music.

As a kid I used to watch the records on my record player go around, and the needle and arm danced the beats from the tinny speakers. The music had form.

You had to care about it, because you had to take care of it. One false move, one carelessly discarded sleeve, and your music was done for: warped, scratched, unplayable. You connected to songs emotionally but also physically. Yes CDs are physical, but they're not quite the same. They look cheaper; they feel a little tackier. The gloriously tactile cardboard canvas of the twelve-inch record, replaced by a smaller, clear square of plastic—it's a bit like watching *Gone with the Wind* on a phone. How would you rather look at *Sgt. Pepper's*, Pink Floyd's *Animals*, or any of the Blue Note covers?

Gone are the hours spent in the record store on a Saturday, leafing through the racks in search of that hidden gem. Replaced with sitting in front of the computer in your underpants, a sad lyric junkie, trolling through the iTunes store getting a thirty-second taste of something that promises to be better than it is. But hey, at 99¢, if it's shit you can always throw it in the trash or stick it in a playlist with the other ten thousand songs you never listen to.

kj

Thanks, dude. Now there's no space for me to write anything. But anyway, well said.

martin

kj

I have a question about the first idea you sent for this MP3 player. I kinda like the crop circles that sort of imitate tape cassette wheels... do they have a function or are they just decoration?

No, it's still there. The album is two parts: one is the individual songs that can be torn out, like a Pantone book, and the second is the album cover that includes digital information for all songs. RFID tag technology allows the sensor to be embedded in the paper.

Yep, decoration. I might try a pattern inspired by some other musical element.

Ahhh...got it. And then you stack the albums on the MP3 player and they can be read by the device?

OK—well for what it's worth, I liked the reference.

Me too. There's a bunch of interesting references between analog and digital to play with.

The MP3 player reads what's stacked on top, essentially a tangible playlist. If the albums are stacked neatly the songs play in order; if they are misaligned then the songs are shuffled. From a technology standpoint the only thing I'm not sure about is if the entire MP3 is stored on the paper or if there's just a pointer to a location on the web where the data is stored and streamed.

Maybe there's some kind of way to build a pattern that connects vinyl record gratings.

Gratings? Do you mean grooves?

Yes...I wasn't sure what they were called. I couldn't think of the right word.

I can talk to Doug Solomon. I don't think you've ever met him. He has worked in technology and social impact in many companies around Silicon Valley, including Apple.

The design's not done yet but I've evolved the basic idea. I was trying to get back to the physicality of music and the cool large-format graphics of album covers.

Cool. Can you ask him about the MP3 player—specifically about whether to embed the whole song or just the online info?

I seem to remember that when we were talking about this idea earlier, there was something about taking an album and tearing off a piece of it to give away or share a single song...the MP3 song would be embedded in the paper, for each song...but maybe that idea went away?

Will do.

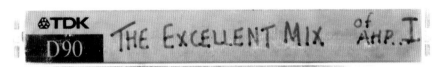

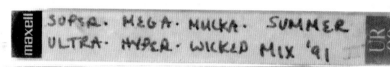

I spoke with Doug about the idea that this MP3 player allows people to create a mixtape of digital music. When I showed him our idea, the first thing he said was, "Why is it twelve inches square? No one is ever going to want that. MP3 players are just going to get smaller and smaller."

I asked Doug to focus on the technology first: we need to get an MP3 song onto the paper that is the album cover. He said that it is easy to embed an RFID memory chip in the paper; it would be cheap enough, and eventually the RFID tag can be printed. The chip holds the data, and the reader bounces radio waves off the antenna and sucks the data off the chip. Then, you can have the player pull the song from a database on the web. The actual data doesn't need to be on the chip, and then I guess if you don't own it, you could be asked to buy it. The RFID chip could have a whole album but right now there's not much space on most chips, barely enough for one song. But in five years this memory should be cheaper and then the chips will be able to hold lots of information.

Doug really is a believer in technology and progress. He said that he thinks that even-

tually even the token that represents music (a tape cassette, a CD, an MP3 file) will disappear and the device that plays your music, will recognize you, find your music and pull it to exactly where you are from some digital storage space. He mentioned that his playlist of Hawaiian songs is better than anything physical: it's just hours of music, and that's all he wants. Then again, he hasn't yet thrown away any of his CDs or vinyls.

I realized, in the middle of this conversation, that Doug and I sort of disagree in some very lovely ways about stuff like this...I don't want everything to disappear in a virtual world. I make things. I want to keep some of the physical stuff around.

martin | kj

Can you tell me more about the album covers you sent?

We need enough to create a stack so that we can talk about the interaction metaphor. Something original using online stock images that have been played with. The band names and albums are all made up. I used an online lyric generator.

I like the idea of having the lyrics there. But today I found myself trying to explain to someone how you make a mix-tape and I really couldn't explain it easily. Could you walk me thru that again?

Cool. I get it. Some of them are by the same artist. Like Ian Quimby has a few, is that right?

You select the tracks on an album that you like, tear them out and place them in a sequence with other tracks, bind them, and send them to your lover. The act of giving away the track is the act of love, because you will no longer be able to play it.

I figured that you would buy a couple of albums from one artist, hence the same name.

OK.

So you have a limited number of copies of each song that you can tear and mix?

We also have to pick one "feature" album that gets songs on the back and lyrics and perforations.

You have only one copy of each song.

You can't have two copies? One you keep and one you mix?

I liked the idea that when you tear off a track, the album art remains, but the lyrics and the music leave you. We could do two, but then there's no internal conflict as to whether to give away the track . . .

I like having two copies better because if you give a song away to someone, you might still want to listen to it, to remind you of that person or just because you like that song. You still have to choose who you want to share the song with, and you only get to pick one person.

You have a point there. I
like that it would be more
like a "jigsaw" piece . . .
so they have something
of you and you have the
"hole" to remind you.

If the album is
twelve by twelve, what
size are the songs?
And how do you bundle
the songs as a mix?
And how does that mix
get played?

I was thinking about
using the cassette case
as a tongue-in-cheek
reference, but I have
to check the dimensions.
The songs slip into the
case, and then the
entire case is placed
on the player . . . The
tape cassette case
is 4.25"×2.75"×0.5".
Those dimensions get
you twelve tracks on
an album.

Done. I'll make a layout
to show how this works.
Maybe you put the pieces
of paper (the songs)
into a cassette tape box,
with room for annotation.
Then you can add song
lyrics, like on old-school
liner notes.

I see—so it's an
array of cassette-
size perfs.

Yeah, and I spent all day
looking for a fucking
perforation machine to
make the proto.

Sweet. I wonder what
the tape-cassette-
sized MP3s would look
like on this player...

That doesn't
sound fun.

Actually, that's a total
lie. It was more like half
an hour.

Also we can add this
idea to music magazines,
where you can tear out
a song and throw it onto
the player.

I think twelve tracks
is OK. Let's lock it
like that.

So were you think-
ing that the black
plastic for the
player would be
some material
that references
the magnetic tape
from an audio
cassette tape?

I want it in the dark
brownish-black that's the
same color as tape.

OK.

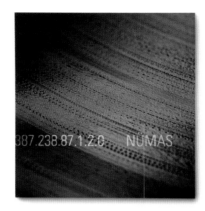

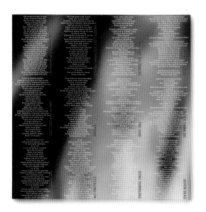

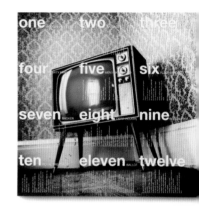

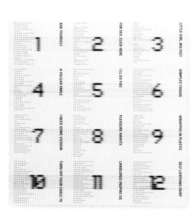

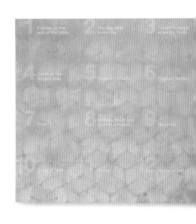

Ideas are not quite the same

open format

PUSH IN
TO LOCK

god's dirty laundry

EXPERIMENT № 11
C60

the cupboards

VHF

CHANGING
CHANNELS

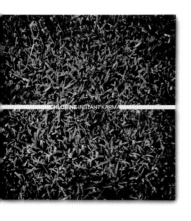

CHLORINE INSTANT KARMA

Boxcar Weekends

IAN QUIMBY UK

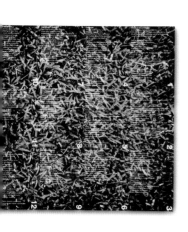

The idea here was to
find a physical represen-
tation of the elements of
modern musical life that
we've come to love (such
as playlists and shuffle),
but not give up on that
retro mixtape, twelve-
inch vinyl physicality.

martin	kj		

kj: I think I pay more attention to lyrics than most people. Is it because I'm a girl?

martin: Ah, music and gender theory.

kj: Now I've really got you going—talking about gender theory, your favorite! ;)

martin: I was talking to someone about lyrics and music the other day . . . can't remember why. She said she likes electronic music—so she doesn't have to concentrate on words.

kj: I think the reason I like mixtapes is related to how I feel about lyrics. Mixtapes let you say something. You create a story as you pick the songs.

martin: Why don't people make mixtapes anymore?

kj: I think that songs make me cry when it's personal.

kj: I have a stack of mix-tapes from high school that I keep in a drawer. But it's an idea that really only existed for tape cassettes...

martin: Do you cry because of the lyrics or because of the memories they evoke?

martin: Yeah, true. With MP3s, you can make a playlist and burn a CD, but it isn't the same. And an e-mail isn't the same as a love letter.

kj: I believe in the idea that music has a resonant frequency... that one note from the Elvis Costello's "Indoor Fireworks," from "Lithium Sunsets" by Sting, from Adrienne Young's cover of the Grateful Dead's "Brokedown Palace"... and then these frequencies "match" with one person in particular, in this case me.

martin: Interesting . . . this could be a difference between men and women. I like the notion that women are somehow more "tuned," and different things can create a dramatic response.

That's an interesting
way to think about
it. If women are more
"tuned," then what
are men?

I agree; that's why
I like running and
driving...those
are the two times
I can isolate myself
with music.

I don't know. Maybe
we're all tuned and the
result is just manifested
differently. Music can
trigger an adrenaline
response. Maybe more in
men. We drive faster with
certain music. We change
our productivity at work
based on music.

Still two things—
driving and music.
Running + music.

There are definitely
some songs that are
driving songs.

Ah, true, I didn't
think of it that
way. How do we get
just music?

AC/DC's *Back in Black*.

When was the last time
you lay on the floor with
some headphones on and
just listened?

There was something
else I wanted to
say about music...
some days, when I've
been busy or distrac-
ted, I realize that
I haven't stopped to
listen to music in
a while, and I rea-
lize that I miss it.

Almost never,
I'd say. Maybe I'll
try that later
today...interesting
challenge. You?

Last time was in Boston
nine months ago. Music is
completely different for
me when I experience it
in the purest way, that
is to say when I isolate
that sense.

It's increasingly hard to
find time to just enjoy
music on its own. It's
like food: if we go to a
restaurant or a gig, we're
focused, but if we're
at home, the TV's on or
we're working, then we
are distracted. Always
two things together.

I would believe
it. But I wouldn't
underestimate the
focus that I can
have on music
while running...
I think I need
better headphones.

I think running is pretty
good at focusing you;
the problem is all the
ambient noise.

Ah, true. The cars,
the people on the
street, etc.

211

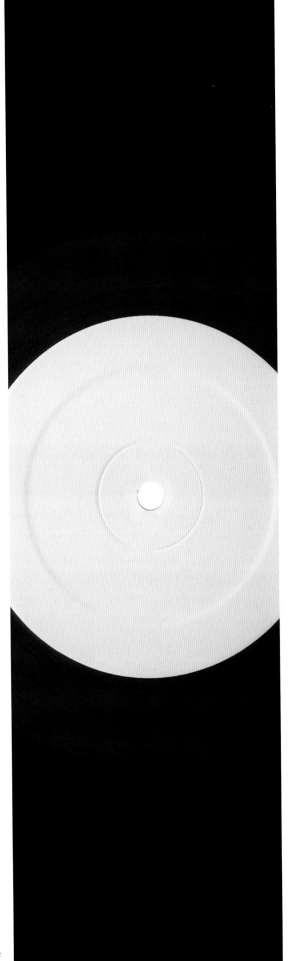

I just want to say
one thing about music
and technology. Music
is the only area of the
entertainment industry
where technology has
been focused on conven-
ience over quality.

I remember you
talking about
this before, about
how technology has
reduced the quality
of music.

Historically the only way
to experience music was
to go to a performance
and hear it live. To hear
Mozart you had to go to
a performance, and the
experience was shared
and social. Then we
recorded sound; it was
nowhere near the quality
of a live performance,
but now it was a business
that could be replicated.
Technology slowly im-
proved the quality to
the point where we
had 33-1/3 RPM LPs. With
the right equipment, this
represented the best
of the recorded medium
but still not the same
experience as a live
performance.

Is 33-1/3 RPM
vinyl still the
best quality
recorded medium?

For a consumer format, I'm
sure the source tape is
still the best. For years
I had followed the analog-
digital debate and read
all the reasons why one
was better than the other.
But most of that was still
science stuff. I wanted
a real-world comparison.

I would guess that
the big wigs in the
music industry these
days are not selling
"sound"; they're
selling "lifestyles"...
so quality of sound
doesn't matter.

Even if we take the motivations of the music industry out of the equation and just concentrate on the technology, I still think analog trumps digital. I had a friend who was a music fanatic and he had an incredible set-up with valve gear, so we did a real-world test with the two formats, CD and LP, and after I heard the two versions it was clear to me that the LP was better.

Nope, I'm 100 percent digital. I traded my soul for convenience.

That's the interesting thing. I love that technology can allow me to be creative with software, editing movies, sculpting form, etc. But with the same technology, I have lost any connection to music, because for me, growing up in a vinyl era, there was a physical connection. It's not the same for film or TV. The quality of those media has increased. And therefore you could argue the connection has gotten better. I love watching Blu-Ray because it's so vivid—you connect with the image in ways that you didn't before.

You're an analog player in a digital world...

:) Actually...that should be a sad face. You shouldn't have to trade your soul. :(

Oh, shit. I forgot to make the point that we went from music being social to it being isolating. More people wear iPods than go to live gigs.

We just finished watching them all back to back. *Arrested* was genius.

Video snacking.

I think we should start using a new kind of descriptor—the Twinkie, Ho Ho, Big Mac . . . like "I totally snacked on a Twinkie of *MASH* last night, dude" . . . does that sound American enough?

I'm gonna Mac out with *The Sopranos* tonight.

Dude.

Australian surfing turtles.

I like the idea of building connections or making them better ...that's what convergence should be about, but it isn't. It's just another stupid buzzword.

My head is hurting from this music talk. I'm going to watch an episode of *Arrested Development* instead.

I like the format of watching half-hour shows, but all the episodes at once. It's like a new form of media, like a movie, but easier to stop and start. Good for those of us who are multi-tasking.

Yes, video snacking. Like it.

Sounds good to me. Like totally.

Righteous.

Like those sea turtle characters in *Finding Nemo*...They say: "Righteous, dude."

Cool.

What if a magazine could speak? Not in a cheesy musical greeting card kind of way, but where the visual experience is enhanced by an audio interview or an exclusive preview of that soon-to-be-released, über cool new collection of tracks by the freshest of beat monkeys, laid down just a week prior, in the basement of a secret, Parisian after hours club. What if these fringes of culture met new technologies to reinvigorate a tired medium like the magazine? What if you came home from the store and instead of tossing the magazine on a table you place it on the player and the content comes to life? Contemporary digital expressions embedded in the chemical signatures of ink. FAKE the magazine.

martin

I fell in love with this idea, maybe even to the point
where I could no longer see if it was actually any
good. In truth I'm not sure if I care whether it makes
sense or not; I just enjoyed it too much. I remember
over the months having many heated discussions with
Dan DeRuntz, an interaction designer, about the fact
that we blindly accept that the only way forward when
it comes to music is the MP3 and all of its future der-
ivations. The joy and love that used to go into making
a mixtape, captured so beautifully in Nick Hornby's
book *High Fidelity* and a rite of passage for any spotty
teenager in love, has now been rendered obsolete.
It's fitting that we're thinking about this stuff now,
the year in which the last cassette tape ever produced dropped onto store shelves, forgotten, like the
final pick in dodgeball. I feel strangely melancholic
that in this shift from analog to digital we somehow
lost something; we traded connection for convenience.
Ultimately this experiment won't change anything;
technology marches on, teenagers in love today play
out their courtship online in their Facebook pages,
not browsing record stacks. But I feel much better
for having done it. My personal last gasp attempt to
regain my musical soul; it's not a pink vinyl edition
of "Cool for Cats", but then few things are.

kj

Of all the products in this book, this is the
one I wish I could actually buy. But it isn't
realistic. As a culture, we've moved on, and
the intangiblity of iTunes is probably our
future. No one will miss the CD. The mixtape
is probably gone forever.

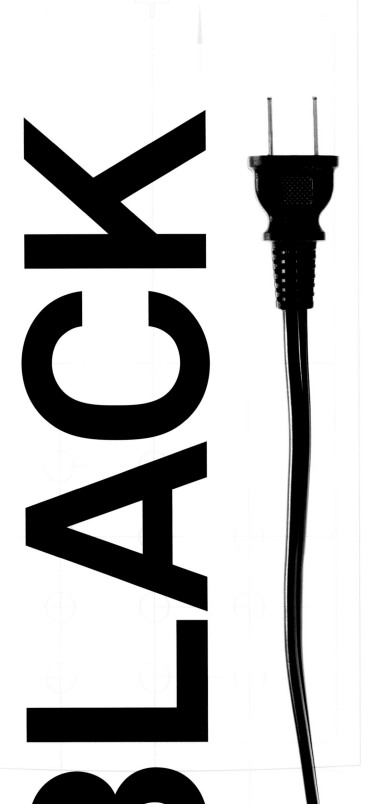

BLACK

4.57

0.5

44.85

36

108

9.3

26

4

The little black dress.
For gentlemen.

---

martin

If we could create a consumer electronics brand from scratch and without any market constraints—no brand baggage, no demographics, no technical or manufacturing restrictions—what would we do? The starting point is three guys, a computer, imagination, and a desire to fake stuff that we would like to see. Sounds like a bad sitcom, maybe, but it's more like fantasy football for design geeks, only we build our offensive line with titanium and carbon fiber. Nothing is real, it's pure illusion. This is the product equivalent of a few hours spent wandering the virtual streets in Grand Theft Auto or perhaps the love child of Superman and Clark Kent, for gadget geeks and übermen alike. Our goal is simple in this fictitious world: to elicit lust with something that's built of bytes and pixels instead of polymers and oxides.

---

kj

I have never been much of a gadget girl. I own a Canon camera, a Samsung printer, an Apple iPod, a BlackBerry. But I don't really care about any of these things. I don't need the latest version as soon as it hits the market. I just need one. And I already have one.

What I do find intriguing is the buzz that's easily created when the market is getting ready for the launch of the next gadget. Maybe we can find a way to rethink these objects and at the same time create our own buzz. Maybe we can build a story around something that doesn't exist. Maybe we can find ways to create a fetish for the mass market. Martin has always wanted to talk to a "fetish professional" in San Francisco, Mistress Morgana, as inspiration for this experiment. She's a friend of a friend who works in San Francisco. I never thought this was part of my job, but I think she can help me understand the role of fetish in product design, and that will certainly help us build strong emotional connections with objects. Even if they don't exist.

221

AN INTERVIEW WITH
MISTRESS MORGANA

Morgana Maye is a BDSM educator and consultant who lives and works in San Francisco.

As a lifestyle BDSM player and a predoctoral candidate in clinical psychology, she has devoted

years to the personal, professional, and academic exploration of the topic of fetish from a unique vantage point. She also has two chickens, named Sophia Loren and Rita Hayworth.

KJ: OK. Let's talk about fetish.

Morgana: I'm kind of a theory slut. It's impossible for me to engage with *fetish* as a concept without really appreciating how ironic it is that we're using it in the way we are today, given where it came from. The term fetish really came into vogue in the mid-eighteenth century, through anthropology, and it had a really specific purpose. It was designed to describe people's religious traditions in West Africa. It described people's orientation to objects as God, their association of objects with special magical powers.

The term didn't come into popular use until Freud wrote about it in 1927. Freud described fetishism as a paraphilia, an atypical or abnormal sexual interest. But before Freud, in the mid-nineteenth century, Karl Marx was writing about commodity fetishism. In many ways, Marx was writing about the object's ability to make a person more worthwhile. So if I have land, if have a home, if I have many ponies, if I have that new pair of Manolo Blahniks, I have elevated myself.

What I find fascinating about the early history of fetish is that the term represents one of the first times historians, anthropologists, and philosophers started looking at humans' relationships to objects and to each other instead of their relationships to God. We go from the worship of a deity to the worship of a thing, and it's a thing that not only stays in the mortal and tangible, but it could be a thing that other humans made.

It's almost the beginning of consumerism on some level.

Absolutely. And I think what's kind of brilliant is that the Marxist notion of commodity fetishism describes where we're at now so sublimely and in a way that I don't think Marx himself could have ever anticipated. The way that these objects are produced, the way that media presents them as the ideal and then as obsolete, even the degree to which they are rubberized or cast in colors that are designed to be sort of sensual and provocative.

A fetish describes a person's profound lust for an object, and that object is the end point—a rubber dress, a stiletto heel—and the person who might be wearing these things is simply a delivery device for the object, and the object is where it ends.

This sounds a bit like Carrie on *Sex and the City*.

Absolutely, who has maybe the largest high-heel fetish of any character recorded on television. There's that wonderful scene where she realizes that she has enough shoes to constitute a down payment on a house. And she's going to become the woman who lives in her shoes, because that's what she's done—she's privileged that commodity fetish over home ownership.

I want to hear more about how the experience of fetish is different from the object of that fetish, or how they relate to each other.

A fetish is something that we could take on at various points in our lives. It could be fleeting, it could last for a week and a half, it could be enduring, it could be something that lasts in ourselves from childhood and persists for our entire lives. And I think any time we've really really wanted any particular object, that new laptop computer, a new car, that fabulous sweater, those jeans that make our ass look great, and we purchase it and we incorporate it and we make it ours, we go through what the fetish cycle is about: identifying the object, attaining the object, and feeling relief afterward.

There is an obsessional and compulsive component to fetishism that can be wielded very sanely and very humanly but does seem to be an undeniable aspect of fetishism, which is to say that there's the need to get the perfect item; there's the need for it to really sort of work the way you want to see it function exactly.

For instance, I have a real fetish for 1950s domestic scenarios. This is a fiction, this is something that never actually existed at any point in time, but it absolutely existed in media, and it existed as a social ideal. So I spend a lot of time on eBay collecting vintage aprons. There's a color palette, there's a language. It's this sort of minutiae of detail that we start creating, and the heat is in the details. The heat is in the objects and the ritual itself. So it's a fetish in the sense that it's a form of sexual expression that has nothing to do with traditional sex. Every tiny little detail makes sense. If there's soap, it's Ivory soap, not Irish Spring.

It reminds me of improv in some respects: you're there to serve the scene, and you're not there to take control.

The objects are there in service of the fetish, as are you. And there's a degree to which you have to kind of love the details, and the fetish is in the details.

What's an obsession and what's a fetish?

I think Marx has held truest in terms of what commodity fetishism means in culture. So when is a thing an obsession, when is it a fetish, when is it something that you really love, when is it a proclivity? We all know what it's like to deeply desire an object. It might not be so overwhelming that it becomes a fetish, but we know what it's like to really want something. And I know the difference between a thing I prefer and a thing that is the only thing I will have. And there's a link there; there's a spectrum on which the volume is a little lower on this end and a little higher on this end.

One of my favorite current uses of the term *fetish* actually is in gaming. There are a series of video games that have fetishes as weapons with magical powers.

What is the future of fetishism?

Multimedia. I think that where fetishism is going is that it operates on multiple platforms at once, and there is a way in which commodity fetishism and sexual fetishism have started to merge. I do think that the beginning stages of that are the incorporation of sexualized imagery in selling products. And I'm not talking about women's bodies to sell beer. I'm talking about the way in which textures and tastes and smells and the visceral experience of an object are connected in the way the object itself is sold.

Is this helpful?

Yeah, very helpful. I wrote a lot of stuff down. Like the very first thing I wrote down was "object is God"...love it. Your first historical reference to fetish sounds a bit like that movie *The Gods Must Be Crazy*.

I love the fetishization of everyday objects, the things that you would naturally have in your house. And you get to invest them with this sort of ritual reality that has no basis in actual reality but that you get to make hyper-real through performing them.

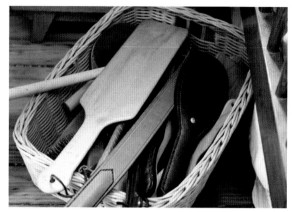

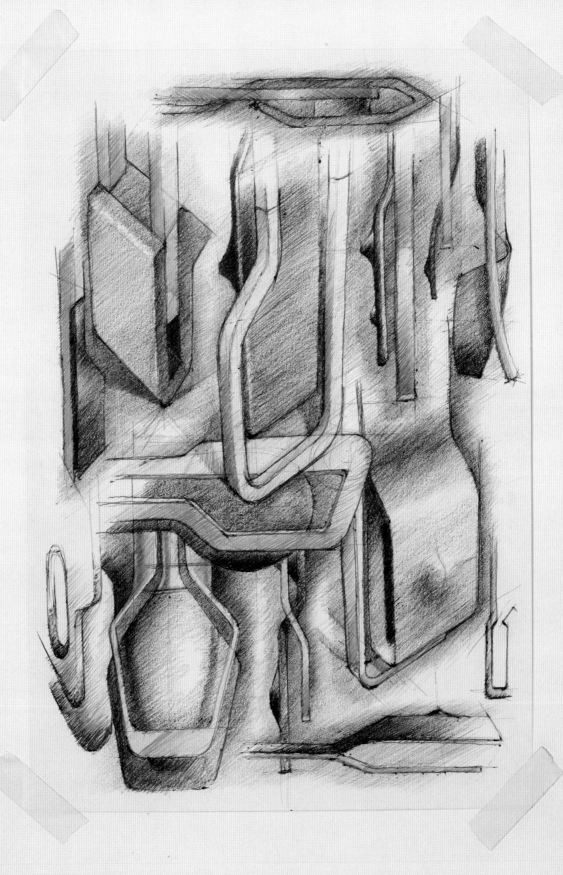

martin	kj

kj: Why did you start thinking about the idea that we could design a brand from scratch?

martin: I'm not sure I was thinking about brand much. I've spent years designing consumer electronics for other people. I just wanted to do a collection of stuff that I was interested in, rather than stuff that had to fit into a preconceived notion of a brand.

kj: So it's about the idea first.

martin: I was interested in the idea that electronics continue to get smaller and smaller but there's a physical human limit to just how small you can get with some stuff. The idea that you could create volume but still represent high-tech seemed like a good place to explore for a while. Enclosing the void, in some way.

kj: And as the technology gets smaller, the product doesn't disappear...it's still human scale.

Another way to give context, without actually building and selling the product and letting people experience it themselves, would be to do a little YouTube video.

Right. The reality is that a company would just fill space with more battery life. But because we're not playing in real life, for this it seemed more valuable to see what you could do with the extra space.

Yeah. That's the other medium where you can blur reality. If you make a bad home movie of a product demo but use post-production techniques so it looks real, then people will react to it as if it is real, hopefully.

You are trying to build the idea of negative space.

If we had more time, we'd do that next, I guess...but the book is due on Tuesday!

The products in some way tell a story about possibilities, but these are firmly rooted in science fiction. What I find compelling is to present these ideas as if they were real, to see how people will react.

Yeah, no Oscars for us.

That's why you made the posters, eh?

Subway posters just provide a possibility for creating context that makes stuff seem more real.

Why did you reference 007?

I don't know. It's kinda stupid. I think the objects look a little like Bond gadgets, I guess.

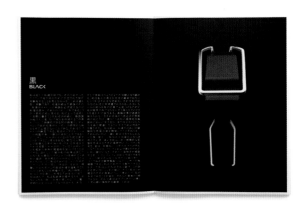

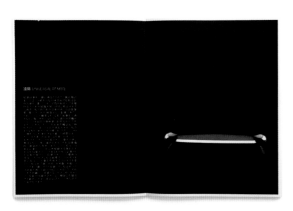

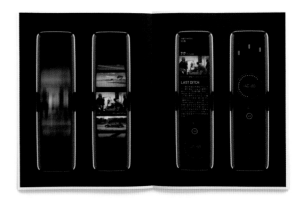

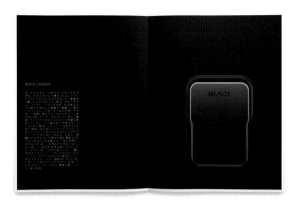

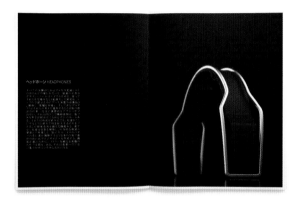

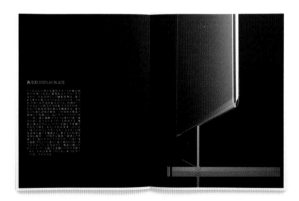

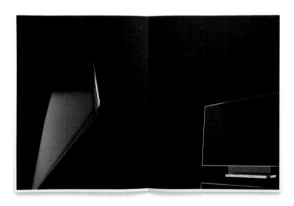

martin

Most consumer products come to market after many rounds of testing with consumers. For a designer, this is a deeply unpleasant experience. You're sitting in a bland room behind a one-way mirror, eating bad food and drinking worse coffee, and watching groups of people pick apart the thing you just poured your soul into for the last six months.

I've always wanted to get the original inventors of the focus group, put them in a room with strangers and see how much they enjoy it. "Can you make your ears smaller?" "Do you come in orange?" "I'd like you to be larger with more capacity and if you could just put an extra finger on each hand that would be great."

Many products die here at this great corporate abattoir-cum-funeral home. Sure some things deserve their fate; many probably shouldn't have even got to this point. But as we continue to generally bland our way across America, what of those moments of

creative genius destined to be a career footnote, overlooked by people who, starved of backstory and context, judge with a preconceived notion of what an air conditioner, a laptop, or a washing machine looks like and sounds like and feels like? Ever wonder why a concept car is so cool and the market version isn't? It's hard to be cool with twelve cupholders and room for a pony. So much great design never makes it out of these rooms. It's like playing blackjack in Vegas, where the decks are stacked against you from the start.

What does any of this have to do with this experiment? All this stuff, this fake brand, was created out of a reaction to focus groups as a way of evaluating design. It's us getting to play at being virtual CEOs and cramming our designs full of details that we love and not those that feel appropriate for everyone else, or even anyone else. But maybe if we cater to our own obsessions without compromise these will be the highly fetishized that others will love too.

kj

This experiment is about creating a brand from scratch. It's about objects that define negative space. It's about creating buzz for something that doesn't exist and probably never will. This series of objects was one of the first experiments that we started, and it has remained, unfortunately, mostly unfinished. We wanted to create a brand, design some products, describe elements of its advertising campaign, post a YouTube video, get feedback from people who look

for this type of thing on the internet, and then tell the story. Our ambitions were greater than the time allowed. But that leaves us in a place where this book is not yet finished, and that's a good thing. It's just a starting point for design.

CONCLUSIONS

martin	kj
I forgot what I was going to type.	
	No problem.
Bugger. Still can't remember . . .	
	You're just getting older... ;)
OK. I'm done. I'll put some more stuff in an e-mail.	
	Sounds good. I'm going to watch *Risky Business* and eat a burrito.
	:)
Now you're just trying to be funny. No one watches *Risky Business* while eating a burrito . . .	
	No—really, I am.
	And stop making me laugh. I guess this is still fun...

martin

The book's not finished, yet I find myself writing the conclusion, which, given that we're coming down to the last few days of getting things together, means I hate everything. I'm sick of typing, I'm sick of my own voice, FTP, publishers, e-mail and most of all, pen-cils. I sure as shit don't miss my pencil now.

There are some designers who sit back at the end and enjoy the fruits of their labour and feel good. And there are some, like me, who only see the screw-ups and the missed opportunities. Oh how I hate that feeling of "if only . . . ." If only we had more time, more money, more everything. If only I had changed that curve, that color, that font. Things can always be better. It's a universal creative truth.

These pages gave me a reason to reconnect to what it is that I love: the process of creation. I've always preferred the journey over the result, and I loved the process of creating this thing. I loved the collaboration, the dabbling in the unknown, the risk of failure. I love that all the content is newly created. It's no retrospective glance at a sparkly career, no lifetime achievement Oscar, and so when it's released it'll be the first time anyone's seen it, warts and all.

I realize now that when we started I had convinced myself that this would be a place devoid of compro-mise, that we would be free to play in our own giant bouncy design castle. For the most part, we did; we bounced around for a while like epileptic frogs and occasionally fell on our arses. But the reality is that design is all about compromises, even the imaginary explorations in this book. Those that aren't imposed upon us by budget and time we place on ourselves by defining the areas in which to play. Design, this unholy alliance of art and commerce, doesn't really seem to work without them. It's these boundaries that provided us with a fresh dialogue on design, an opportunity to push our thinking in new directions and any time that happens it's a good day to be a designer.

kj

There seems to be something inherently human about writing books. I'm sure the publishing industry is probably scared that www-doteverything will replace the printed book. But I think—or at least hope—that this will never happen. Books matter.

Books are the tangible result of ideas and imagination. They give thoughts literal weight and time and space; they are the combination of intangible daydreams and belabored nightmares paired with cover art, font, paper and ink.

To the reader, a book can be a trophy of an accomplishment ("I've read this"), a memento of adventure ("I went here"), an archive of life and style ("I've gone from the clas-sics to the esoteric and then back again"). Together, a collection of books tells a story of their owner. For the author, the story of accomplishment, adventure and archive is the same, only the perspective is different. For Martin and me, this book has been an outlet for the creativity that spills over from our day jobs. It's a meandering story about possibility and failure and the good-ness that comes from both. It's an exploration of materiality beyond the limits of our current projects and clients. And it makes a better story in the end.

I believe you can't fall in love with some-thing you can't touch, and that you can't tell good stories if people aren't emotion-ally connected to what might happen next. As designers, we hope that everything we make is part product, part story. We want those stories to be written by designers and by design itself.

martin	kj
I'm here in the middle of nowhere. No cell reception but I found this wireless network. Not sure how long it will last.	
Testing, testing, 1, 2, 3.	
Nanoo, Nanoo, Mork calling Orson.	
A giraffe's underpants are three times larger than those worn by a zebra.	
One is the loneliest number.	
	Can you see me now?
	Hi...
	You there now?
	Isn't three the magic number?
	Who is Orson?
	Argh.

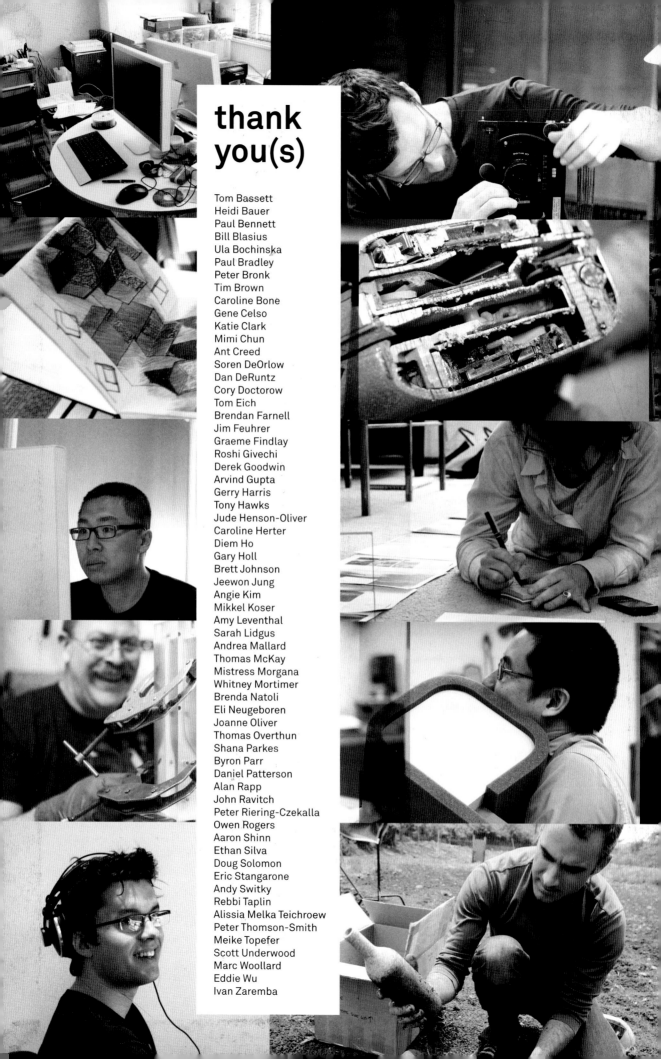

thank you(s)

Tom Bassett
Heidi Bauer
Paul Bennett
Bill Blasius
Ula Bochinska
Paul Bradley
Peter Bronk
Tim Brown
Caroline Bone
Gene Celso
Katie Clark
Mimi Chun
Ant Creed
Soren DeOrlow
Dan DeRuntz
Cory Doctorow
Tom Eich
Brendan Farnell
Jim Feuhrer
Graeme Findlay
Roshi Givechi
Derek Goodwin
Arvind Gupta
Gerry Harris
Tony Hawks
Jude Henson-Oliver
Caroline Herter
Diem Ho
Gary Holl
Brett Johnson
Jeewon Jung
Angie Kim
Mikkel Koser
Amy Leventhal
Sarah Lidgus
Andrea Mallard
Thomas McKay
Mistress Morgana
Whitney Mortimer
Brenda Natoli
Eli Neugeboren
Joanne Oliver
Thomas Overthun
Shana Parkes
Byron Parr
Daniel Patterson
Alan Rapp
John Ravitch
Peter Riering-Czekalla
Owen Rogers
Aaron Shinn
Ethan Silva
Doug Solomon
Eric Stangarone
Andy Switky
Rebbi Taplin
Alissia Melka Teichroew
Peter Thomson-Smith
Meike Topefer
Scott Underwood
Marc Woollard
Eddie Wu
Ivan Zaremba

THE LONDON ST

THE LONDON ST

KEN BLACKER

Capital Transport

First published 2012

ISBN 978-185414-363-1

Published by Capital Transport Publishing Ltd
www.capitaltransport.com

Printed by 1010 Printing International Ltd

CONTENTS

INTRODUCTION

This history of the ST class in London, which delves back into an era of London's transport past now rapidly fading from living memory, has been written as a companion volume to the story of the LT six-wheelers that I completed a couple of years ago. I remember both classes very vividly, admittedly from a schoolboy perspective, but it is often the memories from those schoolboy years that hit home the hardest and linger the longest. The STs and LTs shared the same time slot in history and were clearly from the same mould, and I felt that, having written about one, I could hardly avoid writing about the other.

Not that, in my young days, I liked them equally. I know that I am not alone in feeling a much greater affection for the LTs, partly because with their greater bulk they looked more majestic, but also because – like most London bus types over the years – they were predictable and you knew exactly where they were to be found. On the other hand the STs – at least in post-war times – were almost fly-by-night. For the most part they served as substitutes for all the other double deck classes and in this role they could and often did turn up almost anywhere. They were often pushed from pillar to post, sometimes through official inter-garage transfer arrangements but often as unofficial loans. I can quote a typical

example from 1947, a year in which I kept a full list of every bus I travelled on, the vehicle in question being ST 626. On 26th October I travelled on it working from Palmers Green garage on route 29 and on 6th December from West Green on the 144. In fact it belonged to neither, and when I was at last able to look up its history many years later, I discovered that on both occasions it was officially allocated to Upton Park.

In those far-off days, when every journey could turn out to be a voyage of discovery, I had comparatively few memorable trips on STs partly, I suspect, because I may have avoided them in favour of more favoured classes such as STLs, LTs and Guys. However on one memorable bank holiday I set off by Underground for Hounslow with Windsor as my ultimate goal, having heard on the grapevine (which is all we had in those days) that I might find ST 1139 – the 'holy grail' of STs – working there. From Hounslow the 116 to Staines was a Tilling, my first-ever ride on one, and the onward connection to Windsor was yet another Tilling, this time with a huge 441 chalked on its front dome but no other indication of where it might be going. These two journeys marked the sum total of my rides on open staircase STs, but at least I achieved my goal and saw ST 1139 bustling to and fro between Windsor and Datchet.

Fortunately, over the ensuing years, I have managed to collect a vast amount of information, official and otherwise, on the STs, and I have also recorded the memories of many who worked on and with them, all of which have been invaluable in helping to compile this history. Obviously, after such a long time, there will be gaps in the accumulated knowledge, and there may be odd inaccuracies either in interpretation or even in the source material from which information is taken. London Transport's own records can sometimes be conflicting or inaccurate. However I have done my best with the information available, and I hope it makes enjoyable reading.

It has not been possible, within the space available, to give detailed information on chassis, registration or body numbers. However this information has been readily available for many years and I would recommend those seeking such details to refer to the excellent fleet history on the STs issued jointly by the PSV Circle and the Omnibus Society about 30 years ago.

As always, I would like to express my sincere thanks to everyone who has helped me over the years by supplying

information, memories or photographs without which the compilation of this history would not have been possible. Special thanks go, as they did with the LT book, to Alan Nightingale who has made great efforts to unearth photographs and additional information, and who has kindly taken on the unenviable task of reading and proof checking the final draft. Many of those whose help I freely acknowledge are no longer with us, and the list grows longer with the passing years. Friends from the past who have contributed posthumously to this volume have included the late Peter Aldridge, John Gillham, Ken Glazier, W J (Bill) Haynes, V C (Vic) Jones, Ron Lunn, Prince Marshall, George Robbins, Allen T Smith, Don Thompson and Reg Westgate. To John Aldridge, Alan Cross, Denis Battams, Frank Davis, Fred Ivey, Don Jones, Les Hampton, Anthony Roscoss, Hugh Taylor, Chris Warren and Mick Webber I must say Thank You for your help and also, in some cases, for sharing my interest in London buses over very many years.

KEN BLACKER

CHAPTER 1
ST 1

On Tuesday 22nd October 1929 an impressive new double deck bus was presented at Scotland Yard and tentative approval was given for it to operate in London subject to a few minor modifications being made. These were duly carried out, and on the 31st of the same month the new bus was issued with Metropolitan Police plate number 1242. This marked the culmination of a major project carried out by the London General Omnibus Company's Experimental & Research Department and now, newly registered UU 6614, ST 1 was ready to commence service trials as the prototype of a planned new fleet. It was taken to Hammersmith garage ready to begin an active working life on 1st November. A fresh era in bus history had begun, and from this small beginning the ST class was destined to become a major force on the London bus scene for many years to come.

ST 1 represented, for the LGOC, the latest throw of the dice in its long overdue battle to modernise its fleet. Earlier in the same year it had still been taking delivery of NS class double deckers which were not only thoroughly outdated in appearance but were constructed to a mechanical specification that rendered them incapable of competing in performance with contemporary modern vehicles. ST 1 was the second in a triumvirate of new classes unveiled by the LGOC within a period of four months, all of which were based on the latest range of passenger chassis from the Southall factory of the Associated Equipment Company. Preceding it into service on 6th August had been LT 1, representing the very latest in three axle design based on the AEC Renown chassis, whilst trailing behind as the third of the trio was T 1, a four-wheeled AEC Regal single decker placed into service on 5th December. The AEC Regent chassis upon which ST 1 was based was, like the others, still in its infancy, though in the fullness of time it was to prove so successful that new Regents continued to be built right through to early in 1968, the marque being regularly updated all the while to incorporate design improvements as they came along.

The late nineteen-twenties marked a period of exceptionally rapid development in bus design, and the legend of AEC's emergence from the doldrums of stagnation within a very short time is perhaps the greatest success story of the era. The background to this was the appointment in July 1928 to the post of Chief Engineer at AEC of the highly skilled George John Rackham, whose previous two year spell in the same post at Leyland had turned that company into the clear market leader with his inspired range of Titan and Tiger passenger vehicles. The payment of a phenomenally high salary with which Lord Ashfield lured Rackham across to the Underground group (of which AEC and the LGOC were both subsidiaries) was quickly justified by the remarkably rapid speed at which Rackham worked to produce a series of new designs which transformed AEC's sales outlook within a matter of months.

Within each oncoming phase of new design which Rackham introduced, the similarity to work that he had previously produced at Leyland was very evident, though subtle differences were applied throughout and nothing was a complete replica. First to emerge was a completely new 6-cylinder engine with overhead camshaft driving the valves through rockers. Then came the innovative range of new chassis of which the first to be completed was a Regent, probably in about December 1928. Classified as type 661, the new Regent was very similar to the Leyland Titan – its main competitor – in design and layout, having the same low frame chassis with curved profile over the front and rear axles and a transmission line offset to the nearside to give a level flooring throughout the lower saloon. Small wheels requiring 36x8 tyres helped further to keep the height down. A single servo vacuum braking system acted on all four wheels and Marles type steering was employed which produced a 45 degree lock. The spindly looking semi-floating rear axle was a further copy of current Leyland practice, but the Regent scored by having a much more compact front end design with a bonnet length from the bulkhead to the extreme front of the chassis a full 6 inches less than that on the Titan. This resulted in a wheelbase nearly 1ft shorter at 15ft 6½ins even though the overall vehicle length remained the same at 25ft. The masterpiece of the design was its handsome polished aluminium radiator shell which was thoroughly modern in appearance and set AEC's range of new chassis apart from all others for sheer elegance.

Being within the same family group, the LGOC naturally kept closely in touch with design developments at AEC, and in January 1929 its board of directors approved the purchase of two Regent chassis even though the design was virtually fresh off the drawing board and completely untried. In fact the development of the Regent and its contemporaries was kept fairly hush-hush at the time, and although it was obviously known about within sections of the industry and AEC was willing to take orders if these were placed, no official announcement was made until June 1929. Only one of the two Regents ordered by General was intended for immediate passenger service, a decision having been taken to set the other one aside initially for use as a test and development chassis. AEC, meanwhile, had authorised construction of an initial batch of twelve Regents (chassis 661001-661012), most of which were intended for use as demonstrators. One of these, 661008, was loaned to the Underground group in July 1929 ahead of the construction of the two chassis ordered by the LGOC, and the story of this vehicle – which was subsequently purchased and operated as ST 1139 in the London Transport fleet – is told in chapter 2.

The production run of AEC Regents, which followed on from the original trial run of twelve, was well in hand for provincial customers before the first of the two chassis

ST 1 had already been allocated its official registration number UU 6614 when it posed at Chiswick for its official photographs to be taken on 25th October 1929, but it had not yet been licensed and still carried trade plate 014A. Though not overly modern in appearance compared with some provincial contemporaries, it marked a vast improvement over what had gone before it in the General fleet, and looked fresh and welcoming in the new red and cream livery. Like LT 1 which had posed in a similar position about three months earlier, ST 1 displayed the destination '11A STRAND ALDWYCH' (a short working of the 11E under the complex 'Bassom numbering system), but unlike LT 1, this was the route on which it actually worked once it entered service on 1st November. *L T Museum*

ordered by the LGOC came off the production line. Chassis 661074 was taken into stock on 7th October 1929 as ST 1 by which time a new body that had been under construction for some while was now nearing completion. The second chassis, 661148, arrived from Southall seven weeks later on 27th November, and though initially intended only for use within Chiswick Works, it was allocated fleet number ST 2. In December a redundant K-type body (No. 4647) was installed on it, and this weird looking combination became part of the everyday scene within the works through to May 1931 when a normal ST body was fitted and ST 2 finally joined the operational fleet.

Construction of ST 1's body had begun at Chiswick soon after the order for the chassis had been placed and, in accordance with normal LGOC practice, the main framework was built of fully seasoned English ash. Referred to as a "Pullman" body to emphasise the relative plushness of its fittings, it bore a strong family likeness in its general design to the body fitted to the first AEC Renown six-wheeler LT 1, although it had a neater finish in several respects. Like LT 1, it had a fully glazed box-like driver's cab, the only open section of which was the doorway aperture which, in accordance with usual LGOC practice, was left open. The glazed cab was quite unusual at the time as this was a feature to which the Metropolitan Police was strongly averse on safety gounds. Through its Public Carriage Office the police had a duty to vet and approve all stage carriage designs for use within the metropolis, and although as a matter of course they would allow the windscreen itself to be glazed, they would not extend this facility to the windows on either side. Although some other operators were happy to accept this arrangement, it did not prove popular with the LGOC or its staff when tried out on a number of NSs because of the strong and very uncomfortable draughts that were created, and in fact experimental windscreens on a number of NSs were quickly removed because of adverse staff reaction. However in May 1929 a concession was obtained by General from the Metropolitan Police to fit one hundred new buses experimentally with fully enclosed cabs, and ST 1 was one of these.

The starkly upright rear of ST 1 was functional and businesslike in appearance and it set the style for many hundreds of new buses that were to follow, both STs and LTs. The roller blind destination screen and the registration number plate – the latter back-lit from the saloon lighting – were well sited and clearly visible, but neither were destined to last for much more than a couple of years in these positions. The two unglazed windows on the platform were an even shorter lived feature and may well have been fitted with glass before ST 1 entered service. *L T Museum*

When it appeared a few months earlier, LT 1 had broken new ground in being built to accommodate roller destination blinds in place of the boards that the LGOC had normally favoured. ST 1 was similarly equipped, and it was now clear that General had decided to gradually phase out the use of route boards. The simplicity of blinds, back-lit from inside the bus, did away with the need to stock a host of boards that were bulky to store and cumbersome to handle, although there was a downside to the new arrangement with the reduction in the amount of information that could be displayed. On LT 1, and again on ST 1, a combined destination, route and number aperture was provided at front and rear with a smaller number-only display on the nearside above the platform.

It was evident from the outset that a tremendous amount of thought and design effort had gone into producing the body for ST 1 and its rear end design was particularly ingenious.

Whereas LT 1 had incorporated a conventional outside staircase of the style favoured by the Metropolitan Police, ST 1 was built with an enclosed rear end, flying in the face of the strong police prejudice which had resulted in early members of the LS class having to have their enclosed backs removed. From the point of view of safety and ease of operation, the platform design adopted for ST 1, and the completely straight staircase associated with it, could not have been bettered. The platform was completely uncluttered and free from obstruction over the whole of its 3ft 5ins length. This eased the conductor's job but also helped to speed the vehicle if a passenger was slow climbing the stairs because those behind could stand in the wide vestibule while the bus got under way instead of waiting on the pavement. The big drawback to this arrangement was, of course, its adverse impact on seating capacity, and there was also the problem that no below-stairs provision existed for passengers' luggage.

To overcome any possible police fears that passengers may be trapped inside the upper deck if the vehicle fell on to its nearside, an emergency exit was provided at the back even though this was not required by law at the time. The control handle for this was located behind glass in a box mounted over the centre of the escape hatch. To enable trapped passengers to escape from the lower deck a small 9¾in cut-away was provided in the rear wall of the vehicle. A strange feature of the platform, perhaps also incorporated with ease of escape in mind, was that the rearmost side window and the offside rear window were both initially left unglazed, although there is a strong likelihood that the vehicle did not enter service in this form. Certainly by the start of 1930, but probably much earlier, all the platform window apertures were glazed, the offside one with a sliding section to enable the conductor to reach out and signal to following traffic.

Another unusual feature was that the conventional body riser creating a step up from the platform into the lower saloon was omitted, allowing the floor to continue at the lower level as far as the differential housing. The reason for this arrangement was said to be to allow the conductor to carry out his work without being troubled by standing passengers, although the logic of it is hard to understand.

General was ahead of its time in fitting an emergency window at the rear of the upper saloon. This illustration of the general arrangement was supplied at the belated press launch in February 1930 and shows the control handle situated in a box behind a glass panel.

Looking forward inside the upper saloon, the new type of half-drop window with top-mounted 'push-down' lever can be clearly seen, as can the new style of front ventilator which, having been introduced on ST 1, became a standard fitment for the fleet right through to the first STLs. Two out of the three triple seats can be seen alongside the staircase; the front one of these was later replaced by a conventional double, giving increased circulating space at the top of the stairs. *L T Museum.*

ST 1 was built with a seating capacity of 50, comprising 30 in the upper deck but only 20 downstairs where the stair well occupied much of the space that would normally be available for seating. Forward of the staircase on the upper deck were four rows of frontward facing seats while adjacent to the stairwell were three seats each accommodating three followed by a full width row of five at the back. Downstairs a total of 16 seats faced forward in four rows, behind which was a longitudinal seat for four over the nearside wheelarch facing the staircase panel. The seats themselves were built on a wooden framework reinforced with metal brackets and flitch plates, and had deeply padded backs and "super sprung" cushions with a ridge on the gangway side of the back squab to help passengers stay comfortably in place. They were upholstered front and back in a fawn coloured moquette which matched the grey-green side panels which were covered in scratchproof rexine.

Apart from the side panels, rexine was widely used elsewhere in the interior, in cream at window level, in lightly patterned white on the centre ceiling panels, and in grey-green above the windows and on the various ceiling mouldings. The ample supply of half drop windows, of which there were twelve upstairs and six down, consisted of a new type incorporating a top-mounted easy-to-operate central push-down lever for lowering them, closure being achieved by pushing the frame upwards against the ratchet, a quick and simple operation. All front and rear windows were glazed in unsplinterable glass. Another new feature was the prominent raised ventilator panel at the front of each saloon which was a practical if not particularly attractive feature containing a sliding grid operated by the conductor. In place of the traditional bell cord there were handily placed untarnishable metal plungers for the pneumatic bells on the lower deck and platform with a single one upstairs above the staircase, the pipework for these being hidden beneath the panelling. A pleasant if not entirely necessary or practical touch was the narrow mirror mounted on the lower deck front bulkhead between the windows beneath which the large wooden fareboard was displayed.

Anyone entering the vehicle in daylight could have been forgiven for thinking that no internal lighting system had been installed as there was a complete dearth within the saloons of visible bulbs or bulb holders. These had, in fact, all been hidden from view behind translucent curved ceiling panels made of a non-flammable material called 'Acetaloid' but often referred to as 'Pearlite'. This arrangement was designed to give out a diffused and warm glow after dark whilst reducing clutter to a minimum and it was probably the most advanced and modern aspect of the whole ST body design although it was not entirely new, having already been showcased on LT 1.

In its completed form, ST 1 had an overall length of 24ft 11ins, an unladen height of 14ft 3ins and an unladen weight of 5 tons 11cwt 2qrs. It was powered by AEC's A140 6-cylinder engine rated at 37.2hp with 100mm bore and 130mm stroke giving a capacity of 6.1 litres and developing 95bhp at 2,500rpm. This engine, which incorporated provision for pressure lubrication of both main bearings and big ends, was the same type as used on the larger and heavier LT 1, but though it aroused criticism in the latter vehicle for its lack of pulling power, it proved to be adequate for the ST. The engine was mounted as a unit with the single plate clutch and four speed sliding mesh gearbox. A starter motor was included in the specification, having belatedly been adopted as standard for all new LGOC vehicles more than ten years after Superintendent Bassom at Scotland Yard had given his approval for a self starter on B 1025 at Mortlake garage as far back as 30th August 1918. A theoretically helpful gadget was a detachable fog light for mounting on the nearside dumbiron, though no record exists as to when or how often this was ever used.

ST 1 was originally painted in the same attractive livery as LT 1, employing a large amount of cream except on the lower deck panels which were in standard LGOC red. Black was employed as usual on horizontal mouldings and mudguards, whilst the roof and driver's canopy were silver, the aluminium paint used on them having been found to be heat resistant and long lasting. This livery, which was presumably introduced to give a brighter and more cheerful look to the fleet, was widely dubbed "rhubarb and custard". However it was short lived, and for reasons that are now unknown, the order was given in December 1929 to repaint the vehicle in standard LGOC red and grey style including red panelling on both decks shown in the photo below. It is known from contemporary observations in January 1930 that the livery change had taken place by then.

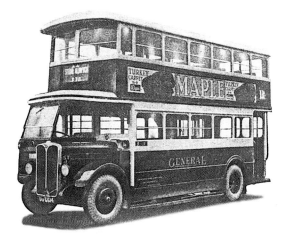

The new bus was photographed profusely at Chiswick Works on 25th August 1929 but the press and public were not present, and nor was anyone invited to its low key entry into service on 1st October. It seems that a deliberate decision was taken to avoid a repetition of the ballyhoo that had attended LT 1's launch into service; in fact its early service days were conducted in such a low key manner that no press reports were made of it and no record survives as to its early performance.

At Hammersmith garage ST 1 was rostered to work purely on route 11E (Liverpool Street–Shepherds Bush). This route was selected as being the ideal one on which to study the vehicle's potential for handling large rush hour crowds, its wide platform being eminently suited to handle the rapid turnover of passengers at busy points, particularly between the City, Strand, Whitehall and Victoria. It also gave an opportunity to compare the performance of the AEC Regent with its close rival, the Leyland Titan, one of which rival operator Chocolate Express had been running on route 11 since 30th July with the delivery of more of them imminent. Such was the Titan's popularity, it was already beginning to make a big impact on Chocolate Express's traffic receipts, and the LGOC no doubt hoped that ST 1 would produce the same benefit in addition to quelling public perception that the Company was not interested in modernising its fleet.

ST 1's sojourn on the 11 was relatively brief and it is unlikely that it extended much beyond January 1930, although it still retained its route 11 blinds when it was belatedly shown off to the trade press in early February. Even then they were not given the opportunity to sample it on the road, and their jaunt on it consisted only of a few circuits inside Chiswick Works accompanied by the usual press hand-out and a photographic session. By this time ST 1 had been reduced to a 49-seater, the frontmost of the three treble seats on the upper deck having been replaced by a double. A purely cosmetic though very noticeable change was that all the cream interior window surrounds had been replaced by a more sombre grey-green whilst a huge mirror now adorned the staircase panel facing the lower saloon longitudinal seat.

On 1st March 1930 ST 1 was put back into service, but now at Hanwell garage which had been nominated as the recipient for the initial batch of production STs, the first eighteen of which had arrived there a day beforehand, on 28th February. Altogether Hanwell was destined to receive no fewer than 98 STs over the course of the next seven weeks. On 16th September 1930 ST 1 went to Chiswick for its first overhaul from which it emerged exactly one month later half a ton heavier at 6 tons 1cwt 2qrs, partly due to the fitment of a very substantial rear bumper. It is highly likely that a conventional lower saloon floor and step entrance were installed at the same time.

At its next overhaul, on 15th October 1931, ST 1 ceased to exist in its original form. On the very same day a replacement ST 1 was supplied ex-overhaul to Hanwell which was a perfectly standard member of the class carrying the body formerly on ST 484. ST 1's own body was rebuilt to fit the LGOC's standard type of Regent chassis, on which the fuel filler was located on the nearside, the opposite to ST 1, and it was thereafter treated as a standard unit of the fleet, appearing with a variety of bonnet numbers during the ensuing years. It is not known what happened to ST 1's original chassis. Possibly it was reconfigured to standard LGOC condition, but it is just as likely that it was dismantled and its parts used for spares.

CHAPTER 2
LONDON'S OLDEST REGENT – ST 1139

The eighth AEC Regent had been fully signwritten for East Surrey but had yet to reach its licensing date of 2nd July 1929 when AEC called their official photographer in to record its existence on film. The projecting brackets at upper waistrail level to support the top of a destination board, and the ungainly lamp swooping over the top to illuminate it, are unmissable features that ruin the appearance of the piano-front styling. The route number aperture at the top is lit from inside but cannot easily be accessed to change the display as the front windows do not open. A feature of Short Bros. outside staircase bodies of this period was the curved glass in the rearmost nearside window of the upper deck.

Although ST 1 is rightly regarded as the precursor of the LGOC's family of highly successful and versatile fleet of AEC Regents it was not, in fact, the first Regent with which the Company had been associated. This honour fell to UU 6610 which later became well known as the unique ST 1139. Although the donkey work of actually testing the vehicle under service conditions was left to two of the LGOC's country subsidiaries, it was the LGOC who actually hired and eventually purchased it and kept a close eye on its performance in the early days.

UU 6610 was one of the very earliest Regents constructed in the spring and early summer of 1929 and distributed to various operators as demonstrators. They came complete with bodies, which were sometimes erroneously described at the time as AEC bodies whereas they had in fact been built by Short Brothers of Rochester using AEC designs. Shorts produced a range of bodies for Regents in both high and lowbridge format with either open or enclosed backs in a styling clearly influenced by the piano-front profile originated and popularised by Leyland. The highbridge version mostly employed an unusual design of upper deck roof embodying a prominent hump along the centre which looked positively bizarre when viewed from a distance, but two exceptions to this were built with an eye to their operation in the Metropolitan Police District where possibly the humped roof would not have found favour at the highly conservative Public Carriage Office, and UU 6610 was one of these. Conservatively shaped though heavily domed roofs were fitted to the two outside staircase bodies on the fourth and eighth Regent chassis which became UU 9161 (chassis 661004) and UU 6610 (661008). The former was licensed on 12th July 1929 as a demonstrator in the London fleet of Thomas Tilling Ltd while UU 6610 was licensed by the LGOC at Chiswick ten days before this, on 2nd July, its registration number immediately preceding that of the first AEC Renown six-wheeler LT 1.

With only very minor differences such as the positioning of route number holders on the side panels, the two Regent demonstrators were virtually identical and both carried red and cream livery with their operator's name posted prominently on the sides. In the case of UU 6610 the operator was destined to be East Surrey, the LGOC's Reigate based subsidiary. General elected not to run this bus in London despite modifications having been made to the normal Shorts body specifically to make it suitable to do so, such as providing an open driver's cab apart from the windscreen itself, and the provision of a tester's tip-up seat above the autovac tank with supporting hand-strap dangling down from above. In anticipation that board indicators would be needed rather than roller blinds (the apertures for which were plated over), an untidy array of brackets was provided at the front which were necessary to hold the top of the route board clear of the bulge of the piano front. Above these, equally untidily, was a lamp

attached to spindly arched supports to provide illumination. A container for the route number plate was mounted at the top, between the two front windows, and was lit from inside.

UU 6610 arrived at Reigate on 4th July 1929. It was a 51-seater with 24 seats downstairs comprised of five transverse rows of double seats plus inward facing seats for two over the wheelarches, while the 27 upstairs seats were in seven forward facing rows, the rearmost one on the offside being a single. The seats were attractively covered in a floral moquette; ample lighting was provided by lamps with jelly-mould covers in each bay, and there were six opening windows of the full-drop type in each saloon. The new bus was soon placed into service on route 414 (West Croydon–Horsham) where it could hardly have failed to impress, being so much more modern than anything else East Surrey had to offer.

After only a brief spell on route 414, UU 6610 returned to Chiswick where it was repainted and re-lettered to work for Autocar Services Ltd, a subsidiary of East Surrey based in Tunbridge Wells. The only visible change carried out at this time was the insertion of a ventilator flap in the front panel of the driver's cab, but other alterations must have taken place as the unladen weight actually dropped slightly from the original 5 tons 13cwt 1qr to 5 tons 9cwt 3qrs. Its stay at Autocar was destined to be of longer duration, and UU 6610 could be found on route 7A (Tunbridge Wells–Tonbridge) from the latter part of August 1929 through to March 1930.

For almost all of 1929 UU 6610 remained AEC's property, a situation which lasted right through to 31st December on which day the LGOC bought it, presumably having negotiated a favourable price. General now had three Regents within its ownership, for while UU 6610 had been working as a demonstrator, ST 1 had come into service and ST 2's chassis was in use within Chiswick Works. No fleet number was given to UU 6610 but it was allocated LGOC body number 10954. In March 1930 it returned back to Chiswick from Tunbridge Wells to be given a protracted overhaul during which it would have been stripped down and closely examined to ascertain levels of wear and tear incurred during its eight months in service. While it was there the seating capacity was reduced to 48 by removing three from the rear of the upper deck, giving greater circulating space at the top of the staircase.

Three months elapsed before UU 6610 was once again ready for use, and it was not until 17th June 1930 that it finally made its way back to Reigate to rejoin the East Surrey fleet back on route 414 where it had worked briefly in the previous year. The vehicle now carried standard East Surrey livery and was allocated fleet number 255, following on from a batch of new Ransomes-bodied Regents currently being delivered, although as the Company was now on the verge of abandoning the use of fleet numbers altogether it was not actually displayed on the vehicle. At an unknown date, but probably at its next overhaul in May/June 1931, the opportunity was taken to replace the destination boards and their accompanying lighting paraphernalia with a conventional roller blind to bring it in line with the many other Regents which the Company was now operating. In order to accommodate a standard-sized screen the front was re-profiled with the bulge of the piano-front styling now occurring higher up than before.

As far as is known, UU 6610 spent the next two years or so working on route 414 and it was still based at Reigate garage on 28th January 1932 when East Surrey was reborn under the new title of London General Country Services Ltd with enhanced responsibility for the provision of services in all of the country districts surrounding London, north as well as south. This was followed, on 7th April 1932, by a re-arrangement of assets under which all the vehicles loaned by the LGOC to East Surrey, and subsequently to LGCS, were formally purchased by the latter, UU 6610 included. On 1st July 1933 its ownership changed once again when it became part of the initial fleet of the Country Omnibus & Coach Department of the new London Passenger Transport Board.

Top left UU 6610 was no doubt a great novelty to passengers and crews alike during its spell on Autocar's route 7A. An obvious pride in it is indicated by the white-walling of the tyres which, though now a little scuffed, help to enhance its overall appearance. The upper destination board which reads 'TUNBRIDGE WELLS-SOUTHBOROUGH-TONBRIDGE' to indicate the full extent of the vehicle's operation is a semi-permanent fixture, which is fortunate in view of its relative inaccessibility. The lower board, which is easier to reach, is used to show the actual direction of travel.

Top right Now under LGOC ownership and back in service with East Surrey, UU 6610 has been painted in a less ornate livery but still carries board indicators. The 'via' board is now a full height one reaching right up to the top retaining bracket, but it is far from clear how the conductor managed to reach the one above it to display the destination 'HORSHAM' without having had access to a ladder at the West Croydon terminus. *A N Porter*

Above Still on route 414, but no longer requiring contortional acts to display the correct destination, UU 6610 has had its upper front panels re-profiled to accommodate a destination blind which can be accessed by the conductor from inside the upper saloon. Although further minor modifications will subsequently be made, the vehicle has now basically adopted the appearance by which it will be instantly recognised for many years to come as London Transport's ST 1139.

CHAPTER 3
FLEET EXPANSION UNDER THE LGOC

Without waiting to find out the results of ST 1's service trials, the LGOC embarked on a major expansion of the class with the intention of getting the first vehicles into service as early in 1930 as possible. This apparently remarkable leap of faith was, in fact, forced upon the Company which badly needed to retrieve as quickly as it could ground lost to many of its independent competitors who were literally cashing in handsomely by placing new Leyland Titans into service. In terms of speed and comfort these were clearly a cut well above the LGOC's most modern offering, the NS, and by the start of 1930 no fewer than 22 Titans could be found in London running for 14 operators (Claremont, Chocolate Express, Essex, Gordon, Peraeque, Perkins, Pickup, Pioneer, Premier, Reliance, Renown, Standard, Triumph and Westminster) with the delivery of several more imminent. Not only were the Titans capable of running rings around General's slow and ponderous NSs, but they exposed vividly the broad generational gap between the new Leylands and the numerous open-top solid-tyred K and S double deckers which, with 960 and 834 respectively still on books, made up so much of the LGOC fleet. Through being within Underground group ownership along with AEC, General was in no position to buy Titans of its own so it had to trust that the AEC Regent would come up to the same high standard. AEC, on its part, depended upon the LGOC placing orders to help recover the huge capital outlay involved in developing its new range of models and also to provide it with the strong customer base essential to keep it in business.

Before proceeding further with the story of the growth of the ST class, it is appropriate to look at the LGOC's order book for vehicles of this type to help understand how the fleet was intended to develop. This is a complicated subject because what was planned was not always put into practice for a variety of reasons. In August 1929 the LGOC announced publicly that it had placed an order with AEC for no fewer than 270 new chassis of which 120 were to be Regents. In fact no order stipulating 120 Regents was ever placed, but over a period of months a succession of contracts was sealed covering the delivery of 836 ST class vehicles (including the two chassis already received) as follows:

Contract		
918(1)	ST 1	plus 1 chassis for testing and development (ST 2)
979	ST 3-101	
?	ST 102-301	
1010	ST 302-501	to include 25 Strachans and 33 Short Bros bodies
995	ST 502-516	for National Omnibus & Transport Company, Watford
918(2)	ST 517	training school chassis
1032	ST 518-817	to include 25 Strachans and 17 Short Bros bodies
1051	ST 818-821	for National Omnibus & Transport Company, Ware
1047	ST 822-836	for Overground

It can be seen from studying the capital requisition numbers that orders were not always placed in fleet number sequence. In the case of ST 102-301, no specific order number has been traced and it is presumed that these were supplied as an extension to contract 979.

Except where stated, all the above were to be bodied at Chiswick. In addition, the body shop at Chiswick was commissioned to supply a total of 28 spare bodies ordered in three separate contracts, 9 at the same time as the order for ST 3-101 was placed, a further 9 along with ST 502-516, plus a subsequent and final order for 10. In fact only 24 were used as intended, three being diverted for use on Daimler chassis (DST 1-3) and another cancelled, probably to counter balance the purchase of a previously unplanned experimental body from Metro Cammell.

New STs flooded into service from Hanwell garage at an astonishing rate in the early months of 1930. ST 73 was one of four licensed for service on 24th March at which time 62 were already at work there, and within the next two days they had been joined by a further fourteen. ST 73 was recorded at Oxford Circus on its second day in service. *L T Museum*

The LGOC also ordered 63 chassis on behalf of its subsidiary companies in three separate batches, none of which were allotted fleet numbers in the ST series.

981   30 with bodies by Ransomes, Sims & Jefferies for East Surrey

1055   30 with bodies by Short Bros for East Surrey

1115   23 with LGOC bodies for London General Country Services

As will become evident in the following chapters, the original plans for allocating fleet numbers quickly fell by the wayside. The instructional vehicle intended to have been ST 517 was actually ST 169. The fleet for National at Watford was delivered earlier than originally planned and occupied a miscellany of fleet numbers between ST 107 and ST 163. The only STs for Overground were ST 822-826, and ST 833, 834 were supplied new to East Surrey. In London Transport days all 83 vehicles covered by capital requisitions 981, 1055 and 1115 finally received fleet numbers ranging between ST 1032 and ST 1132.

When authorising its new vehicle purchase programme the LGOC Board envisaged, and actually approved, the placing of two separate orders for Regents to take the fleet up to ST 301. This arrangement was reflected in associated orders to the coachworks at Chiswick which allocated 100 body numbers (10377-10476) to the first batch and 200 (10503-10702) to the second. Only 299 chassis were required (the 300th body being for ST 2) and these were allocated numbers in a single sequence, 661211-661509. As mentioned in chapter 1, nine spare bodies were subsequently ordered (10955-10963) to form an overhaul float, and spare chassis would have been purchased too for the same reason, but as always in the case of float chassis these were not ordered as complete units, but were covered within the requisitioning of supplies and spare parts accompanying each chassis supply contract.

Interestingly, numbered between the first and second body contracts was ST 1 which carried body No. 10493. It is presumed that the allocation of a body number to this vehicle was overlooked at the time it was ordered and built.

Once the ST chassis for the LGOC began rolling off the production line at Southall they did so at a prodigious rate. Similarly the body production plant at Chiswick was mass producing and stockpiling bodies which could be mounted on new chassis almost as soon as they arrived. First into service was a batch of sixteen on 28th February 1930 (ST 3-15, 17, 19, 23), all at Hanwell garage where they were joined next day by ST 1. Thereafter the monthly output varied wildly but in some months significant numbers of new STs joined the LGOC fleet with the maximum input of 72 being achieved in March 1930, followed by almost as impressive figures in April with 57 and July with 68.

When purchasing ST 1 the LGOC appears to have been happy to accept a perfectly standard Regent chassis, but for its bulk order certain modifications were stipulated, the most noticeable of which was the removal of the petrol tank from its normal offside position to the nearside, the space vacated on the offside being used to carry the vehicle's two 6 volt batteries in preference to placing them inside the body as was more commonly the case. For some unknown reason – perhaps to save weight – the rear chassis overhang was cut a little shorter than normal. On most, the mechanical specification was the same as for ST 1, although the first six chassis were initially fitted with a 7:1 rear axle ratio instead of the normal 6¼:1 for comparative purposes.

The standard Chiswick body for the production run of STs fairly closely resembled that on ST 1 although certain major modifications were clearly apparent. The most obvious difference lay in the fitment of an open driver's cab, no further permission having been obtained from the Metropolitan Police to extend beyond the original trial run of 100 buses with fully glazed cabs. The square contours of ST 1's cab were

In a busy traffic scene at Marble Arch, ST 55 looks strikingly modern compared with all the other buses in view. Even the covered-top NSs look positively dated, and so great have been recent advances in bus design that it is hard to believe that older vehicles, such as K 364 seen carrying METROPOLITAN fleet names, are barely a decade old. *L T Museum*

View inside the lower deck of ST 50 show that, apart from the use of grey-green rexine on the window surrounds instead of cream, there was little difference between the interior of prototype ST 1 and the standard production body. Two plungers for the pneumatic bell system can be clearly seen, but the most notable feature is the large mirror on the staircase wall. *L T Museum*

abandoned in favour of a neat, rounded lower cab structure designed for quick modification once fully enclosed cabs became permissible, which was seen as being only a matter of time. Above cab level the black band around the vehicle's centre was now flat in profile and not convex as on ST 1. Internally, the excellent straight staircase was modified with slightly wider treads which meant that the bottom step now protruded into the platform area by a few inches but not enough to affect the overall air of spaciousness. The unusual lower saloon floor arrangement on ST 1, with the riser positioned about 2ft inside, had probably constituted a trip hazard for many an unwary passenger and was eliminated by placing the step up from the platform conventionally in line with the bulkhead. Like ST 1 in its modified form, the standard ST was a 49-seater employing the same very comfortable type of seats in exactly the same layout.

Climbing inside one of the new STs, you could hardly miss one prominent feature which was a huge mirror occupying the whole upper half of the staircase partition. Passengers sitting in the longidudinal seat had the pleasure – or embarrassment – of looking at reflections of themselves throughout their journey whilst those heading for the forward facing seats in the lower saloon were presented with tantalising glimpses of themselves as they passed by! This quickly became known officially as the 'mirror panel'. Inside the saloons the décor copied that applied to ST 1 in its modified form with grey-green scratchproof rexine covering the mouldings around the windows as well as the body sides. At 5 tons 10cwt 0qr the unladen weight of the complete vehicle was just a little less than ST 1.

A couple of features inherited from ST 1 were quickly to prove troublesome and might perhaps have been avoided if the prototype vehicle had been allowed to undergo a longer gestation period before the production design was finalised. One was the system of diffused lighting within the saloons which came in for criticism from both sides, customers and staff. From a passenger's point of view the mellow, warm glow, though pleasant enough, was inadequate to read by in comfort, whilst staff were confronted with a rigmarole of removing numerous screws and items of moulding whenever a bulb needed to be changed. The second less than satisfactory feature was the pneumatic bell system. The plungers, or 'pushes' as the LGOC called them, often needed some force to operate which was inconvenient for passengers but was frequently overcome by conductors who resorted to hitting them with the end of their ticket racks, a practice which continued despite exhortations from management that this spoiled the appearance and could render the plungers inoperative. Managers also had to take drivers to task for trying to reduce the ringing noise from the bells by stuffing the pipes with paper.

It is interesting to recall that the average cost of producing each of the first batch of production bodies was £571 6s 11d. This compared very favourably with a final cost of £1,422 12s 0d for the prototype body on ST 1 and illustrates graphically the cost benefit of mass production as against building one-offs. AEC's charge for each ST chassis was £700, which meant that each complete ST was bought for a fraction over £1,270.

From new, two of the earliest STs were involved in an interesting though ultimately unsuccessful experiment aimed

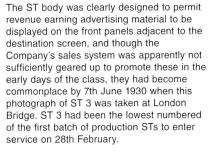

The ST body was clearly designed to permit revenue earning advertising material to be displayed on the front panels adjacent to the destination screen, and though the Company's sales system was apparently not sufficiently geared up to promote these in the early days of the class, they had become commonplace by 7th June 1930 when this photograph of ST 3 was taken at London Bridge. ST 3 had been the lowest numbered of the first batch of production STs to enter service on 28th February.

As originally built, the rear end of the standard ST body closely resembled the prototype ST 1 except that radiused corners were omitted from the bottoms of the windows. When ST 112 was photographed at Holborn in September 1930, plans were already afoot to reconfigure the rather bulbous looking lower deck styling. By the time ST 112 was licensed for service on 12th April 1930, the flow of new STs into Hanwell had almost ceased. *L T Museum*

Highly organised teams of coachbuilders were employed at Chiswick to produce new bus bodies on an industrial scale. This picture shows how the lower saloon structure was lowered into a pit to allow the separately constructed upper deck to be attached without needing the use of ladders or gantries. As the upper deck is being lowered into position, workmen are already beginning to cut the canvas to shape for gluing to the driver's canopy. *L T Museum*

at achieving greater refinement in performance than was achievable from even AEC's smooth running 6-cylinder unit, which was acknowledged to be one of the best on the market. The LGOC's Development Engineer, Owen Watson, was particularly interested in exploiting the potential of the 8-cylinder in-line engine, having witnessed its smooth running in high class cars such as the Hillman, Lanchester and Wolseley. He obtained permission to commission AEC to construct five such engines at Southall to LGOC specification and set about installing them in all three examples of AEC's new chassis range. The first two entered service in Renowns LT 35 and LT 41 on 22nd January 1930 and another was used on Regal T 43. The other two were both present in new ST chassis when these were received from Southall, entering service at Hanwell on 28th February and 7th April 1930 respectively as ST 4 and ST 84. The engines are believed to have been a modification of the standard overhead camshaft A 140 with a reduction from the usual 100mm bore down to 87mm to theoretically achieve the same swept volume. Being, obviously, longer than the normal engine, permission had to be obtained from the police to extend the radiator forward by a few inches to accommodate it. Although in theory the 8-cylinder engine should have been a refined but equally powerful variation on the 6-cylinder version it was actually rated at only 85bhp, a reduction of 10bhp, because mixture distribution proved to be less satisfactory than anticipated using a single carburettor on such a long engine. The benefits hoped for were not achieved and, one by one, the five vehicles involved were fitted with standard 6-cylinder units. STs 4 and 84 were both dealt with in December 1930 and the experiment ended when the last two, LT 35 and T 43, were converted in January 1931.

After the massive injection of 98 new STs into Hanwell garage, it was time to start an equally large programme at Hammersmith. In fact the two overlapped a little, the first intake at Hammersmith being on 27th March 1930 whilst Hanwell received its last on 17th April. Fleet numbers well up into the ST 150s could now be seen, but meanwhile 15 vehicles were withdrawn from the roster of those scheduled to go to the LGOC and were sent instead to work on services operated on the Company's behalf by the National Omnibus & Transport Company at its Watford garage. These were early replacements for the vehicles originally ordered for National which would have been ST 502-516. Nine of them (ST 107, 111, 116, 129, 132, 135, 143, 152, 159) were needed urgently at Watford to counter direct competition from the Lewis Omnibus Company which had managed to put new AEC Regents on the road ahead of National, and the remaining six (ST 136, 140, 141, 157, 162, 163) were destined to receive special lowbridge style bodies to permit the speedy conversion to double-deck operation of the busy service from Watford to Berkhamsted via Chesham. The full stories of these two batches are told in chapters 5 and 6.

Hammersmith garage began to receive an enormous batch of new STs in late March 1930, and ST 127 joined the fleet there on 12th May. The LGOC commissioned this colour view of it in 'as new' condition, which shows how attractive these vehicles looked in the plain but functional General livery. *L T Museum*

The fleet modernisation at Hammersmith was even more ambitious than that at Hanwell with no fewer than 101 STs due between March and the completion of the intake on 1st July 1930. During this period a number of changes were made to the bodywork specification, the first of many introduced throughout the course of the ST construction programme. It all seems to have been done on a piecemeal basis, and if documentation ever existed to show exactly where in the construction programme each change was implemented this has long ago disappeared. To those who remember the LGOC STs in the nineteen-forties, when several hundred vehicles all looked basically the same, it might come as a surprise to learn that, by the end of 1931, a whole host of bodywork variations could be found which gradually disappeared as the vehicles were modified and their specification standardised.

The first external variation became apparent in June 1930 when a simple metal visor appeared on the front of the canopy ahead of the driver, the dual purpose of which was to cut down glare from the sun and also to keep out some of the rain on wet days. It was presumably introduced as a result of unsatisfactory service experience with the open cab as originally designed, but though all future new vehicles were fitted with visors prior to the eventual introduction of full windscreens, no attempt was made to retro-fit the 150 or so STs already in service. At about the same time, or possibly even a little earlier, the use of translucent panels to cover the internal lighting was discontinued, no doubt primarily as a result of unsatisfactory service experience but probably also to cut production costs. Metal coving panels were now used upon which the light bulbs were mounted in conventional holders with neat looking jellymould-style glass covers over them. Vehicles which had been built with the original concealed lighting were modified to the new form on their first overhaul, which meant that all traces of the original arrangement had been eliminated as early as June 1931. Yet another contemporary move was the elimination of the huge mirror on the staircase panel, not just from vehicles coming off the production line but also from those already in service. The mirrors, which must have been extremely expensive to purchase in the first place because of their large size, were claimed to be a distraction to passengers, although there might also have been a pressing financial motive behind their removal as the LGOC proceeded to derive considerable benefit from marketing the former 'mirror panel' as a popular site for advertising material.

One particular modification which can be specifically dated was confined, at first, to a single vehicle, ST 161, which entered service at Hammersmith on 7th June 1930. This modification was nothing to do with unsatisfactory service experience or dictated by new design whims, but was done to pre-empt a forthcoming change in the law. Since 1929 a major new Bill had been going through Parliament which was destined to have a huge impact on the whole bus industry, including the mighty LGOC, and it duly received Royal Assent as the Road Traffic Act on 1st August 1930. Included within its numerous provisions affecting passenger service vehicles were new Construction & Use Regulations amongst the nineteen pages of which was a clause rendering it illegal to construct ST bodies to the existing design from an implementation date in 1931. This forthcoming change in law related to the width of the cut-away at the rear of the platform, the purpose of which was to allow passengers to escape in the event of a vehicle tipping over and falling on to its nearside. Under the forthcoming regulations the 9¾ inch gap provided in the current ST design would be inadequate and a wider aperture was needed.

It was decided to construct an ST which could comply with the forthcoming regulation and to try it out in service. A standard body fresh off the production line, no. 10541, which had been mounted on the chassis of ST 161 soon after the latter had been received from AEC on 7th April, was set aside for experimental rebuilding. The Chiswick drawing office had redesigned the lower half of the rear end of the body to achieve a 1ft 9in cut-away, and accompanying this was the substitution of the existing two window arrangement by a single pane of glass, giving an altogether much neater appearance. This revised design was subsequently adopted as standard for the ST fleet, and for LTs too, but not until October 1930 and new ST bodies continued to be built to the old design until then.

Outside the finishing shop at Chiswick the final touches are given to a row of brand new STs. The side advertisements have already been applied, and destination blinds will also be fitted before the vehicles are sent out for service. More significantly, the individual identity of each vehicle has still to be determined and marked upon it in the form of fleet and registration numbers, the former being in strict numerical sequence with the AEC chassis numbers. *R W Kidner*

At about the same time that all these changes were being implemented, the LGOC entered into what might be called its 'bumper' phase. Somebody appears to have persuaded the Company that it would be a good idea to fit bumpers to its buses – both front and rear – presumably to minimise collision damage and insurance claims – and the STs were at the forefront of this programme. (Initially they were referred to as 'buffers' but before long the more usual term 'bumper' came into regular use.) The first manifestation of the new vogue appers to have been with ST 153 which was fitted on 13th May 1930 with rear corner springs, and it entered service with these at Hammersmith on 2nd June. Presumably the springs were similar to those later fitted to London United's 'Diddler' trolleybuses, but the idea was not pursued any further. The sprung bumper would have been mounted on the bodywork itself, but the LGOC appears to have wanted something much more substantial for the backs of its vehicles independent of the bodywork. The designers came up with nothing less than a bolted extension to the chassis frame which curved upwards beyond the rear of the body to support a quite handsome bumper consisting of three horizontal bars, one above the other. This was an extremely heavy and cumbersome arrangement which pushed the unladen weight of the vehicle up by just over 11cwt to 6 tons 1cwt 2qrs and must have been detrimental to fuel consumption. This arrangement was installed on ST 286 which entered service on 1st August, and it must have impressed the LGOC's management sufficiently for it to become a standard feature on all vehicles entering service from 16th September onwards. In addition, a crash programme took place between September 1930 and January 1931 to fit rear bumpers to all 287 STs that had previously entered service without them including the prototype ST 1.

ST 161 was employed during April and May 1930 as the guinea pig for a revised rear end incorporating a wider door cut-away designed to comply with forthcoming legislative changes, and it introduced the classic styling to which all of the LGOC's STs eventually complied. The colour photograph also shows a three-tiered rear bumper arrangement which was being experimented with at the time, although it is not thought to have still been on this vehicle when it entered service at Hammersmith on 7th June. The blue, triangular 'Four Wheel Brakes' emblem was another innovation about the same time, but it quickly fell into disuse. *L T Museum*

Front bumpers were in vogue too. Although officially intended as bumpers they would be better described as radiator guards as this seems to have been their prime function. Uncertainty appears to have prevailed over how best to mount a front bumper and some were bolted directly to the radiator shell which, on the face of it, would not have provided much in the way of impact resistance in the case of a collision. More commonly, bumpers were supported in holders welded or riveted to the top of each dumbiron. In some cases the tubular bumper structure rose vertically from the dumbiron to about three quarters of the way up the side of the radiator and then around the front to complete the bumper effect, and in others it projected directly outwards from the dumbiron itself. The first vehicle to be fitted was ST 286, at the same time in July 1930 that it received its rear bumper, making it the first fully bumper equipped vehicle in the fleet, and from about the middle of September STs began entering service displaying the new front bumpers. In the absence of any contemporary documentation, the effectiveness of these can only be speculated upon, but it was probably not very great as fitment ceased from about December 1930 and no attempt was ever made to fit them on STs already in service. Surprisingly the dumbiron attachments continued to be present but unused on all new chassis until the end of the production programme, and they could also be found in large numbers on LT six-wheelers even though none of the latter class ever had front bumpers fitted to them.

The delivery of new STs to Hammersmith, which took three months to complete, had witnessed not only several deviations from the original body specification, but it also saw the introduction of the fleet name METROPOLITAN on a sizeable number of the new vehicles. Although operated as an integral part of the LGOC fleet and carrying standard General red and grey livery, the vehicles concerned had been bought and paid for by the Tramways (M.E.T.) Omnibus Company Ltd which, although fully owned by the Underground group, was not an LGOC subsidiary. However under an agreement of 25th July 1919 covering the post-war reinstatement of the MET fleet, followed by several subsidiary agreements made over the years, the LGOC operated the fleet on the MET's behalf. The LGOC did everything from

providing garages, management, crews, petrol and tyres, vehicle maintenance and insurance to obtaining licences, arranging schedules and fixing fares. In return, MET agreed to restrict its operations to 11.33% of the total fleet of General and its associated companies for which it received 11.33% of gross receipts. The supply of new vehicles was arranged by the LGOC on the strict understanding that the price paid for them could not be any greater than the LGOC itself paid. By an agreement of 8th May 1931 backdated to 1st January 1928, the MET proportion of the total fleet was reduced to 8.32% of which 34 of Hammersmith's STs formed part.

When Hammersmith's share of the new ST fleet was completed, it was time for Seven Kings to take over as the next major recipient of new vehicles, of which it was destined to receive 96 between July and September 1930. Between them, Hanwell, Hammersmith and Seven Kings had absorbed all available new STs within the batch ST 3-301. In fact Seven Kings' requirement was only fully satisfied by the inclusion of 18 vehicles from the next two orders, which differed mechanically from their predecessors in having AEC's own design of worm and nut steering which was lower geared and lighter than the Marles arrangement used previously. This was the first of a number of improvements made to the mechanical specification during the ST construction programme, and the updated steering was fitted to all existing STs at their first overhaul. Following on from ST 301 and well out of fleet number sequence came ST 502-516 with chassis 661783-661797. This was the batch originally intended for National and it was augmented by ST 517 (661798) which had been originally earmarked as the instructional chassis but was not eventually used as such. The final three deliveries to Seven Kings, on 18th/19th September 1930, were the first of the next series of 200, ST 302-501 (661800-661999). Fifty-eight of these were due to have bodies built by outside coachbuilders Strachans (who were to provide 25) and Shorts (33), but delivery from these factories was not planned to commence until late November. Meanwhile the nine Chiswick-built float bodies ordered along with ST 3-301 had not been needed as such since the first overhaul programme had not yet commenced, so they were mounted instead on new chassis as the latter arrived from Southall.

The LGOC was fond of depicting impressive line-ups of new and recently overhauled vehicles in its works at Chiswick and this row of fifteen – with brand new vehicles at the front and old open-toppers at the back – was arranged for the photographer in July 1930. The two STs that can be identified, ST 218 and ST 252 at first and third positions in the line respectively, both entered service at Seven Kings on the 10th of the month. *L T Museum*

Canopy visors had come into use to shelter drivers from the very worst of the sun's glare and to provide a slight relief from driving rain, in time for the big ST allocation to Seven Kings starting in July 1930. ST 264, seen at High Holborn, started work on 25th July 1930 and, like much of the initial Seven Kings fleet, transferred to Norwood about a year later. *L T Museum*

At the time of completion of the initial order for 300, four STs from this batch remained outstanding for entry into service. One never appeared. This was ST 169 which, after being taken into stock on 7th April 1930, was set aside four days later as the training school instructional chassis, replacing in advance ST 517 which had been notionally reserved for this purpose. Over the ensuing years countless newly recruited drivers came into contact with ST 169's chassis as they passed through Chiswick while undergoing training, before it was finally disposed of in August 1950. Even earlier in the fleet numbering sequence, ST 154 had not been delivered as it should have been in April 1930 because its intended chassis (661362) had been diverted by agreement with the LGOC to another customer. This was Chariot Omnibus Services Ltd. of Shepherds Bush in whose service it received a Birch outside staircase body and ran as GJ 8501. On the face of it, the LGOC's acquiescence in letting a chassis go to one of its competitors may have seemed odd, but from AEC's point of view any opportunity to penetrate a market heavily dominated by its main competitor, Leyland, was too good to miss. It proved to be a vain effort because, in common with various other manufacturers, AEC failed to garner any substantial sales to the London 'pirate' operators. The loss of chassis 661362 was subsequently made good by sending the LGOC chassis 661799 which was licensed as ST 154 at Seven Kings on 17th September 1930.

ST 211 disappeared from the scene almost as soon as it had been taken into stock on 19th June 1930. Its destination was Metro Cammell's works at Birmingham where arrangements had been made for it to receive an ST style body using the MCW patented form of 'all metal' construction. The body took almost four months to complete, but the finished result (numbered 11535 in the LGOC body series) was a passable if rather plain and workmanlike copy of the standard body, recognisable mainly through its square topped windows and flat lower body panelling. Though destined to be the only one of its type on an ST chassis, the 'all metal' body offered sufficient potential for 25 generally similar bodies to be ordered on Dennis Lances for LGOC subsidiary Overground Ltd. Despite its steel based construction, ST 211 was only half a ton greater in weight than a standard ST at exactly 6 tons, although almost immediately after it arrived at Chiswick from Metro Cammell a back bumper was added which pushed the unladen weight up to 6 tons 12cwt 0qr. ST 211 entered service on 20th October 1930 and its distinctive body remained a feature of the ST fleet for the next 18 years under the guise of various fleet numbers which, in pre-war years, changed after each overhaul.

The last of the 'missing' quartet to enter LGOC service was ST 174. This had been received in chassis form at Chiswick on 29th April 1930 and, as part of the normal sequence of things, a new body was mounted on 3rd May. Thereafter the vehicle disappeared from sight, at least from Londoners. It was hired to AEC who promptly shipped it off to Sweden as one of a number of British double deckers working at the great Stockholm Exhibition held in the eastern-central suburbs of that city between May and September 1930. The Exhibition, an enormous and influential affair attracting 4 million visitors, showcased Sweden's

No photograph is known to exist of the Metro Cammell all-metal body with open cab as fitted to ST 211. This advertisement depicts the body in its second guise as ST 379 alongside a similar looking Dennis Lance in the Overground fleet.

Almost inevitably, the use of translucent internal lighting panels was discontinued, probably in June 1930, the replacements being conventional lamp holders covered by neat jellymould-style shades. These are depicted an ST 513 which joined the fleet at Seven Kings in September 1930. *L T Museum*

No doubt much to the pleasure of General's management, the relative plushness of the STs' well-padded interior even reached the pages of the popular satirical magazine 'Punch'. This cartoon is a very good depiction of the platform end of an ST, complete with jellymould lamps, and shows a conductor in typical pose with his punch and rack at the ready.

Gentleman (on latest de luxe motor-bus) : " Lummy, this is a bit of orlright, ain't it ? 'Ave yer got beds upstairs ? "

Rear bumpers were finally adopted as standard in September 1930 and an early vehicle to carry them was ST 513. The bumpers came in two styles, some with a central vertical strip and others without, and, as on ST 513, it was not unusual for these to partly obscure the BP advertisement on the lower panel. ST 513 was one of the last to enter service with the original double window platform arrangement. *L T Museum*

latest products and crafts along with its designs for modern living. Strong emphasis was also placed on transport including cars, buses, trains and aeroplanes. ST 174 finally made its way back to Chiswick on 14th January 1931 whereupon it was put through overhaul having, presumably, worked quite hard whilst overseas transporting visitors to and from the Exhibition. Still retaining its original body, it finally entered service on 7th March 1931.

Once Seven Kings had been fully stocked with its planned quota of STs on 19th September, a pause ensued before the next garage began to receive an influx, which was Leyton whose first one went into service on 10th October. This was the first pause in what had so far been a headlong rush of STs into service at an almost breathless rate, and it marked the break between the end of the first requisition for Chiswick built bodies and the start of the next one, which was for 109 including 9 spares. Starting with the Leyton batch the revised rear end first tried out on ST 161 now became standard, vehicles built with the new style back comprising ST 303, 306-501, 515 and 518 onwards, plus 'all metal' ST 211 which joined Leyton's fleet on 20th October 1930. Leyton was another garage where part of its fleet consisted of Tramways (M.E.T.) vehicles, and some one hundred of the massive fleet of 171 new STs allocated there were given METROPOLITAN fleet names.

Up to this point the STs had been characterised by the substantial inflows of vehicles into a few select garages. On one intermediate occasion when a comparatively small alloca-

tion of STs had been needed elsewhere consisting of 18 at Cricklewood in August 1930, the requirement had been met not with new vehicles but by transferring used STs from Hammersmith. However a change of policy now became detectable with future deliveries being earmarked for specific routes rather than complete garages, and this started when Norwood received 14 new STs between 31st October and 4th November. Chalk Farm then gained 18 between 4th and 13th November, Elmers End 15 from the 13th to 19th November and Nunhead 17 between 20th and 24th November.

At Nunhead the first standard STs bodied by an outside manufacturer made their appearance in service on 20th November in the form of ST 348 and ST 551 bodied by Short Brothers Ltd at their factory in Rochester, and others quickly followed. Soon afterwards, on 29th November a second delivery of STs to Nunhead included ST 310 which was the first from the North Acton factory of Strachans Successors Ltd. These outside orders had been placed to relieve pressure on the Chiswick body shops despite the cost of each body being some 27% higher than if they had been built in-house. In total, each manufacturer was contracted to build 50, body numbers being allocated in blocks as 11435-11484 to Strachans and 11485-11534 to Shorts. These, and the bodies concurrently built at Chiswick, were totally intermingled as far as fleet numbers were concerned and apart from the manufacturer's transfer – which was obliterated by paint on first overhaul anyway – there was no way of distinguishing the Strachans and Shorts bodies from the Chiswick product.

Front bumpers are fitted to STs 470 and 489, seen in a line-up outside the Public Carriage Office in Lambeth Road in November 1930. ST 470, at the front, entered service at Nunhead on 24th November while ST 489 started work a day later at Leyton. The bus at the very back, behind the S-type, is one of a pair of Dennis Lances bought by the Reliance Omnibus Company, the first of their type in London. *C F Klapper*

Seen 'at home' in Hammersmith garage and with the front bumper prominently in view, is ST 123 which was fitted with bumpers on 29th September 1930 as part of an ongoing installation programme. Another feature, about which nothing is known, is the driver's mirror attached to the offside at waistrail level. Driving mirrors did not come into general use on the LGOC until about July 1931, and when they did so they were mounted much higher than this, possibly to render them less vulnerable to sundry knocks. *Ken Blacker collection*

The supply of chassis under the current contract was now drawing to a close and AEC began gearing up for the start of a new batch of 300 (6611163-6611462) which were to become ST 518-817 in the LGOC fleet. These were built to an improved specification in having triple rather than single servo vacuum braking, and they also incorporated AEC's latest D124 gearbox with constant mesh third gear in place of the D119 with its sliding mesh third gear arrangement. Both features were retro-fitted to all earlier vehicles in due course. STs placed into service with LGOC-built bodies all employed the new batch of chassis from 4th December 1930 onwards, but Strachans and Shorts continued to supply bodies on the previous chassis batch for a little longer. Both ran out of these during the first week of January 1931 after which there was a pause of roughly a month before they resumed production using chassis from the latest order. The final Shorts bodies (on ST 603, 618) were placed into service on 16th February 1931 and the last Strachans (ST 638, 640) followed suit on 5th March with the exception of a late straggler (ST 619) on the 31st of the same month.

The next garage to receive new STs after Nunhead's requirements had been fulfilled was Seven Kings which received a batch of 23 at the start of December. STs were, of course, no stranger to Seven Kings but several were, in fact, outstationed at Romford which did not have an allocation of its own. Renamed Hornchurch in early London Transport days to avoid confusion with the Green Line (ex Hillman) garage of the same name, Romford was one of a number of small outer suburban LGOC garages with minimal facilities of their own which relied on larger, better equipped garages to provide their vehicle fleets and the maintenance for them.

The use of double deckers on Romford local work had become possible as a result of a service revision on 3rd December 1930, and one of the STs used on this was of particular interest. ST 510 had been delivered to Chiswick as a new chassis back in August but was not promptly prepared for service. Instead it was used as the guinea pig for a planned change in destination blind layout which resulted in the rear

display being removed entirely and re-sited at the side above the doorway in place of the route number aperture located there previously. This resulted in a reduction from three to two in the number of roller blinds required for each bus and freed up the large back panel for commercial advertising. When adopted as standard practice, it also resulted in a furore from the general public the like of which the LGOC had not predicted because of the total absence of route information on the rear of new vehicles. ST 510 was also provided with a thick wooden horizontal strip around the lower panels to provide greater protection against casual knocks than the normal half-round metal moulding had provided. After all this was done, ST 510 was used as the prototype for the fitment of an enclosed driver's cab which is reported to have been installed by 17th October. The finished result, based on the standard rounded lower cab structure, looked very similar to the design already familiar on Green Line T types and was clearly carried out as a trial run pre-empting the Metropolitan Police's relaxation over the use of enclosed cabs on stage carriage vehicles which was now viewed as inevitable within the not too distant future. ST 510 was licensed for service on 3rd December 1930, the first day of ST operation on route G1 between Collier Row and Upminster (Corbets Tey on Sundays). In this far eastern corner of the LGOC's operating territory it could discretely operate without offending the sensibilities of the Public Carriage Office as the Metropolitan Police District boundary stopped short of Romford.

Although it had pioneered the revised blind layout ST 510 was not the first to display it in service. The new arrangement was adopted as standard for all new Chiswick built bodies from early in November 1930 although the two outside manufacturers, having geared up to build the earlier design, continued to do so until the completion of their contracts in February (Short Bros) and March (Strachans) 1931. The last garage to receive STs in 1930 was Forest Gate which gained an allocation of 46 between 6th and 16th December, after which all new deliveries for the remainder of the year went to enhance further the already large fleet at Leyton.

Once formally adopted, the revised rear blind layout was applied to earlier vehicles as they went through overhaul. A typical example of this is ST 506, carrying the body formerly on ST 284 after overhaul in July 1931. As well as providing advertising space – for Dunlop in this case – where the rear blind box once was, a tidying-up down below has now provided space for a reasonably sized advert at lower deck level. *L T Museum*

ST 510 was a trial vehicle in September 1930 on which the back destination screen was removed to free-up advertising space, and re-sited above the platform entrance. Posed here, alongside Metropolitan S 263, it graphically illustrates the difference in floor height between the two types of AEC chassis and emphasises the wide generation gap between them. ST 510 did not enter service in this form but was further rebuilt in October with an enclosed cab for experimental operation in the far eastern reaches of the LGOC's empire. *Ken Blacker collection*

December 1930 saw the introduction of the revised lower saloon interior with five, instead of four, transverse seats on the nearside, and also of the new 'bucket' type seat backs with their curved outer edges. For the time being the narrow vertical front mirror still survives and the ceiling mouldings are still picked-out in a contrasting colour, but the lamps are now unshaded and basically the body depicts the appearance that will persist throughout the remaining life of the STs. The vehicle is ST 768, new to Kingston garage on 18th April 1931. *L T Museum*

Before moving on to review events in 1931 it is necessary to pause here to recall two noteworthy engine experiments which took place in 1930. In response to demands from a number of operators, of which the LGOC was almost certainly one, AEC began developing by early 1930 a more powerful version of its standard A140 6-cylinder petrol engine. Various early production versions appeared, but the design finally settled down as the A145 with 110mm bore and a swept volume of 7.4 litres. The A145 was eagerly adopted by the General for its LT class six-wheelers which had proved under-powered with the 100mm engine, but the first recorded use within the LGOC of the larger engine was actually on ST 121 at Hanwell as early as 27th September 1930. At this stage no change was made to the existing back axle ratio of 6¼:1, but when a second Hanwell vehicle, ST 104, was converted on 11th April 1931 it was allied to a 6¾ axle ratio. It is doubtful if the fairly small and lightweight ST ever really needed this extra power, but over the years that followed, and indeed right up to the final days of the class, there was always a small minority of vehicles fitted in the same way as ST 104.

Much talk within the bus industry at the time was over the development of the compression ignition engine powered by heavy oil. AEC was very much to the forefront in the development of the diesel engine, or "oil engine" as it was generally known at the time, and the LGOC was a keen backer of it too, being anxious to exploit the economies of operation that the new technology offered. In October 1930 AEC announced the availability of its A155 6-cylinder overhead valve oil engine employing the German Acro air-cell combustion chamber. With a bore of 110mm and stroke of 142mm, a swept volume of approximately 8.1 litres was produced, the rated power output of 95bhp at 2,400rpm being exactly the same as the 110mm bore petrol engine used on ST 121. The LGOC ordered twelve of the new AEC-Acro engines and decided that the first three should be installed in ST chassis.

Three new chassis, those of ST 462, 464 and 466, were supplied on 27th October 1930 with oil engines already fitted, and after being promptly bodied they were sent back on loan to AEC on 30th October. The manufacturer was keen to exhibit and demonstrate them, along with other vehicles, on the occasion of a visit by the influential Municipal Tramways and Transport Association, with the hope that firm orders would result. The three were immediately distinguishable from other STs by the 'snout' effect at the front caused by the almost 5 inch projection of the radiator to accommodate the oil engine which was longer than its petrol counterpart. The larger engine brought the vehicle's unladen weight up to 6 tons 8cwt 0qrs, as a result of which the seating capacity had to be reduced to 44 to come within existing regulations.

When it had finished with them, AEC sent the three STs back to Chiswick one by one, starting with ST 462 on 7th November. The chosen garage for their operation was Willesden, where ST 462 was the only ST in stock at the time of entering service on 1st December 1930. It was joined on the 17th by ST 466 and on 2nd January 1931 by ST 464. These three remained the only oilers in the LGOC fleet until the first of nine similarly powered LTs started work on 28th February. Their progress was carefully monitored and it soon became clear that all was far from well. The engines proved extremely smoky when operating under heavy injection and public complaints poured in about the poisonous smelling exhaust fumes, which were found to be at their worst when the engines were cold. Surprisingly, the engines were ungoverned as to their maximum speed, and it was partly because of this that they were highly prone to bearing and crankshaft failures. Their fuel consumption in the region of 7mpg was much less favourable than had been hoped for, and they were unpopular with staff because of sluggish performance and general unreliability. On 7th October 1931 the three ST oilers were transferred to Harrow Weald where all the LGOC's

oilers were currently being concentrated, but their time on route 183B was destined to be short. AEC had now developed an improved design of oil engine using the Ricardo head, and the LGOC had decided to convert its twelve AEC-Acro engines to the new format, but not for use in STs where the loss of seating capacity rendered them uneconomic. The three were due for overhaul anyway, and the vehicles that replaced them at Harrow Weald bearing the identities of ST 462, 464 and 466 were normal petrol engine STs. The last to run as an oiler was ST 464 which went into overhaul on 31st December 1931.

As 1930 drew to a close the current requisition for new ST bodies from the Chiswick coachbuilding shop was nearing completion and construction of the next batch (12010-12327) began. Fewer than one hundred of the latest style body had been built when yet another design change occurred starting with body 12098. For a reason that is not immediately clear, as it seems to have achieved no practical gain, the seating arrangement on the lower deck was revised although the total capacity remained the same. Whereas previously the inward facing seat over the rear wheelarch had accommodated four, this was now shortened to two with an additional forward facing seat substituted on the nearside ahead of it. In order to make this possible the spacing between the

forward facing seats on the nearside had to be reduced from a comfortable 2ft 7 ins down to 2ft 4 ins, although the offside ones naturally retained the old wider spacing. A new type of seat came into use, albeit with the same familiar fawn moquette. Referred to officially as a 'bucket' seat, it had a reprofiled back with curves at the outer edges, presumably intended to follow the contours of the human body. Although not immediately obvious, the wooden seat frame was of lighter construction than the earlier design, but it was clear that the cushions were a little less deep and well sprung than before. Even so, there was little or no noticeable difference in comfort between the old style of seat and the new; with their high backs and well padded upholstery both could justifiably claim to be up to private car standard. The first vehicles with modified interiors to enter service were ST 578, 589, 592 at Leyton on 31st December 1930 whilst the last Chiswick built bodies of the old type were licensed, also at Leyton, on 2nd January 1931 as ST 553, 567, 568, 571, 576.

By this time the use of decorative jellymoulds to cover the internal lighting bulbs had ceased although it is not known when this occurred, and the shades were removed from all the vehicles that had formerly carried them leaving the bulbs exposed and readily accessible but giving a less stylish and more utilitarian appearance to the vehicle interiors.

January 1931 saw new 'float' bodies brought into use when the first ST overhaul cycle commenced, and Hanwell's ST 7 was one of the first to receive one of these. The photograph was taken at Beaconsfield prior to the start of ST 7's long 2hrs 22mins summer Sunday run on route 98 to the Aldwych. The body started life with an open driver's cab but had been modernised by the time the photograph was taken. *J F Higham*

Right A chance shot at Holborn at the end of 1931 finds three STs at a time of transition. Seven Kings' ST 515 on the left, and Forest Gate's ST 529 on the right, have both recently been fitted with windscreens but carry different designs of front bumper, both of which will soon be dispensed with. The newer, centre vehicle in the Metropolitan fleet is Middle Row's ST 719. This was one of the very last batch of open cab vehicles to enter service on 23rd February 1931 and is still in this condition; it never carried a front bumper. Both ST 515 and ST 529 will be moving to pastures new in March 1932 when new Bluebird LTs are received for the 25 and 26 group of routes. *Ken Blacker collection*

The start of 1931 saw the commencement of overhauling for the earliest vehicles which were now approaching one year old. In fact the first, ST 3, went into Chiswick on the last day of the old year, after which a continuous programme was maintained. Float bodies were now required for the first time starting with a batch of six which appeared as ST 3-8 between 5th and 16th January. These were taken from the current production run (nos. 12104-12109) and were amongst the earliest with the revised lower deck seating layout. The first overhauled body to reappear was the one formerly carried by ST 3 and now on ST 9. It re-entered service at Hanwell on 19th January and demonstrated that the back end had now been rebuilt to match current styling with a wider platform cut-away and single window, and minus the rear indicator box which had now been relocated at the side. Thereafter every ST in the LGOC fleet was updated in the same way as it went through overhaul.

Towards the end of 1930 news was received that the Metropolitan Police was about to reverse its policy of objecting to the fitment of windscreens and side glasses to the cabs of public service vehicles operating within its territory, with March 1931 being rumoured as the month when relaxation of the rules would be introduced. In fact the LGOC appears to have received the go-ahead very early in February, or perhaps even before this, and plans were immediately put in hand to modify production arrangements accordingly. At the time, in addition to the ST programme which was in full swing, the first batch of enclosed back LTs was just coming into service which had an identical driver's cab arrangement to that of the ST. Although no record now exists of when this decision was taken, first priority was given to fitting enclosed cabs to new LTs in preference to STs with the result that the final open cab LTs were put into service on 6th February whereas STs continued to be licensed in this form right up to the 23rd of the month. On that date the last eight new open cab vehicles entered service at Middle Row garage (ST 688, 696, 710, 719, 728, 735, 738 and 744), and although these all carried METROPOLITAN fleet names, they effectively marked the end of an era for General and its bus operations in the Metropolis.

No more new STs were licensed until 2nd March when ST 676 and 831 began work at Middle Row. These were fitted with enclosed cabs of exactly the same type as the one installed on ST 510 some months earlier, as were all future deliveries to the LGOC and Metropolitan fleets. They were not, however, the first windscreen fitted LGOC STs into service as overhauled vehicles had begun emerging from Chiswick in this form a week earlier, starting with ST 25 and 46 at Hanwell on 26th February. At the changeover time five new STs were still outstanding from Strachans where their completion was delayed for windscreens to be fitted prior to delivery and these were all placed into service in March. Very soon afterwards a programme commenced for the fitment of enclosed cabs to all vehicles which did not have them, but it was not pursued systematically or, apparently, with any great haste, and although some STs were dealt with quite promptly, others continued to emerge from overhaul as late as January 1932 with their open cabs still intact. Although no record exists to confirm this, it was probably not until the autumn or even early winter of 1932 that the last open cab was eliminated.

New deliveries of STs for General were still arriving thick and fast at the start of 1931, but this was destined not to last. The Company had become wedded to the higher capacity of the three axle LT class, and no more orders for STs were placed. January saw the licensing of 35 new STs; February saw a final huge burst of activity with 101, followed by a fall to a still respectable 68 in March. Thereafter April and May saw 39 and 35 STs licensed respectively, and that was more or less the end. Three latecomers in June and one in July brought the programme to its close.

However, early in the year the LGOC benefited from the addition of nine STs to its fleet which it had not expected to get. Earlier on, it had placed an order with AEC for 15 STs (chassis 661463-661477) for its Potters Bar based subsidiary Overground Ltd. With standard Chiswick built bodies painted in Overground colours, these were allocated fleet numbers ST 822-836. The LGOC's plans for its own fleet ended at ST 817 and the Overground batch was numbered to follow on from four vehicles (ST 818-821) ordered for use by National at its

Ware garage (which actually had later chassis numbered 661478-661481). Only ST 822-826 were actually delivered to Overground before it was decided to order a fleet of new Dennis Lances for the company instead, placing a question mark over the future of the STs at Potters Bar. In fact one of them – ST 824 – was returned to the LGOC as early as 26th February after only three weeks with Overground, presumably because it was surplus to the latter's immediate requirements, and it was promptly put into General colours and placed into service at Leyton on 5th March. Most of the remaining STs originally intended for Overground were diverted instead to General during March with the exception of ST 833 and 834 which joined the East Surrey fleet.

A very interesting vehicle entered service on 14th March 1931. As its comparatively low fleet number ST 307 indicates, it had been in stock for quite a while before being put to use. ST 307 had, in fact, been received from AEC on 11th September 1930 and a Chiswick built body was fitted to it almost immediately afterwards. It was then set aside to become a test bed for an air-cooled engine which the Chiswick development staff had procured from the USA and were keen to try out. General had a long history of studying transatlantic automotive developments, and the air-cooled engine range produced by the Franklin Automobile Company of Syracuse was of particular interest to them. Franklin was a builder of very high quality motor cars but was also involved in the aviation market, and its speciality was its range of air-cooled engines, notably its 6-cylinder model of 1930 which was reputed to have more power per cubic inch of cylinder capacity than any other engine of its time. In theory, at least, air cooling offered many advantages quite apart from the obvious fact that such an engine had no freezing or boiling points. An air-cooled engine was more thermodynamically efficient than a typical water-cooled one and offered notable weight reduction through needing no radiator or fan; it also promised worthwhile fuel economy. There were, of course, disadvantages too, and apart from the complexity of all the ducting, baffles, fins and oil coolers there was the problem that air passages could coke up with oil and dirt. Above all, there was the louder noise inherent in this type of engine.

ST 307's Franklin 95hp engine had bore and stroke of 3½ ins and 4¾ ins respectively, and it received an RAC rating of 29.4hp. Ignition was provided by another American manufacturer, Delco of Dayton, Ohio, using that company's ring ignition system in place of the magneto usually favoured by the LGOC. For its service application, ST 307 was given a rear axle ratio of 7:1 in place of the 6¼:1 of a normal ST. Although ST 307's new engine was fully operational by October 1930 and its existence was common knowledge, its much delayed entry into service at Hammersmith garage on 14th March 1931 tends to indicate that the commissioning process had not gone smoothly. It can also be presumed that the vehicle did not perform as satisfactorily as had been hoped, for after only three months it was converted back to standard ST format, officially on 23rd June 1931.

Typical of the STs that entered service from new with enclosed cabs is ST 674, fist licensed on 30th March 1931 and photographed on 19th August. Officially allocated to Seven Kings, it carried RD plates for operation from Romford garage on route 66. It is recorded as being officially transferred to Romford in March 1932 which is presumably when the latter progressed from being an outstation to a garage in its own right.

Back at the start of 1931 Leyton garage was still under-going an influx of new STs. Streatham was due to receive its first small intake of eleven in January and February but these were not new and all came from existing fleets at Leyton and Hammersmith. In receipt of brand new STs were Willesden and Middle Row which amassed fleets of 32 and 52 respectively concurrently during February and March, the great majority at both garages carrying METROPOLITAN fleet names. In March Hammersmith received another small allocation, including Franklin engined ST 307, whilst Turnham Green's first 15 arrived a little later in the same month. The spread of STs continued during April and May with 15 for Kingston, although this garage was in fact no stranger to the class, having borrowed STs from Hanwell since as early as March 1930 to provide modern rolling stock for weekend route 620 to Guildford which was suffering intense competition from coaches on the Portsmouth Road. New deliveries were now drawing to a close, and after Hammersmith received yet another batch, this time of 22, on 11th May and Kingston's final vehicle had been received on the 21st, very few remained still to be placed into service.

The end of new vehicle production did not completely halt the onward march of STs into new territory, but from now onwards the main catalyst for change was the arrival of new LTs which flooded into service at a prodigious rate, displacing STs in their wake as well as eliminating many time-expired K and S types from the fleet. By this means Hendon garage began receiving STs from the middle of May 1931, 36 of which arrived from Leyton over an eight week period. Five late stragglers from the new bus programme were received too, including ST 777 which was the last one of all to be newly licensed for service with General on 11th July 1931. Although officially allocated to Hendon, many of these recently received STs could also be found running from Edgware garage which, like Romford, was a small outer suburban location treated as an outstation with no specific rolling stock allocation of its own.

In total, 808 STs had been taken directly into the General and Metropolitan fleets between the start of the construction programme in February 1930 and its end in July 1931, an average of more than 47 per month and a notable achievement by any standard. This excludes ST 169 which remained in chassis form throughout its life. The great majority started work without windscreens and, for the record, the 148 that entered service with enclosed cabs were ST 2, 307, 510, 583, 594, 597, 601, 611, 619*, 622*, 629*, 638*, 640*, 643, 645, 648, 650, 651, 654, 656, 658-660, 663-667, 671-676, 679, 680, 682-687, 689-692, 694, 701-703, 705, 709, 715-718, 721-724, 729, 730, 734, 736, 737, 740, 742, 743, 746-817, 827-832, 835, 836. All were Chiswick bodied except those marked with an asterisk which were built by Strachans.

Three noteworthy specimens were included amongst the last few STs to enter service. One of these was ST 2 which was no longer required for engineering purposes at Chiswick and had shed its temporary K-type body in favour of a standard ST one. Carrying a registration number contemporary with vehicles numbered in the seven and eight hundreds, it joined the fleet at Norwood garage on 23rd May 1931.

New into service on 3rd June was ST 746 which was an experimental vehicle carrying a Wilson epicyclic gearbox manufactured by Daimler and coupled to a Daimler fluid flywheel. The LGOC had been interested in the preselective gearbox for some time and had obtained Scotland Yard approval for one fitted to NS 2015 on 24th January 1930. The promise of quietness, high efficiency, long life and ease of gear changing that the combination of preselect gearbox and fluid flywheel offered had induced the LGOC to purchase three Daimler CH6 chassis (DST 1-3) which were placed into service at Harrow Weald in February 1931. Now, for comparative purposes, the Company wished to try the same equipment in a standard Regent chassis, and ST 746 was put to work alongside the DSTs on route 18, making it the precursor of a huge number of preselector equipped AECs to serve London for several decades to come. However it

In the looming presence of the Crystal Palace on the Saturdays-only 2B, and with enclosed-back 'tunnel' NS 2235 standing behind, Hendon's recently overhauled ST 409 displays its new 'camel back' body. As originally installed, this arrangement had the disadvantage that the blind could not be turned from inside the body but required the conductor to clamber on the nearside dumbiron to do so, but the winding gear was later transferred into the cab. The majority of these vehicles could be found at Hendon garage in their early days. Seen at the Golders Green terminus of route 183B and about to return back to Pinner, Harrow Weald's ST 466 shows its projecting snout indicating that this is one of the three AEC-Acro oilers, but not for much longer. A standard petrol engined ST will emerge to take its place when it goes for overhaul on 17th December 1931. An enclosed cab has been fitted for this latter part of its career as an experimental oiler.

remained unique within the LGOC fleet whose engineers preferred to use the LT class when taking the experiment further. The first LT preselectors entered service in July 1931, and when ST 746 went for overhaul in June 1932 it was converted to standard crash gearbox transmission.

ST 802, which was licensed at Hendon on 25th June, was noteworthy because it introduced, for the first time, a really new look to the ST class, at least when viewed from the front. There was no mistaking it, because although body 12327 had been constructed to exactly the same box dimensions as all the others, the front had been drastically restyled with the destination box mounted integrally with the canopy over the driver's cab. No logical explanation has ever been given as to why this was done. The new style destination box was no larger than the old one and had the disadvantage that, whereas previously the conductor could change the destination blind from inside the vehicle, he now had to clamber on to the front nearside dumbiron to do so. The only possible advantage may have been that the screen was a little closer to eye level in its revised position, but the suspicion lingers that the change was made purely for styling's sake and nothing more. The destination box formed a pronounced hump over the driver's canopy which encouraged some to refer to it as the 'camel back' design. The LGOC must have been pleased with its new styling and introduced it as a standard feature into the LT class, the first of which entered service on 2nd July, although unlike ST 802 the LTs also embodied another new feature in that the upper deck tapered inwards to give a slightly more modern rounded contour than before.

ST 802's was not the only camel back ST body; ten more followed carrying body numbers 12345-12354, the highest in the LGOC's ST fleet. These were built specifically to complete the float of bodies required for full scale overhauling of the STs. An earlier stockpile of eight float bodies numbered randomly between 12235 and 12255 plus 12923 had been

used up between March and May 1931 on ST 57, 59, 90, 102, 108, 120, 155, 199, and more were now needed. The ten new bodies were constructed in September 1931, four months after the main ST construction programme had ceased, just in time to meet enhanced overhaul requirements anticipated to take effect from that month onwards. In appearance, the ten new bodies were exactly like the one on ST 802 except that they incorporated a long, narrow combined route number and destination screen at the rear above the platform window, displacing the registration number which was re-sited at the top of the bulkhead window above the platform. The ten new bodies were placed into service in September and October 1931 on newly overhauled chassis, the majority appearing at Hendon (and its Edgware subsidiary) as ST 409, 420, 477, 537, 547 and 550. Two (ST 363, 492) went to Harrow Weald and one (ST 494) to Seven Kings. The last ST body of all to enter service was also the highest numbered, 12354, on Hendon's ST 550 on 16th October. Over the ensuing years the eleven camel back vehicles inevitably stood out distinctively from the rest of the very standard looking ST fleet and, thanks to the Chiswick overhauling system, the range of fleet numbers that they carried fluctuated widely, ranging between ST 9 and ST 823.

The last body to be built was of particular interest because it heralded a swing in emphasis away from comfort and ease of passenger movement towards the commercially minded approach of maximising seating capacity. Gone from ST 550 was the uncluttered platform, the offside part of which was now occupied by the staircase which was placed further back than before. The staircase itself still retained the redeeming feature of being completely straight except for the very bottom riser which was now set at a right angle to the remainder. Its repositioning left space for a rearrangement of the seating on both decks. Upstairs there were five rows of double transverse seats on the offside and seven on the nearside. At the very back on the nearside was a seat for three

Two different approaches to increasing seating capacity are illustrated here. The new float 'camel back' body on ST 550 relies on retaining an almost straight staircase placed one bay further back, whilst the overhauled body on ST 538 has a more traditional rounded staircase. In both instances the single seats which became so popular on pre-war London buses have now made their appearance. *L T Museum*

adjacent to the stairwell, and in front of this were placed two single seats with space between them to gain access to the seat behind. Downstairs four transverse seats on the offside and five on the nearside were both followed by an inward facing pair seating two over the wheelarches. With an upstairs capacity of 29 and a lower deck seating 22, the total capacity of 51 was, in fact, only two more than on a standard ST, but even this minor gain could be crucial if replicated on every vehicle working high frequency, busy services, a benefit already exploited by Thomas Tilling with its 52-seat AEC Regents and by the many independents whose Titans and Lances never seated fewer than 51 and often carried as many as 56.

ST 550's conversion represented a halfway house between the old order of things and the complete reappraisal of bus body design then taking place within the LGOC, culminating in the famous Bluebird body on the LT class. In fact the prototype Bluebird body was already under construction at Chiswick at the same time as ST 550's body was being prepared during late September and early October 1931. A feature common to the two, and perpetuated throughout the remaining pre-war years on the STL and STD classes, was the twin single-seat arrangement at the back of the upper deck which always proved very popular with passengers preferring to sit alone. It must be assumed, however, that the revised internal layout on ST 550 did not meet the complete satisfaction of the LGOC management, for within a few months the modification of another ST was under way to a somewhat different design.

In November 1931 a body was chosen at random from the overhaul line to form the basis for a renewed attempt at increasing seating capacity in the standard ST body. Body 12037 was removed from ST 490 upon its arrival at Chiswick from Seven Kings on the 13th and its internal reconstruction appears to have begun straight away. The concept of a

straight staircase was now completely abandoned and a conventional curved one of the type familiar on outside staircase vehicles was installed instead. Being sited further to the rear than the staircase on ST 550, it was well clear of the offside wheelarch, leaving space for passengers' luggage beneath it for the first time on an ST. The lower deck was now virtually clear of all staircase obstruction, allowing the offside longitudinal seat to accommodate three and the transverse seats in front of it to be spaced out to give much more leg room than usual. The wide spacing of the offside seats was repeated on the upper deck too, but the extra seat gained downstairs was lost upstairs because the rear nearside one had to be reduced from three to two to take account of the more intrusive stairwell. The conversion was completed in time for the finished result to be officially photographed on 4th December, and on the 11th newly overhauled body 12037 entered service at Forest Gate under the guise of ST 538. As with the body on ST 550, it was destined to remain unique. Undoubtedly the sheer amount of work involved and the high cost implications associated with it would have acted as strong deterrents to carrying out any more conversions of this kind when all that could be achieved was two extra seats.

While the small scale and ultimately fruitless experiments to increase seating capacity were keeping the drawing office and coach factory staff busy, a massive and quite costly rebuilding programme was initiated that was to affect almost every ST in the General fleet. Right from the very early days of the ST class, and of the LTs too, complaints had been received about the route and destination information shown on the roller blind displays which were perceived by the travelling public to be grossly inferior to the boards carried on NSs and earlier classes. The complaints gathered such momentum that they sometimes dominated letters pages in the press, and the matter was even raised in Parliament.

The final ST body to be built for the LGOC's use, no. 12354, was the one originally on ST 550, and the revised positioning of its staircase can be seen through the lower deck windows. However this view was taken after its first overhaul in October 1932, and it now graces Camberwell's ST 519 as it prepares to set out from Victoria for Ladbroke Grove.

The LGOC tried various ways to combat the problem such as printing the route number in black on a white rectangle in order to emphasise it and, later, by displaying a very large route number at the expense of omitting all the intermediate points, but all to no avail. In July 1931 the Metropolitan Police issued an edict that improved displays must be provided, and this included the backs of vehicles where latterly nothing had been shown. The LGOC's response was to order many hundreds of prefabricated destination boxes, complete with winding gear and internal lighting, that could be reasonably easily installed as vehicles passed through Chiswick during their annual overhaul. At the front, a large box was to be attached to the outside of the bodywork which, because it could no longer be accessed from inside the vehicle, had to be wound from the driver's cab whenever the display needed to be changed. This was, in fact, a two man task because no periscope was provided and the conductor had to stand in front of the vehicle to give the driver guidance.

At the back, a wide but narrow combined route number and destination screen was built into the bodywork above the platform window with the winding handle projecting at the end. This quickly led to the everyday sight of conductors leaning out of the back of the bus as it went along, with one hand grasping the hand rail and the other winding the blind mechanism, a process which the LGOC tried to stamp on as dangerous but which persisted as long as the STs and LTs were around. This box displaced the registration number plate which was re-sited on the platform bulkhead window whence, in turn, it displaced a route number stencil that had been located there latterly and which was moved to a new position at the foot of the rearmost nearside window. The nearside blind box remained physically unaltered but now displayed only the major via points.

Quite apart from the cost of manufacturing and installing all the new equipment, there was also the huge logistical task of providing all the new roller blinds coupled to the unavoidable waste involved in scrapping all the existing ones ahead of their life expiry. The only STs not touched by the rebuilding programme were those with camel back bodies (except that ST 802 needed a rear blind box to be installed), and the massive programme also included well over three hundred LTs as well as the small DL and DST classes. As far as the camel back bodies were concerned, it was clearly not feasible to attach a larger front destination box, so in common with LTs built to the same style, brackets were attached to the main bodywork above the destination bulge to which a painted board listing intermediate points could be attached. The very first standard ST to appear in service with its new rear blind box in place was ST 381 at Seven Kings on 26th August 1931, and the last ST to be modified in this way left Chiswick Works just before Christmas 1932. Surprisingly, the front and rear blind box modifications were not co-ordinated with the result that they were often carried out on individual vehicles at different times. Thus it was possible on some STs for the front one to be dealt with first whilst the back one took priority on others. Coupled to the ongoing conversion from open to closed cab configuration, which was carried out equally haphazardly, this meant that for a year or so it was possible to find STs carrying all sorts of modification combinations.

A notable feature of 1931 was the gradual diminution from May onwards in the number of STs carrying METROPOLITAN fleet names. This was a deliberate process dating from the 8th May 1931 agreement mentioned earlier, of absorbing the Metropolitan vehicles into the main fleet "to secure the most economical and efficient management". Arising from this, permission was obtained from the Ministry of Transport and the Metropolitan Police for General to absorb the schedules and licences provided that it placed "on the chassis or some external part" of each vehicle a plate indicating that it was

The installation of new, rear destination screens, which was achieved without the loss of any advertising space, was a massive task undertaken in 1931/32. ST 561, which was converted in November 1931, shows the new arrangement and the consequent repositioning of the registration number plate on the bulkhead window where it is far less visible than it had been previously. Old Kent Road's ST 529, which was dealt with a month later, still retains the old style of destination blind in its side indicator box instead of the intended intermediate point display, a common occurrence throughout the fleet pending delivery of the correct blinds. *L T Museum/ E G P Masterman*

the property of the Tramways (M.E.T.) Omnibus Company. This arrangement undoubtedly permitted complete flexibility of operation, and it was a relatively simple matter to credit the Metropolitan company with its agreed 8.32% of gross receipts at the year's financial end. It is not known whereabouts on each vehicle the stipulated ownership plate was placed or, if indeed, this was done at all. The METROPOLITAN fleet names were not removed immediately but gradually disappeared as each vehicle went through overhaul. The result was that, by the end of 1931, out of about 253 STs originally carrying METROPOLITAN names, only about 108 still did so. The last (ST 793, 794, 812) disappeared from Hammersmith garage in January 1932; ST 603 was the last at Leyton in February, ST 827 at Willesden in early March, and finally ST 619 at Middle Row which went for overhaul on 23rd March 1932. After this, the only vehicles still carrying the METROPOLITAN name were some NSs at Clay Hall which did so for a few weeks longer.

Allocation changes affecting the ST class came about at an almost breathtaking speed in the second half of 1931. Harrow Weald received its first ST on 3rd June but this was a one-off in the form of preselector equipped ST 746. However by July standard crash box ones were being received in quantity from Leyton whilst, on 7th October, the three oilers formerly at Willesden joined the mixed bag at Harrow Weald. After running STs for a little over six months, Nunhead lost its entire allocation in June and July, most of which went to bolster up the fleet at Seven Kings, and in the latter month Shepherds Bush is recorded as having received three STs from Leyton. These may, in fact, have officially been on Hammersmith's strength to which Shepherds Bush was merely an outstation at the time, although this arrangement was shortly to end. In any case, two of these departed in October to Hendon along with a small batch of Hammersmith STs and the other went, along with more Hammersmith STs, to Elmers End in January 1932, marking the end of Shepherds Bush's tenuous connection with STs in the pre-war era. Next to receive a first time allocation was Hounslow in early September 1931 when eight were transferred in from Streatham and Hammersmith, and these may also have been used at Uxbridge which was an engineering outpost of Hounslow at the time. Conversely, Romford's position as an

outstation ceased during the latter half of the year, and it had an allocation of 20 STs of its own by the end of 1931. The next big event saw the removal to Middle Row of all of Cricklewood's STs between 20th October and 4th November after which Cricklewood remained an ST-free zone for the rest of the decade. Finally, on 2nd December, two STs were officially based at the East Surrey garage in Slough specifically for use on LGOC operations in the area, with four more following on 11th May 1932.

On 21st October 1931 the LGOC's fleet of STs was augmented by four when Overground's ST 822, 823, 825, 826 were transferred to the parent company upon arrival at Potters Bar of the first of the new Dennis Lances. This concluded a momentous year for General whose fleet had been transformed thanks to the arrival of so many new STs and LTs. Progress had been such that the last of the ancient-looking open-top S class double deckers were removed in December and a final few of the even older K types were now hanging on by a tenuous thread because a weight restriction on route 90 dictated their retention at Twickenham garage.

It might have been expected that, with the construction of new STs at an end, 1932 would have been a year of quiet consolidation for the class, but this was not so. Major reallocations came as thick and fast as they had done in 1931 thanks to the constant flow of new LTs into service, causing STs to be redeployed in many more locations new to them. First on the minus side was Streatham whose last STs left on 5th October, whilst November saw the departure of the final remnants of the once huge fleets at Hammersmith and Hanwell along with the whole of the smaller allocation at Chalk Farm. The fleets at most of these garages had been gradually run down over several months and, along with a large though not total exodus from Seven Kings and Forest Gate, this permitted the permanent introduction of the class at five new locations. From 26th February an intake from Forest Gate tackled the last remaining bastion of regular open top NS operation at Old Kent Road which went on into early March. A huge exodus from Seven Kings and a lesser outflowing from Forest Gate formed a substantial fleet at Clay Hall between March and May, with an impressive though not quite so large number at Camberwell in March which was further augmented later in the year from Hanwell

The design detail of the all-metal ST body, and also of the Dennis Lances, resulted in a more substantial looking destination box being fitted than was normal. Now in its third guise, the Metro Cammell body is seen on Leyton's ST 478 outside the Royal Forest Hotel, Chingford working the timings of a former independent proprietor on route 511A. *W J Haynes*

and Hammersmith. Upton Park came next with intakes in June and October followed by Sidcup which was stocked with STs at the end of July, mainly ex Hanwell. Out of the ordinary was an allocation of STs to Sutton in June ready for the main Epsom racing season, at the end of which they all departed on 4th July. A similar arrangement was adopted in 1933. Towards the end of 1932, throughout the month of November, an exodus of STs from the General fleet saw 27 repainted on overhaul into Overground livery and sent to Potters Bar, barely a year having elapsed since Overground's earlier STs had been returned to the parent fleet.

A subtle change in appearance took place on a number of STs in 1932 when a few began to emerge from overhaul with new back axles of the fully floating type which were stubbier and more substantial-looking than the spindly and rather outdated design normally associated with the class. The first three are thought to have appeared in this form in February 1932 and at least seven STs were finally converted, possibly more. Changes of identity at each overhaul make it impossible to be certain exactly how many chassis were involved, but a final reference in May 1935 would make it seem that the experiment had then ceased as far as the STs were concerned although the fully floating axle had, of course, by then been standard on the STL class for more than two years.

In the autumn of 1932 an innovative experiment got under way to assess the feasibility of using fuel derived from coal as a means of lessening dependence on the use of imported petroleum products. Research tests had been going on for some time at Chiswick and it was known that the LGOC had enjoyed some success in using gasworks creosote during bench tests. The time had now come to conduct in-service road trials and it was decided that, as a first step, an ST would be modified to run on creosote. A chassis was taken from the overhaul line on 23rd September 1932 and modification of its engine had been completed by the 30th. Bearing fleet number ST 403, the newly overhauled vehicle was dispatched on 1st October to operate from Mortlake garage, the only ST ever to do so during the nineteen-thirties. The experiment was widened in January 1933 when ST 403 was joined by a creosote powered LT, and a second was converted in April. The two LTs were reconverted to petrol operation in May and ST 403 was finally recorded as having ceased its trial running on 12th June although it may, in reality, have done so much earlier. The results were pronounced as being disappointing, the conclusion drawn from the trial being that existing engines were unsuitable for modification and that a special engine would need to be designed if home produced fuel was to be utilised in a satisfactory way.

The larger front indicator boxes undoubtedly allowed a more informative display to be shown, but made blind-turning a two-man job because with no periscope provided, the driver had to rely on signals from the conductor for guidance. Harrow Weald's ST 144 was photographed at South Harrow station in January 1933. *J F Higham*

White drivers' coats and the presence of Bluebird LTs indicate that it is now the summer of 1932. Hanwell's ST 20 passes construction works for a new entrance to Chancery Lane station and it is evident that, even at this late stage, it still carries the original open cab and small front destination blind.
A new back indicator box had, however, been installed in November 1931.
Ken Blacker collection

During 1932 the London Passenger Transport Bill was making its way through Parliament and it was clear that the days of the LGOC as a privately owned undertaking were numbered. However this did not deter the management from continuing to innovate, and towards the end of the year the decision was taken to experiment with yet another type of engine in an ST chassis. The ST had by now become an obsolete model, having been overtaken by the 16ft 3ins wheelbase STL which made full use of a relaxation dating from early 1932 in the maximum length and weight regulations for two axle double deckers which could now be 26ft 0ins (instead of 25ft 0ins) in length and 10 tons (previously 9 tons) in laden weight.

The first 60-seat STLs entered service at Clay Hall in December 1932, the precursors of a massive class more than 2,600 strong whose unstoppable progress was destined to continue until war intervened in 1939. However for the experiment that the LGOC had in mind the smaller, lighter ST was ideal. AEC was marketing a range of 4-cylinder oil engines of the overhead camshaft type using a similar valve gear arrangement to that employed on contemporary petrol units. These were principally intended for use in its Regal 4 range of single deckers, but the LGOC's engineers wished to test its suitability for double-deck bus use in the right circumstances, no doubt with the achievement of maximum fuel economy in mind. The engine selected was the A166 which was the least powerful version on offer and had the same 146mm stroke as the 7.7 unit and a bore size of 108mm giving a swept volume of 5.35 litres. The compactness of the engine meant that it could be housed under the existing bonnet, avoiding the need for any structural modification, but its extra weight meant that the seating capacity of the selected vehicle, ST 42, had to be reduced by two to 47 by removing a double seat from the upper deck.

Installation of the new engine was completed on 3rd January 1933 and, after a period of testing, ST 42 was put to work at Hanwell on the 31st of the month. This was the garage where all of the LGOC's oil engined vehicles were now housed but where ST 42 was the only vehicle of its type, the last remnants of Hanwell's once large ST fleet having been sent away shortly before Christmas. The Company's oil engined fleet now stood at 106 all of which, except for ST 42, were LT six-wheelers. Looked at in retrospect, the experiment was a strange one to have undertaken as its basic concept flew in the face of all the Company's recent experience which had amply proved that buses powered by 6-cylinder engines were far better suited to London conditions than the ponderous 4-cylinder NS and others that they had replaced. It was a far cry from the experiment with 8-cylinder engines four years earlier. The experiment lasted only until 3rd June 1933 when the 4-cylinder unit was removed. Official reports on the experiment have been lost in the mists of time but it can be safely assumed that it was not a success. The vehicle would almost certainly have proved too slow to keep up with modern urban traffic and would have been something of an anachronism at a time when schedules were being speeded up to take advantage of the greater performance offered by modern 6-cylinder vehicles. On 6th June 1933 ST 42 went to work at Harrow Weald back in its old petrol engined form, and no further conversions to diesel were carried out on the ST class until 1949.

Additional to the major and visible experiments, many small ones were carried out on the STs during the period 1931-33 on a variety of matters involving brake linings, tyre sizes, rubber mudguards, adjustable drivers' seats, and the use of Dunlopillo instead of sprung seat cases, few of which had a long term impact on the class. The fitment of sweeping-out traps with rectangular spring-loaded flaps in 20 vehicles

The end of an era approaches. It is summer 1933 and soon the LGOC will exist no longer. In the final days of the Company's operation two of Turnham Green's STs pass on the busy route 65 at Ealing Broadway District Line station. ST 675, on the left, is nearing its terminus at Argyle Road whilst, outside the station itself, ST 673 picks up on a 65A short working to Hook. *Alan Nightingale collection*

distributed amongst various garages in October 1931 produced no labour saving and their use was soon cancelled.

The first spate of action in 1933 resulted from the introduction of new STLs at Clay Hall which saw the departure of all 51 of its STs by early April. An impact of this was felt at Athol Street which took in its first ST allocation between 5th and 28th January, totalling 18 STs in all. Such was the general state of flux within the fleet at the time that all 18 moved out again on 1st March and LTs came in instead. The same day saw a start of ST operation at Holloway and the end of LGOC operation from Slough, these being part of one of the massive shake-ups that the LGOC indulged in from time to time which, in this instance, saw large transfers of STs into Camberwell and Old Kent Road balanced by reciprocal movements of NSs into Norwood, Middle Row, Harrow Weald and Nunhead.

During March and April 1933 West Green received its first STs as a result of the ongoing influx of new STLs into Clay Hall. It was during this time, on 13th April, that the London Passenger Transport Act received royal assent with a vesting date set as Saturday 1st July 1933. Before this day arrived one final act took place within the ST class under LGOC auspices when, on 31st May, Norwood swapped eleven of its STs with Nunhead in exchange for LTs, reintroducing STs to Nunhead for the first time since the last of its previous allocation left in July 1931.

The London General Omnibus Company came to a close at the end of June 1933, 78 years after it had first arrived on the London bus scene. On its final day, 30th June, STs could be found operating from 24 of the Company's 46 garages. Fleet utilisation was incredibly high with a full one hundred per cent licensed for service, a figure achievable because of extremely high standards of maintenance backed up by the famous production line overhauling system at Chiswick Works where an ample stock of 'float' chassis and bodies ensured that vehicle identities could be kept permanently active and fully employed. The LGOC era ended with STs dispersed amongst garages as follows:

Camberwell (Q)	46
Elmers End (ED)	36
Forest Gate (G)	9
Hammersmith (R)	35
Harrow Weald (HD)	35
Hendon (AE) / Edgware (EW)	68
Holloway (J)	23
Hounslow (AV) / Uxbridge (UX)	36
Kingston (K)	14
Norwood (N)	45
Nunhead (AH)	11
Old Kent Road (P)	65
Romford (RD)	14
Seven Kings (AP)	16
Sidcup (SP)	38
Sutton (A) *(for Epsom races)*	6
Turnham Green (V)	60
Upton Park (U)	22
Leyton (T)	78
West Green (WG)	24
Middle Row (X)	60
Willesden (AC)	46

CHAPTER 4
RANSOMES FOR COUNTRY SERVICE

In October 1929, at the same time that the LGOC board of directors approved the purchase of 100 STs for the Company's own use, it also authorised the placing of a substantial order for 60 more Regents to be shared between its country subsidiaries, East Surrey and Autocar. It was envisaged that delivery would commence in April 1930 by which time the production of ST 3 upwards would be in full swing, leaving no spare capacity at Chiswick to produce bodies for the country vehicles within the required timescale. External tenders were therefore issued, as a result of which Ransomes, Sims & Jefferies Ltd of Ipswich were contracted to build the 60 new bodies at a price of £725 each. This inevitably incurred an unavoidable premium over the average cost of £594 6s 0d for the Chiswick product but the latter did not have to bear the element of profit required by outside coachbuilders or some of their other fixed costs. Oddly, the chassis specification was for a completely standard AEC product and not a modified one that would have included a nearside fuel tank as was required for General's own fleet.

The new modern rolling stock was badly needed by both companies. In the case of Autocar it was required to massively update the service to meet competition on its trunk Tunbridge Wells–Tonbridge corridor, whilst on the much larger East Surrey operation a general upgrading could no longer be deferred. The Company ran a substantial fleet of double deckers which, with the exception of a solitary NS received as recently as July 1929 to replace a vehicle destroyed by fire, consisted solely of open-toppers that were clearly no longer suitable for the major country operations to which they were allocated.

Although the 60 new Regents were covered by a single order, this masked the fact that ownership of them was to be divided three ways. Eighteen were to be supplied to and owned outright by Autocar, whilst of the remaining 42, 30 would be the property of the LGOC and would be loaned to East Surrey whose livery they would carry, and only 12 would be owned by East Surrey itself.

When the new vehicles began to arrive from Ipswich in April 1930, it was immediately apparent that Ransomes had not been supplied with plans for the current ST body but had instead copied the design of the prototype ST 1 which they had faithfully followed in almost every detail. They had the same square driver's cab which was fully glazed. As on ST 1, the side lights were mounted on the driver's canopy and the between-decks black moulding strip was convex rather than flat. An improvement over the prototype in its original form was that all the platform windows were now glazed with the last offside bay being provided with a half-drop unit rather than the now standard sliding type used for ease of conductor signalling. A notable variation was that fixed glazing was installed in the front upper deck windows. Drivers were provided with a half-height door, and at the back the rear indicator box protruded slightly from the main bodywork

instead of lying flat against it. Inside, the idea of using translucent lighting panels was jettisoned in favour of much more conventional individual tungsten bulbs mounted in the ceiling panels and covered by rectangular glass shades. The unladen weight of the completed vehicle, 5 tons 11cwt 2qrs, was exactly the same as that of ST 1.

The chassis numbers allocated by AEC were lower than those of the main LGOC batch, occupying the series 661143-661209, interrupted only by two chassis for Southern General, four for Newcastle Corporation and the LGOC's ST 2. However Ransomes were rather slower than Chiswick in producing the new bodies with the result that the first complete vehicles were not ready for licensing until 13th April 1930, and it was the end of July before the final ones were placed into service. Both Autocar and East Surrey received vehicles concurrently and their chassis numbers were intermingled, although responsibility for licensing them lay with their respective managements. The Autocars were registered in Kent as KR 3032, 3881-3897 with fleet numbers 113, 125-141 whilst the East Surrey vehicles were registered appropriately in Surrey as PG 7593, 7724-7728, 7836, 7963-7997. Although fleet numbers were allocated by East Surrey (not in registration number order) as 213-254 they were not carried on the vehicles. East Surrey had formerly been obliged to use fleet numbers by certain local council licensing authorities, but was now in the process of abandoning their use and relying purely on registration numbers for identification. The twelve vehicles in the batch which were the Company's own property were PG 7724-7728, 7836, 7963-7967, 7980. The remainder, in true LGOC fashion, were allocated body numbers 11105-11134 but, like the theoretical fleet numbers, these were not issued in numerical sequence and were never used for any practical purpose.

Top right PG 7968 (which became ST 1103 in London Transport days) was still in fairly pristine condition on 4th August 1930 when this manufacturer's publicity shot was taken, three months after it first entered service with East Surrey. The close similarity to the body on ST 1 is very evident, the only real point of difference being that the front upper deck windows are non-opening on the East Surrey version. *J M Aldridge*

Right A line-up in the sunshine outside Leatherhead garage shows two of the earlier East Surrey Regents looking at their very best with the decorative black markings that were omitted from later members of the batch. The Regent nearest the camera is PG 7728 (the future ST 1096), one of the vehicles owned by East Surrey itself. Also present in addition to a second Regent are an ex-LGOC K-type single decker, a brand new AEC Regal and a pair of PS-type open toppers now on pneumatics. *L T Museum*

45

The first few vehicles delivered to East Surrey looked particularly splendid with their red and cream livery enhanced by ornate black decoration on the red panels of both decks, an embellishment shared with a batch of new Hall Lewis bodied AEC Regals delivered at about the same time. However this was soon discontinued and most entered service in a plain, unadorned livery. The Regents were dispersed to three garages, Reigate, Leatherhead and Crawley, from which they monopolised the Company's operations into Kingston via route 406 and also began making inroads into the substantial network of services radiating southwards from West Croydon by taking over routes 405 and 408. Although Autocar's traditional livery had been a striking purple and yellow, its Regents were also delivered in red and cream, but nevertheless they looked very modern and attractive when newly delivered to their operating base at Tunbridge Wells. At their first overhaul, which was carried out at Chiswick, the vehicles in both fleets were repainted in the standard LGOC colours of red and grey. At the same time their back offside lower corner panels were fitted with two horizontal reinforcement bars, presumably as protection against accident damage, but they never received the substantial back bumpers as fitted to the General fleet.

Although it was an occurrence apparent only to the accountants, a change took place on 1st August 1930 when six of the East Surrey-owned vehicles were sold to the LGOC as a result of a financial readjustment between the two companies, leaving just six out of the 42 still in East Surrey ownership. The transferred vehicles were PG 7963-7967, 7980 which then received LGOC body numbers 11537-11542 in that order. Interestingly, the last of these had worked as an East Surrey owned bus for merely one day before being sold. A rather more visible change of ownership came about on 2nd January 1931 when the LGOC purchased four Regents from Autocar. Autocar had found itself able to provide work for only 14 double deckers, and with no hope of finding work

Tonbridge High Street on a very wet day finds Autocar's KR 3896 working route 11 between Tunbridge Wells and Hadlow. Following its first overhaul in 1931, this bus – in common with all Autocar and East Surrey Regents – now carries a greater expanse of red on its lower panels. The bus coming the other way is an Albion of Redcar Services Ltd, Autocar's main competitor. *Alan Nightingale collection*

within the Company for the other four, it made sense to re-allocate them elsewhere within the group. The LGOC immediately put the four on loan to East Surrey in whose livery they were repainted and under whose auspices they remained in Kent to operate trunk route 402 out of Dunton Green garage. The four were KR 3886, 3892-3894 and their allocated LGOC body numbers were 12358/12355-12357.

An East Surrey board meeting held at 55 Broadway on 14th December 1931 heralded a big change ahead when a proposal was adopted to extend the Company's jurisdiction to include the operations north of the Thames currently contracted out by the LGOC to the National Omnibus & Transport Company. Under the changed circumstances the East Surrey title would clearly no longer be appropriate and at an Extraordinary General Meeting on 20th January 1932, it was agreed to rename the business 'London General Country Services Ltd'. The change of name took effect eight days later, and from 27th February the new title began to appear on the Company's vehicles. For a few months, ownership of the vehicles remained divided as it had been in East Surrey days with part of the fleet owned by LGCS itself and the remainder by the LGOC. However this situation changed on 7th April 1932 when all the LGOC vehicles were formally sold to LGCS. The new undertaking now took complete charge of its own affairs which were henceforth handled entirely from its headquarters at Bell Street, Reigate. Unfortunately, from this point onwards, detailed records of the fleet and its movements cease to be available, leaving gaps in our knowledge of what occurred during the next three years.

The fleet name adopted by the new company was GENERAL written in bold letters on a rectangular silvery grey base with the smaller wording COUNTRY SERVICES below it. The LGOC's livery of red and grey continued to be used for about a year when, in an abrupt change, a base colour of green was adopted in March 1933. This was done in advance of the creation of the London Passenger Transport Board, the decision having already been taken that its country area buses would be green to distinguish them from the central area red. The actual livery chosen was a copy of that already used for Green Line coaches of sage green enhanced by black horizontal reliefs and mudguards, silver roof and orange wheels. The earlier style of fleet name was replaced by the single word GENERAL in gold lettering. The Reigate management pursued the same policy as Chiswick of overhauling each vehicle annually, either at its splendid new Reigate garage opened in January 1932 alongside the old one, where extensive overhauling facilities existed or, if an overflow was needed, at Watford High Street garage inherited from National, and it did not take long for the new green livery to begin making its mark.

The Reigate overhaul works were capable of dealing with 21 complete vehicles a week drawn from a very mixed LGCS and Green Line fleet. Once it became well established the Reigate maintenance regime appears to have thrived as an independent overhaul works with very little Chiswick influence or input. The Chiswick production line system requiring a float of spare chassis and bodies was not replicated; in fact Reigate functioned in much the same traditional manner as did the central works of most major provincial bus operators, resulting in each vehicle maintaining its own chassis and body integrity.

None of the identity or livery changes affected Autocar which continued running unchanged. Its separate identity was retained in the prior knowledge that, under the terms of the London Passenger Transport Act, the outlying nature of

Autocar's operating territory stretched well beyond the scope of the London Passenger Transport Board when it was formed in 1933, and saw Regents regularly heading as far afield as Uckfield. KR 3895 continued on these workings when ownership of Autocar was transferred to Maidstone & District. *J F Higham*

its operating territory would place it almost wholly beyond the remit of the new authority. When, in due course, the London Passenger Transport Board came on the scene on 1st July 1933, the ownership of Autocar passed on the same day to Maidstone & District Motor Services Ltd which inherited the 14 Regents along with the rest of the undertaking, leaving only operating rights for the section between Tonbridge and Sevenoaks to pass to the LPTB. By November of the same year Autocar vehicles had begun appearing in Maidstone & District green, and on 1st May 1935 Autocar ceased to exist as a separate entity with its fleet merged into that of the parent company. The Regents became 1 to 14 in the Maidstone

& District numbering series but their end was already approaching. In June 1937 the whole batch was traded into AEC following upon the purchase of new vehicles and, as far as is known, none ever used again in its original form. Some subsequently appeared with various coach companies as single deckers but only one (KR 3897), now with a new Burlingham coach body, is known to have survived any length of time into the post-war era, remaining active until as late as 1957. The Ransomes Regents owned by LGCS were destined to lead far longer working lives in their original form, and their story under London Transport ownership is resumed in chapter 15.

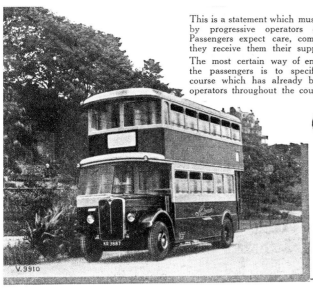

This is a statement which must always be borne in mind by progressive operators of motor coach services. Passengers expect care, comfort and courtesy, and if they receive them their support can be relied upon.

The most certain way of ensuring absolute comfort for the passengers is to specify Ransomes coachwork—a course which has already been taken by experienced operators throughout the country.

Ransomes
COACH AND OMNIBUS BODIES

OUR NEW ILLUSTRATED BROCHURE, giving full particulars and details of our coachwork, will gladly be sent on application.

**Ransomes, Sims & Jefferies, Ltd.,
Ipswich, England.**

V.3910

Ransomes were justifiably proud of gaining a prestigious order for 60 double-deck bodies. It was a big scoop for them in a very competitive market and they lost no time in advertising the fact. The vehicle depicted here, Autocar's KR 3887, entered revenue service in June 1930.

Bromley North station is the terminal point for East Surrey's KR 3892. As its Kent registration number suggests, this was one of the four Regents transferred from Autocar to East Surrey in January 1931 when barely six months old. In London Transport days it became ST 1086. *C F Klapper*

The future ST 1087 was also photographed at Bromley North, still on route 402 on which all four of the ex-Autocar Regents stayed put in pre-LPTB days. Now carrying the short-lived insignia of London General Country Services, it shares the stand with the LGOC's 'Scooter' LT 1200 and a pair of LGCS PS-types working route 410 to Reigate on which conventional covered-top double deckers could not operate.

CHAPTER 5
NATIONAL

Just to the north of London, outside the Metropolitan Police District and covering a wide area between Aylesbury and Brentwood, were a host of LGOC services operated on its behalf by the National Omnibus & Transport Company Ltd. This arrangement could be traced back to a formal agreement signed by the two parties on 21st July 1921 although it had commenced earlier, and certainly by 25th May of that year when National assumed control of General's garage in Watford. It was a good arrangement for both companies. The LGOC supplied the vehicles and garages while National provided the management and everything else necessary for the operation, and both shared the profits on an agreed basis. By the end of 1930 the LGOC had 128 buses on loan to National which was fifteen more than were with East Surrey at the time. Interestingly, and in stark contrast to East Surrey, National always referred to the hired vehicles by their LGOC fleet numbers.

By 1930 it had become imperative that outdated open-toppers based at Watford should be replaced with new rolling stock and General decided to set aside 16 of the current order for STs for this purpose. Fleet numbers ST 502-517 were reserved for the National vehicles with an anticipated availability for service in August and September 1930. However this plan was changed at an early stage, probably at National's insistence. Updated vehicles were needed more urgently than this to compete with the Lewis Omnibus Company's impressive new AEC Regents on trunk route N1 between Rickmansworth and St Albans (see chapter 14). National watched Lewis creaming off most of the trade from this potentially highly profitable corridor and realised that there would be very little left if they had to wait until mid-summer for the promised new buses to materialise.

A revised plan was adopted. Nine newly built STs would be diverted from current LGOC deliveries as soon as possible and sent to National for the N1. This would leave a balance of seven from the originally planned allocation of sixteen and special lowbridge bodies were be ordered for six of these from an outside manufacturer to enable them to work on National route N6 (Watford–Berkhamsted). Although National was now going to receive one ST fewer than originally planned, the net financial outlay would be approximately the same taking into account the substantial additional cost of each of the six lowbridge bodies. As for ST 502-517, these were ready for service as planned in the summer of 1930 and were added to the LGOC's own fleet where their bonnet numbers were well ahead of existing deliveries which had only just reached the 300 mark.

This chapter deals only with the nine standard STs supplied to National, the lowbridge ones being described in chapter 6. All nine were scheduled to operate from National's Watford garage situated in the Lower High Street. Built by the LGOC in 1925, this was where the management for National's outer London operations was based and where

extensive engineering work was carried out. The new buses were taken seemingly haphazardly from within current deliveries, the first to arrive at Watford being ST 116 on 7th April 1930. All nine were in position by 2nd May, the others being (in order of fleet numbers but not delivery dates) ST 107, 111, 129, 132, 135, 143, 152 and 159. Apart from carrying the NATIONAL fleet name and 206 Brompton Road SW3 legal address, they do not appear to have differed in any way from STs working for General.

Their arrival in Watford would undoubtedly have helped restore National's fortunes on route N1. The new STs may not have looked quite as impressive or as modern as the Lewis vehicles thanks to their rather conservative body shape, and their open drivers' cabs must have appeared positively outdated to the travelling public of Hertfordshire, but at least National was now able to operate on equal terms for comfort and speed.

Its Watford based bus operation on behalf of the LGOC was, in fact, the only one still directly carried out by the National Omnibus & Transport Company which had hived off all its other operations to subsidiaries with shared railway ownership, and it was now largely a holding or investment company. Less than a year after the STs entered service, in February 1931, Thomas Tilling Ltd acquired the whole of its share capital, though no outward sign of change took place as a result of this.

February 1931 was also the month in which National augmented its stock of Chiswick built STs by four to replace the same number of open-top S-types which it still operated from its garage in Ware, located in the old Harvey & Burrows premises behind the town hall in the High Street. They were required specifically for route 310 (Hertford–Enfield Town) which meant that, unlike the STs at Watford, these entered into Metropolitan Police territory, hence the 'Bassom' style route number. ST 820 was the first into service on 13th February followed by ST 818 on the 19th and finally ST 819 and 821 on 2nd March. These dates spanned the crucial weeks when new STs changed from having open driver's cabs to enclosed ones with windscreens. Theoretically ST 819 and 821 should have been built with enclosed cabs but in fact all four arrived at Ware with open fronts, giving ST 819 and 821 the dubious honour of being the last buses supplied for use anywhere within the Underground group's orbit without windscreens. Instead they were fitted with a unique style of deep metal visor which extended the whole width of the vehicle and was presumably an experiment in providing a moderately draught-reduced environment for the driver without going to the extent of supplying a fully glazed cab.

Under the terms of the joint agreement, the vehicles on loan to National were all returned annually to Chiswick for overhaul, and planned programmes were issued from Chiswick Works covering this. Whilst there, some of the modifications planned for the LGOC's own fleet were also

AEC Regents meet in head-on competition in Watford High Street, giving passengers a choice of comfortable speedy transport along the main road to St Albans. National's ST 111, pausing for a crew changeover, is still relatively clean and new, but the Lewis Omnibus Company's UR 5508, which is probably about to overtake it, might be viewed by discerning passengers as the more impressively modern looking of the two. *W Noel Jackson*

Inexplicably, National clung to the concept of open drivers' cabs long after most other operators, including the LGOC, and its Regents were still open fronted when they passed, via London General Country Services, to the LPTB. The extra-wide metal screen fixed below the canopy on ST 821 can hardly have been adequate compensation for the lack of a fully glazed cab. *A G Newman*

applied to the National vehicles, and as a result the STs delivered in 1930 duly received a rebuilt rear end to provide a wider platform cut-away and with the rear destination screen repositioned at the side. In some cases they were also given rear bumpers. They were not, however, provided with the larger front destination screen subsequently specified for LGOC vehicles and, more notably, were not fitted with windscreens. It appears that National preferred to retain the open cab format. Nor were National STs slotted into the normal factory line process employed at Chiswick, resulting in each vehicle keeping its own specific identity with no body or chassis exchanges taking place.

The creation of London General Country Services on 28th January 1932, with the intention of combining all of the Underground group's country operations into one unit forming, in effect, a ring around London, spelt the end of the working agreement with National. Negotiations with National led to the latter accepting a payment of £2,500 in respect of loss of profits arising from the termination of its contract, and formal administration of the National services was transferred to LGCS on 1st March 1932 on which date the vehicles received the new owner's fleet name and legal ownership lettering. Initially the fleet itself remained on loan from the LGOC, but this changed on 7th April 1932 when – together with the vehicles formerly loaned to East Surrey – they were formally sold to LGCS. Henceforth the administration and overhauling of the vehicles was all centred at Reigate, and in line with current LGCS policy the use of fleet numbers was discontinued. However a northern divisional office was retained at Watford High Street garage where heavy mechanical work and some repainting was carried out on vehicles based at northern garages.

CHAPTER 6
LOWBRIDGE REGENTS

Although there were only eight of them, the STs with lowbridge bodies are among the best remembered and individually most photographed of all, not just because of their totally non-standard appearance but because they outlasted the rest of the class, even to the extent of receiving diesel engines in their late old age. They originated from two different sources, but are dealt with together in this chapter because they were all of similar appearance and were always treated as a single batch after coming together under London Transport ownership.

Six of them received brief mention in chapter 5 because their chassis were included within the fifteen Regents diverted in the spring of 1930 from within the LGOC's initial batch of one hundred to provide an urgent updating of the services worked on behalf of the LGOC by the National Omnibus & Transport Company in the Watford area. One of these services was the picturesque N6 between Watford, Chesham and Berkhamsted which was heavily patronised and needed double deckers but was precluded from being worked by normal height covered top vehicles because of the low Black Horse bridge on the Metropolitan & Great Central line near Chalfont & Latimer railway station. Short Brothers of Rochester had prior experience, albeit limited, of constructing low height bodies on AEC Regent chassis and were contracted by the LGOC to provide six of these as quickly as possible. The first chassis was received from AEC on 29th April and by 31st May five out of the six had received bodies and were licensed to start work on that day. These were ST 136, 140, 141, 157 and 162, and they were followed into service on 5th June by ST 163.

The bodywork provided by Shorts was basically to their own standard design, unsurprisingly as it would not have been worth the LGOC's time and expense to design and build its own bodies for such a small batch of vehicles. Distinctive external features of the Shorts body were its exaggerated and very boxy style of piano front surmounted by upper deck windows formed in a pronounced V-shape, but minus the projecting front peak favoured by General. At the back, the single rear window on each deck was heavily rounded on all four corners, and a specially distinctive Shorts feature was an oval window on the offside illuminating the staircase. Small concessions to LGOC requirements were the fitment of a rounded driver's cab which, in profile, was not unlike that specified for standard STs although, unlike them, it was glazed. Another LGOC requirement was the fitment of opening windows at the upstairs front which had to be of the half drop type as the full drops fitted elsewhere on the body could not be used in this position. Because the chassis came from an LGOC batch, the petrol filler was on the nearside rather than being offside mounted as was more normal on the Regent chassis. The vehicles were delivered to Watford garage in standard General red livery but carrying NATIONAL fleet name and legal address.

Climbing aboard, the striking difference – apart from the use of copious amounts of polished wood for internal trimming rather than the LGOC's much favoured rexine – was the seating layout employed to achieve the desired overall low height. Leyland had established and patented the use of a sunken offside upper deck gangway to achieve this end; Shorts avoided infringing Leyland's rights by installing

The earliest known photograph of one of National's lowbridge Regents is this one of ST 162 taken in Chesham, carrying the 1933 green and black livery of London General Country Services and with its former fleet number now obliterated. With the exception of the driver's cab, which has been constructed to comply with the LGOC's requirements, the bodywork is otherwise recognisable as being a completely standard Short Bros product, right down to the oval window on the offside. *J F Higham*

gangway troughs on both sides, leaving space along the centre of the upper deck for eight rows of seats each accommodating three passengers and resulting in a somewhat claustrophobic atmosphere downstairs with ceiling wells projecting into the saloon on both sides. In one way this arrangement was an improvement over the Leyland design which employed bench seats for four where three passengers often had to move to let the fourth one out, but getting from one gangway to the other was by no means convenient as it meant stooping very low to cross the raised floor in the centre. A seating capacity of 50 was achieved initially, but this was later reduced to 48 distributed evenly with 24 on each deck. At £790 13s 0d each the bodies were not cheap, but this was the price that the LGOC was obliged to pay to obtain specialist bodywork from an outside contractor.

The other two very similar vehicles originated with the Amersham & District Motor Bus & Haulage Company Ltd. Based, as its title suggests, in Amersham and with another garage in High Wycombe, this company had, in fact, been 50% owned since 1929 by the LGOC through a nominee company, West Nominees Ltd. Managed since its inception by William Randall, Amersham & District was an unusually well run and highly profitable company, and such was the high regard in which the LGOC held its management that it did not even trouble to exercise its option to nominate anyone to serve on the board of directors. Except where its interests immediately coincided with those of the LGOC, Amersham & District was left to go completely its own way, and it was pursuing its independent course when its directors decided to purchase two new double deckers in 1930.

Passenger numbers had built up to the extent that double deckers were needed as a matter of urgency to work local services in High Wycombe on weekdays and on the main Chesham to Windsor run on Sundays and bank holidays, and approval for the purchase of two new ones was given at a board meeting on 2nd April. Noted for its opportunistic vehicle purchases, the Company quickly scanned the market and found that AEC could supply two Regents at very short notice. One was, in fact, already built and could be supplied fully painted in a week's time, on the 9th, whilst a chassis could be released immediately for the other. The already-built

one was, like many AEC stock vehicles, bodied by Shorts, and it carried the lowbridge version of this company's standard body which, in most respects, was the design to which the six for National were being constructed. Low height vehicles were not specifically needed but this one was accepted because it happened to be what was available at the time, and when Amersham & District turned to its preferred body supplier, Strachans, for the second one to be built it specified the same type of body for convenience of operation.

The first of the two Regents was licensed on 9th April 1930 as KX 4656, carrying fleet number 29. The vehicle from Strachans, KX 5055, followed on 30th May and became no. 30. Strachans was adept at copying other coachbuilders' designs, and in general appearance this closely resembled no. 29 especially at the back where Shorts' trademark rounded windows were replicated almost exactly. There were differences however. A more pronounced rake was given to the front upstairs windows, a lower doorway was provided over the platform, and the side lights were mounted on the mudguards instead of on the driver's canopy. Originally the oval staircase window was omitted, although one was later fitted at an unknown date. The biggest difference, however, was that KX 5055 was about 1½ins taller than KX 4656. The Strachans vehicle was also dearer, costing a total price including chassis of £1,730 whereas the other had been obtained for £1,696. Both were smartly finished in Amersham & District's green and cream livery which, even down to the semi-ornate style of fleet name, was a close copy of the livery used by the similarly titled but much larger Aldershot & District. They were built as 48-seaters, and the only real structural differences between them and the National batch were their square driver's cab and standard Regent offside filler cap.

When it entered service on 9th April KX 4656 was, in fact, the very first of the lowbridge Regents to operate in the area. Even KX 5055 managed to start work one day ahead of the first Nationals on 30th May. Both of the Amersham & District Regents were based at the Company's High Wycombe garage, and whilst their weekday operations were initially on locals as planned, they were released from this role in February

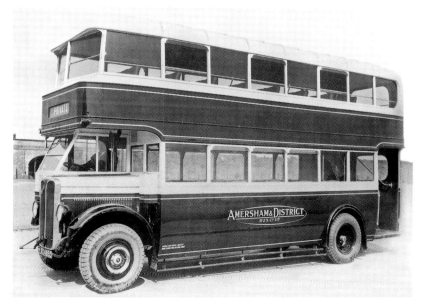

The Shorts standard cab profile and distinctive very rounded rear windows can be clearly seen on this manufacturer's study of Amersham & District's KX 4656. The central bench-type seats, mounted high on their raised central platform, are clearly visible in the upper deck.

1931 when replacement double deckers were acquired in the form of a pair of second hand Guy six-wheelers. Thereafter the Regents could be found daily on the Chesham–Windsor run, meeting up at Chesham with the six National vehicles which, fate was to decree, they would work alongside for many years to come.

On 1st March 1932 the six National vehicles came under the control of London General Country Services, passing on 1st July 1933 to the London Passenger Transport Board. Because of its Underground group shareholding, Amersham & District was also scheduled for compulsory acquisition by the Board, but there was a general feeling at 55 Broadway that its absorption into the main fleet should be delayed in order to give time for the host of major problems that were expected to arise during the months immediately following the Board's formation to be sorted out first. Well before the July vesting date, the Amersham & District directors were approached and asked if they would be prepared to keep the Company going beyond 1st July and until further notice, which they agreed to do provided that this would have no adverse impact on subsequent compensation claims. The stay of execution lasted until 29th November 1933 when Amersham & District's vehicles, services and property were finally absorbed into London Transport, uniting all eight lowbridge Regents within a single fleet.

This view at the Strachans factory provides an opportunity to compare KX 5055 (ST 1090) with its sister vehicle. The rounded back windows have been faithfully replicated but the upper deck front has a more pronounced rake and the slightly increased depth between decks has resulted in the upper saloon seats being mounted slightly lower in relation to the window line. The side lights were mounted on the mudguards from new on this bus. *Ken Blacker collection*

Top right The upper saloon of KX 5055 when new presents a slightly Spartan appearance with the single-skinned panelling revealing the roof structure and only very limited use of features such as polished mahogany to offset the utilitarian effect. The use of a brighter and more strongly patterned moquette rather than the popular but mundane 'lozenge' design would probably have improved matters. The nearside sunken gangway was of little practical value because it led nowhere and a clamber across the raised centre section was necessary to reach it. *Ken Blacker collection*

Right Windsor Castle provides an impressive backdrop for KX 5055 in a photograph presumed to have been taken early in its life judging by the vehicle's still pristine condition. The crew are taking their layover prior to setting off on a return run to their base at High Wycombe. An end of life view inside ST 136 shows the claustrophobic effect within the lower saloon created by the twin sunken gangways. It is interesting to note that the LGOC specified the fitment of its own peculiar type of front ventilator panel into the otherwise standard Short Bros interior. Despite the warning notices on the bulkhead and the seat backs it was a common occurrence for passengers to bump their heads when standing up to alight. *Alan B Cross*

CHAPTER 7
MORE REGENTS FOR EAST SURREY

The arrival of the 32 new Ransomes bodied Regents between April and July 1930 had done much to reinvigorate the East Surrey fleet but a quartet of major services radiating south from West Croydon still remained in the hands of AEC PS-type double deckers which, though only between four and six years old and now on pneumatic tyres, retained their open tops and looked hopelessly outdated. In the autumn of 1930 it was decided to replace them as soon as possible with a further injection of new Regents, and an order went out from Chiswick for the supply of 30 with bodywork by Short Brothers. Twenty-eight of these were covered by an LGOC sanction with the intention of placing them on loan to East Surrey, whilst the remaining two would be East Surrey's own vehicles. All would be constructed to more or less the same specification as the latest STs built for the LGOC itself with 100mm engines and triple servo brakes, and they would have windscreens from new.

New chassis began to be received towards the end of February 1931, and the first complete vehicle from Shorts was supplied to Reigate ready for licensing on 16th March with input continuing steadily thereafter. East Surrey had now fully abandoned the use of fleet numbers and relied totally on registration numbers for identification purposes. The actual licensing was carried out at Chiswick using registration numbers taken from current LGOC batches with the result that they were issued entirely haphazardly, the 30 vehicles being GN 4699, 4707, 4715, 4725, 4726, 4732, 4761, 4762, 4780, 4789, 4796, GO 635, 636, 646, 647, 654, 698, 700, 5132, 5146, 5152, 5181, 5182, 5188, 5193, 7108, 7109, 7115, 7136, 7156, 7157. The two East Surrey owned vehicles were GN 4761 and 4762 and they were amongst the first to be received even though their chassis numbers (6611511, 6611512) followed on at the end of the LGOC-owned batch (6611483-6611510). The last one to be put into service was GO 5132 on 8th July 1931, bringing the total of Regents on loan to East Surrey from the LGOC to an impressive maximum of 71 in addition to the eight which East Surrey owned in its own right. The LGOC gave body numbers 12359-12386 to the 38 buses that it owned, although these were never referred to or carried on the vehicles and were superseded by new numbers in London Transport days.

The 30 new Regents were allocated principally to Godstone garage with smaller numbers at Reigate, East Grinstead and Chelsham. In appearance they were easily distinguishable from the Ransomes batch in having round rather than square cabs, whilst at the rear there was no destination box and the platform cut-away was to the regulation new standard. In fact they differed very little from the final STs delivered to General except in having a half-height driver's door and in dispensing with the cumbersome back bumper, substituting three neat raised bumping strips on the back corner panel instead. They even had nearside fuel tanks, totally the opposite to the Ransomes batch with their offside fuelling arrangement.

Having already had experience of constructing 50 standard ST bodies for the LGOC, it was inevitable that Shorts' second batch of 32 for East Surrey service would conform to almost exactly the same design. The only modifications to suit East Surrey requirements were the addition of a driver's half-door and the provision of three rubbing strips on the back corner panel in preference to fitting a full sized rear bumper. GO 7115 (later ST 1066) was placed into service in June 1931 and looked almost brand new when photographed at West Croydon on the 414B to Capel. *E G P Masterman*

GN 4732 was one of only two Regents to be allocated an ST number in East Surrey days, and it would have been displaying its identity as ST 834 when photographed in Dorking High Street at the far end of its regular run from Morden. The LGOC-built bodywork was identical in all respects to the Short Bros bodies on the much larger batch. *Alan Nightingale collection*

The new Regents brought a welcome degree of comfort and modernity to passengers on routes 403, 409, 414 and 459, but in truth they struggled to perform adequately over certain sections of these. The problem lay in the hilly terrain that they served, and besides the notable Reigate Hill there were others that caused even more difficulty including the hills between Upper and Lower Caterham and from Forest Row to East Grinstead. In fact Godstone's GO 636 was completely destroyed when still less than two years old after it caught fire on Reigate Hill on 6th May 1933. An acceptable solution was found to lie in the modification of the back axle ratio from the standard 6¼:1 to 7:1 to improve hill climbing ability, and this was subsequently used whenever vehicles were based at Godstone and East Grinstead garages and sometimes also at Reigate.

Quite early on in the delivery process of the new STs from Shorts, a couple of other vehicles arrived from a different source. The requirement for them on East Surrey had not been foreseen at the time that the batch of 30 was ordered, but had arisen subsequently as part of a scheme for transferring route 70D (Morden–Dorking) along with the whole five bus allocation at Crayford garage from the LGOC to East Surrey, who could operate them more economically. The planned starting date for the scheme was Wednesday 1st April 1931, and on 24th February a letter went out from the Licensing Superintendent ordering two STs from the existing new bus programme to be prepared with East Surrey sign-writings in readiness for the transfer of operations which also involved five overhauled open-top NSs and five unoverhauled T-type single deckers. The new vehicles selected were ST 833, 834 which formed part of the ST 822-836 batch originally intended for Overground. They were licensed on 24th March 1931 (at which time only three of the new Shorts batch were in stock) for service at Dorking garage, and they came carrying their allotted ST fleet numbers, the only Regents in the East Surrey fleet ever to do so.

Apart from the loss of GO 636 by fire, the two 1931 intakes of Regents led an uneventful existence prior to the formation of the LPTB, passing meanwhile into London Country Bus Services ownership in January 1932 along with the rest of the East Surrey fleet and making a start in adopting the new green and black livery from March 1933 onwards. At the start of the Board's days in July 1933 they were still serving exactly the same territories as when they were new.

The second batch of Regents carried East Surrey identity for less than a year before the London General Country Services regime took over. GO 5193, photographed in April 1932, was one of those fitted for hilly route operation, and as ST 1063 under the London Transport numbering scheme, it was destined to work from Godstone garage for many years to come. *J F Higham*

CHAPTER 8
OVERGROUND

Overground Ltd was General's unique subsidiary, a former independent undertaking still surviving under its old name and under its original management. Large in stature, the forceful Walter James Dangerfield entered the London bus business in 1923 and sold out to General on 8th June 1927, but by mutual agreement the Overground name was retained and Dangerfield continued to run the Company as a largely self-contained organisation which retained its own pay and conditions for staff and its own scheduling arrangements. The continuation of Overground as a separate entity with Dangerfield remaining as manager and licensee were conditions that General had been forced to accept in order to remove a sizeable business with 38 buses from the field of competition, but it proved to be a prudent move because Overground was tightly run and consistently returned a healthy level of profit. Finance for the purchase had been provided to the extent of 91.68% by the LGOC, the remainder being held by the Tramways (M.E.T.) Omnibus Company.

Overground's rolling stock requirements were organised from Chiswick although the vehicles carried their own dark red and off white livery and had their own numbering scheme. The Company possessed its own heavy maintenance and repairing facilities which, from 28th May 1930, had been based at a splendid new garage in Potters Bar owned and provided by the LGOC, and in most instances it overhauled its vehicles there although on occasions some were dealt with at Chiswick. Here the old family atmosphere inherited from former days at Camden Town still prevailed and Walter Dangerfield – who in his former days had been a farmer at Mill Hill – still sold potatoes and other vegetables to his staff.

Representing the first, abbreviated allocation of STs to Overground and showing '285 Victoria' as its destination, ST 822 carries standard LGOC red and grey livery modified only by the fleet names and the reference to Walter James Dangerfield as manager. The offside route number box is a mystery, and it is not known if ST 822 was a one-off or whether others were similarly fitted. *W Noel Jackson*

The Buckingham Palace Road stand at Victoria was a favourite place for photographing Overground buses, and two Regents are present on this occasion with one of Chocolate Express's Dodson bodied Leyland Titans standing in between. The Overground number for ST 412 was 21. *D W K Jones*

Not all Overground Regents displayed their ST number, and sometimes when they were shown on the bonnet side they had come from a different vehicle. Overground 16, alias ST 544, was photographed outside the Piccadilly Line extension station at Enfield West soon after its opening on 13th March 1933. *C F Klapper*

By the autumn of 1930 it had become apparent that an updating of the Overground fleet could not be delayed much longer. The sparkling new premises at Potters Bar contrasted strongly with the fleet which now consisted almost entirely of elderly bonneted open-top Leyland LB types. Most of these originated from a variety of acquired operators and had been drafted in only comparatively recently to replace Overground's own Dennises which, after being overhauled by their manufacturer at Guildford, had been re-employed within General's own fleet. The condition of the Leylands varied widely; some were quite sturdy but others were in a poor state and urgently needed to be replaced. For a start an order was placed for 15 Chiswick-bodied STs. A letter from AEC dated 3rd January 1931 confirmed that chassis numbered 6611463-6611477 had been set aside for Overground and would be ST 822-836.

The new STs began to come on stream in February 1931. ST 824 was received first, on the 2nd of the month, and was presumably immediately put to work training Potters Bar's staff. The next four were licensed, ready to immediately enter service, on the 17th and 18th. These were ST 822, 823, 825 and 826, but that was where the programme abruptly ceased. ST 827 onwards were diverted to General and ST 824 joined them on 26th February, leaving just four Regents at Potters Bar. A change of plan had occurred, and it subsequently transpired that a completely separate order was being placed on behalf of Overground for 25 Dennis Lances with all-metal Metro Cammell bodies similar to the one currently being experimentally tried out on ST 211. The Lances, when they came, were Overground's own property, but the four Regents remained in LGOC ownership and a temporary loan agreement was drawn up to cover them whereby Overground was to pay General a hire fee of £20 per vehicle per month. It was agreed that the four STs would stay at Potters Bar until the new Dennises arrived.

By sheer chance the body of 12 (ST 447) was carrying the OVERGROUND name for the second time when it arrived newly overhauled for service at Potters Bar in November 1932. It had formerly operated there as ST 822 between February and October 1931 but had since lost the offside route number box shown in the earlier photograph opposite. *J F Higham*

The first Dennis Lance was licensed on 6th October 1931 and, with the exception of one late straggler, all were in service by 4th December. On 21st October the four STs were dispatched to Chiswick where they were quickly repainted into General colours for operation within the main fleet. They had not long gone when, for some unknown reason, ST 500 was sent to Potters Bar, but it stayed only until 30th December and may never have received Overground colours.

Just about a year later, a renewed attempt was made to update the Overground fleet by sweeping away all the remaining first generation double deckers still contained within it. By this time the passage of the London Passenger Transport Bill through Parliament was sufficiently advanced for it to be clear that Overground Ltd. had only a limited future ahead of it, so it was decided to supply the Company with used STs, newly overhauled in Overground colours, which would remain on loan until it ceased to function. The first arrived on 31st October 1932 and the last on 1st December, and there were 27 in all. Fleet numbers 1 to 27 were allocated by Overground in order of arrival and were displayed in small white numerals. The Company never referred to the vehicles by their ST numbers even though these were also displayed on many of the vehicles. They could not, in any case, be relied upon since the bonnet covers, on which the ST numbers were displayed in raised metal numerals, were sometimes exchanged between vehicles. The 27 STs are listed below, and it will be noted that two of them were appearing in Overground colours for the second time.

Overground No.	ST	Date received at Potters Bar	Overground No.	ST	Date received at Potters Bar
1	456	31/10/32	15	826	15/11/32
2	825	31/10/31	16	544	16/11/32
3	531	7/11/32	17	4	17/11/32
4	431	7/11/32	18	417	18/11/32
5	357	8/11/32	19	467	18/11/32
6	397	8/11/32	20	525	21/11/32
7	378	10/11/32	21	412	22/11/32
8	515	10/11/32	22	14	25/11/32
9	3	10/11/32	23	510	23/11/32
10	36	10/11/32	24	529	24/11/32
11	343	11/11/32	25	16	25/11/32
12	447	11/11/32	26	546	29/11/32
13	468	14/11/32	27	6	1/12/32
14	393	14/11/32			

The Regents and Lances were completely intermixed on the five services worked by Overground, presenting a good opportunity to witness the performance of the two competing models side by side, although strict comparisons could not always be made as 16 out of the 27 STs were equipped with 110mm engines which put them in a different power category from the Lances. The latter, with their smooth running

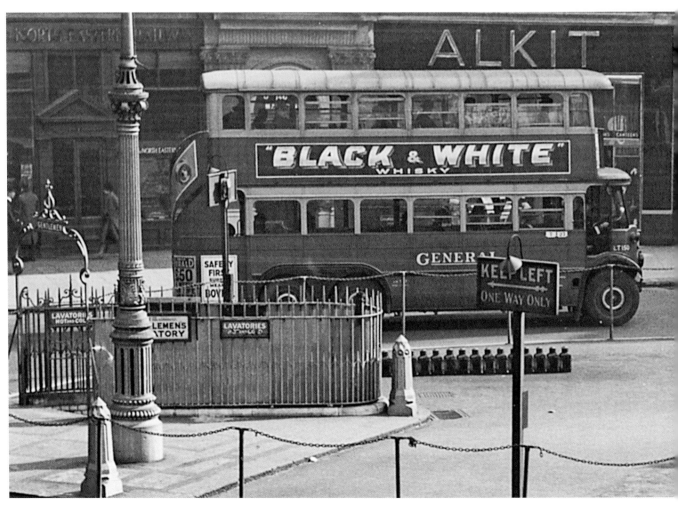

60

Potters Bar garage was noted for the large and well-tended garden in front of it. Across the foliage, no. 24 (ST 529) can be compared with D 19, one of Overground's famous fleet of Dennis Lances, and the Regent is clearly the taller of the two. *D W K Jones*

engines, consistently prevailed in terms of economy of fuel consumption but they were less resistant to being worked hard in London traffic and much more prone to boil up, especially if pushed to their maximum through the gears.

As the vesting date of 1st July 1933 drew near when ownership of Overground and all its assets would be transferred to the London Passenger Transport Board, the Central Bus department expressed its eagerness to absorb the Overground operations as quickly as possible. Aware of the massive task that lay ahead in integrating all its acquired operations, Frank Pick felt that it would be advisable to leave Overground alone for a while to enable other, more pressing matters to be handled, and wrote: "Can't you leave Mr. Dangerfield in control at Potters Bar, securing any adjustment you want through him? I am not at all sure we should gain anything by disturbing the family Party at Potters Bar at this moment." This was one of the rare occasions when his advice fell on deaf ears, and on 7th July 1933 Overground's operations were absorbed by the LPTB.

Traces of the Overground regime did not stay around for very long. Having been at Potters Bar for the best part of a year, the STs were all approaching the time when they would be due for overhaul, and from September 1933 they began going into Chiswick Works to be replaced by others in standard fleet colours. This process was carried out strictly in fleet number order, and when no. 27 (alias ST 6) departed for Chiswick on 27th November a brief but interesting episode in the history of the ST class came to an end.

The scene is Cambridge Circus, and Overground 22 (ST 14) scuttles down Charing Cross Road while General's LT 150 – the highest numbered of its class with an outside staircase – heads for Shaftesbury Avenue. The date is 14th March 1933 and takeover by the LPTB lies only a little over three months away. *Ken Blacker collection*

CHAPTER 9
THE BLUEBIRDS

During its short span of life, London General Country Services received only one intake of new vehicles. These arrived in August 1932 and consisted of 23 Regents plus 2 Renown single deckers, all of which had been ordered in the previous April. In line with the Company's current policy, which it had inherited from East Surrey, they were not given fleet numbers.

The contract for their purchase was placed on the Company's behalf by the LGOC and they were allocated registration numbers within a large series reserved by the latter for various purchases, GX 5314-5336 for the Regents and GX 5337/5338 for the Renowns. Body numbers were also allocated: 13441/42 for the Renowns and 13443-13465 for the Regents. The bodies for all 25 were built at Chiswick.

Probably fresh off the Chiswick production line in August 1932, GX 5317 appears to have been photographed in haste before the correct blinds had been printed for it, and an LGOC set has been installed to fill the empty spaces. As ST 1073, this Bluebird was destined – by a fair margin – to be the last of its class to survive. *L T Museum*

Only the ten GX registered vehicles could be found immediate work and two of these, including GX 5323 (later ST 1079) ended up at Reigate. It was photographed at West Croydon in the company of an older Regent, laying over before its southbound departure to Crawley.
J F Higham

The subsequent history of the two Renown single deckers is covered in the companion volume on the LT class. The Regents, when they emerged from Chiswick, resembled nothing else in the LGCS fleet. In fact they were a shortened copy of the Bluebird type LT six-wheelers placed into service in large numbers by General from February 1932 onwards, and they featured the same blue internal décor that gave the class its name. The two most notable design features of the Bluebird LT had been the lengthening of the upper saloon compared with its predecessors by utilising the space above the driver's cab, and the introduction of a traditional style curved staircase at the rear in place of the straight stairs and wide, clutter-free platform now so familiar on the LGOC and its associated fleets. The overriding reason for these changes had been to maximise seating capacity, which on the Bluebird LT was 60, but this advantage was completely lost on the LGCS Regents which carried only 48 (22 downstairs and 26 up) and, remarkably, was one fewer than on the standard type of ST despite the additional floor space available and the fact that the Bluebird body was 2½ins longer. As a result the upstairs seating was unusually spacious, though this did not totally compensate for the deliberate reduction in standards of comfort brought about by using a new cheaper and lighter type of seat. This was a low backed unit using Dunlopillo rather than sprung cushions which was far less well padded and was set lower and at a less comfortable angle than on earlier vehicles.

Until the arrival of the 23 Regents London General Country Services and its predecessors had not been notably preoccupied with providing extensive destination displays on their modern vehicles in the same way that General had been forced to do; in fact all LGCS Regents still carried their original destination boxes and had not been upgraded in line with those in the LGOC fleet. The Bluebirds, with their extensive displays including roof mounted number box at the front, brought the imparting of route information to a new high level and reversed the short lived policy of not showing a destination on the back of the bus. In constructing the Bluebird bodies, Chiswick had pared weight down to a bare minimum with the result that the complete vehicle weighed only 6 tons 5cwt 0qrs even though the body was larger than what had gone before, and this frugality was destined to cause problems in years to come. Strangely, though the Bluebird style of body looked impressive and even majestic when mounted on the six-wheeled LT chassis, the same did not seem to apply on the LGCS vehicles. The angular styling appeared to lose some of its impressiveness when scaled down to the shorter, two-axle model.

The LGCS batch was the last to be ordered from AEC by any operator to employ the now outmoded 15ft 6½ins version of the Regent chassis. At the 1931 Olympia motor show AEC had exhibited its new, 16ft 3ins version in anticipation of a relaxation of the Construction & Use Regulations to permit two axle double deckers to be up to 26ft in length and 10 tons in laden weight. These new regulations had been in force since early in 1932, and there is no obvious reason why the now superseded specification was chosen for this batch of vehicles, especially as the LGOC was itself actively pursuing the purchase of the longer wheelbase version to form its STL class. In all other respects the new chassis reflected the continuous improvements that AEC had made to the Regent since its introduction which now included Lockheed hydraulic operation of the brakes from a vacuum servo unit. The customary 100mm bore engine was specified as was the favoured rear axle ratio of 6¼:1.

The Underground group had been working for some time towards confining the LGOC's sphere of operation within the boundaries of the Metropolitan Police District and had developed a policy of transferring services projecting beyond this to lower-cost subsidiaries. An example of this had been the 1st April 1931 transfer of the Crayford garage operations, and also of the Dorking section of route 70, to East Surrey. The

23 Regents were bought specifically to pursue this policy further. However a major scheme to transfer services running southwards from Morden to Epsom, Lower Kingswood and Walton on the Hill on 31st May 1932 fell through, removing a potential source of employment for them. Upon delivery they had been stored at Reigate, but when the first ten (GX 5314-5323) finally entered service at the end of August 1932 only two were actually used at Reigate. The remainder were sent to Watford garage where they were used initially on the Rickmansworth–St Albans run in direct competition with the modern Regents of the Lewis Omnibus Company, displacing the older and more old fashioned open-cab ex National STs that had worked on it until then.

This left 13 new vehicles surplus to requirements, and with no work in prospect for them they remained in store for the remainder of 1932. Early in January 1933, still with no work on the horizon, their booked registration numbers GX 5324-5336 were reallocated to new STLs and Dennis Darts.

With just four months' existence ahead of it, London General Country Services managed to find a niche for the APC registered batch at Windsor garage when the major Slough/Windsor area reorganisation was implemented on 1st March 1933. Photographed at Slough was APC 163 (the future ST 1033) and *opposite top*, at Windsor, APC 162 (ST 1032) and one other, all on route 481. *Alan B Cross/D W K Jones*

The chance for some to be activated finally came with a large reorganisation on 1st March 1933 when the LGCS took over various LGOC operations in the Slough and Windsor area. Eight new Regents were required at Windsor garage, a splendid new building which had opened as recently as 18th January. Their original registration numbers having been forfeited, it was necessary to obtain replacement ones, which the Reigate office set about doing. As a consequence these were issued in Surrey as APC 162-170, the only instance of three letter registrations within the ST class. At about the same time – it is not known exactly when – the residue of five was found work at the one-time National garage in Ware, principally on route 310 between Hertford and Enfield. In this instance the LGCS's northern divisional office at Watford was tasked with obtaining registration numbers from Hertfordshire County Council who issued JH 4646-4650. Thus this small batch of 23 vehicles uniquely ended up with registration numbers issued in three different counties. They spent little time with their original operator, LGCS, before passing to the LPTB on 1st July 1933.

The JH registered Bluebirds likewise enjoyed only a brief working existence for London General Country Services. Ware based JH 4648 (ST 1082) waits at Enfield Town for its departure to Hertford North. The conductor has re-set the destination blind above the platform but appears to have forgotten the one at the back. *D W K Jones*

CHAPTER 10
ST LOOKALIKES

Although their roots dated back to the end of the nineteen-twenties, the STs – and their associated LT and T types – were basically a thirties phenomenon and, above all, they were distinctly and instantly recognisably 'London' in appearance. This was in sharp contrast to the previous decade when AEC and the LGOC had jointly been prepared to sell their chassis and body products to any customer who came forward, and even to operators overseas, which meant that the body styles designed by General could theoretically appear anywhere and were not specifically confined to London. Now, with the Chiswick body shops unable to cope with demand from within the Company, and General having to augment its output through placing contracts with outside suppliers, the concept of body styling unique to London began to take hold.

The distinctive ST body styling made a number of well recorded appearances in 1931/32 both in London itself and outside. The first internal instance occurred early in 1931 when three newly constructed bodies (12078-12080) were taken directly from the ST production line and modified for fitment to Daimler CH6 chassis to form DST 1-3. These three chassis had been taken into stock in December 1930 specifically to try out the combination of the Wilson preselective gearbox, which was being actively marketed by Improved Cars Ltd and manufactured under licence by Daimler, with the patented Daimler fluid flywheel. These offered an ease of driving much better suited to London's ever worsening traffic than the conventional combination of clutch and crash gearbox. The Wilson box promised quietness, high efficiency and long life whilst also easing the driver's job through the advantage of being able to select a gear before it was needed, giving a faster gearchange and the useful ability to use the gear as a brake. The fluid flywheel, which contained no major wearing parts, virtually eliminated the destructive effects and shocks of bad gear changing on the gearbox, propeller shaft, differential gear and axle shafts.

Fortunately the Daimler CH6 chassis had the same wheelbase as the AEC Regent and a very similar front end layout, which meant that it was quite a simple matter to install the standard ST body on it with only minor modifications necessary to details like floor traps. The mechanical specification, in addition to the Siddeley-built Wilson gearbox which was mounted amidships, included Daimler's CV35 6-cylinder 5.76 litre sleeve valve engine with bore and stroke of 97mm and 130mm respectively and rated at 85bhp, giving somewhat less output than a standard ST. Differing rear axle ratios were adopted, 6¼:1 on DST 1 and 3 and 7¼:1 on DST 2, presumably to assess variations in performance. At 6 tons 2cwt 0qrs the completed bus, with open cab body, was roughly the same in unladen weight as the contemporary ST. The LGOC chose to operate its newest type of bus from its newest garage, Harrow Weald, which had opened as recently as 9th April 1930 and was well equipped to handle experimental vehicles. DST 1 was licensed for service on route 18 on 2nd February 1931 with the other two following three days later.

Although no fleet number is carried on the nearside, this Daimler CH6 is DST 3. For its first six months in service DST 3 ran with an open-fronted cab which differed from those on contemporary STs in having no vertical side bars fitted. The front bumper, projecting immediately outwards from the dumbirons, is similar to one of the versions fitted to STs.
C F Klapper

The combination of Wilson gearbox and fluid flywheel quickly confirmed all that was expected of it, but otherwise the vehicles were not a success. The sleeve valve engine, with its typical trail of bluish exhaust, had already been proven as not up to the job of powering a double decker reliably having already been unsuccessfully fitted to some vehicles in the LS class, and it fared no better on the DST. In 1931 Daimler began offering a 6.56 litre 90bhp 103mm x130mm poppet valve engine using the same crankshaft as the sleeve valve unit, and the LGOC purchased one of these for DST 3 in March 1932, amending the axle ratio at the same time to 7¼. It did not lead to any further purchases.

Meanwhile enclosed cabs had been fitted in August and September 1931 as part of the ongoing fleet programme, and in line with the modifications to indicator layouts on the LTs and STs, DST 2 was fitted with the enlarged front box and rear display in September 1932 with the other two following in November. After only four years' service, DST 1-3 were deemed to have served their purpose and were taken into Chiswick works and delicensed on 11th February 1935. Accompanying them was a Birch bodied CH6 taken over from the Red Line service of E Brickwood Ltd and now numbered DST 5. The bodies were removed from all four and subsequently installed on new, specially shortened STL chassis, the ST style bodies being placed on STL 1260, 1261, 1263 and the Birch body on STL 1262. The redundant Daimler chassis were sold to a dealer and all four subsequently served as coaches with a variety of owners.

Looking superficially like an ordinary ST apart from their fully floating rear axles, the STLs with ST bodies struck an incongruous note with CLE registrations. In August 1944 the fourth of the quartet also became ST bodied after the Birch body on STL 1262 was destroyed by enemy action, although having had a standard STL cab with sloping windscreen grafted on to it, STL 1262 remained easily distinguishable from the other three. This state of affairs lasted only until February 1947 when STL 1262 was rebuilt yet again, this time as a normal wheelbase STL with roofbox body, leaving the other three to soldier on, still looking for all the world like STs, for two more years.

DST 3 is seen at London bridge after a windscreen had been fitted at the end of August 1931, showing the squarer style of cab adopted on these vehicles to suit the Daimler radiator. As in the previous photograph, it is about to embark on the long 1hour 50mins run to Harrow Weald garage on route 18, but now carries a later style of destination blind omitting all mention of via points.

An early post-war view of STL 1263 finds it at Colindale accompanied by STL 1227, both operating from Cricklewood garage. Apart from the lack of an autovac tank and a fully floating axle, STL 1263 looks for all the world like a standard ST. Withdrawn in January 1949, it was in fact outlived by many STs.
John House

Overground Lances galore at Victoria where three be seen on the stand for the 284, 285 and 629 groups of routes. D 8, which leads the line-up, is still in as-delivered condition with small front indicator box. Body numbers 13030-13054 were allocated but not carried in sequence, and the registration numbers for the 25 Lances were taken at random from within a current LGOC allocation. *E G P Masterman*

A rear view shows the general similarity of the Metro Cammell body to the LGOC's standard design. When seen from the back, Overground's final livery presented a picture of unrelieved red. Photographed on the Black Bull stand in Whetstone fresh out of overhaul in March 1933, D 4 is on a suburban 307 working to Enfield. *C F Klapper*

The second and somewhat larger batch of ST lookalikes purchased by General consisted of the 25 Dennis Lances ordered in 1931 for the Overground fleet. The Lance had proved reasonably successful in the service of some of the LGOC's competitors and, though no background papers survive to explain exactly why Dennises were bought, it can be surmised that General wished to try some out for itself and that the self-contained Overground operation at Potters Bar was an ideal place to do so. At the same time the opportunity was taken to gain further experience of the patented MCW method of body construction employing flanged box section drawn steel pillars following the trial of a single body on ST 211 (ST 379 from September 1931), and bodies of this type were ordered for construction by Metro Cammell. In appearance they were very similar to the all-metal body on the ST except that the radiused top window corners favoured by the LGOC were now featured. However the longer wheelbase of the Lance meant that these were not interchangeable with ST bodies and resulted in a shorter rear bay and slightly narrower platform, while the dash panel design was modified to suit the Lance radiator. They were fitted with windscreens from new.

The Dennis 6-cylinder 6.1 litre 110-mm x 130mm engine rated at 100bhp was allied to a 4-speed crash gearbox, the whole combination promising to give a road performance equivalent to that of the AEC Regent. In fact, despite drawbacks which became apparent in service and a higher unladen weight of 6.13.1, they performed economically to produce a better mpg rate than the STs. Numbered D 1-25 by Overground, the complete batch entered service at Potters Bar between 6th October and 4th December 1931 with the exception of D 25 which, for some unknown reason, was delayed until 4th February 1932. Upon absorption of the Overground fleet into the LPTB on 7th July 1933, the Lances remained at Potters Bar but were now known as the DL class. Under the Overground regime annual overhauls and repainting had been carried out in the modern premises at Potters Bar, and for a few months into the London Transport era the Lances continued to be dealt with there. The last to be out-shopped was D 25 on 12th December 1933; from the start of 1934 this work was transferred to Chiswick.

Under London Transport auspices the seating capacity on the upper deck was reduced by one in 1934 on 16 of the DLs to bring the total down to 48, while a further reduction in 1934/35 rendered all of them 47 seaters, only to return back to 48 in 1936/37. It is not known why any of this was done. There was also some tinkering with the axle ratios on some of them, modifying the original 6¾ to 6¼ and then reverting to the original, again for reasons unknown but presumably to improve road performance.

The first Lance to lose its Overground livery under LPTB auspices was this one, which appeared carrying the GENERAL fleet name but its old Overground number D 9 on 27th July 1933. It demonstrates the large front indicator box now fitted to these vehicles which, because of the bulbous nature of the driver's roof canopy, has a downward slope at the top from front to back. Chocolate Express Titan UW 6157, standing behind, is destined to remain in private ownership until August 1934. *D W K Jones*

In London Transport days the original 25 Overground Lances were joined at Potters Bar by eight more taken over from independents and numbered DL 26-33. These were a mixture of Dodson and Birch bodied vehicles, the former being DL 26 ex Claremont, DL 27 ex CC, DL 30 and 31 ex Ambassador and DL 32 and 33 ex Reliance. Birch had bodied DL 28 for Red Rover and DL 29 for Ambassador. DL 26 and 27 had outside staircases; the rest were fully enclosed at the rear. The Lance era at Potters Bar began to disintegrate on 3rd November 1936 with the transfer of a number of vehicles southwards to Sutton, and during the next four weeks the remainder followed, the last on 2nd December. Once again, the reason for this mass exodus is not recorded, but it may be assumed that the vehicles had been deemed better suited to Sutton's purely outer suburban operations than to those at Potters Bar, many of which penetrated deep into central London.

It is probable that, when the Lances moved as a complete class to Sutton, it was planned that they would last much more than a year there. However a strike by busmen in May and June 1937 put a completely different complexion on their fate. The severe loss of passenger traffic that ensued, and subsequent reductions in service levels to meet the reduced demand, brought forward the demise of non-standard types such as the Dennises, with the result that withdrawals of the DLs began on 29th November 1937 and proceeded rapidly thereafter, with the last of the ex-Overground contingent – DL 3, 14, 16, 23 – being delicensed on 1st January 1938. All 33 Lances were moved for storage into Chiswick tram depot to await a buyer, and they were subsequently sold to G J Dawson of Clapham Road SW9, a leading scrap merchant of the day. It would seem that, despite the potential working life still left in them, all the vehicles were purchased for their high metal content and were melted down accordingly.

Now in full London Transport colours as DL 7, this Lance shows the Chiswick influence now prevailing through the use of standard AEC front wheel rings which have replaced Dennis's own type, while the large back hub is no longer picked out in silver. The polished surround has now disappeared from the radiator and so has the Lance badge. *A D Packer*

Unlicensed and running under trade plate 309H, JF 223 appears to be in use by AEC as a back-up vehicle at an event of some sort. The canvas banners proclaiming that it is a 110hp Regent service vehicle hide the fact that the upstairs windows are unusual full-depth sideways sliders. The full-drop ones on the lower saloon can be more clearly seen. *Ken Blacker collection*

As well as the 28 lookalikes created for London service in the early nineteen-thirties, a further 18 were built for use outside the capital. Their story is, in reality, an unusual post-script to that of the Regents built for East Surrey and Autocar by Ransomes Sims & Jefferies, for it was from the latter's Ipswich works that all saw the light of day. Although no evidence to this effect survives, its seems fair to assume that Ransomes agreed to pay a royalty to the LGOC for using its designs, an outlay which would have been to Ransomes' advantage as the Company stood to avoid incurring design and tooling costs in fulfilling what were only very small orders.

One of the 18 was ordered by AEC itself to go on a Regent chassis which it intended to use as a demonstrator promoting the recently introduced 110mm engine. With chassis number 661129, it was slightly ahead of the 60 ordered by the LGOC, and the Ransomes body was built concurrently with them. Externally, apart from livery, it was identical to the East Surrey and Autocar vehicles in all respects except that it incorporated a very unusual arrange-ment of opening windows. These were of the full-drop type in the lower deck, which obviously necessitated a modification of waistrail design to accommodate them, whilst the upper saloon was equipped with unusual, full height sliding windows reminiscent of those fitted on the upper decks of NSs but not really best suited to the British climate. Registered JF 223 in anticipation of a booked demonstration spell with Leicester Corporation which took place in June 1930, it was also shown during the next 18 months to the municipal operators at Birmingham, Walsall, Exeter, Bury and Hull, and also to Devon General and T White & Company of Cardiff and possibly others, none of whom purchased it. JF 223 was bought by E W Campion & Sons of Nottingham in August 1932, passing to Barton Transport in January 1936 when it took over the Campion business. The following year appears to have been its last.

The two West Bridgford Ransomes-bodied Regents carried impressively large shaded gold fleet names when new. The offside view of 18 and the nearside one of 19 show their almost total similarity apart from livery to the East Surrey/Autocar batch. All that was missing was the tester's tip-up seat and leather strap which were not needed for provincial use.

No. 17, photographed before it was registered as FJ 7411, typifies the Ransomes Regents supplied to Exeter Corporation. On these, the frontal style was modified to accommodate the local destination display arrangements, and the cab side was redesigned to provide a wider, fully glazed driver's door.

Also built alongside the East Surrey/Autocar batch were VO 3877/3878, which entered service with West Bridgford Urban District Council in June 1930. Apart from livery, these appeared identical in all obvious respects to the original LGOC specification. They worked in West Bridgford until 1940, during part of which time they would presumably have met up on occasions with JF 223 during their frequent trips into Nottingham. From October 1940 until July 1941 they ran on loan to London Transport working from Norwood garage and it is a great pity that they were not photographed whilst doing so. Although now considered redundant by West Bridgford UDC they went on to lead just as long lives as their London Transport contemporaries. After a subsequent wartime loan to Grimsby Corporation they were finally sold in March 1947 to Nottingham Corporation which was desperate for additional rolling stock at the time. They remained in service there until as late as September 1949.

After a lapse of a few months, Ransomes began building some more ST lookalikes, this time for Exeter Corporation. The Corporation had become disenchanted with trams and the growing problems being encountered by them on the narrow streets and single track sections of its 3ft 6ins gauge system. JF 223 was one of the buses tried out as a demonstrator to determine suitability for tram replacement and it must have impressed the Council's Transport Department which placed two orders with AEC and Ransomes for a total of 15 similar vehicles. The Corporation must have been particularly impressed with the straight stair layout of the LGOC design as it specified the same arrangement on a batch of Leyland Titans with Brush bodies ordered at about the same time. The new Regents were built as 48-seaters and the first batch (fleet numbers 16-21, FJ 7410-7415) came at the end of 1930 in time to take over from trams on the Alphington Road–Whipton route in January 1931. Resplendent in Exeter's Napier green and yellow, they were almost identical to the earlier Ransomes Regents apart from the use of a full rather than half-height driver's cab door and modifications to the front panelling to permit the fitting of the operator's own indicator displays. A second identical batch (22-30, FJ 7820-7828) was delivered in the spring of 1931 and licensed on 4th August to permit the final demise of the trams on the 19th of that month. These were the last AECs ever to be purchased by Exeter Corporation and the last Regents to be bodied at the Ipswich factory.

All except three of Exeter's Regents were withdrawn from service in 1938 but many found ongoing use elsewhere, mostly as single deckers and none with its original Ransomes body. Odd ones survived well into the nineteen-fifties. Of the three that escaped the 1938 cull, two (nos. 29 and 30) joined the West Bridgford pair on loan to London Transport between October 1940 and July 1941. No. 30 spent most of this time alongside the West Bridgford vehicles at Norwood, leaving no. 29 as the only ST lookalike to be based north of the Thames at Palmers Green. This pair were subsequently owned by Bristol Tramways and then Crosville from 1945 onwards, lasting in service until 1951 albeit carrying replacement double-deck bodies very unlike their Ransomes originals.

CHAPTER 11
THOMAS TILLING'S LONDON STs

Second only to the LGOC in its contribution of buses to the ST class, Thomas Tilling Ltd was a long established and substantial bus business with headquarters in the heart of Westminster at 20 Victoria Street SW1. A very old company which pre-dated the LGOC, it could trace its jobmaster origins back to the 1840s and had expanded into the bus business by 1851, the year of the Great Exhibition. It later became renowned for its fleet of Tilling Stevens petrol electrics which had served the Company well, bringing it mechanical reliability and financial prosperity. Outright competition with the LGOC had been eschewed by sharing in the London Omnibus 'Pool', the first written agreement having been signed by the two parties on 15th May 1912. Although much of Tilling's subsequent development of its bus interests was achieved by gaining financial control of established operators throughout the British Isles, it continued to maintain its London business, and also a branch in Brighton, as a directly controlled operation under its own name.

In mid-December 1929 Tilling announced that it had placed a substantial order for 100 AEC Regents with which to start replacing the now ageing petrol electrics that comprised its London fleet. This decision must have come as a big disappointment to Tilling Stevens who had pinned its hopes on its latest petrol electric model, the TS17A, one of which had been supplied to Thomas Tilling for trial running in London. Registered GU 6488 and carrying Tilling's own 52-seat bodywork, it had started work on 18th May 1929. For the trial period it ran in headlong competition with Shorts bodied AEC Regent demonstrator UU 9161 which entered service in June and was, numerically, only the fourth of its type to be built carrying chassis number 661004. A second Tilling Stevens TS17A was subsequently tried out in Brighton where a Leyland Titan TD1 and a Daimler CF6 were also trialled, but none of these impressed sufficiently for any orders to be placed, and the Brighton fleet was also renewed with AEC Regents.

When they began entering service in June 1930, Tilling's new Regents were seen to carry the same livery styling as the demonstrator apart from the fleet name which was in an updated form, and they also carried the same very informative six-line listing of intermediate points at front and rear. Less easy to read from some angles were the destination boards which were slightly angled behind glass inside the upper saloon. Running from Bromley garage, 6019 (ST 843) was photographed at Marble Arch, looking far more sprightly than the Gas Light & Coke Company's Sentinel steamer crossing the wide roadway alongside it. The permanently open unglazed front section of the nearside cab window caused such a draught that it was commonplace for drivers to feel more comfortable with the windscreen wide open. On Tilling's Regents the tester's tip-up seat was fitted in front of the autovac tank, unlike the LGOC where it was located above. *G J Robbins collection.*

AEC Regent demonstrator UU 9161's trial period on route 36 starting in May 1929 convinced the Tilling management that the way ahead lay with Regents and not petrol electrics. Seen well loaded on a journey to Hither Green, it was fully fitted out as a Tilling bus including livery and running number plates, and carried current advertising material.

The original order for 100 Regents was soon augmented by another 36 which were announced as being for the Brighton section. However there must have been a subsequent change of plan, for the first 12 were all reserved for service in Brighton and not London, after which the London section received the whole of the remaining 124. Tilling possessed extensive coachbuilding facilities which enabled it to construct its own bus bodies, but these facilities were not sufficient to cope with all the new Regents at their planned rate of arrival. To make up the balance, a contract was placed with Christopher Dodson (1930) Ltd to construct bodies to Tilling's design in their works at Cobbald Road, Willesden.

A very favourable rate was negotiated with AEC for the chassis for which Tilling paid only £800 each, a reduction of about 30% on the official list price which clearly reflected the benefit of buying in bulk. (The LGOC did better still and paid £100 less than this for its STs, but its bulk-buying power was even greater and the fact that both were within the same group of companies may also have had an influence on price.) Tilling managed to produce its own bodies for about £560 apiece which was roughly the same amount that a Chiswick built body cost the LGOC. It is not known what price per body was paid to Dodson, although these would inevitably have been dearer once a profit margin had been factored in.

The typical offside view of a Tilling Regent, with the driver's half height door and exaggerated curve of the bodywork above it, is shown by 6097 (ST 921), a November 1930 delivery to Catford garage. Tilling's operations were controlled on the road by LGOC inspectors such as the gentleman posing jovially in front of the bus. *R K Blencowe collection*

The Tilling operation in London for which the new Regents were licensed from 17th June 1930 onwards was an unusual and complex set-up. It was unusual in that it employed no inspectors or timekeepers, these services being hired in from the LGOC who were also contracted to provide tickets, waybills and punches. The LGOC was also responsible for deciding which services Tilling's buses would operate and their frequency. The total extent of the Tilling operation was governed by periodically renewed agreements, the most recent of which, signed on 11th November 1929 and valid for ten years, stipulated that Tilling would work five per cent of vehicles within the London Omnibus Pool. General was also in charge of setting fares though Tilling retained all the receipts on services worked solely by itself, these being aggregated where services were jointly worked. In addition to Tilling's own fleet, it also operated by agreement a substantial number of LGOC owned petrol electrics painted in Tilling livery, which were referred to by both operators as "transferred omnibuses". Tilling's three operational garages were also owned by the LGOC. Those at Bromley and Catford had been purchased from Tilling under an agreement of 12th April 1923, and such was the closeness of the arrangements between the two that Tilling loaned the LGOC about £100,000 repayable over a fixed period to make the purchase possible. A further loan was arranged to enable Croydon garage to be bought under an agreement of 26th March 1926.

On the engineering side of its affairs, Tilling operated completely independently of the LGOC, both in regard to the vehicles within its ownership and also to those supplied by the LGOC which it treated as though they were its own. In 1930 this comprised 114 LGOC owned buses out of a total Tilling fleet of 364. The hub of the operation was Bull Yard, an extensive site in High Street, Peckham where, in addition to a range of administrative offices, there was a large works in which the Company's bus and commercial vehicle chassis were overhauled and all major mechanical work was carried out. Under the ultimate control of Bull Yard but with their own specialist management were three coach factories, the most distant of which was the Obelisk Works at High Street, Lewisham, sometimes called Salisbury Yard. This served partly as a coachbuilding factory, for which purpose the roof was raised in 1929 to accommodate covered top double deckers, and it was also responsible for overhauling open top bodies. Closer to Bull Yard, in Peckham Road, was the Pelican Yard, part of which comprised a modern extension, including a widened approach road built in 1927-30. This was where the main body stores were located, and later in Tilling days this factory mainly specialised in overhauling covered top bodies. Like the Obelisk Works, it also employed staff on new body construction. The most westerly and largest of the three coachworks was a former stable block in Wren Road, Camberwell Green, where the factory manager and his staff were located. This works carried out body overhaul and repair works of all kinds.

Construction of the new ST bodies was mainly a joint effort between the Obelisk Works and Pelican Yard and it is said that, between them, they had the ability to produce four new buses a week. Well over sixty per cent of the staff at each of these two factories were employed on new body construction whereas at Wren Road only 16% were engaged on new works which were probably mostly confined to tasks such as machining parts for the other factories rather than the complete construction of new bodies. The Obelisk Works was the reception point for new chassis, but in the main only the lower decks and upper saloon floors of the new bodies were constructed there. After painting, these were mounted on the new chassis and driven to Pelican Yard where separate upper decks were jig built and painted. The two decks were then joined and the staircases and fittings added to produce the complete vehicle.

Tilling commenced a new fleet numbering system for its Regents starting at 6001. The initial batch of 100 (6001-6100) was allocated registration numbers GJ 2001-2100 with the subsequent 36 (6101-6136) following on as GK 1001-1036. Fleet and registration numbers were kept strictly in sequence with each other, the Tilling management clearly seeing no value in adopting the LGOC policy of aligning fleet and chassis numbers which resulted in registration numbers being allocated haphazardly. In common with the LGOC, Tilling allocated body numbers to its buses which, in the case of the 124 London Regents, were 5184-5307. These were issued in strict numerical sequence upon arrival irrespective of which factory a body had been built in, but they quickly became jumbled as Tilling pursued a similar policy to the LGOC of exchanging bodies between chassis at overhaul.

The lowest numbered of the new Regents, 6001-6012, were allocated to the Brighton department, although most of them entered service there later than the first of the London batch 6013-6136. Six of the Brighton vehicles and all of the London ones carried new Tilling designed bodies of a very distinctive styling quite unlike that favoured by the LGOC. Notable features included the heavily domed roof and the use of pronounced swoops linking the front bulkhead with the driver's canopy and replicated at the back, though in a slightly less prominent manner and on the nearside only, between the rear bulkhead and the short platform overhang. Overall the design was a strange mixture of old and new, the old being represented by the open staircase, the three-window front end upper deck layout, and the retention throughout of destination boards rather than roller blinds which were now in

The second, less heavy livery for Regents, employing cream around the upper deck windows, succeeded in giving the vehicles a brighter appearance. No. 6085 (ST 909) received this livery at its first overhaul and is seen at Rennell Street, Lewisham running from Catford garage on the semi-rural route 146A to Keston. The contrast with the Tilling Stevens petrol electric standing behind it could not be more stark.

vogue. A reversion to 1920s styling was the shallowness of the skirt panels, exposing the offside petrol tank and other components and necessitating a three-layered wooden safety rail to fill the gap. A windscreen was fitted and so was a half-height driver's door, but to meet police requirements the nearside of the cab was unglazed at its forward end. As was so often the case with this arrangement, a strong draught was created around the driver when the vehicle was in motion and this, coupled with the lack of a windscreen wiper, meant that drivers tended to keep the windscreen wide open most of the time, totally nullifying the point of having it.

At 52, the Tilling Regent seated three more than its LGOC equivalent, 25 downstairs and 27 up. The seats were packed more closely together downstairs than on the upper deck where spacing was very generous, especially on the offside. The downstairs layout consisted of facing seats for three over each wheelarch forward of which were five rows of transverse seats, an unusual feature being that the front one on the nearside was only a single. The upstairs arrangement was also unusual in that the very back seat on the nearside, which accommodated three, was inward facing, presumably to provide maximum circulating space at the top of the stair-case. From the popular corner seat there was a spectacular view looking back as well as a chance to inspect everybody coming up the stairs! The seats themselves were deep and well sprung and upholstered in Tilling's own design of moquette with leather edgings, and the backs were covered in repp as were all the side panels.

Whereas General preferred to employ large areas of rexine on its internal coverings, the Tilling body was more opulent in appearance with generous use of mahogany on all the window surrounds and main mouldings, brought to a high gloss finish by being cellulose sprayed to maximise wear resistance. Like the LGOC, however, Tilling installed bells of the Numa air-operated type. Particular thought had been given to ventilation which used the "Ashanco" patented system of extracting air by means of six fittings which allowed a complete air change to take place approximately every four minutes when the vehicle was in motion. The intakes were under the front canopy and the outlets along the roof on the upper deck, the lower saloon extractors being prominently situated in the side panels immediately above the windows and clearly visible from the outside.

Apart from incorporating the more usual offside fuel tank position, the Regent chassis supplied to Tilling differed from those bought by General in having a longer rear overhang (7ft 2ins beyond the rear axle as opposed to 6ft 10ins), presumably better to accommodate the weight of the stair-case which was placed much further back in the Tilling model. Whereas the LGOC preferred batteries to be mounted on the chassis (in the position occupied by the fuel tank on the Tillings), the latter accommodated them inside the body. Both specified similar gearbox and clutch arrangements although gear ratios differed slightly, and both opted for a rear axle ratio of 6¼:1. A peculiarity of the Tilling fleet was that both single and triple vacuum servo systems were used for braking with no apparent preference for one or the other, being spread roughly on a 50:50 basis throughout the batches in no particular sequence. Another difference from current LGOC practice was that Tilling did not require the fitting of self starters. In an apparent endeavour to secure the max-imum fuel economy, the Company specified engines with a bore of only 95mm, which would undoubtedly have produced a rather muted road performance especially under a full 52 passenger load. This was a specially downrated version of the A140 engine (coded A140E) which, with sleeved Specialloid pistons, produced a swept volume of only about 5.5 litres. As built, the new buses weighed in at 6 tons 1cwt 2qrs, rather more than their LGOC contemporaries in original guise.

Eight new Regents (6013-6020) were licensed and ready for service at Bromley garage by the time that operation commenced on Friday 27th June 1930. Looking unusually tall and slim thanks largely to the effect created by their deeply domed roofs, they presented a rather more drab appearance than their LGOC counterparts thanks to the darker red of the Tilling livery relieved only by two below-windows cream bands and silver roof. They introduced a new, updated style of fleetname using block capitals instead of the former script lettering whilst still retaining the traditional rectangular background to highlight the Tilling name. Their first sphere of operation was on route 36, on which the Regent demonstrator had also shown its paces in the previous year, but as deliveries proceeded apace the new Regents rapidly spread to other services and beyond Bromley garage to firstly, Catford, and lastly, to Croydon, all the time sweeping away open-top petrol electrics.

No. 6158 (ST 982) carried the second livery from new. Allocated to Croydon garage, it is seen leading General's LT 685 around the Parliament Square one-way working. The Tilling bus is on the 12A and the LGOC on 112A, both of which are interworked and are variants of the main route 12 under the convoluted numbering of the Bassom scheme.
D W K Jones

The first Tilling Regents had barely been in service for a month when new vehicles began coming off the production lines demonstrating a major change of policy with regard to the display of destination information. Gone were the destination boards from inside the front and rear windows as were the separate route number stencils including the one mounted prominently over the driver's canopy. Instead, roller blinds were provided with a simple destination display and a rather small route number side by side in rectangular boxes projecting from the bodywork front and rear and accessed from within the upper saloon. The via points were still painted on detachable boards but these were reduced in height. It is not known at what point in the production programme the change took place or whether the Tilling and Dodson factories changed over at the same time. Photographic evidence shows no. 6042 in the original form which suggests that somewhere in the region of fifty may have started work without roller blinds. All of these appear to have been converted to the later format at their first overhaul if not before.

Two further modifications took place at about the time deliveries reached the one hundred mark. One was a purely cosmetic attempt to lighten the original rather drab and heavy appearance by painting the upper deck window surrounds cream. The other came in an endeavour to improve air circulation in the upper deck which had formerly relied on inconspicuous intake grilles mounted under the roof overhang. A much more sophisticated and visible air scoop, resembling a large mouth organ, was mounted in line with the top of the central front window. Although the revised livery was quickly applied to all earlier vehicles, the new style of air intake was not fitted to those bodies delivered without it, so both styles of body could be found operating side by side right to the end.

In service, the new Regents quickly proved far superior to the ponderous and ancient looking petrol electrics once the drivers had fully mastered the intricacies of handling clutches and gearboxes. However Tilling's parsimony over horsepower would not have gone unnoticed by drivers who would have been well aware that General's STs had a little more 'poke' than their own vehicles. It was probably this unfavourable comparison that eventually led Tilling's management to specify fifteen of the September/October 1930 deliveries with 100mm engines, theoretically putting them on a par with the Generals. The outcome of the trial was 'no change', and Tilling continued to specify 95mm engines for its London fleet of Regents.

Long before the last of the 124 vehicles destined for London had been delivered in January 1931, a further batch of 62 was ordered, delivery of which followed on without a break. Meanwhile one of the last to be built under the earlier contract, 6130, was sent to operate in Brighton on 30th January 1931 and did not return until 25th June making it, as far as is known, the only one of the London fleet ever to run there. The specification for 6137-6198 (GK 6237-6298) was the same as before with bodies constructed by both Tilling and Dodson and numbered 5326-5328, 5332-5390, although new deliveries from about February 1931 onwards were fitted with fully glazed cabs and windscreen wipers to which the remainder were duly converted. Following on from 6198 came two further Brighton batches, 6199-6126 (GK 6299, GN 6200-6226) and 6227-6250 (GP 6227-6250). The first batch was bodied by Dodson and the other by Tilling, including a few built in the Brighton section's works at Hove. Yet more followed purely for Brighton use, 6255-6300 (GW 6255-6300), and by the time these entered service between January and July 1932, bringing the Brighton fleet of Regents up to 110, their body styling really did look very dated.

Tilling 6016 (ST 840) waits at the East Dulwich stand for its return to Shoreditch on route 78A, a short working of the much longer 78 through to West Wickham. The decorative moulding seen curving downwards just ahead of the badly fitting route number plate is believed to be the only feature distinguishing Tilling built bodies from those constructed by Dodson which did not have this fitment. *C F Klapper*

Its independent days over, the gold LPTB fleet number of ST 898 stands out particularly prominently against the black of the Tilling bonnet side. Having been one of the very last vehicles to be overhauled under Tiling ownership, ST 898 subsequently became one of the last to display the Tilling name which it did until October 1934. LGOC-style garage and running number plates have now replaced the originals, and the side route number plate has been replaced by the typical LGOC stencil type mounted at the foot of the window. London Transport preferred to use white on black intermediate point boards rather than vice versa, perhaps on legibility grounds. *C F Klapper*

No. 6225 (ST1023) was photographed outside Westminster Abbey working from Catford garage soon after being transferred to the London section from Brighton in April 1933, with the front board advertising Tilling's Private Hire Service. The fresh air intake at the top of the centre front window, common to all bodies built after about December 1930, is clearly seen in this view. *E G P Masterman*

When Tilling placed the order for 6137-6198, the Company also announced that five spare bodies were to be built to serve as an overhaul float. Only four are traced as actually having been built (body nos. 5511-5514) and these were all used in London. In the spring of 1933 five of the Brighton vehicles were transferred permanently to the London fleet starting with 6226 and 6227, which were plated at Scotland Yard on 13th April. They were followed by 6228 on 8th May, 6230 on 13th May and 6236 on 30th May. On arrival, it was found that they all had the more powerful 100mm version of the AEC engine, which had probably been essential for the hilly terrain encountered in Brighton. With the receipt of these five, the London fleet of Tilling STs reached its maximum of 191.

The demise of Tilling's London operation was specified within the London Passenger Transport Act and it was fully expected both at 55 Broadway and 20 Victoria Street that a takeover date of 1st August would be achieved. However failure to reach an initial agreement over the extent of transfer and huge acrimony over compensation terms meant that this date was missed, and it was not until 15th September 1933 that an Order from the Minister of Transport fixed Sunday 1st October 1933 as the Appointed Day. Passengers first learnt about it from a notice pasted on Tilling's fare-boards on 25th September. At the takeover Tilling handed over 224 licensed buses of its own (including the 191 short wheelbase Regents) plus 104 which London Transport had already owned since 1st July as well as 36 unlicensed petrol

electrics (26 belonging to Tilling and 10 to the LPTB). The 191 Regents were immediately allocated fleet numbers ST 837-1027 in exactly the same sequence as their Tilling numbering. Their bodies were numbered 13847-14037 in the order that they were carried at the time and thus not in the same sequence as their Tilling numbers, with the four bodies currently unallocated to chassis added on at the end as 14038-14041. Within a few days of takeover the new fleet numbers began to appear in gold transfers on the vehicles themselves where they stood out particularly prominently on the bonnet sides which, under Tilling's livery, were painted black. Interestingly the fleet number ST 837 had been briefly used before, mistakenly, for the first of the Tilling operated but LGOC owned 16ft 3ins wheelbase Regents delivered in October 1932, but this error was soon rectified and the vehicle was more appropriately numbered STL 51.

It had been previously agreed that only two of Tilling's properties would pass into the Board's ownership: Bull Yard and the Obelisk Works, the other two remaining with Thomas Tilling Ltd. Early on, London Transport decided that, in order to gain detailed experience of Tilling's maintenance and overhauling methods, Bull Yard would remain open for the overhauling of chassis as well as continuing to hold stores for the former Company garages at Bromley, Catford and Croydon. In fact the Bull Yard works were looking a little underused with staff working on short time owing to the comparative newness of the fleet. Of the two body shops which were not due to pass to London Transport control, Wren Road had already ceased carrying out maintenance work for the London fleet and it was arranged that, as soon as all outstanding work had been completed at Pelican Yard, this would close. All body overhauling work on the ex-Tilling fleet would henceforth be carried out at Lewisham where new body construction would cease as soon as four spare STL bodies currently being built were complete. Meanwhile all repainting carried out on former Tilling vehicles would in future be completed as near as possible to LPTB standard.

This plan was quickly changed after an inspection carried out at Bull Yard on 30th October by Frank Pick who decreed that both this and Lewisham should be shut down as soon as possible. January 3rd 1934 was duly set as the date for closure of both premises except for a token presence which would continue at Lewisham until the 8th. Thereafter all plant and machinery was to be dismantled and sent from there to Bull Yard by 25th January to render the works empty and rate free. Meanwhile the first few newly overhauled STs to emerge from the former Tilling works did so wearing their old livery style, repainting of them having commenced prior to the takeover, although GENERAL fleet names were now carried. The first to appear in full LPTB red and grey livery is recorded as ST 905 on 19th October 1933. As the time approached for the closure of the Tilling overhaul shops the intake of vehicles slowed, with the last two ST chassis entering Bull Yard late in December; ST 949 on the 27th and ST 952 on the 29th. Four bodies still remained at Lewisham at the start of 1934 from which they emerged newly overhauled on 9th January (ST 952), the 11th (ST 955, 957) and, last of all, ST 949 on the 12th. The works then closed permanently, a few days later than planned. At the end, the long established Tilling system had ceased to function smoothly and it had been necessary to bring overhauled chassis across from Chiswick in order to get ST 955 and 957 back on the road.

The first complete Tilling ST to emerge newly overhauled from Chiswick was ST 951 on 19th January 1934. To achieve Chiswick style flexibility of chassis overhauling, three buses were removed from the licensed fleet to form a float in January and February 1934, those initially selected being ST 975, 976, 991. Armed with spare chassis and a body float which stood temporarily at seven units, it had become possible by the end of February to emulate with the Tilling STs the long established LGOC practice whereby each bus could theoretically emerge from overhaul on the same day as it went in, or at least within two or three days of it.

Running concurrently with the overhaul programme were a couple of improvement schemes, one of which was to the

An odd man out with a vengeance, Croydon's ST 839 was photographed at the Black Horse, Addiscombe terminus of route 12 on 21st May 1939, eighteen months after making its debut in its revised form. Peering through the lower deck windows, the two-tone STL-style interior colour scheme can be clearly seen. *J Bonell*

driver's cab and notably the windscreen, and another was to replace the air bells with electrically operated ones. On the mechanical side, Frank Pick agreed with the Transport & General Workers' Union on 31st October 1933 to fit anti-backfire starting handles as quickly as possible to bring the STs in line with ex-LGOC vehicles. What the Union really wanted, however, was for self starters to be fitted, work which began with Catford's ST 989 on 26th February 1934. When in position, the self starters and other modifications added 7cwt to the weight of each vehicle which would probably have been even greater had the rear bumpers not been removed at the same time. Perhaps unwisely, management promised that every bus would be fitted with a self starter by 1st October 1934 without first ensuring that an adequate supply of these could be obtained in time. When 1st October came and only 14 out of 88 vehicles at Bromley garage had been dealt with (this figure included T and STL types as well as STs), a one day strike ensued. The programme was finally completed on the STs on 25th October.

Under the LGOC engineering structure to which the Tilling garages were transferred in 1934 much greater efficiency was expected, and the number of spare buses at the three garages was reduced from 10% to 8% to produce a substantial saving of six STs. Better performance was expected on the road too, and to achieve this the LPTB set about replacing the 5.52 litre engines on the STs fitted with them – all except 20 in fact – with 6.26 litre units common in the main ST fleet, a task which had been completed by the end of 1936. This was followed, during 1937/38, by the fitting of triple servo braking systems to the roughly half of the class not already so equipped.

Under London Transport auspices the Tilling STs led a remarkably static existence for the remainder of the pre-war era, and though inter-garage transfers inevitably occurred, these never took the vehicles beyond the former Tilling trio of garages. However by the middle of the decade it was already becoming increasingly apparent that there was a problem with the bodywork leading to an ever increasing number of distorted and sagging waistrails. These were found right across the Tilling ST fleet irrespective of where the bodies had been built and almost certainly indicated a defect in the actual design rather than in the materials used or the standards of workmanship. It is interesting to note that in Brighton, where Tilling reorganised its operations under the title of Brighton, Hove & District Omnibus Company Ltd in November 1935, the same problem was tackled by completely rebodying a number of vehicles, 16 of its Tilling STs being dealt with by 1936/37 followed by many more during the war.

London Transport did not envisage carrying out such a drastic solution. Instead its experimental department took the matter in hand and devised a scheme for rebuilding the lower deck structure to a stronger format. On 6th October 1937 it removed body 14006 from ST 1008 which had just arrived at Chiswick for overhaul, and commenced what amounted to a complete reconstruction of the lower saloon. When it emerged as ST 839 just over six weeks later, on 20th November, it had been transformed into one of the most odd looking hybrids that London had ever seen. Not content with just strengthening the Tilling body, keeping its original shape with odd minor modifications, the experimental shop had produced a replica of the current STL lower body structure, albeit retaining a six bay layout to match up with the original Tilling underframe. Both inside and outside, all the current STL features were there including the standard windscreen with its gentle lower curve and even, on the offside, the streamlined extension to the front mudguard so typical of the class. In total contrast, the upper deck remained pure Tilling and the original outside staircase was still there completely unaltered.

It probably came as no surprise to anyone that ST 839 remained a complete one-off, with no further attempts being made to extend the lifespan of the Tilling bodies in such a drastic and unrealistic way. In all probability, when the result of the experiment was reviewed, the expense that the conversion inevitably incurred was deemed unjustifiable on vehicles which, with outside staircases and thus basically obsolete anyway, could only have a limited life span ahead of them. Instead the Tilling STs were pencilled in for disposal as soon as practicable as part of the ongoing fleet renewal programme. Meanwhile a scheme was put in hand to help drivers by repositioning the side lights from the canopy to the conventional position much lower down, but this was tackled in a half-hearted way and many vehicles still remained to be dealt with when war broke out.

On 1st August 1939 an influx of diesel STLs into Catford resulted in the start of what was expected to be a phased withdrawal of the whole fleet of Tilling STs. Eighteen of them, selected from amongst those with the 'oldest' overhaul dates, were delicensed and parked up in Chiswick tram depot pending disposal. It was fully anticipated that all 191 would have left the fleet well before the end of 1940 but history was,

of course, destined to change the whole scheme of things following the onset of war just over a month later. Eventually all except two of the eighteen had to be reinstated to cover wartime emergencies leaving the unfortunate pair, ST 853 and ST 876, to share the doubtful honour along with ex-independent ST 1028 (see chapter 13) of being the only members of the ST class to end their public service career through natural causes before the outbreak of war.

On 2nd September 1939, just one day before war was declared, a number of Tilling STs were transferred away from their home territory for the very first time. Sixteen were involved, all Catford based ones, and the Country area was their destination with nine going to Northfleet, four to Swanley and three to East Grinstead. As with the ex-LGOC STs dispatched south temporarily from Old Kent Road as recorded in the last chapter, their purpose was to fulfil evacuation and other war related duties. The war, and the austerity years that followed it, were to see many Tilling STs reprieved from the early demise that had been planned for them, in some cases with a stay of execution that lasted for almost ten years, more than doubling their originally expected lifespan.

The last new route to be introduced before the outbreak of war was the 119 on 9th August 1939. Worked from Bromley garage, it provided a new link between Hayes and West Wickham on its journey between Bromley North and Croydon. Seen in Hayes, ST 984 was typical of the rolling stock on the 119 in the closing days of the pre-war era. By 1936 the side lights on the Tilling vehicles had been lowered by a few inches and are now fixed to the front of the driver's canopy instead of being above it. *C F Klapper*

CHAPTER 12
CENTRAL BUSES 1933-1939

Saturday 1st July 1933 was a momentous date in London's transport history when the London Passenger Transport Board came into being charged with the task of providing "an adequate and properly co-ordinated system of passenger transport" within the London area. On 18th September it adopted the abbreviated title 'London Transport' as the public face of the organisation which, from May 1934, was also used as a fleet name on all its rolling stock. This was the start of an era of monopoly in the provision of road passenger services within the Metropolitan Police District augmented by extensive rights of compulsory purchase beyond its boundaries, a position which placed the new Board heavily in the public spotlight for there was no-one else to blame if anything

went wrong. Its extremely strong management team led by Lord Ashfield and Frank Pick, supported by very able senior management inherited mostly from the Underground group and the London County Council, led London Transport through its glorious years in the nineteen-thirties when the eyes of the world were upon it and transport authorities from many countries came to learn how things were done. There were detractors, of course, such as the Communist Party of Great Britain who loudly demanded that the whole Board should be sacked, but often these were politically motivated and their efforts in no way deflected London Transport from the major attempts at service co-ordination and the massive modernisation schemes that it successfully carried out.

The decision to retain GENERAL as the fleet name in the early days of the LPTB was perhaps unfortunate as it gave the incorrect impression that nothing much had changed. Apart from the revised wording on the legal ownership panel, this is how things would have looked to passengers boarding Holloway's ST 273 in Hampstead Garden Suburb. In fact the vehicle had already been modified by the removal of the tester's tip-up seat upon overhaul in December 1933. In contrast to the earlier paucity of information on ST destination blinds, every road travelled by route 608 on its short 25 minute run between Archway and Golders Green is now listed. *L T Museum*

The Board's road services were provided by three distinct departments: Central Buses, Country Buses & Coaches, and Trams & Trolleybuses, and the whole of the LGOC's STs, with which this chapter deals, was merged into the first of these. In fact, apart from the new legal ownership details which appeared on all vehicles within the first few days, there was little initial sign on the vehicles themselves that anything had changed. They were still run by the old LGOC management and still carried the GENERAL fleet name. The bus purchasing programme inherited from the LGOC continued unabated with new STLs arriving in service at an average rate of 17 per month for the rest of 1933 and with inevitable repercussions on the STs. In most instances STs were not directly replaced by new vehicles but by consequential transfers of LTs and NSs, but the result was that by 4th October 1933 Forest Gate had lost all its STs with Hammersmith following suit by 18th December.

An early manifestation of the LPTB's monopoly position was the absorption of the Potters Bar based Overground fleet on 7th July 1933, bringing its 27 STs under the same control as the remainder, whilst the takeover of Thomas Tilling's services on 1st October was followed by the transferring-in to the ex-Tilling garage at Catford of no fewer than 31 LGOC type STs between 10th October and 5th December to replace obsolete open top petrol electrics. Every one of these STs came direct from overhaul at Chiswick and they would have made an interesting comparison with Tilling's own outside staircase Regents which had now been numbered in the ST class.

Not a single year elapsed during the remainder of the nineteen-thirties without a garage somewhere on Central Buses either receiving STs for the first time or losing them all, such was the constant state of flux. In some instances a garage that had lost all its STs got some back either during or after the war, but not in every case. Sometimes, as had happened in LGOC days, garages would gain and lose STs all within the same year, this being Battersea's experience when seven arrived in July and departed in October 1934. However the biggest event of 1934 came right at the start of the year on 17th January when, in one of the grand reallocations of which the LGOC had been so fond, all 45 of Upton Park's STs departed overnight (on paper, at least, but it may have taken a few days to achieve) to a host of other garages. Twenty-four LTs were lost too, the replacements for all of these being ex-independent TD class Leyland Titans most of which still carried a miscellany of liveries and fleet names. Croydon was a second ex-Tilling garage to receive standard STs with 11 arriving in April, though none ever reached the third of the Tilling garages, Bromley, until after the outbreak of war. Enfield gained STs as replacements for single deck LTs on 4th July 1934 whilst Tottenham received its first, in place of STLs, during August.

On Turnham Green's ST 289 the tester's seat is still clearly in position as it passes tram track removal work in Richmond Road, Kingston on 8th August 1933. When the seat is removed at the next overhaul the tax disc holders accompanying it will be moved too, into the driver's cab. The tramway to Ham Common had last been used on 2nd May 1931 and was never converted to trolleybuses. *John Aldridge collection*

84

This was the period in which several small physical changes were made to the STs to bring them to the condition in which they would remain for the bulk of their lifespan. Starting in November 1933, or possibly even a little earlier, their fixed starting handles were removed and replaced by detachable sprung type ones carried in a wooden block on the cab floor just to the right of the footbrake, with a fastener to keep the handle in position. A constant problem for the LGOC had been drivers who would not ensure that the handle was secured by the leather strap provided, allowing it to obscure part of the registration plate and thereby rendering the Company liable to prosecution; this was now effectively overcome. At about the same time, removal began upon overhaul of the tester's tip-up seat from above the autovac tank and its associated safety strap now that these were no longer officially required. From about July 1934 removal of the back bumpers commenced, their simple replacement being a pair of raised mouldings at the foot of the rear panel adequate for cyclists – who commonly enjoyed travelling in the slipstream of a bus – and others to bump up against. No great hurry seems to have been attached to the bumper removal with some lasting in use well into 1936, and the same was the case with the replacement of the original water filler cap by a flatter type which similarly took a couple of years or more to achieve.

All of the above changes involved every vehicle, but one particular modification carried out on overhaul from about July 1934 onwards was confined solely to STs carrying bodies of the camel back style. A common complaint from the travelling public was that the lettering on the wooden boards listing intermediate points – which had themselves been provided as an afterthought – could not be read at night as no illumination was provided. To put this right, a programme was commenced of attaching a somewhat ungainly looking lamp to the front pillar above the board which was linked to the vehicle's lighting system and shone down upon it at night. As a modification to the vehicle's wiring was involved this was not an entirely straightforward operation, although with only 11 vehicles to be dealt with it did not impact anywhere near as strongly on the ST class as it did on the LTs of which there were 358 camel backs.

An experiment, which may have been initiated in a small way by the LGOC as early as October 1932, was expanded to a more meaningful level in 1934, possibly embracing up to as many as fifteen standard STs. Each was fitted with the smallest version of the AEC 6-cylinder petrol engine with bore of only 95mm, rated at about 5.5 litres. This engine was used by Thomas Tilling on the bulk of its London STs, and presumably the Board's engineers wished to test the feasibility of employing it on a wider scale. A number of garages were involved but principally Elmers End, Harrow Weald and Willesden. The results of the trial have not survived, but it appears to have ceased by March 1935.

In LGOC days the Company had pursued a policy of transferring services outside the Metropolitan Police District to its country subsidiaries whose costs were lower, and this was continued by London Transport with route 370 (Romford–Grays) which, until the abandonment of the Bassom route numbering system on 3rd October 1934, had been known as the G1. Country Buses had, in any case, been present on the route since 1st August 1933 having taken over Eastern National's former workings. The date selected was 5th December 1934 and, in circumstances that were to remain unique, three STs that had operated on it in Central Bus days were temporarily loaned to the Country Bus department to continue their same employment. The losing garage was Hornchurch (the former Romford recently renamed) and the vehicles concerned were ST 175, 374 and 399. They spent almost six months at Grays where they continued to operate in standard red and grey livery, returning to the Central Bus department on 28th May 1935 where they joined the large ST contingent at Turnham Green.

At about this time Hornchurch garage was building up a fleet of its own instead of being dependent on Seven Kings to supply its rolling stock, which effectively brought the allocation of STs to Seven Kings itself to an end. Similarly, at an unknown date during the mid-thirties, the other suburban garages at Edgware and Uxbridge became self-supporting units too. In a continuation of LGOC practice, garages continued to be arranged for purposes of docking and major repairs into groups of two or three with one in each group nominated as the 'parent shed' where all the major work was carried out, but each had its own specific vehicle allocation and the former practice of treating a few smaller ones as outstations was never again pursued.

March and April 1935 found Streatham garage in receipt of a substantial number of STs for a second time, having lost its last ones in 1932, and by June 1935 Tottenham had lost all the STs received less than a year earlier and was not destined to get any more until 1938. 1936 saw Twickenham garage's first STs arrive on 29th April and depart again on 6th May, while 15 of the class at Putney Bridge lasted just a little longer, from 4th March until they gradually drifted away in July. Two closely related southern garages, Elmers End and Nunhead, both lost all their STs on 29th April, whilst the two former Tilling garages, Catford and Croydon, had both lost all their standard STs by 1st December 1936. STs were now being concentrated in larger batches at a smaller number of garages, and in 1937 this resulted in Hendon losing its last ones in May followed by Enfield in October. Contrary to this, 14 returned to Hendon in November 1938, only to depart again by May 1939, while Tottenham rejoined the ranks of ST users with a fairly substantial batch of 22 in October 1938, five months after Catford had begun receiving a further intake in May.

Top left Photographed primarily to show the fine green passenger shelter, of which London Transport erected many throughout its territory, West Green's ST 334 was far from its north London home in Shooters Hill Road on its way to Welling. By March 1935, when this photograph was taken, the GENERAL fleet name was fast disappearing. ST 334 has acquired a new filler cap, but the back bumper is still clearly in place as is the starting handle which, in this instance, is strapped up – as it is supposed to be – to prevent it from partly obscuring the registration plate. *L T Museum*

Left September 1935, and ST 294 stands at Victoria terminus with its conductor apparently attending to the back destination display. Inter-garage loans were very common at this time and, though operating from Tottenham garage, ST 294 belongs to West Green which, under the engineering arrangements in force at the time, was – along with Enfield – a subsidiary to Tottenham where all major dockings and repairs were carried out. *G H F Atkins*

On 23rd May 1936 Turnham Green's ST 61 made the news when it was hit side-on by a lorry just outside Leatherhead, causing it to topple over, slightly injuring several passengers. The assembled crowd enjoyed a rare opportunity to study the underside of an ST while arrangements were in hand to get it uprighted. The damage to ST 61 was not great and it was back in service within a few days. *Ken Blacker collection*

A visit to Uxbridge garage on 22nd September 1936 shows the Spartan nature of the structure with only primitive pit facilities on hand. Larger vehicles, such as T 4 (on the far left) and ST 765, were supplied from the parent garage at Hounslow, the only vehicles officially allocated to Uxbridge being a few small Dennis Darts such as DA 6 and DA 13, although in this instance DA 13 (the right hand one of the pair) is also on loan from Hounslow. *L T Museum*

Caught up in the ever changing allocation of STs was Enfield garage which had some on books between July 1934 and October 1937 when new STLs replaced them. ST 772 was seen on 23rd January 1937 negotiating overflow waters from the River Lea in Hall Lane, Chingford. *Alan Nightingale collection*

1937 saw in increase of two in the size of the Central Bus ST fleet. This came about after the Country Bus department agreed to release them in exchange for two double-deck Q-types (Q 2, 3) which had been operating since 1935 from Middle Row garage on route 52 to test their suitability on a central London service. Despite their modern appearance, the position of the entrance ahead of the front wheels on the Qs is alleged to have resulted in constant confusion at busy stops which would not be a problem on country area work. Two one-time National STs were selected for the swap, ST 819 and 820 being sent to Chiswick works for overhaul and conversion on 7th June 1937 from Windsor and Hatfield garages respectively. Whilst at Chiswick they were equipped with Central Bus standard indicators and winding gear at front and rear and were repainted in red livery before being sent for service at Holloway on the 22nd (ST 820) and 23rd June (ST 819). As with all former ex-National STs, their original bodies and chassis were kept together at this and subsequent overhauls, but to all outward purposes they now looked identical to all other standard STs in the Central Bus fleet.

This was a time of great change. As well as the huge numbers of new STLs flooding into service – 798 in 1937/38 alone – the STDs were making their impressive mark at Hendon. STs directly swept away the last NSs – from West Green garage – on the night of 30th November 1937, and although they were not immediately involved, STs were still a major force in the fleet when the last DL class Dennis Lances were ousted just ahead of the NSs and when the first concerted effort to remove the TD class Leyland Titans in the closing days of 1937. Such had been the transformation that, within only five years from the formation of London Transport, the STs had moved from being one of the more modern types in the fleet to one of the oldest and most outdated, with the planned start of withdrawals not far off. The withdrawal plan envisaged the outside staircase Tilling and independent STs going first, and none of the ST class was expected to remain within the fleet beyond the end of 1941.

An interesting experiment, well ahead of its time, was the automatic bus recording trial carried out on route 44. A series of photographs was taken on 12th March 1938 to show the roof-mounted induction coil fitted to some of Holloway's STs and the overhead receiving coil beneath which they passed when entering Victoria bus station. The conductors of both ST 496 and ST 103 appear to have been asked to pose – rather self-consciously as it turned out – on the platform. In the case of ST 103 it looks as though a thorough washdown with soap would not come amiss to remove the ingrained dirt from the upper panels.
L T Museum

The Board's quest for modernity led it to conduct an interesting if low key experiment which is thought to have begun towards the end of 1937. A notable feature of its tram and trolleybus operations was the series of recording clocks which could be found in various public places, most notably in the foyer of 55 Broadway, and also within depots, showing on paper clock dials the passage of vehicles past certain contact points and illustrating graphically any bunching or gaps appearing in service. With their immediate contact through skates on the electrical supply, the provision of this information was a relatively simple matter on trams and trolleybuses, but the Board now wished to investigate extending the principle to motor buses even though these were remote from any electrical source. The method adopted to achieve this was to harness direct induction between a coil placed on the bus and a receiving coil fixed at the recording point above (or under) the roadway, the connection between the receiving coil and the office where the printer would be kept being via the telephone wires. A service trial was planned on route 44, a short self-contained operation between the main line stations at King's Cross and Victoria worked by STs from Holloway garage, which had the advantage that a receiving coil could be strung across the Board's own roadway at the entrance to Victoria bus station, avoiding the need to involve local authorities in the experiment. A minimum of eight STs was required to be equipped to cover the basic service plus a few more to cover for maintenance requirements, so probably up to a dozen were kitted out for the experiment, but with identities changing upon overhaul it has not been possible to determine exactly how many were done. A cast aluminium case carried inside each bus carried the receiving transformer and condensers, the current from the transformer being carried to the transmitting coil mounted on the roof which was about 4ft square and could just be seen from certain positions at ground level.

The experiment continued throughout the whole of 1938, but by the December of that year the Board had begun seeking a way of reducing the costs associated with developing it further, perhaps to the extent of individual vehicle recognition. The General Electric Company was approached but showed no interest in proceeding with commercial research on such a project, and with air raid and other war related precautions now on the agenda, this was probably not a propitious time to pursue the matter further. The experiment appears to have ceased early in 1939 but no documentation survives to show exactly when. The experimental equipment was removed from the buses except that, in the case of a couple of STs, the transmitting coil remained on the roof and could occasionally be glimpsed for the next ten years as a reminder of what might have been.

In view of the short residual life span planned for them, it was perhaps a little surprising that a limited programme was started in 1938 of modernising a number of vehicles with flush panelling on the lower deck and, in some cases at least, with modern STL-style brown, yellow and pale green interior décor instead of the uniform drab allover grey into which most of the Central Bus ST interiors had now descended. From the start the reconditioning scheme was focused much more strongly on the generally similar LT bodies rather than STs, but six of the latter are known to have been dealt with between July and October 1938. Rebuilding continued for several months beyond this but only on LTs, and it is presumed that the order had gone out to cease further work on STs as this was not financially worthwhile.

A livery simplification towards the end of 1938 saw the elimination of the black surround to the driver's cab as well as the black line under the lower saloon windows. A November 1938 recipient of the revised colour scheme was Hounslow's ST 651, seen here on temporary loan to Staines Country Bus garage for what is probably a bank holiday working to Burnham Beeches. The temporary masking of the destination box presages the widescale implementation of this measure a couple of years later as part of the wartime economy drive. *J F Higham*

In 1939 a further minor modification to the livery resulted in the whole of the front bulkhead being painted red. More noticeable was the blanking-out of the staircase window, a feature quickly adopted on the whole ST fleet. ST 664, a June 1939 overhaul, stands at Edgware where the north colonnade of the once handsome station building has been demolished as part of the planned extension of the Northern Line. ST 664, formerly on Hendon's books, had become a permanent fixture at Edgware when this garage finally received an allocation of double deckers in its own right. *C F Klapper*

A more positive updating programme for the Central Bus STs was strongly implemented in 1938. At the start of the year 153 out of the original 300 built with single servo braking systems were still in this form, although changes of identity at overhaul meant that those still with single servos now occupied fleet numbers haphazardly throughout the whole range between ST 7 and ST 835. In a crash programme between January and July, with a few stragglers beyond then until October, all had their braking systems improved to the now standard triple servo arrangement. This work was carried out with a minimum of interruption as part of the overhaul process on about two thirds of them, but the vehicles not scheduled for overhaul during this period had to be called to Chiswick specifically for the work to be carried out.

With cost saving high on the agenda, a simplification of the bus livery was introduced towards the end of 1938 when the driver's cab window surrounds and the ledge below the lower deck windows ceased to be picked out in black. A couple of months later a further small modification was made by painting the whole of the nearside bulkhead panel red instead of picking out the window surround in grey. Also at about

this time the use of raised metal fleet numbers ceased on the bonnet cover with more conventional gold transfers being used instead. None of these changes proved detrimental to the appearance of the vehicles; in fact they probably achieved an improvement in giving a less fussy overall appearance.

January 1st 1939 heralded the official loss of one seat on the former LGOC STs when they were downgraded overnight to 48-seaters. The only exceptions were the two built with experimental staircases which had now become known as ST 195 and ST 294. The former was the one with the camel back style body and this had been modified since new and was now only a 50-seater following the removal of one of the single seats from the upper deck. The big changeover was merely a money saving device to bring the vehicles into a lower taxation category, and no immediate physical change was made except to amend the sign above the back seat on the upper deck to show that it was now intended for only 4 passengers instead of 5. Later, however, some received small armrests at each end of the long seat to physically restrict its seating potential.

By late summer 1939 war with Germany had become

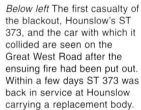

In 1937/38 the traditional square Metropolitan Police stage carriage plates were replaced by much smaller oval-shaped ones as illustrated here on ST 50. Deep in Country Bus territory, it stands at the Leatherhead terminus of route 65. In front of ST 50, in two-tone Country green livery, is Leyland Cub C 52 working a 462 local journey to Fetcham.
L T Museum

Below left The first casualty of the blackout, Hounslow's ST 373, and the car with which it collided are seen on the Great West Road after the ensuing fire had been put out. Within a few days ST 373 was back in service at Hounslow carrying a replacement body.

inevitable. Long drawn up plans for evacuation of women, children, the sick and vulnerable, and movement of troops and of essential medical and other personnel to their war stations were now activated, and on Friday 1st September blackout regulations were introduced. On the same day, in readiness for the evacuation work which they were to perform and in anticipation of the probable withdrawal of the Green Line network, many double deckers were temporarily transferred to Country area garages to augment their existing fleets. Although STs were not generally included within these arrangements, Old Kent Road garage dispatched 17 to garages in the southern country area, three each to Dartford, Dunton Green and Crawley, and no fewer than eight to Reigate. As if in an omen of things to come, Hounslow's ST 373 was involved in a collision with a car on the Great West Road during the very first evening of the blackout whilst doing evacuation work, and its body was completely burnt out in the fire that ensued. The body was quickly replaced and the bus promptly returned to service, the first of many such urgent body replacements that were to happen in the war years that lay ahead.

CHAPTER 13
'PIRATE' REGENTS – ST 1028-1031

Almost immediately after it came into being, the London Passenger Transport Board turned its attention towards acquiring the 51 independent bus companies scheduled for compulsory acquisition under section 5 of the London Passenger Transport Act; the legendary 'pirate' operators that the LGOC had regarded with scorn for the past decade. On 14th July 1933 a letter went out to the owners of each of them requesting detailed information on every aspect of their business in order to enable the acquisition process to commence and to determine the subsequent compensation to be paid. A great deal of feverish work went on at 55 Broadway to study accounts, contracts and staff details of each operator, whilst physical inspections had to be made to ascertain the extent and condition of their rolling stock, premises and spares holdings. Despite the immensity of the task, the first round of acquisitions was ready to take place on Wednesday 1st November 1933, just four months after the Board's inauguration.

From 1929 onwards the independents had invested quite heavily in modern double-deck rolling stock and especially in Leyland Titan TD1s and TD2s of which they had collectively amassed an impressive total of 118 (plus a further 12 Titan 'Specials' owned by the City Motor Omnibus Company based on the very similar Tiger TS3 chassis). Insignificant in comparison, the number of AEC Regents which passed into the Board's ownership amounted to a mere ten of which four were of the short, 15ft 6½in wheelbase variety and were absorbed into the ST class. The remainder became STLs. There had been no reluctance on the part of AEC to sell to the 'pirates', and the latters' clear preference for the Titan was no doubt partly influenced by the fact that it had come on the market first, but undoubtedly its main selling point was its cheaper list price of £1,075 (though this was subject to negotiation) compared with £1,125 for the Regent. Another point in the Titan's favour was its reputation for being slightly more economical in fuel consumption. The only other real contender to the Titan and Regent was the Dennis Lance, but only eight of these were purchased by London independents.

All four ex-independent STs entered the Board's stock in November 1933, receiving fleet numbers ST 1028-1031 following on from the substantial batch recently acquired from Tilling. ST 1028 and 1029 came with the very first acquisitions on 1st November when ten operators were absorbed, whilst ST 1030 and 1031 arrived just over a week later, on Friday 10th November, which was the second major takeover date. They came from four different operators and inevitably each one had distinctive characteristics of its own.

This manufacturer's photograph depicts Chariot's brand new Regent in all its pristine glory before entering service. Fully signwritten at Birch's works with advertisements and destination information, there is even a slip board above the autovac tank proclaiming that the bus serves two of the major department stores of the time, Whiteleys and Selfridges. Lamps are fitted to both front dome and driver's canopy to illuminate the route information and the driver's cab is completely unglazed.

Reviewing the four in fleet number order, the first and theoretically the oldest was ST 1028 with AEC chassis number 661362. It had, however, been preceded into service by ST 1031 with the much later chassis number 661771. Registered GJ 8501 and licensed for service on 16th June 1930, ST 1028's origins pose something of a mystery because its chassis was diverted from the middle of the LGOC's first big batch within which it had already been allocated fleet number ST 154. The exact circumstance under which this vehicle, alone, was diverted to another operator, and to one of the LGOC's competitors, will probably never be known, but the chassis certainly carried all the signs of having been destined for the LGOC even to the extent of the positioning of its batteries and the nearside location of its petrol tank.

The owner of GJ 8501 was Chariot Omnibus Services Ltd of Shepherds Bush. Chariot's registered office was the Goldhawk Garage at 165 Goldhawk Road, which was where the vehicle was garaged. This was, in fact, a petrol filling station on the corner of Brackenbury Road owned by Tankard & Smith Ltd and it was also home to Chariot's only other bus, a 1924 Dennis which was demoted to use as spare vehicle upon arrival of the Regent and was one of the few Dennis 4-tonners to pass into LPTB ownership still on solid tyres.

Chariot's owner, Ernest Davison, bought GJ 8501 for £1,939, having negotiated a price of £1,219 with AEC for the chassis plus £720 to Birch Brothers Ltd who constructed the 56-seat outside staircase body at their works in Cathcart Road, Kentish Town. In fact Davison paid well above the usual list price for the Regent chassis, perhaps because he was in a hurry and wanted quick delivery, and this may give a clue as to why the LGOC was happy to acquiesce in forgoing it in the knowledge that a replacement could easily be scheduled on the production line at a later date.

The Birch body was based on that manufacturer's standard 5-bay layout and incorporated the Company's quirky arrangement whereby the pillars on the lower deck were not in line with the ones above, a clear indication that the two sections of body were built independently. Styling features distinct to Birch were the shallower than normal windows on each deck and a notable downward tilt to the front of the driver's canopy, the latter being claimed as offering improved weather protection where no windscreen was fitted as well as reducing sun glare. As built, the cab was completely open, although it had been enclosed with the fitting of a windscreen and side glasses by 1932. The shallowness of the windows was emphasised by the use of continuous metal rain strips on both decks

A busy traffic scene finds Chariot's Regent recently repainted and with its freshly whitened tyres showing just the first traces of scuffing. The mud splash arrangement attached to the back mudguard has a very make-do-and-mend air and blends badly with the general appearance of the vehicle. *Omnibus Society collection*

and GJ 8501 was relatively unusual for a London 'pirate' bus in having half drop windows throughout in preference to the more normal full drop type. The upstairs front three-window arrangement was typical of most independent double deckers with half drops provided in the two outer panes through which it was possible for the conductor to change the route number and destination boards, both of which were located in the centre window and illuminated from outside, the route number from above and the destination from below. GJ 8501 carried the red and white livery plus silver roof favoured latterly by the majority of the remaining independents, with the fleet name CHARIOT emblazoned in gold boldly on the sides copying – as did many of the 'pirates' – the style favoured by General on which the first and last letters were larger than the underlined ones in the centre.

At its second overhaul in June 1932, Chariot seriously considered transforming the vehicle by grafting an enclosed back end on to it. Birch offered this as a form of conversion kit which a number of independents took up, and Ernest Davison was given a quotation of £78 to undertake this work, including complete repainting of the vehicle. He declined the offer which was, perhaps, fortunate as Birch's similar work on other vehicles subsequently proved structurally unsound and had to be removed.

ST 1029, which was also taken over on 1st November, was a slightly newer vehicle, having been licensed as VX 7487 on 4th September 1930 by Frederick Kirk, a one-time LGOC employee, of 109 Mildenhall Road, Clapton, who used the fleet name Empire. Kirk's was the archetypal one-man one-bus business, with the bus being paid for through a monthly hire purchase agreement and there being almost no other assets to speak of. A weekly rental secured a place for it in the Empress Garage at Canal Sidings, Cambridge Heath and all maintenance work on it was carried out there. The Empress Garage was the property of Empress Motors Ltd, another London 'pirate' operator which, after its buses had succumbed to the LPTB, continued to be a highly successful coaching business that continues to the time of writing.

VX 7487 looked very different from the rather spindly Chariot Regent, thanks to its more solid and substantial 6-bay bodywork supplied by Dodson. A 54-seater (30 upstairs and 24 down), the complete vehicle weighed in at 5 tons 19cwt 3qrs, substantially more than the 5 tons 10cwt 0qrs of Birch bodied GJ 8501. It was also a faster vehicle, having the 110mm version of AEC's 6-cylinder petrol engine compared with the less lively if more economical 100mm variant on the Chariot bus. In normal Dodson fashion full drop windows surmounted by glass louvres were used on both decks, and for the benefit of the driver an opening windscreen was fitted although the sides of the cab were left unglazed to comply with Public Carriage Office requirements.

Frederick Kirk's Empire Regent carried the fairly sturdy six-bay type of Dodson body favoured by many London independents, albeit more usually found on a Leyland Titan chassis. VX 7487's passengers wait patiently in Hoe Street, Walthamstow, while its driver appears to be having a chat with an acquaintance. Although the only Empire bus, it carries fleet number 2. *J F Higham*

When the third Regent, ST 1030, entered the Board's fleet on 10th November it was seen to be structurally and mechanically almost identical to ST 1029. In fact Pro Bono Publico's VX 7553 carried the next chassis number to VX 7487 (VX 7487 – 661109; VX 7553 – 661110), and their unladen weights and engine specifications were identical. Unusual in being a pair of Regents amongst a sea of Titans, there is a suspicion that the two east London operators colluded to order them together, perhaps to receive minor reductions in price. The only real difference was that the Pro Bono Publico vehicle seated one passenger fewer at 53 (30 up and 23 down). It was also visually more attractive in carrying a handsome brown and cream livery complete with ornate lining-out whereas the Empire vehicle was in the more prosaic red and white. Pro Bono Publico's new Regent was licensed for service on 11th September 1930, exactly one week after the Empire bus had taken to the road. A year later, and again in common with the Empire Regent, it had been fitted with glazed cab sides now that these were permitted by the Metropolitan Police.

Pro Bono Publico Ltd was controlled by another ex-LGOC man, John Frederick Brown, and all shares in the Company were held by the Brown family. Its operation was double the size of that of Empire, comprising a fleet of two which were garaged in the premises of Whittington, Cox & Company at 736 Lea Bridge Road, Leyton. VX 7553's companion vehicle was an elderly Dennis 4-tonner until April 1932 when a second modern double decker was bought. However the Company's experience with VX 7553 was obviously not sufficiently encouraging to convince it that another Regent was desirable, and when brand new Dodson bodied EV 5860 arrived it was based on a Leyland TD2 chassis.

Pro Bono Publico's Regent carried the same type of Dodson body as one supplied to Empire, but its appearance was enhanced by gold lining-out. In original form VX 7553 was provided with a windscreen but both sides of the cab were left completely open. The underside of the tester's tip-up seat is used to proclaim that the vehicle goes "To and From Essex County Ground". *J M Aldridge collection*

Edward Gilchrist's brand new Pembroke Regent displays clearly the droopy cab line associated with Birch-built bodies. Six months later GJ 3020 was back at the coachbuilders for the lower deck framework to be strengthened. An unusual styling feature is that the front tyre is picked out in white whereas, at the back, it is the wheel itself and not the tyre that is painted white.

The highest numbered of the independent STs, 1031, had in fact been the first of the four to enter service in London, on 8th May 1930, and it was the only one based south of the Thames. GJ 3020 was the sole vehicle in the Pembroke fleet and its owner was Edward Gilchrist Hope whose office address was 143 Railton Road, Herne Hill. He garaged his bus in the haulage contractor's yard of J J Wise & Son at 43 Effra Road, Brixton. Until shortly before the arrival of GJ 3020, Hope had traded in partnership with George Frith, and the two of them had jointly scoured the market to find a suitable new double decker as a replacement for their ageing Dennis. They had seriously considered the merits and prices of the Leyland Titan and Daimler CF6 before deciding to go for a Regent with 56-seat Birch bodywork.

The body on the Pembroke bus displayed several of the same typical Birch features as the one on Chariot's Regent including the high waist rail, non-aligning pillars and downward curved front canopy. However it lacked the narrow but prominent lower deck waistrail of the Chariot, carried full rather than half-drop windows on each deck, and was equipped with a windscreen but no side glasses. Inside, the fairly shallow windows combined with plentiful use of polished wood and high backed leather seats all served to give an air of opulent cosiness. With an unladen weight of only 5 tons 7cwt 0qrs, this 56-seater was the lightest of the four independent STs, and it shared with ST 1028 the use of the lower powered 100mm engine. The lightness of weight may have indicated a flimsiness in bodywork construction, and as early as 24th November 1930 GJ 3020 was back at Birch's for alterations to be carried out. When the vehicle returned to service it was apparent that the lower deck had been rebuilt to a much more substantial format, completely new and much more substantial waistrails having been installed of a type which precluded the continued use of full-drop windows, the latter having been replaced with 'Quicktho' half-drops. The upper deck, however, remained unaltered.

GJ 3020 faced stiff competition on route 184 and was only lightly loaded as it set out from Southall on its way to Oxford Circus. Looking a little dowdy, it demonstrated clearly the half-drop windows fitted to the lower saloon during its reconstruction in November/December 1930. The cab sides remained unglazed through to London Transport days.
J F Higham

London Transport's November 1933 acquisitions were made in such haste that it was impossible immediately to assimilate the acquired vehicles, staff and scheduled operations into its main fleet, so arrangements had to be made with the former proprietors to continue running their businesses exactly as before until an orderly transfer could be arranged. They were each paid an agreed weekly salary for this purpose, the amount of which depended upon the size of their fleet. As a result the Chariot, Empire, Pro Bono Publico and Pembroke Regents continued running throughout the remainder of 1933 displaying little visible clue that anything had changed apart from the Board's name and address replacing that of the previous owner. With one exception this arrangement continued up to and including Tuesday 16th January 1934; on the 17th the LPTB took over fully whereupon the acquired STs were all housed together for the first time in Camberwell garage. The exception was VX 7487 (the future ST 1029) whose former owner did not stay until the appointed day and ceased to operate as Empire a week early on 8th January. The now-redundant Regent was removed from its Cambridge Heath base to Chiswick Works where its overhaul was immediately put in hand.

Although ST 1028-1031 were all officially transferred into Camberwell garage on 17th January, ST 1029 did not actually arrive there until its overhaul was completed on the 31st of that month. The other three were all immediately given their appointed fleet numbers, fitted with standard running number holders, and operated as an integral part of Camberwell's 45-strong ST fleet. The three that still bore their old liveries and fleet names continued to do so until they could be absorbed into the Chiswick repainting programme.

The Chariot fleet name has been seen on the streets of London for the last time. Chiswick Works is the location of this photograph of ST 1028, parked close to a Bluebird LT body and awaiting its turn to be overhauled and repainted in standard London Transport colours. *G J Robbins collection*

Newly arrived at Camberwell garage, VX 7553 must have seemed an odd sight on route 43 in Pro Bono Publico livery. Standard LPTB running number plates have been added and complete sets of destination boards have been produced for this and other ex-independent Regents now allocated there. Its new fleet number, ST 1030, is barely visible in gold numerals on the cream background of the panel below the driver's window. *D W K Jones*

The only Regent out of the four 'pirate' ones to receive GENERAL fleet names was ST 1029, the one-time Empire vehicle, seen here arriving at its terminus by Clapham Common station. It masqueraded as a General bus until October 1934. Interestingly, black on white route boards were supplied by London Transport for the independent Regents, the very opposite to what was done with the Tilling STs.

Whilst in the works at Chiswick, ST 1029 was stripped down to ascertain its structural condition, repaired where necessary and fitted with a self starter, in the process raising its weight by 6cwt. It duly emerged in standard red and grey fleet livery, suffering the ultimate indignity of displaying the fleet name GENERAL, the implacable enemy of the London independents whose very existence was now being extinguished.

Next into Chiswick works, in late April 1934, was ex Pro Bono Publico ST 1030 which, though not scheduled for a complete overhaul until the following October, was repainted into fleet colours and equipped with a self starter. As in the case of ST 1029, no substantial change was made to the Dodson bodywork which even continued to carry a full set of board indicators, probably to the irritation of staff at Camberwell garage whose entire fleet apart from the four ex-independent STs was fully equipped with roller blinds.

Five days after ST 1030 arrived back from Chiswick, ex-Pembroke ST 1031 departed for there on 9th May 1934, but in this case a full overhaul was called for. As with the previous two, a self starter was now installed, and the opportunity was taken to add glazing to the cab sides as this had not been done in Pembroke days. Yet again the Birch bodywork was beginning to display structural weaknesses despite the strengthening that had taken place early in its career. The solution chosen by the Chiswick staff was to attach external metal bracing to all the vertical pillars on the lower deck, though other work was probably carried out too since, when it emerged from overhaul on 19th May, ST 1031's unladen weight had substantially increased by more than one ton to 6 tons 8cwt 1qr. In order to keep within the laden weight regulations, this necessitated a reduction in seating capacity to 52 which was achieved by removing four seats from the upper saloon which now held only 28.

STs 1029 and 1030, with their typical Dodson bodies, had looked very similar to each other in 'pirate' days and the similarity was emphasised even more strongly once they both carried standard London Transport colours. Photographs of ST 1029 at Caterham and ST 1030 at the Swan & Sugar Loaf, South Croydon typify this pair as they appeared throughout the second half of the nineteen-thirties. ST 1029 was destined to be the only one of the four ex-independent Regents to survive a full decade in London Transport ownership.
D W K Jones/J Bonell

ST 1031 retained its mix of full and half-drop windows throughout London Transport days and also its droopy canopy and square-cut cab, the latter now glazed on the sides but retaining its original outline. In the nearside photograph, taken at Forest Hill, the driver's canopy gives the distinct impression that, because of the lack of support below it, the structure is collapsing towards the nearside. The offside view, at Caterham Valley, shows clearly the strapping applied by London Transport to give strength to the pillars, despite which distortion of the framework is becoming apparent over the rear wheelarch.
J Bonell/D W K Jones

It is not known for certain which of the four STs was the last to carry its original livery. Theoretically the strongest contender for this honour was ex-Chariot ST 1028, which was not officially recorded as having been called in for overhaul until 7th June 1934, but it is known to have already been resident at Chiswick Works on 19th April and may well have been there for some time before that. If this was indeed the case it would have left ST 1031 as the last to represent the 'pirate' era in its Pembroke colours. Like ST 1031, it emerged from Chiswick substantially heavier than it went in, though no outward change had taken place to alter its physical appearance. The seating capacity had been reduced at the same time from 56 to 54, although by the time ST 1028 re-entered service on 22nd June 1934 this had been reduced further to 52.

The remainder of the nineteen-thirties proved largely uneventful for the four Regents. ST 1029 was derated with a 100mm engine in October 1934; ST 1031 and ST 1028 were upseated to carry 54 in September 1936 and November 1938 respectively, whilst ST 1029 became a 56-seater at an unknown date. Only in the case of ST 1028 did any subse-

quent change to external appearance take place. It is not known exactly when or why, but probably in about January 1938 as a result of a collision the whole of the typical Birch 'droopy' canopy was removed and replaced with a conventional straight one, below which was fitted a standard ST rounded cab with open doorway. Amazingly, all four Regents continued to carry their wooden destination boards and metal route number stencils for the rest of the decade.

Up to 21st August 1935 ST 1028-1031 could commonly be found on a variety of central London routes worked from Camberwell garage, but on this date they switched to a largely suburban routine as a result of a reallocation to Croydon. In exchange Camberwell received a quartet of ex-LGOC STs, a type which had been very much in the minority at Croydon compared with its large contingent of 49 of its native Tilling type. Even when Croydon lost the last of its LGOC STs on 1st December 1936 the four 'pirates' stayed on. The first batch of scheduled ST withdrawals on 1st August 1939 saw the demise of ST 1028 along with several of the Tilling type, but the other three were still active at the outbreak of war.

ST 1028 demonstrates its full London Transport livery after being transferred to Croydon garage in August 1935, where full sets of boards were available to enable the four acquired Regents to roam over all the widespread territory served from there. When photographed at the Camden Gardens terminus of route 59 it still carried its original canopy and square profiled cab. The later view, taken on 23rd April 1938 at Caterham, demonstrates the new straight canopy and ST-style cab. The unusual oval staircase window, which ST 1028 retained to the end, was a feature more normally associated with Short Bros bodies. *J F Higham/D W K Jones*

CHAPTER 14
LEWIS OMNIBUS COMPANY

Although they were amongst the highest numbered of the ST fleet, five out of the six AEC double deckers acquired from the Lewis Omnibus Company Ltd of Watford had, in fact, been some of the very first Regents to run in the London area. The only ones to precede them were the East Surrey/Autocar UU 6610 (later ST 1139), the LGOC's ST 1, and a couple of demonstrators used by Thomas Tilling and by Lewis themselves. They were ordered in December 1929 for the earliest possible delivery in readiness for a new service which Lewis planned to operate between Rickmansworth, Watford and St Albans. AEC was able to supply them from stock with bodywork by Short Brothers and they were ready for licensing on 28th January 1930 as UR 5506-5510.

The Lewis Omnibus Company was the most substantial of a number of independent operators based in and around Watford and the majority of the shareholding in it was held in equal proportions by Frederick Lewis, its founder, and the Metropolitan Railway through its subsidiary, the North West Land & Transport Company Ltd. This was a very efficient and harmonious arrangement, with the two sides getting on very well together and sharing a mutual dislike of the Combine and its various subsidiaries. Their fleet was garaged mainly in a former wartime munitions factory in Cassiobury Park Avenue, near the Metropolitan Railway's Watford station, although a garage right in the town centre at 25 Market Street was used as an overflow.

The five Regents, which looked very smart and modern in Lewis's maroon and white livery, were 51-seaters purchased for £1,790 each. They carried the current style of standard fully enclosed Shorts body with exaggerated piano front arrangement on which the upper deck windows came to a very distinct V-formation over the destination box. Other distinctive Shorts features were the small oval staircase window on the offside and the very rounded corners, top and bottom, of both the upper and lower deck windows at the rear. Inside they were fitted out very attractively with plenty of polished woodwork enhancing the semi-bucket seats which

were upholstered in red leather with brown 'Scratchproof' rexine backs matching the side lining panels. There were 24 seats downstairs and 27 on the upper deck. An interesting feature specified by Lewis and fitted before delivery was a 'via' board below the driver's canopy which normally displayed 'VIA WATFORD' and was illuminated by a small lamp installed above it. The mechanical specification included the standard 100mm engine and a rear axle ratio of 6¼:1. Some of the five entered service on 28th January 1930 between Rickmansworth and Watford, a licence to run to St Albans having not yet been received, and the full service finally commenced on Tuesday 11th March.

Fleet numbers R 1-5 were allocated to the five Regents in registration number order and were displayed on the bonnet side (R presumably standing for 'Regent'). The new Rickmansworth–St Albans service proved so successful that it soon became necessary to buy a sixth Regent to augment the original five, and as a result R 6 (UR 7879) was licensed on 30th October 1930. This was very slightly more expensive than the others at exactly £1,800 but, as a 54-seater, it carried three more passengers. Although also bodied by Shorts, it was of a slightly more modern styling and thus easily recognisable. The main improvement was at the front where both the piano-front section and the windows above it were gently raked backwards to give a more streamlined effect, whilst the upstairs front windows themselves were surmounted by neat inward-opening hopper type sections to provide improved ventilation to the upper saloon. A route number aperture was provided adjacent to the destination box at front and rear, but this feature was not needed by Lewis and was never used. At the back, the windows on both decks were now radiused only on their upper corners whilst the upstairs one was incorporated into an emergency exit, a feature not provided on the earlier vehicles. This body shared with them, however, the very shallow platform cut-away at the back which was soon to be outlawed under revised Construction & Use regulations.

A manufacturer's study of Lewis R 3 (the future ST 1135) clearly illustrates the 'boxy' nature of Short Bros' interpretation of the 'piano front' styling copied by several manufacturers from the Leyland original. In building above the driver's cab, better use was made of potential floor space than was achieved by the LGOC in its ST design. *Ken Blacker collection*

Right The North Orbital Road was a major construction work in the early nineteen-thirties to speed traffic to and from Tilbury Docks. Vast amounts of earth had to be excavated alongside the existing road where R3 is seen passing a bull-nose Morris car while making its way to St Albans. The rounded back windows so typical of Short Bros bodies of the era are clearly demonstrated and the registration number is shown twice, once in the back window and again at the bottom corner. *Ken Blacker collection*

R 3 again, this time in service at Watford when still very new and demonstrating the illuminated 'via' board carried by the Lewis Regents. These had been removed within about a year having possibly formed an impediment to the driver's forward vision towards the nearside. *W Noel Jackson*

Centre Lewis's final Regent, R 6, was easily distinguishable from the others through various minor modifications to the design. With less emphasis given to rounding-off the corners of the back windows some of the 'character' was lost, and the destination box (with the unused number aperture adjacent to it) was mounted lower than on the main batch.

To meet a continuing demand for greater carrying capacity on its trunk service, Lewis placed an order in September 1931 for the supply of additional seats to increase the capacity of R 1-5 by four to 55 through inserting an extra row on the upper deck, achieved by moving all the existing seats closer together. This move had been made possible by an amendment to the Construction & Use regulations to permit a laden weight of 9½ tons, an increase of 10cwt, making the higher capacity legal. Short Brothers were contracted to supply the extra seats at £4 14s 0d each, but due to serious manufacturing delays fitment of them did not commence until May 1932. At about the same time Shorts were called in to seal the roofs, which had begun to leak. This was done, but in spite of Lewis's high standard of maintenance, further problems began to manifest themselves and it became abundantly clear that the bodies were defective both in their design and construction and that further remedial work would eventually become necessary.

The formation of the London Passenger Transport Board in 1933 placed the Lewis company in an unusual position. Although it worked outside the Metropolitan Police District, Lewis was specifically designated under the Act for compulsory acquisition by virtue of the Metropolitan Railway's holding in it. The railway company was absorbed by the Board on its very first day of existence, 1st July 1933, and from the same date the Board inherited the former Metropolitan shareholding in Lewis. However it could exercise no control within the Company even though its stake was equal to that of Frederick Lewis, because this fell just short of a fifty per cent shareholding thanks to the existence of a few minor shareholders. Frederick Lewis continued running the Company under his long term contract while the Board was forced to go through the same formal procedures for acquisition as applied in any other case. When, in due course, its officers examined the Lewis fleet to ascertain the mechanical condition and value of each vehicle, they were quick to realise the problems that the bodywork on the Regents was now causing. They found that on most, if not all of them, the front bulkheads had worked loose, causing the vehicles to sway at speed and the cabs to droop. The lower saloon floors needed strengthening, and there was a clear tendency for the upper saloon floor above the driver to rot, almost certainly as a result of the ingress of rain. The six vehicles were mechanically fine and ran well, but at the very least the bulkheads needed urgent bracketing to eliminate the worst of the bodywork problems.

The Lewis Omnibus Company passed into complete London Transport ownership on 1st October 1933. However the Board's management at Watford was not ready to absorb the Lewis business immediately despite having had ample notice of the event, so it was arranged that the Company would continue as before, with Frederick Lewis at the helm, until such time as the ex-National Watford High Street garage could cope with the extra work. This gave the Company a six-week reprieve with the handover of assets finally occurring on 15th November 1933.

Due to the lack of detailed records covering the Country Bus & Coach fleet during the period 1933-35, the immediate fate of the six ex-Lewis Regents after the takeover cannot be confirmed. They were allocated fleet numbers ST 1133-1138 in the same order in which they had previously been R 1-6, and they received these numbers between April and June 1935 as they passed through overhaul at Chiswick. They had, however, undergone an earlier overhaul at Reigate roughly a year beforehand during which their Lewis livery was eliminated in favour of Country Bus green. At the same time the bulkheads were bracketed and they were fitted with larger, standard sized destination apertures front and rear. Their seating capacity was reduced to 48, leaving just 20 seats on the lower deck and 28 on the upper, probably to reduce stress on what was perceived to be rather flimsy bodywork. By the middle of 1935, with the keeping of detailed records resumed, the six vehicles were well dispersed across the Country Bus fleet. ST 1133 was then based at Reigate, ST 1134 at Tring, ST 1135-1137 at Hertford and ST 1138 at St Albans.

In 1936 someone, somewhere at Chiswick (or perhaps at Reigate or both) must have taken another look at the six Lewis Regents and their potential for carrying more than the 48 seats they were currently fitted with subject to the bodywork being strengthened sufficiently to do so. In July 1936 ST 1136, then based at Watford High Street but undergoing overhaul at Chiswick, was upseated to 54 by adding four seats on the lower deck and two upstairs, and ST 1135 – also by then at Watford High Street – was dealt with similarly in

October of the same year. In December the entire batch of six was transferred to Grays where, in the event of them all being converted to 54-seaters, their extra capacity would be valuable on the hard-pressed Grays–Purfleet road. Exactly what happened next is not known except that all six were delicensed on 31st January 1937 and relicensed again on 1st March, by which time every one of them had been converted to the higher seating capacity. It seems likely that some other work was also carried out during the month that they were off the road, details of which will probably never be known.

Despite the various rectification jobs carried out on them during their London Transport days, the Lewis Regents were never modified from their original appearance, and they continued to retain their full-drop windows, their narrow platform cut-aways and their lack of an upstairs emergency exit (except on ST 1138 which had had one from new). However by 1939 the end was drawing near for the still troublesome Shorts bodies. Three of them (ST 1133, 1134, 1138) had passed through their routine overhaul at Chiswick when it was decided, in March 1939, not to spend any more time or money on them. When the next one – ST 1135 – emerged from overhaul on 30th March it carried a standard ST body taken from Central Bus float but modified for Country use by applying two-tone green livery and by adopting the standard Country Bus indicator box layout consisting of a small screen at the front and none at all at the rear. At the same time the fuel filler point was relocated from the standard LGOC nearside position to the offside to suit the ex-Lewis chassis. ST 1137 was dealt with similarly in May 1939 followed by ST 1136 in June. Interestingly, the latter differed from the other two in now sporting a nearside fuel tank, which almost certainly indicates that it was not actually on a Lewis chassis at all but on a standard LGOC one taken from stock. The fate of the Shorts bodies removed from these three is not known, but it is assumed that they were sold for scrap shortly afterwards. With the advent of war, the remaining three managed to retain their original bodies until 1941/42 as recorded in chapter 18.

St Albans in May 1935 with ST 1138, the former Lewis R 6, demonstrating its more streamlined frontal profile compared with the other five. A standard London Transport front indicator box has now been fitted and the vehicle has recently been repainted into the latest Country Bus livery. *J F Higham*

CHAPTER 15
COUNTRY BUSES 1933-1939

July 1st 1933 came, and London General Country Services was absorbed into the Country Bus & Coach department of the London Passenger Transport Board. In much the same way that the Central Bus organisation was a virtual extension of the LGOC, so the Country Bus & Coach section in its early days bore striking similarities to the LGCS. There were no immediate plans afoot for the purchase of new double deckers apart from 12 which became known as the 'Godstone' type lowbridge STLs, so the 125 Regents inherited from LGCS formed the backbone of the modern fleet. The LGCS system of managing without fleet numbers for its vehicles remained in force and, for the next year or so, all vehicle matters were dealt with at Reigate where the main overhauling facilities gradually became overwhelmed under the burden of the expanding fleet as numerous private operators were acquired.

Unfortunately for the historian, Reigate's record keeping was not as meticulous as that at Chiswick and much of what there was has not survived, so large gaps exist in the detailed knowledge of vehicle movements in the early days of London Transport.

The new country bus livery of green and black which had been introduced in March 1933 in readiness for the setting up of the new organisation quickly made its mark and had become universal within about a year. Initially the fleet name GENERAL continued in use as it did on Central Buses, until the classic LONDON TRANSPORT insignia was introduced on bus sides in May 1934. As time went by, the removal of competition through the acquisition of many small operators made possible the introduction of major service co-ordination schemes in several towns, sometimes resulting in the relocation of STs to garages from which they had never previously operated. The acquisition of territory not formerly served by the LGCS, such as Thames-side services in Essex and Kent acquired from Eastern National and Maidstone & District respectively, also opened up potential new operating territory for them. By 1934, for instance, the prototype Regent UU 6610 (which later became ST 1139) had become a regular performer on the Grays–Purfleet road. At the start of 1935 the Regents could be found in varying numbers at all Country garages operating double deckers except Epping and Weybridge.

The green and black livery introduced in May 1933 was initially retained by the Country Bus department together with the GENERAL fleet name. Amongst the many inter-garage transfers that resulted in unusual vehicles going to pastures new was that of UU 6610 to Grays. Yet to gain its identity as ST 1139, this unmistakeable vehicle was photographed at Grays war memorial about to set out on a G40 journey to Romford.

With ever more independents being acquired, the Country Bus & Coach department was faced with the massive task of maintaining a diverse fleet, disposing of vehicles that could not usefully be retained and integrating the remainder with those acquired from London General Country Services. The modern overhaul works at Reigate were initially crucial to this effort and some of the mixed fleet that had to be handled are seen here. AECs and Gilfords predominate, and on the right a coachmaker is seen attending to the bulkhead pillar of a Wycombe bodied Gilford coach. Right at the back lowbridge ST 136 is undergoing overhaul while, nearer the camera, an unidentified Bluebird is present. The photograph was probably taken in about May 1934. *Ken Blacker collection*

Under the Reigate maintenance regime very little physical alteration was made to any of the Regents except that the driver's cabs were brought up to a modern standard on a few of them. Most noticeably deficient in this respect were the former National STs which, surprisingly at this late stage, still had no windscreens. In December 1933 authority was given for the fitment of enclosed cabs to eight of the 1930 batch (numbered in the ST one hundred series) and the four 1931 vehicles (ST 818-821). The earlier batch consisted, in fact, of nine buses, so it is presumed that one of these had been dealt with earlier. One other Regent in need of updating was UU 6610 which, though it had carried a windscreen from new, still had no side glasses or windscreen wiper. This omission was rectified in about May 1934 during its routine overhaul.

One further job carried out in early London Transport days was the modification of the destination boxes on the two ex-Amersham & District lowbridge Regents and the six ex-Lewis vehicles to bring them in line with the main fleet. As built, all carried single line displays which needed to be replaced by deeper screens. An ad-hoc approach by the Reigate coachbuilding staff resulted in variations in the treatment meted out to various vehicles as witnessed by the two low height ones on which it would have been logical to treat both identically. Instead two different approaches were taken. On KX 5055 (which later became ST 1090) the existing front box was enlarged in height within the existing front panelling but not narrowed to meet the new requirements, which meant that the glass had to be masked on either side. On KX 4656 (the future ST 1089) a completely new box of the

correct height and width was constructed, not tidily within the existing panelling but projecting above it to break up the symmetry of the piano front. These turned out to be merely the first of many alterations to bodies on the lowbridge STs which finally resulted in almost every one being different in appearance from all the others.

Signs that times were changing, and that the Country Bus & Coach department was to become more like its Central Bus counterpart, appeared towards the end of 1934 when vehicles began to be fitted with holders for garage plates and running number stencils. Code letters were allocated to garages (and in certain cases subsequently amended when it was found that they clashed with ones already in use in the Central area), and by the start of 1935 all were fully in use. The lack of fleet numbers was also rectified. Plans were drawn up for the transfer of Country Bus overhauls to Chiswick with the first intake in January 1935, and this required vehicle types to be recognised by class letters, their registration numbers being too varied and haphazard for use with Chiswick's sophisticated system of control. With regard to the Regents, the 13 highbridge and 6 lowbridge STs originally operated by National retained the numbers that they had originally been allocated and, in some cases, still carred in raised digits on their bonnet sides. East Surrey STs 833 and 834 kept their original numbers too. The remainder were numbered to follow on from the STs acquired from the London independents, not logically by age or by grouping together in batches of identical vehicles, but by order of their registration numbers. Taking those with the lowest starting letters first, the Country Bus fleet was numbered as shown overleaf.

ST 1032-1039	Ex-LGCS Bluebirds	APC 162-166, 168-170
ST 1040-1069	Ex-East Surrey, Shorts-bodied	various between GN 4699-4796, GO 635-700, GO 5132-GO 5193, GO 7108-7157
ST 1070-1079	Ex-LGCS Bluebirds	GX 5314-5323
ST 1080-1084	Ex-LGCS Bluebirds	JH 4646-4650
ST 1085-1088	Ex-Autocar Ransomes	KR 3886, 3892-3894
ST 1089, 1090	Ex-Amersham lowbridge	KX 4656, 5055
ST 1091-1132	Ex-East Surrey Ransomes	various between PG 7593 and 7979
ST 1133-1138	Ex-Lewis	UR 5506-5510, 7897
ST 1139	Ex-demonstrator	UU 6610

Thus, by this strange system of numbering presumably set up by a bureaucrat rather than a practical person, the oldest vehicle paradoxically received the highest fleet number and the 23 identical Bluebirds were split up into two separate batches. The system also failed to recognise that former East Surrey GO 636 no longer existed, and ST 1051 was allocated to it in the correct sequence as though it was still in the fleet. Vehicles began to appear displaying fleet numbers as they emerged from their Chiswick overhaul from February 1935 onwards, and a few months later a small suffix letter B or C began to accompany the fleet number to denote whether the vehicle was officially classified as a bus or a coach. In the case of the STs, of course, all carried the suffix B.

The use of body numbers was also extended to the Country Bus & Coach fleet although any that had been allocated in earlier days were now discarded with new ones issued in their place. Here a complete lack of prior planning was evident. Each vehicle was allocated its new body number as it went through its first Chiswick overhaul with the result that numbers were completely jumbled between vehicle types and they were also intermixed with batches of new vehicles as these came off the production line. The lowest ST body number – 15342 – was issued to the first one out of the Chiswick overhaul shops on 11th February 1935, which was Bluebird ST 1070, whilst the highest – 16821 – went to the last in the cycle, square-cab ST 1130 on 25th May 1936.

After little more than a year in its original red livery, ex-LGCS Bluebird GX 5314 (later ST 1070) gained Country area green and black colours in about February 1934 and, like most vehicles in the fleet, lost them after a year in favour of a revised two-tone green scheme. Standing behind the Bluebird at Watford is Central Bus ST 364 operating from Harrow Weald garage. *J F Higham*

For a short while in May 1934 vehicles emerged from overhaul with no fleet name pending availability of the new LONDON TRANSPORT transfers. Ransomes bodied PG 7976 (ST 1111) was a Reigate based bus at the time. *Andrew N Porter*

The classic new fleet name was applied to APC 163 in August 1934 at which time the use of running number plates had still be to introduced on Country Buses and the vehicle had still to be allocated its fleet number ST 1033. Originally at Windsor, APC 163 had been transferred to Hemel Hempstead in early London Transport days but was operating from Watford High Street when photographed at Rickmansworth en route to Garston. *J F Higham*

For a few months in early 1935 Country Bus vehicles carried running number plates but had yet to receive fleet numbers. The future ST 1139, still at Grays, was one of the last to be overhauled in the old green and black colours. Whilst being dealt with at Reigate, glazing was provided for the cab sides (apart from the cab door) which meant that drivers no longer needed to proceed with the windscreen wide open to achieve a reasonably draught-reduced journey. *D W K Jones*

Still carrying GENERAL fleet names but now fitted with running number plates, Bluebird GY 5323 (soon to become ST 1079) was the only one of its type operating south of the Thames in early London Transport days, and it remained at Reigate garage through to November 1936. In the meantime it has had a standard sized destination box grafted into the large aperture normally used to display intermediate points, with the result that it now displays the main items of information twice.

Soon after fleet numbers came on the scene a small letter B was added to denote that a vehicle was a bus as distinct from a coach. Inside Reigate garage, square cab ST 1097B displays the new identity on its bonnet side. In the background can just be glimpsed ST 1139, now in later livery and also on Reigate's rolling stock inventory. *H J Snook*

Quite early in its existence London Transport decided that the travelling public might have difficulty differentiating between buses and coaches because both carried the same livery, and the decision was taken to adopt a different colour scheme for the former. Although the problem of possible confusion only existed with single deckers, a new livery was tried out on double deckers too, on which it proved particularly effective. Although mid-green was maintained as the main colour, it was relieved by large areas of pale green, the two being applied in the same manner as red and grey were used on the Central Bus fleet, retaining the narrow central black band and mudguards and silver roof. Trial vehicles appeared in this style as early as October 1933, but more than a year elapsed before it began to be used regularly with the switch of overhauling from Reigate to Chiswick.

With the Country fleet now under its control, Chiswick lost no time in bringing the Ransomes STs up to a standard more compatible with that of former LGOC vehicles. Tasks that had been carried out on the LGOC STs some years earlier were now put in hand as each bus became due for overhaul in a process which occupied the remainder of 1935 and continued into the early part of 1936. As no works float existed for these vehicles, each had to be dealt with individually and some were off the road for several weeks at a time while the work was carried out. Much of it was electrical and largely hidden

from public view as it involved the replacement of the pneumatic bell system by an electric one run off the batteries. Far more apparent was the rebuilding of the back platform to provide the now standard 1ft 9ins cut-away at the rear. This resulted in the insertion of a single platform window to replace the former twin window arrangement, but unlike earlier LGOC programmed alterations, it was not uniformly carried out with the result that some vehicles ended up with square cornered tops to their windows whereas others were rounded. In all cases the rear registration plate was removed from above the back window although there is no obvious reason why this was thought to be necessary as the space vacated was not required for anything else. In almost every instance it was re-sited on the platform, although there were a few exceptions where the number plate was more conventionally built into the bottom right hand side of the back panel while at least two cases existed of vehicles with registration plates in both positions. The small route number indicator box above the platform was plated over but the back indicator box was left in place and remained an easy recognition feature of the Ransomes bodies when viewed from the rear. The repositioning of the back registration plate was extended to all other ex-East Surrey and National STs too, again for no obvious reason since, in its new position, it was far less visible than it had been previously.

Top left Amongst the very first STs to appear from overhaul at Chiswick in the new livery was Autocar ST 1088, a Hatfield based vehicle. A few very early two-tone green repaints were given black fleet numbers to which, in this instance, a gold B has subsequently been added.

Top right and above left By 1935, and probably much earlier, the two Amersham & District Regents had been fitted with destination boxes to match the ex-National vehicles. The different results achieved on the two vehicles can be seen by comparing Short Bros bodied ST 1089 with Strachans ST 1090. Unusually ST 1090 now displays a Short Bros style oval window which it did not have when new, whereas the similar unit on ST 1089 has clearly been plated over and was later removed completely. Both now have their side lights conventionally mounted on the bodywork instead of on the mudguards. *J F Higham*

Above right The rebuilding of the rear ends of the Ransomes bodied STs produced a number of variations on a general theme, but common to all was the widened door aperture and the replacement of the half-drop in the last offside bay by a sliding window. The double rubbing strip arrangement at the foot of the back panel could now be found on most of them. Guildford's ST 1103 has a square topped platform window but this was not always the case. *Andrew N Porter*

The mid-thirties found the ex-Lewis STs distributed around the country fleet until they were all gathered together at Grays in December 1936. ST 1133 spent about three years as an odd man out at Reigate displaying a neat new front destination box with rounded corners and accessed from within the upper saloon. *J F Higham*

Jumping ahead in livery styles to 1939, this view of ST 136 in Watford shows the final frontal condition to which six out of the eight lowbridge STs had been re-profiled by the outbreak of war. ST 136 had been the first to be rebuilt in this way and was unique in being the only one to retain opening front windows on the upper deck. *D Evans*

Even more major work was carried out on the lowbridge STs as these were called into Chiswick works, one by one, from the middle of 1935 onwards. Three had already been overhauled there and had escaped relatively unscathed before a programme of drastic action got underway, presumably partly inspired by what had been discovered when dealing with these three. It had become evident that the body frames needed strengthening, coupled to which came a desire to bring the bodies up to modern construction and use standards by widening the platform cut-away and inserting an emergency window at the rear of the upper saloon.

The first vehicle tackled was ST 162 which went into Chiswick on 11th June 1935 and was stripped down to its bare framework. As part of the general strengthening the full drop windows, which gave an inherent weakness to the frame, were removed and half-drops were inserted instead along with the more sturdy waistrails that were feasible now that the windows did not have to drop through them. At the back the whole structure was stripped away including the windows on each deck with their heavily rounded corners which had been such a strong feature of the Short Brothers bodies. A new platform (and probably a new staircase) was built as was a new back platform wall, while up above an opening emergency window with two square cornered panes of glass was inserted in the widened aperture. During repanelling the mid-decks horizontal moulding was omitted and provision was inserted for drainage of the upper saloon gangways. The job took several weeks to complete, and after it was done similar rebuilding was carried out later in 1935 on ST

141 and ST 1089. When the work was finished and the vehicles had resumed service they were recognisable at a glance by the half-drop windows and the replacement of the former glass louvres above them by continuous metal rain strips, whilst when viewed from the rear the transformation was complete and they looked nothing like they had before.

This turned out to be only the first phase of the rebuilding programme on the lowbridge STs. Stage 2, which began with ST 136 in June 1936, saw a much more ambitious reworking to alter the entire body profile at front and back. Plans had obviously been prepared in the drawing office at Chiswick to give the bodies an updated appearance by eliminating the excesses of the angular piano front whilst relieving the uprightness at the back by introducing a curved aspect above the top deck waistrail. After rebuilding, the front above the driver's cab gently sloped backwards leaving at the top only the slightest hint of the old piano front styling. Most noticeable at the back, in the more rounded rear dome, was the insertion of an STL style emergency window with its typical Y-shaped central bar. Most remarkably, in view of all the other rebuilding that had taken place, ST 136 emerged still carrying its old Short Brothers rounded downstairs window and narrow platform entrance, which it continued to display for the rest of its life and was the only one of the eight to do so. ST 1090 was converted to the new, modernised profile over a 6½ week period starting at the end of October 1936. Once all the work had been carried out the new unladen weight of about 6 tons 12cwt marked a substantial increase of about 14cwt over the original.

The third and final phase in the modification of the lowbridge STs began with ST 157 in September 1937 whereby, upon repanelling, standard ST raised waistrail panels were now used on the lower deck in place of the original flat panels with their secondary, lower moulding strip. The customary thick wooden rubbing strake was also fitted half way down, and this meant that, for the first time in their career, the lowbridge STs began to look as though they had a family connection, however tenuous, with the main ST class. ST 163 was similarly treated later in 1937 and, last of all, ST 140 in November 1938, whilst meanwhile already rebuilt STs 162 and 1090 were brought up to this final standard with new side panelling when they returned for their next overhaul in September and November 1937 respectively, although ST 162 retained its more upright rear end and the original emergency windows fitted in 1935, never gaining a Y-type one. The net result of all this rebuilding activity was that, by the time war broke out, the only ones still carrying their original bulbous piano fronts were ST 141 and 1089. The latter was unique, however, in having lost its oval staircase window which had been plated over in about 1934 and was later removed entirely. It was now the only one of the ex-Amersham & District pair still with its square cab. These two, plus ST 136, were the only ones still carrying original style lower deck panelling, but ST 136 differed from all others in having gained rounded tops to all its opening windows and in having retained its front half drops, which had been removed from all the other ex-National vehicles. Only ST 141, 162 and 1089 managed to retain their original, more upright rears.

Under London Transport ownership the eight lowbridge STs led a fairly uneventful existence operationally, being divided for most of the time in equal numbers between Watford High Street and Amersham garages for operation on route 336 (to which the N6 had been renumbered in January 1934). The eight were more than adequate to serve route 336 so no hardship arose when individual vehicles were absent over long periods of time for rebuilding. The only exception to the established pattern came on 13th May 1936 when the 336 was cut back from Berkhamsted to Chesham as part of a scheme of service alterations in the Amersham and High Wycombe area and ST 162 was reallocated to High Wycombe where it is thought to have been employed on route 326 worked jointly with Thames Valley (the latter used only lowbridge double deckers). It returned to Amersham on 31st December of the same year, after which no further transfers occurred during the pre-war era.

ST 1138, seen carrying Tring (TG) running plates but actually allocated to Hemel Hempstead, has a conventional front-opening destination box projecting slightly at the top from its gently sloped front panels. The side lights on this vehicle have been removed from the front canopy and re-sited lower down. *Alan Nightingale collection*

The only STs other than the lowbridge ones that did not wander were those with low axle ratios specifically allocated to Godstone and East Grinstead for their hill climbing ability. Typical of these was ST 1068 which was on Godstone's books for many years and was photographed on the 409 stand at West Croydon. *J Bonell*

Unique amongst Country area STs in exchanging bodies upon overhaul – a practice commenced in October 1937 – were the square cab Ransomes bodied vehicles. Watford High Street's ST 1128 was carrying the body formerly on ST 1109 when it was photographed on the terminal stand at New Barnet station. The side lights have now been removed from the front canopy to occupy conventional positions lower down. *D W K Jones*

Things were less settled for the rest of the Country Bus ST fleet with new front entrance STLs coming on stream between February and July 1935 followed by a second batch during the second half of 1936. The extent of subsequent ST reallocations can be judged by looking at the Ransomes vehicles of which, in late 1935, 33 out of the 42 originally supplied to Reigate, Leatherhead and Crawley garages were still at these locations whereas, by the time war broke out, only one remained (at Reigate), the rest being scattered far and wide with the largest concentrations being 12 at Watford High Street, 6 at St Albans, 5 at Northfleet and 4 each at High Wycombe and Windsor. ST 819 and 820 were lost to the department altogether in June 1937 when they were transferred to Central Buses in exchange for Q 2 and Q 3.

Whereas the various ex East Surrey and National vehicles found themselves scattered fairly indiscriminately throughout the fleet, the Bluebirds tended to be concentrated in groups and led a more static career. Their different mechanical specification was probably a reason for this. For the most part, the Hertfordshire registered batch remained in their original haunts throughout the decade although they moved from Ware to Hertford when the new garage opened on 2nd January 1935. As for the remainder, with one exception they had all been concentrated by 1935 to work within the Watford area and principally from there on the corridor north-westwards to Hemel Hempstead and Aylesbury for which purpose eight were garaged at Watford High Street, seven at Hemel Hempstead and two at Tring. Later in 1935 almost the entire Watford High Street contingent was transferred to Hemel Hempstead which thereafter was the most important base for the Bluebirds for the remainder of the nineteen-thirties. An exception to this was ST 1079 which could be found at Reigate, the sole example of the class at a southern garage, but even this moved north to join the others at Hemel Hempstead in November 1936.

One after another various Country garages lost their last STs as the decade wore on: Guildford in February 1936, Crawley in July 1936, Leatherhead and Dorking in November 1936, Dunton Green in February 1937, Chelsham in August 1938, Hatfield in January 1939 and, lastly, Dartford in August 1939, the consequence being greater concentrations of the class at other locations. Meanwhile more reconditioning schemes took place, all of them quite major in the scale of work undertaken. ST 1139 was one recipient of Chiswick's attention. It spent two quite long periods in overhaul in 1936 and again in 1937 and at one, or perhaps both of these, strengthening work was carried out on its Short Brothers bodywork which, on this as well as other vehicles in the fleet, had not stood the test of time too well. To strengthen the main framework, the full-drop windows were removed and replaced in the same apertures by half drops. In addition, all the pillars on the lower deck were braced externally by steel straps. The side lights were lowered from the canopy down to waistrail level, and the driver's cab was provided with a small window to the rear of the doorway, slightly inwardly inclined and reducing the width of the door aperture which no longer had a half-height door attached to it. This unique vehicle led a slightly unsettled existence. Latterly at Reigate, it was transferred to Windsor in January 1938, passing to Godstone in April of the same year. In common with all of Godstone's ST fleet it was equipped with a 7:1 rear axle ratio to assist hill climbing and, because of 'sleeping out' arrangements on the route 409 schedule, it could often be seen carrying East Grinstead (EG) garage plates instead of its GD ones.

By 1937 the Ransomes bodies were also beginning to show signs of fatigue despite the work carried out on them at Chiswick a couple of years earlier. Unlike Maidstone & District which, faced with the same problem on its ex-Autocar fleet, had decided to dispose of the vehicles despite their relative newness, the Board opted for a policy of subjecting the

ST 833 was one of the pair diverted when new from the LGOC to East Surrey at Dorking, where it remained until new STLs cleared all Dorking's STs away in November 1936. It is not known when or why it received the large front destination box (ST 1062 was similarly modified), to which a smaller display screen has been fitted to suit the Country Bus department's blinds. The new thinner, curved moulding which has replaced the original deeper, flat one around the cab area was a feature installed on many green STs, especially those in the ST 1040-1069 batch, over a period of years. The reason for it is not known, though it may have occurred when re-canvassing of the canopy roof was carried out. *Alan B Cross*

bodies to a heavy overhaul to prolong their lives by a few more years. The planned work meant that each body would be out of action for longer than usual while undergoing rebuilding, and to accommodate this the unusual step was taken of commandeering standard Central area body 12216, latterly on ST 730, to act as a float. This was converted to Country area standard with small front indicator box and with none at all at the rear, and was rebuilt structurally to accommodate an offside fuel tank. Freshly repainted in two tone green, it started work as ST 1087 at Hertford garage on 6th October 1937 where it was readily distinguishable from the real Ransomes STs by its round cab and opening front windows.

From then onwards each overhauled Ransomes body was mounted on the next appropriate overhauled chassis. As a result of this all except three of the batch (ST 1091, 1111, 1114) changed chassis at least once and sometimes twice, until war intervened and the practice ceased in October 1939. A visible sign of the rebuilding was that the side lights were removed from the front canopy and mounted lower down. On the nearside the autovac tank was found to have been mounted lower on some vehicles than on others, which meant that in some cases the repositioned nearside light could be bolted direct to the front bulkhead whereas in others it had to be attached to the front of the autovac tank. Many, but not all, lost their driver's door and in at least two cases (ST 1115, 1119) standard round cabs were fitted. When the programme was completed all vehicles weighed substantially more than they had done before, probably through the use of more and heavier timber in the body framework, although the resultant weights were by no means uniform and could vary considerably between 7-5-0 and 7-16-0. In March 1939 the former LGOC body found its way on to ST 1118 where it stayed for the rest of its working life, whilst the final Ransomes body to be lifted at overhaul before the programme ceased – it was

The new Lincoln green livery, with pale green relief confined merely to the window frames, began spreading quickly through the Country Bus fleet in 1939. ST 1139 emerged from overhaul carrying this colour scheme on 3rd March, and it also displayed a modification to the driver's cab which had lost its door but gained a narrow window adjacent to the bulkhead. Like many other vehicles originally with high mounted side lights, ST 1139 has now had them lowered. Although based at Godstone garage, East Grinstead (EG) plates are carried on this occasion as a result of the 'sleeping out' arrangements included in the route 409 schedule. *W J Haynes*

removed from ST 1112 on 26th September 1939 – was never needed again and was ultimately scrapped.

In common with their far more numerous six-wheeled counterparts, the Bluebird STs had only been in service for a comparatively short time when structural defects started to become apparent. The most serious problem was with the roofs which needed to be completely stripped down and rebuilt to give greater rigidity. The visible clue that this had been done was the replacement of the thick black band above the windows by a thinner half-round moulding painted in the roof colour of silver. Another modification, introduced in 1939, was the provision in the rear offside bay on the lower deck of a built-in route stencil holder in the style of later STLs. A structured programme for this work was initiated on the Bluebird LTs by November 1937 but less urgency was applied to the STs on which work probably did not begin until 1939. Even then the approach was completely haphazard, in complete contrast to the normal Chiswick approach, and as a result only a minority were treated to both the roof reconstruction and the offside stencil modification; some were given one or the other, and there was at least one on which no visible modification work was carried out at all.

As the pre-war era drew towards a close the Country fleet began to take on a new appearance through the adoption from about July 1938 of a much darker shade of green for the main panelling on all its buses and coaches. The old colours, which looked very attractive when newly applied, had proved to be prone to very quick deterioration through fading. This problem had been known about for some time but it came to a head in January 1938 when Frank Pick carried out a tour of inspection of Country garages and was appalled by the unsatisfactory appearance of many of the vehicles that he saw. Things were found to be particularly bad at Northfleet garage, probably because of the nearby cement works. Pick directed that a body colour must be found which would wear better, and as a result of various tests the famous and attractive Lincoln green was adopted and subsequently used right through to the end of London Transport operation in the Country area. Initially Lincoln green was applied just to the main panels where the sage green shade had previously been used, but from January 1939 the central expanse of Lincoln green was extended downwards on double deckers to just above the lower deck windows, reducing the amount of light green relief and eliminating the need for a central black band. This rather less attractive and somewhat heavy styling had spread quite widely throughout the Country bus fleet by the time war began.

The final act of the peacetime era was played out for Country Buses immediately before the outbreak of war. Additional rolling stock was vital to cope with the expected sudden withdrawal of the Green Line network along with evacuation and other wartime duties, and more than 300 double deckers of various types were drafted into Country Bus garages from the Central area to augment their fleets on 1st and 2nd September 1939. STs were, in fact, very much in the minority, but 14 of the standard LGOC model were sent from Old Kent Road to Reigate, which received five, and Dartford, Dunton Green and Crawley with three apiece. Croydon garage dispatched 16 Tilling vehicles to Northfleet (9), Swanley (4) and East Grinstead (3). This was just a preliminary to the great upheavals within the Country Bus ST fleet that were to take place in the war years that lay ahead.

CHAPTER 16
CHISWICK AND THE CODING SYSTEM

Right from the early days of the ST class it was intended by the LGOC that it would develop into a fleet several hundred strong in which all vehicles would be reasonably compatible with each other. This would ensure that they fitted comfortably within the well established overhauling system used to present the Company's huge fleet in a condition which met the exacting demands of the Metropolitan Police's Public Carriage Office. The way Chiswick Works functioned is described in some detail in the companion volume on the LT class and only salient points need to be repeated here.

It suffices to record that overhauling was carried out at Chiswick on an industrial scale with vehicles being called in annually until the middle nineteen-thirties when the interval between overhauls was increased to approximately every 15 months. Bodies were always lifted from their chassis and overhauled on separate lines, and because bodies almost always took longer to overhaul than chassis, it seldom happened that the same two would be married back together after overhaul unless there was a specific reason, such as the presence of special experimental features, for doing so.

On the stand at Rennell Street, Lewisham, Sidcup's ST 64 is about to depart on a Sundays-only 132B trip to Bexley Mental Hospital. During its long 19½ year working life span ST 64 appeared carrying nine different bodies, all of them outwardly identical. However all the body changes were confined to the pre-war period, and body 10564 which was fitted in November 1938 stayed with the vehicle for the rest of its life. *Omnibus Society*

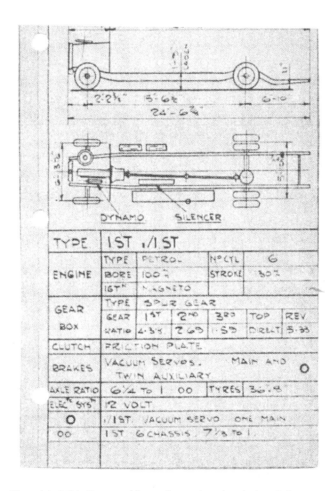

TYPE	1ST./1.ST					
ENGINE	TYPE	PETROL.		N° CYL	6	
	BORE	100 ?		STROKE	30?	
	IG⁺ᴴ	MAGNETO				
GEAR BOX	TYPE	SPUR GEAR				
	GEAR RATIO	1ST	2ᴺᴰ	3ᴿᴰ	TOP	REV
		4·3?	2·6?	1·5?	DIRECT	5·3?
CLUTCH	FRICTION PLATE					
BRAKES	VACUUM SERVOS. MAIN AND TWIN AUXILIARY.					O
AXLE RATIO	6¼ TO 1 00		TYRES	36·8		
ELEC SYS⁺ᴹ	12 VOLT					
O	1/1ST. VACUUM SERVO ONE MAIN					
OO	1ST 6 CHASSIS 7⅛ TO 1					

To assist staff in the use of the coding system, handy descriptive cards were drawn up early in 1934 showing chassis and body dimensions plus other relevant information. Examples shown here are the chassis data sheet for standard LGOC STs (types 1ST and 1/1ST) and a body sheet with its unmistakable drawing of a Tilling (ST7) body (overleaf).

As far as the ST class was concerned the coding system had strict limitations which resulted in it being applied as originally intended to hardly any Country Bus STs. Hatfield's ST 1085, for example, emerged from its Chiswick overhaul with the purely nominal coding 2/1ST9, the same as was given to most other STs in the Country fleet irrespective of mechanical or body specification. *J F Higham*

Always highly cost conscious with regard to everyday operating matters, the LGOC considered it financially important to extract maximum benefit from the payment of road fund tax and arranged its system to ensure that each disc was in active use as nearly as possible for the full twelve months of each year. This was done by inserting 'floats' of both bodies and chassis into the overhauling process. By this means each disc, and the vehicle identity that went with it, could be transferred from a bus arriving at Chiswick to a newly overhauled one about to depart, often on the same day or certainly within a day or two afterwards, ensuring that the earning capacity of the disc was lost for the shortest time possible. The same system was continued by London Transport after its formation and persisted up to the outbreak of war when conditions beyond the Board's control mitigated against its continuance. Throughout the nineteen-thirties a policy was followed of returning each fleet number to the garage whence it had come after overhaul even though it was now carried by a different vehicle. Within classes such as the LTs and STLs, where clear bodywork differences existed such as variations in destination displays, it was sometimes obvious that the newly overhauled vehicle was not really the same one as before, but on the LGOC's STs this was much less apparent since – with the exception of the few camel backs and the Metro Cammell all-metal body – they all looked the same.

The only observable feature that remained constant was the body number painted under the canopy, which stayed with each individual body throughout its life. All other features, including the chassis number stamped on a brass plate affixed to the dumbiron from 1934 onwards, were altered upon overhaul to comply with each change of identity. It is difficult, today, to envisage that such a system operated at Chiswick and the scale on which it was perpetrated, although the mind does not have to be cast back too far to Aldenham Works in the nineteen-fifties and sixties to recall an almost identical system in operation with the RT family.

Taking just one example as typical, ST 64 which was new in March 1930, appeared with no fewer than nine different bodies prior to the outbreak of war, its overhaul history having been as follows:

Garage	Date into overhaul	Date out of overhaul	Body number
Hanwell			10439
Hanwell	5/3/31	12/3/31	10436
Hanwell	11/2/32	12/2/32	11476
Sidcup	1/2/33	1/2/33	12183
Sidcup	1/2/34	1/2/34	10396
Elmers End	6/3/35	8/3/35	10424
Sidcup	8/5/36	13/5/36	10619
Enfield	14/7/37	14/7/37	12141
West Green	10/11/38	17/11/38	10564

Although the overhauling system using stocks of spare bodies and chassis worked with great precision, there were times when it could be thrown out of kilter because of delays on the body overhaul line resulting in insufficient of them being available when needed. Sometimes this occurred when a programmed series of modifications had to be incorporated within the overhauling process causing it to take longer than

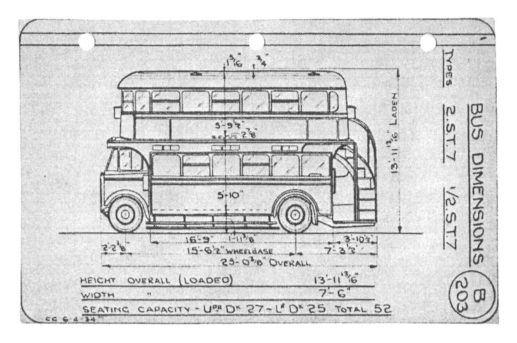

usual, and when this happened a system was adopted of delicensing a few vehicles and allowing their identity to disappear until the position had improved whereupon they could join the licensed fleet once again. Buses temporarily withdrawn from the system for this purpose were officially known as 'floats'. Between 1934 and 1939 this system was adopted several times on LTs and frequently on STLs, but the ex-LGOC fleet of STs managed to escape completely unscathed. The only STs to 'disappear' as floats were Tillings, four of which were out of service from January and February 1934, returning at various dates up to May 1936, augmented by another two for a short period between August and October 1935.

Soon after its formation, London Transport's engineers began to develop a quite ingenious coding system under which various categories of body and chassis could be easily identified when going through overhaul, and also for the benefit of garage staff when determining and specifying their spare parts requirements. Each principal chassis type was allocated a number preceding its class letter. For example 1ST was the code given to ex-LGOC STs carrying triple servo braking systems. Bodies were also coded but in this case the classification followed the class letters, thus ST2 denoted an ex-LGOC body of the second type with revised seating layout. The two were then put together for record keeping purposes as 1ST2. If a minor difference needed to be denoted, either on the chassis or body, it was shown with a stroke. Thus 1/2ST2/1 would denote a vehicle with single servo braking and a camel back body. Only certain types of chassis and body were compatible with each other and the code system enabled staff at Chiswick to distinguish instantly those which could be married together.

Work on organising the system took place throughout the early weeks of 1934 in time for it to be introduced in March, and for the next year or so each chassis and body was coded as it went through the overhaul shops. At the same time the chassis code for each vehicle was engraved on a brass plate for fixing to the nearside dumbiron, and similarly a brass plate with the body code was attached to the cab side just below the driver's nearside window near the water filler cap.

A third brass plate, giving fleet and chassis numbers appertaining to the vehicle at that particular time, was screwed to the offside dumbiron.

The coding system worked well when applied to other major classes such as LT and STL and, in times to come, to the RT family, but its application to the STs was, at best, half-hearted. It worked satisfactorily on the ex-LGOC fleet and also on the Tillings which were also highly standardised and had operated with a system of floats from new. It emphatically did not work on vehicles acquired from other operators, even if these had originally been ordered by and in many cases owned by the LGOC on behalf of East Surrey or National. When responsibility for the Country Bus & Coach fleet passed from Reigate to Chiswick in early 1935 these vehicles were given purely nominal codings which bore no relationship to variations in either chassis or body specification and served merely to warn the overhaul shops against trying to mix and match them. Perhaps the staff at Chiswick responsible for allocating codes were too unsure of what modifications might or might not have been made to individual vehicles under the Reigate regime even to attempt allocating codes with any degree of precision; whatever the reason, the method they adopted made a complete mockery of the system. Code 2/1ST, for example, lumped together chassis with single and triple servos, and with both left and right hand petrol tanks. In similar vein, body code ST9 embraced almost every type of highbridge body in the Country Bus fleet including the bodies on the six Lewis vehicles which were of 6-bay construction and bore no physical resemblance to any others. Even more remarkably, even the open staircase body on ST 1139 was lumped within the ST9 category. When, in October 1937, a standard LGOC ST2 body was diverted to permit heavy overhauling of the 46 Ransomes bodies to take place, it too was given the generic code ST9, and when the six ex-Lewis chassis received LGOC bodies in 1939 and 1942 they retained their old classification of 2/1ST9 even though they were now entirely different in appearance from the way they had been before. The only highbridge Country Bus vehicles to escape the blanket 2/1ST9 categorisation were the Bluebirds which were 3ST4.

The ST codes were as follows:

CHASSIS		Fuel tank position
1ST	Ex LGOC with triple servo braking	Nearside
1/1ST	Ex LGOC with single servo braking	Nearside
2/1ST	Country Bus with triple or single servo braking	Nearside or offside
3/1ST	Lowbridge bus with triple or single servo braking	Nearside or offside
2ST	Ex Tilling with triple servo braking	Offside
1/2ST	Ex Tilling with single servo braking	Offside
2/2ST	Ex Chariot ST 1028	Nearside
3/2ST	Ex Empire ST 1029	Offside
4/2ST	Ex Pro Bono Publico ST 1030	Offside
5/2ST	Ex Pembroke ST 1031	Offside
3ST	Ex LGCS later type chassis for Bluebird body	Nearside
4ST	1ST temporarily converted to gas propulsion (wartime)	Nearside

BODIES			
ST1	Body 10493 with square cab	Nearside	(a)
ST1/1	Standard LGOC body	Nearside	(b)
ST2	Standard LGOC body with revised lower deck seating	Nearside	(b)
ST2/1	Camel back type body	Nearside	(b)
ST3	Metro Cammell 'all-metal' body 11535	Nearside	(c)
ST4	Bluebird type	Nearside	(d)
ST5	Not used		
ST6	Body 10237 with revised staircase	Nearside	(b)
ST6/1	Camel back body 12354 with revised staircase	Nearside	(b)
ST7	Tilling body with outside staircase	Offside	(e)
ST8	Birch outside staircase body ST 1028	Nearside	(h)
ST8/1	Dodson outside staircase body ST 1029	Offside	(h)
ST8/2	Dodson outside staircase body ST 1030	Offside	(h)
ST8/3	Birch outside staircase body ST 1031	Offside	(h)
ST9	LGOC body ex National and East Surrey	Nearside	(f)
	Ransomes body ex East Surrey and Autocar	Offside	(g)
	Shorts body ex East Surrey	Nearside	(f)
	Shorts 6-bay body ex Lewis	Offside	(f)
	Shorts outside staircase body ST 1139	Offside	(f)
	LGOC body used as float for Ransomes & to replace Lewis	Nearside or offside	(h)
ST9/1	Shorts or Strachans lowbridge body	Nearside or offside	(i)

Notes
(a) Code never used, probably indicating that body 10493 had been rebuilt to standard specification by the time coding system was introduced
(b) Compatible with 1ST and 1/1ST chassis and often interchanged between chassis pre-war and occasionally afterwards
(c) Originally compatible with 1ST and 1/1ST chassis but remained with same chassis as ST 150 after being back at Metro Cammell works between July and October 1936
(d) Compatible with 3ST chassis but bodies always stayed with their original chassis
(e) Compatible with 2ST and 1/2ST chassis and often interchanged between chassis pre-war and occasionally afterwards
(f) Linked generically with 2/1ST chassis but always remained with their original chassis
(g) Linked generically with 2/1ST chassis. Bodies exchanged between chassis during 1937-39, but only those chassis which had always carried Ransomes bodies
(h) Formerly coded ST1/1 or ST2
(i) Always stayed on their original chassis

CHAPTER 17
ST 1140

Long after the last ST had been built, and only just over a year before the first withdrawals from service began, the ST class was temporarily augmented by one more vehicle when a newcomer appeared on service trials in west London. ST 1140 was destined to experience only the briefest of careers, but its importance in London bus history cannot be underestimated for it heralded the development of the phenomenally successful RT class. In fact it was RT 1 in disguise.

Probably as early as 1935 London Transport had initiated the process of drawing up a specification for a completely new chassis to form the basis of its double-deck fleet for the nineteen-forties under the direction of two highly skilled engineers, A A M Durrant, Chief Engineer (Buses & Coaches) and J W Wicks who was in charge of development. Their task was to create a bus that would be more than a match for an operating environment which was becoming increasingly more onerous in terms of traffic levels and congestion, whilst securing economies in operation and maintenance which the Board badly needed to ease the financial pressures that were bearing down on it. Working closely with AEC's design team at Southall through a joint experimental committee, the design gradually evolved to the extent that a prototype chassis was built. Perhaps for reasons of commercial sensibility, the joint committee appears to have worked in the utmost secrecy, and no records of their deliberations and decisions appear to have survived, if they were kept at all.

From the outset it was accepted that a successor to the STL would need greater engine power along with other enhancements to operating performance such as improved braking and gear changing. In order to reduce running costs, improvements in fuel consumption, maintenance requirements and operating reliability were needed too. Particular attention was focused on the adoption of air pressure systems both for braking and for gear changing in the preselective gearbox. So far, vacuum brakes had been standardised upon aided on more recent vehicles by hydraulic systems, and the use of air braking on motor vehicles meant treading new ground. Although London Transport was building up extensive experience of air braking on trolleybuses, this was confined only to low speeds after the regenerative and rheostatic electric retardation systems had taken effect, and the provision of smooth air braking at all levels of the speed range remained a problem.

In regard to engine power and performance, the policy of London Transport, and of the LGOC before it, had been to provide just enough power to meet the most stringent of operating environments. However a new line of thought was developing that the provision of substantially greater power than was strictly necessary would result in engines working less hard, giving a resultant decrease in unit wear and the prospect of a longer life for the engine as a whole, with little or no accompanying increase in fuel consumption.

Another strand of investigation was into whether the employment of indirect injection in the combustion chambers of diesel engines, favoured up to now by both London Transport and AEC on the grounds of smooth running, was really better than direct injection which appeared to offer better fuel consumption. A major influencing factor proved to be the placing into service at Hendon garage between April and July 1937 of a new fleet of Leyland Titans, STD 1-100. These vehicles were fitted with Leyland's standard 8.6 litre direct injection diesel engine which was steadily winning converts right across the industry, and was renowned for its smooth running especially towards the top end of the speed range. The STDs proved an instant success, both with drivers for their road performance which well outshone the STL, and also with engineers for their incredibly low rate of service breakdowns and for their ease of maintenance. When London Transport carried out in-depth investigations into the performance of the STDs after the class had been in service for a few months they disbelieved the initial results because these were so extraordinarily good. The tests were taken again, merely to confirm the original findings as being correct. With a miles per gallon figure of 10.36 in 1938 they outshone even the legendary Gardner 6LWs in LT 1417-1426 (at 9.95mpg), whilst their mileage operated between breakdowns was a staggering 2½ times better than the STL. Above all, the STDs provided proof, if such was still needed, that the provision of higher power could be both beneficial and economic for in-town operation. They also emphasised the wisdom, already demonstrated by the 6LWs, of employing direct rather than indirect injection in combustion chamber design to achieve worthwhile fuel economy.

The prototype chassis was quietly assembled at Southall during 1937 and numbered O6616749 in the Regent series. It embodied a new frame design and, though evolutionary rather than revolutionary, included such novelties as automatic brake adjusters and automatic lubrication in addition to the air braking and gear operating systems, plus an improved driver's position, higher and further forward than hitherto. With the radiator and bonnet mounted much lower than usual, the driver's view of the road ahead and of the nearside kerb promised to be superb. A completely new design of 8.8 litre engine was constructed the first of which – out of an authorised batch of seven – was bench tested in October 1937. This engine, though retaining the familiar bore and stroke of 115mm and 142mm respectively, was designed for greater durability by distancing the cylinders slightly further apart and by giving a greater bearing area for the crankshaft, which was itself strengthened. Crucially, allowance was made within the design for a future increase in bore size to 120mm to produce the 9.6 litre output which became the ultimate goal for the new model. A tidier front end was achieved by using gear rather than chain drive for the timing, which produced an engine only marginally longer than the 7.7 despite the wider spacing of the cylinders. The design allowed the use of a number of different combustion chamber arrangements. This was probably a reflection of differences of opinion between various members of the design teams at Chiswick and Southall, and initially an indirect Ricardo Comet III type head was fitted both to the test-bed engine and also to the one ultimately installed in the prototype chassis.

On 6th December 1937 a model of the new bus complete with body was shown to London Transport's Engineering Committee chaired by Frank Pick from which, after a number of subsequent small and mostly cosmetic modifications, the finalised design developed. It was probably then, or some time very soon afterwards, that the type letters RT were adopted. Construction of RT 1's body was put in hand at Chiswick soon after the basic details were settled, but with its anticipated completion date some months ahead, the decision was taken to commence service trials with the new chassis using a second hand body as a stop-gap measure. A meeting on 28th April 1938 officially approved a Special Expenditure Requisition for "1 AEC RT chassis with oil engine and fluid transmission and for the building of one special double deck body for fitting to this chassis" at a projected cost of £3,750, and, at the same meeting, the withdrawal of a surplus Leyland Titan bus was sanctioned which, without this being specifically stated in the accompanying minute, was to provide the temporary body for mounting on the new chassis. Now in full running condition, RT 1's chassis was delivered from Southall to Chiswick on 23rd May 1938, and it formally became London Transport property on 30th June.

Meanwhile a suitable body had been selected to mount on the chassis of RT 1. To simplify matters as far as possible, a body built to accommodate approximately the same 16ft 4ins wheelbase as the RT was needed, and the obvious solution was to select one from a collection of ex-independent Leyland Titans now in storage in the old AEC works at Walthamstow as these were built to a wheelbase of 16ft 6ins and would thus not need too much modification to suit the new chassis. The first mass withdrawal of these had taken place in the final days of 1937 but none had yet been authorised for disposal. TD 111 was selected, though whether this was an informed choice based on the known condition of its bodywork or merely that it was perhaps the vehicle closest to the exit gate is not known. As early as 8th April 1938 TD 111 was extricated from the Forest Road yard and driven to Chiswick where its body would have been promptly removed for overhaul and subsequent modification to adapt it to its new use.

It is perhaps unfortunate that the body chosen to grace the new chassis, albeit temporarily, was a particularly old fashioned and ungainly looking one. TD 111 had been one of a batch of six Leyland double deckers placed in service by the City Motor Omnibus Company Ltd of Astbury Road, Peckham in March 1931 and numbered T 1-6 in the City fleet (TD 111 having formerly been T 2, registered GO 1348). Unusually, they had been based not on the standard Leyland Titan TD1 chassis but on the Tiger TS3 single decker (although they were sometimes referred to as TD Specials), and they therefore lacked the usual dropped chassis frame extension behind the rear axle found on the Titan. This meant that the platform floor was at the same height as the lower saloon gangway, resulting in an awkward two-step arrangement for passengers boarding and alighting. The unusual specification was demanded by Walter Crook, joint

Managing Director and co-owner of the City business, who also designed the outside staircase bodywork. This was built by Dodson at their Cobbald Road works but bore almost no relationship to that Company's standard product. The City vehicles looked tall and ungainly, an effect emphasised by the unusually high skirt rail which harked back to designs of the mid-twenties, although City's very ornate brown and cream based livery helped to ameliorate the outdated appearance to a certain degree. Internally, City managed to squeeze in 56 passengers with 26 on the lower deck and 30 upstairs. Comfortable if cramped high back seats were fitted but the general internal appearance was spartan thanks to City's predilection for painting everything above the waist line in a clinical white. Surprisingly, City placed a further six almost identical new vehicles into service in February 1932 by which time they really did look outmoded.

City was a highly profitable company and it possessed superb maintenance facilities at its north London depot in Leighton Road, Kentish Town, so the twelve Titan Specials would have been in excellent condition when taken over by London Transport on 7th November 1934, as was the rest of the City fleet. However London Transport was unimpressed by the rear end layout of these vehicles which it envisaged contributing to platform accidents especially on the very busy routes 15 and 101 to which many acquired Titans were allocated having been concentrated at Upton Park garage, and it lost no time in taking them all off the road for modification. Between 13th and 30th November 1934 all twelve were sent to Chiswick for the rear ends to be rebuilt. This was quite a major job as it necessitated the provision of a lowered chassis extension to support a normal height platform, the difference in height resulting in an extra riser on the staircase. In the case of TD 111, it went to Chiswck for rebuilding on 14th November and returned back to Upton Park on 10th December, the second of the batch to see service in its new form.

It is by no means clear why London Transport wished to operate RT 1 incognito in its early days under the guise of ST 1140 but this is what it chose to do. Presumably those in charge of the project during its design and construction stage wanted the secrecy that had surrounded it to permeate into its initial phase of trial operation, and there may well have been a reluctance to unveil it as RT 1 until the modern body specially created for it was ready and the maximum impact could be achieved. The ST class designation was not really an appropriate choice as this denoted a short Regent chassis with a 15ft 6½in wheelbase, but possibly London Transport thought it best to avoid nominating a fleet number in the more appropriate STL series as this was still being added to at the time. Newly repainted body 14722 was mounted on the new chassis on 1st July 1938, and although it retained all the main elements of City's original design, it was clear that major modification had been necessary at the front to make it compatible with the RT chassis. The front axle was placed 2ins further back, but the new square-looking driver's cab reached further forward than the old one to meet up with the RT radiator. The bottom line of the new windscreen was roughly the same as on the old one with no attempt made to take full advantage of the handsome low bonnet and radiator. The latter, incidentally, lacked the usual starting handle shaft, thereby providing a clue to the fact that the vehicle had a flexibly mounted engine. A new floor trap would obviously have been installed to gain access to the centrally positioned preselector gearbox, but it is not known what, if any, other modifications had been necessary. The newly completed ST 1140 initially weighed in at 6 tons 17cwt 0qrs unladen, though even before it entered service this was reduced to 6 tons 14cwt 1qr, but how this was achieved is not known.

ST 1140 was licensed as EYK 396 on 9th July 1938 and was delivered to Hanwell garage four days later in preparation for its entry into service. This came on 23rd July after familiarisation training was completed for drivers and engineering staff, and it took up designated duties on route 18C between Hanwell garage and Wembley Empire Pool. With a running time of only just over half an hour and its operating garage at one end, this was about the least risky operation it could be put upon, and it was only on Sundays that it would have been scheduled to run further afield as far as King's Cross. Despite its misleading fleet number, there seems little doubt that the vehicle's true identity was widely known, indeed an entry even appeared in the Board's Allocation Book stating, "An experimental vehicle known as RT 1 occasionally operates on service 18C from Hanwell garage". For internal record purposes it was generally referred to as ST/RT or similar, and the very lively and observant trade press of the time must have been fully aware of its existence although internal self-censorship – perhaps at the behest of AEC who was a regular advertiser in trade magazines – resulted in nothing about it being published.

It was perhaps just as well that ST 1140 was allocated to Hanwell garage, which was only a short distance away from AEC's Southall works, for its progress on the 18C was plagued with uncertainty. The few scanty records that survive show that, during the test period that ST 1140 was in service, it managed to average only 686 miles between road calls. No doubt some of the calls for assistance from drivers could be ascribed purely to unfamiliarity with the vehicle, but many

must have reflected genuine problems, the scale of which can be put into perspective when compared with the LT class whose comparable average figure for 1938 was 8,625 miles (excluding punctures) or the STLs which were even better at 9,128. It is probable that much of the trouble lay with the new technology surrounding the air system, though no contemporary documentation survives to confirm or deny this.

In view of the mounting evidence in favour of using direct rather than indirect injection for the combustion chamber, it was perhaps surprising that ST 1140's engine employed the latter. However this was soon to change. Clearly there were forces at work favouring both methods, but a rather disappointing initial fuel return of 9.4mpg was probably the reason why the engine was modified after only a short time in service. The indirect injection Comet III combustion chamber was replaced by a direct injection one of the Leyland pot cavity type which brought about an immediate improvement in ST 1140's performance to a much more respectable 10.2mpg. Interestingly, three STLs at Hanwell, STL 2513-2515, had been fitted from new with the same experimental type of engine, and their conversion to direct injection which occurred at about the same time produced a very similar result.

The City Motor Omnibus Company's T 7, one of twelve TD Specials purchased for route 536, demonstrates the totally outdated appearance of these vehicles which seemed completely at odds with the go-ahead nature of one of London's most enterprising independent operators. In City's final year its vehicles were repainted into standard London Transport red livery which further emphasised their antiquated appearance. The high floor level at the rear, to which London Transport took immediate exception, can be clearly seen. *Omnibus Society*

TD 119 (the former City T 10) illustrates the new platform arrangement installed by London Transport together with a destination box of the standard Central Bus type. Like LT 160 standing behind, it was based at Upton Park garage and was about to turn on to the stand at the White Horse, East Ham, when photographed.
D A Thompson

On 10th October 1938, after just 78 days of theoretical availability for service, ST 1140 was taken the short distance from Hanwell garage to AEC's works, officially for "repairs", though it was destined never to enter service in its current form again. Its abrupt and premature demise no doubt came as a big disappointment to everyone concerned, but the harsh truth was that it had only managed to clock up 4,802 miles on the 18C, producing a level of serviceability only slightly more than half of what would have been expected from a standard oil-engined STL. ST 1140 spent the next three months with AEC, presumably undergoing further modification and tests, and it did not return to Chiswick until 30th December 1938. Upon arrival there its Dodson body was promptly removed. The chassis alone, still referred to internally as ST 1140 at this stage, went back to AEC on 3rd

January 1939 and was returned to Chiswick on 22nd March. It is presumed, but not confirmed, that during these three months the engine was either modified to 9.6 litre condition or replaced by another of that capacity.

This is where the brief story of ST 1140 ends. The new body that had been purpose built for it was mounted on 27th March 1939, transforming a really ugly duckling into an object of great beauty proudly bearing its true identity as RT 1. Meanwhile the surplus Dodson body had been added to the disposal list and is recorded as having been sold to Steel Breakers & Dismantlers Ltd on 12th April 1939. Even in its true guise, the chassis of RT 1 enjoyed only a short life and was dismantled on 4th September 1946 although, as is well known, its body survives in preservation to this day at the London Bus Museum in Weybridge.

This photograph of ST 1140 appears to have been taken immediately after the chassis and body were united, and the fleet number had yet to be applied. At this stage the handsome, low-mounted RT radiator had still to reach its final form, and the boxy new cab structure above it, with its high window line, made no attempt to capitalise on the excellent forward and nearside visibility that the RT design offered.

CHAPTER 18
THE WARTIME YEARS

The story of the second World War and its major impact on passenger transport within London and the Home Counties has been told in print many times, and for the most thorough overall coverage of events during this era, Ken Glazier's book *London Buses and the Second World War* (published by Capital Transport in 1986) is highly recommended. The following narrative relates purely, and in depth, to the ST class upon which the events of the war impacted far more severely than any other class of double-deck bus within the London Transport fleet.

War was officially declared on Sunday 3rd September 1939. The era of blackout restrictions, including a 20mph after-dark speed limit, was already in force, and within a few days all vehicles carried their mandatory white markings at front and rear, and lamps were masked to emit the minimum of light. To make them less visible from the air, bus roofs were repainted from their reflective silver to a more sober grey. Fuel rationing for motor vehicles was introduced on 23rd September, and to help cope with a 25% cut in petrol and diesel fuel supplies, about one third of all stopping places were eliminated from sections of route where fixed stops applied and these were rapidly introduced in all areas where they had not been in force.

Unseen by the general public, but destined to be of great historic importance in the overall story of London's transport, was the government's decision to remove the power of the London Passenger Transport Board to be its own master and to place it under the control of the Ministry of Transport through its Railway Executive. The truly great days of the LPTB were over after less than a decade during which it had not only transformed London's transport but had also built up an enviable reputation worldwide.

Even before war was officially declared London Transport had undertaken a massive scheme requiring 490 double deckers to transport staff of the 1st, 2nd and 5th Anti Aircraft Battalions to their battle stations between 24th and 28th August. On the whole, STs with their comparatively low seating capacity stayed back to provide a much denuded passenger service within London, but very long journeys to territory completely new to them were undertaken by 23 STs from Middle Row to points as far afield as Stiffkey (Norfolk), Ferrybridge and Sheffield, whilst 12 Tilling and 5 LGOC STs from Catford went to Portsmouth and Corsham and 19 Tillings plus ST 1031 from Croydon reached Southampton and Avonmouth. To their credit only one failed to complete its mission, Middle Row's ST 319 having to be replaced at Royston by green ST 1086 which was provided by Hertford garage to complete the run to Orgreave and Sheffield.

Almost inevitably, with a huge commitment thrown upon it to transport evacuees, essential personnel, troops and many others, London Transport found itself in a state of turmoil for the first four weeks of the war with many garages working vehicles of types that they would not normally be allocated. Throughout September 1939 the 32 STs transferred to Country Buses from Old Kent Road and Catford on 1st and 2nd of the month stayed put with the exception of the three LGOC type vehicles at Crawley which were removed on the 12th, with two joining those already at Reigate and the third returning to its former base at Old Kent Road.

Although the planned withdrawal of STs had commenced on schedule just before the outbreak of war, none had yet been disposed of and most were still in a state where they could be put back into service if necessary. Of the 1,138 STs inherited by London Transport in 1933, 1,112 continued to be

The scene is serene, but Godstone's ST 1041 carries the wartime trappings of masked headlights and white-tipped mudguards. Fresh out of overhaul only a few days before the war began, it wears the rather sombre all-green 1939 livery with the dark, Lincoln shade predominating which, under wartime conditions, is soon to be phased out. *Michael Rooum collection*

licensed for service, the balance of 26 inactive but still in stock comprising the 17 Tillings and 1 independent withdrawn on 1st August plus a few others delicensed after accidents and for other engineering reasons. The actual composition of the ST fleet on 3rd September 1939 was:

(1) In service Central Area
(2) In service Country Area
(3) Total Licensed
(4) Total in stock

	(1)	(2)	(3)	(4)
Ex-LGOC	798	16	814	817
Ex-Tilling	155	15	170	191
Ex-LGCS	-	111	111	112
Ex-Lewis	-	6	6	6
Ex-Independent	3	-	3	4
Lowbridge	-	8	8	8
Totals	956	156	1112	1138

The operational fleet was distributed amongst 21 (out of 52) Central Bus garages and 19 (out of 30) Country Bus premises. The Central Bus organisation contained a number of garages whose double-deck requirement was satisfied solely by STs such as Middle Row, Turnham Green, Hounslow, West Green and Potters Bar, and hefty allocations of the class could be found at all of these. At the other extreme were Kingston and Uxbridge which had very few double-deck workings but which relied solely on STs to fulfill their tiny double-deck requirements. The 3rd September disposition of STs within the Central Bus fleet was:

Middle Row (X)	94	Hornchurch (RD)	42
Turnham Green (V)	89	Bromley (TB)	39 (c)
West Green (WG)	71	Willesden (AC)	31
Croydon (TC)	71 (a)	Holloway (J)	29
Hounslow (AV)	71	Camberwell (Q)	28
Catford (TL)	64 (b)	Streatham (AK)	24
Potters Bar (PB)	63	Tottenham (AR)	23
Old Kent Road (P)	48	Edgware (EW)	23
Leyton (T)	47	Kingston (K)	4
Harrow Weald (HD)	46	Uxbridge (UX)	4
Norwood (N)	45		

(a) 68 ex-Tilling and 3 ex-independent
(b) Includes 34 ex-Tilling
(c) All ex-Tilling

In comparison with the Central Bus fleet, the STs in the Country area were more widely dispersed amongst garages although in much smaller numbers, with the 19 at Watford High Street representing the greatest concentration to be found anywhere. Indeed the ST content at more than half of the garages did not reach beyond single figures. The position at 3rd September was:

Watford High Street (WA)	19 (a)	Windsor (WR)	6
Godstone (GD)	15 (b)	East Grinstead (EG)	5 (g)
Hemel Hempstead (HH)	14	High Wycombe (HE)	5
St Albans (SA)	14	Staines (ST)	5
Northfleet (NF)	13 (c)	Tring (TG)	5
Reigate (RG)	12 (d)	Crawley (CY)	3 (h)
Grays (GY)	10 (e)	Dunton Green (DG)	3 (h)
Hertford (HG)	8	Dartford (DT)	3 (h)
Amersham (MA)	7 (a)	Luton (LS)	2
Swanley (SJ)	7 (f)		

(a) Includes 4 lowbridge
(b) Including ST 1139
(c) Including 8 ex-Tilling temporarily transferred from Central Buses
(d) Including 7 ex-LGOC temporarily transferred from Central Buses
(e) Including 6 ex-Lewis
(f) Including 4 ex-Tilling temporarily transferred from Central Buses
(g) Including 3 ex-Tilling temporarily transferred from Central Buses
(h) Ex-LGOC temporarily transferred from Central Buses

The turmoil that engulfed the London Transport fleet for the first few weeks of the war, resulting in types of vehicles appearing temporarily at garages to which they would not normally be allocated, passed the ST class by almost entirely. Apart from the instances already noted of standard types ex-Old Kent Road and Tillings ex-Catford moving temporarily to garages in the southern Country area, nothing else untoward occurred to affect the STs. However this was merely the lull before a huge storm that was destined to eliminate the class almost entirely from the London scene, albeit temporarily, the cause of which was a series of severe service cuts plus some complete route withdrawals rendering over 800 buses surplus to requirements, the first of which

The first month of the war found many red double deckers operating temporarily from Country Bus garages. One of these was ST 234 which was transferred from Old Kent Road to Dunton Green on 1st September 1939 and was photographed in Sevenoaks bus station covering a 402 working to Bromley North.

was implemented on 23rd September 1939. When determining which double deckers to delicense, the axe inevitably fell upon the STs which, being petrol engined, were inherently less economical to operate, besides which petrol was regarded as more valuable to the war effort than diesel fuel, making its conservation a matter of prime importance. The low seating capacity of the STs also counted against them, and it was with these factors in mind that plans were rapidly drawn up to eliminate the entire class from service as far as practicable.

The first major batch of ST withdrawals officially occurred on 30th September 1939 when a staggering total of 756 members of the class were delicensed, comprising 639 from Central garages and 117 in the Country area. In order to achieve this, and the incredible number of inter-garage transfers that had to be co-ordinated, this huge logistical task was mostly tackled over a four-day period beginning on 28th September. By the time it was over, the number of Central

With so many STs suddenly made redundant, finding suitable storage sites for them presented a real problem. In these scenes at Chelsham garage STs 934 and 984 are standing at the front of the premises while at least seven others are parked up at the back. In January 1940 they were all moved into covered storage at the South London Coaching Station in Clapham Road. *J Bonell*

garages operating STs had diminished from 21 to just seven (Hornchurch, Hounslow, Middle Row, Potters Bar, Tottenham, Turnham Green and West Green), and all remaining ex-Tilling and independent STs were out of use. Inter-related movements of note included the first allocations of modern oil-engined STLs to Willesden, Streatham, Edgware, Harrow Weald, Kingston, Catford and Uxbridge, while petrol vehicles of the same class were used to eliminate STs from Bromley and Croydon. LTs were employed as ST replacements at Norwood, Old Kent Road and Leyton. The quite substantial ST holdings at Holloway and Camberwell were eliminated without replacement.

In proportion to its size, the Country Bus stock of STs was less heavily decimated by the 30th September withdrawals than the Central Bus fleet had been. The temporary allocation of red vehicles obviously ceased, but two categories existed within the Country fleet for which no suitable replacements were available and this meant that, however desirable it may have been, no target could be set for eventual withdrawal of the entire ST class as was the case in the Central area. The larger of the two exceptions embraced the 19 vehicles at Godstone and East Grinstead equipped with special rear axle ratios. One of these was the unique ST 1139 which remained the only outside staircase ST in service after 30th September. The smaller batch of special vehicles comprised the eight lowbridge STs based at Amersham and Watford High Street, and though one of the Amersham contingent of four was delicensed on 30th September, the rest all remained active throughout the war.

In the main, red STLs were used either directly or indirectly to replace all STs at Dunton Green, Dartford, Grays, High Wycombe, Luton, Reigate, Swanley, Staines and Tring. Included within the 30th September delicensings were all six of the ex-Lewis STs and almost all of the Bluebirds. The 38 vehicles which remained in service thus comprised 28 of the 'standard' Country types (ex-National and East Surrey), 2 Bluebirds, 7 lowbridge vehicles and ST 1139. These were distributed amongst eight garages with Godstone having by far the largest holding at 16; the others were Watford High Street 6 (including 4 lowbridge), Hertford 5, Amersham 4 (including 3 lowbridge), East Grinstead 3, Windsor 2, Northfleet 1 and St Albans 1.

1st November 1939 was set as the next major changeover date on which the final elimination from service of the red ST

Redundant after being delicensed on 30th September 1939, a row of STs stands unwanted alongside the cemetery in Elmers End Road. Most, including the lead vehicle ST 938, are Tillings, but the sloping canopy of the second in the line identifies it as ex-Pembroke ST 1031. Most if not all in this row subsequently went for storage at Bull Yard, Peckham, where they were destroyed in the air raid of 7th September 1940. *J Bonell*

fleet would be accomplished. It proved possible to displace all the remaining 308 STs by reactivating STLs and oil engined LTs which had been delicensed at the earlier great changeover. Thus two big bastions of ST operation, Turnham Green and Hounslow with 76 and 62 respectively, switched over to STL virtually overnight, and the same class of vehicle was also sent to Hornchurch to displace its final 36 STs. Various other movements within the STL ranks enabled petrol STLs to sweep away the remaining 49 STs from Middle Row. At Potters Bar an influx of LTs ousted its last 45 STs and a first time allocation of the same class ousted West Green's 35 STs. A small residual allocation of five STs at Tottenham was disposed of as part of a wider ongoing operation to change this garage's fleet over from STLs to LTs. Just over ten years after the first ST entered service, the streets of central London and the inner suburbs echoed to their sound no more.

The Country Bus fleet went largely untouched by the 1st November 1939 changes which saw a mere three STs being delicensed, bringing the operational fleet down to 35. These reductions included the sole remaining ST at Northfleet, one of the pair remaining at Windsor, and a Bluebird which had so far managed to hang on at Hertford, leaving just one Bluebird still operational at Watford High Street.

Typical of the many STs hurriedly relicensed in the closing weeks of 1939 was ST 336 which returned to service at Tottenham on 13th December. Seen against a wintry background, it displays a destination blind with pre-Johnstone type numbers which was becoming a rarity by this time. *Michael Rooum collection*

In the Central area it quickly became apparent that the massive range of service cuts which had seen the withdrawal of 1,266 buses from the scheduled fleet had been far too deep, and from mid-November through to January 1940, well over 400 workings were restored, mostly as scheduled extras. Although some of these could be met by relicensing stored STLs and LTs, it was inevitable that many STs would need to be put back into service, and the first move in this direction came on 15th November 1939 when the entire fleets at Turnham Green and Hounslow were subjected to change once again. Out went the STLs and in came relicensed STs, 78 at Turnham Green and 67 at Hounslow. The Central Bus fleet had managed without STs for just a fortnight!

A week later, on 22nd November, Hornchurch's double-deck fleet was replaced by 41 STs whilst 25 were relicensed at Middle Row. On 21st December a further 21 were relicensed at Hanwell and six at Willesden, but within a week all 27 had been transferred to Middle Row. Finally for 1939, on 13th December, a variety of garages received STs in varying numbers, establishing a pattern that was to persist for the remaining life of the class whereby STs would be used almost anywhere and everywhere to meet surges of demand, shortages of other types of vehicle, or any other exigency that might arise. The 13th December moves swept away the small and short-lived STL allocations from Kingston and Uxbridge besides spreading the ST class to Tottenham, Holloway, Willesden, Catford, Bromley, Croydon, Chelverton Road, Battersea and Upton Park. The last three had not been included amongst those running STs when the war began, whilst at Bromley the standard ex-LGOC ST was a new feature, its previous allocation having been focused on the native Tilling version. The number of 'standard' STs back in service with Central Buses by the end of 1939 totalled 391.

The Country Bus fleet also needed augmenting, but in a very much smaller way, and this was met during the second week of December 1939, mostly on the 11th, by the relicensing of 13 vehicles at Windsor (4), Hemel Hempstead (4), Reigate (2), and one each at Dunton Green, Hertford and Watford High Street. Interestingly, seven of these (the 4 at Hemel Hempstead, 2 at Windsor and 1 at Hertford) were Bluebirds, and it may have been that a conscious effort was made to restore these newest members of the class back into service. On 19th December the four Hemel Hempstead vehicles were transferred to Watford High Street, but the remainder stayed as they were into 1940.

Even before this, two STs had been placed into service at Leatherhead on 1st November, ST 132 and ST 1100, but these were a special case having been fitted out for gas producer operation. A third, ST 1119, joined them later in the month. These proved to be the precursors of a much larger gas producer fleet established from 1942 onwards, and details of the whole producer gas era and its major impact on the ST class can be found in chapter 20.

Although in excess of 500 STs were in service at the close of 1939, this still left an even larger number out of use and the storage of these presented a huge logistical problem. Apart from Potters Bar and Hounslow, few central garages could offer much space for storing unlicensed vehicles, and although a number of Country premises were able to help out, this still left a sizeable proportion of the unused ST fleet requiring secure housing. Non-operational premises including Chiswick tram depot, the former Tilling works at Bull Yard in Peckham, and the one-time AEC premises at Forest Road, Walthamstow were pressed into use as were the closed garages at Slough and Weybridge. This still left many vehicles parked on the public highway at so-called 'dispersal points' with their steering wheels locked to prevent tampering.

In January 1940 easement was obtained through the availability of the former South London Coaching Station at 80 Clapham Road which was owned but no longer actively required by Red & White Services Ltd. At least 50 Tilling STs were placed there during January 1940 followed later by 13 more, and most remained there until they were needed again towards the end of the year.

Very early in the war it became clear that Chiswick Works, with its increasing commitments relating to the war effort, would be unable to sustain the vehicle overhauling programme at anything like its pre-war level. A widening of the period between overhauls was unavoidable, and from about January 1940 onwards vehicles were programmed for overhaul on a two-yearly cycle. Even this proved too ambitious for the Chiswick body shop where manufacturing for the war effort had quickly taken priority, and a backlog rapidly began to form of bodies awaiting overhaul. The only way to alleviate this was to decentralise the work to other premises and by March 1940, body overhauling at Chiswick had virtually ceased. The process is described in fuller detail in the companion volume on the LT class, and it suffices to record here that, for the bulk of the war, body overhauling was carried out at Chiswick tram depot and also in garages at Alperton, Elmers End and Reigate.

Chassis overhauling continued at Chiswick, and whilst bodies were still lifted to enable mechanical work to be carried out, each one was normally reinstated on the chassis that it had come into the works with. Except in certain specific cases, none of which applied to the ST class, the former 'float' system was abandoned. This created a spares bank of bodies which were stored outdoors at Chiswick Works and, where reusable, were mainly employed as replacements for war damaged bodies.

From about the start of 1940 a notable change in the appearance of the Country Bus fleet began to take place when green liveried vehicles began emerging from overhaul freshly repainted in an identical manner to the Central Bus fleet except that green was substituted for red on the lower and mid-decks panels. The use of pale green paint was eliminated entirely, and window frames and surrounding areas were now in what was still officially called grey although it now looked to all intents and purposes more like off-white. The final vestiges of the earlier, unsatisfactory pre-1939 two-tone green were quickly swept away, and most of the STs in the later Lincoln green style were duly repainted green and white as the war moved on, although a few were missed out and still carried the 1939 version of the Country Bus livery right through to when peace was resumed.

The first ten months of hostilities – sometimes referred to as the "phoney war" – brought none of the anticipated bombing, although emergency call-outs for the London bus fleet were common especially from May 1940 onwards as floods of homeless refugees from continental Europe required transporting to rest centres such as those at Wembley and Alexandra Palace. With the threat of attack from the air becoming ever more pressing, a small fleet of around 40 unlicensed STs – mostly Tillings – was distributed to a host of locations for use by Air Raid Precautions (ARP) as control centres and guard rooms. Their destinations varied widely from ST 926 in the relative peace and quiet of far flung Tunbridge Wells to ST 896 at Athol Street in the epicentre of where the fiercest bombing would be expected when it finally came. Though most were stationed at bus garages, there were exceptions and an ARP guard room was even allocated to the Forest Road premises at Walthamstow where a large number of unlicensed buses were stored.

One of the first Country Bus vehicles to receive the new green and white livery was Godstone's ST 1067 in February 1940. In this instance the green on the between-decks panels reached right up to the windows but those that followed were painted to match Central Bus style with a deeper area of white. *Alan B Cross collection*

Included amongst the many Tilling STs relicensed in the autumn of 1940 was ST 908. Officially allocated to Bromley but running on loan to Catford, it displays the most rudimentary of route information for route 75. Standing alongside it at Norwood Junction is Norwood's LT 327.
G E Baddeley

The massive influx of Tilling STs into Watford High Street garage in October 1940 included ST 851 which is shown being diligently washed down by three women general hands in a photograph taken to show ladies covering men's duties under wartime conditions. At the time a programme was in hand for lowering the side lights on the Tilling STs, and the removal of the nearside one from the canopy of ST 851 has enabled a rear view mirror to be provided in its place.

With so many STs inactive, it was no problem to lend the chassis of ST 237 to the War Department in January 1940 for instructional purposes from which it did not return until two years later. Meanwhile mundane matters still had to be attended to. ST 1139 was taken out of service at Godstone on 1st February 1940 and the conductors on the sole outside staircase vehicle in the Country Bus fleet were probably not sorry to see it go. However it was clearly not the Board's intention to dispose of this non-standard vehicle just yet, as later in the same month it was converted back to a standard rear axle ratio of 6¼:1 even though it was not immediately required for use, and was placed in store at Windsor. A few months later, on 10th May 1940, the very first ST disposals took place when Tilling ST 841, 901, 1013, 1014 were sold to the British Broadcasting Corporation. The sale address given was 87 Kings Avenue, Clapham but this was just one of the decentralised locations that the BBC was now occupying and the four STs were required for the daily movement of staff from the railhead at Edgware to Aldenham House at Elstree.

German bombers finally reached London in daylight raids on 6th July 1940, heralding the start of the Blitz that was to last virtually unabated through to June 1941. Just before this, on 1st July, London Transport had started to withdraw temporarily from service the bulk of its brand new but troublesome RT class pending modifications to their braking systems. Vehicles from Chelverton Road garage were de-licensed initially, their replacements being STLs from a variety of locations but principally from Tottenham where 14 STs, mostly taken from unlicensed stock, were used to make up the deficiency. The next and much bigger batch of RT withdrawals came on 1st August by which time the horrors of war were being fully felt on the home front. This time no fewer than 54 relicensed STs were sent directly to Chelverton Road, displacing not only RTs but also the STLs received earlier which now moved the short distance to Putney Bridge, the only other garage currently running RTs.

The first ST casualties of the war came on 11th August when fire spread through a group of ten unlicensed Tilling vehicles officially in the care of Leyton garage but actually parked away from it on a dispersal site. The use of dispersal sites by bus operators was encouraged by a government directive aimed at minimising damage from bombing and it is ironic that, in this instance, the vehicles would have been safer if they had been parked in Leyton garage itself. The ten vehicles were soon towed to Chiswick Works where the extent of the damage could be assessed and in every case the body-work was declared to be fit only for scrap. Most of the chassis were set aside for re-use after overhaul but in one instance, ST 840, the chassis was also dismantled rendering it the first bus to be completely written off as a result of enemy action.

The introduction of peak hour express services in October 1940 provided work for many STs including Tillings such as ST 852. Bromley based, and equipped with a full destination display including an EXPRESS BUS notice in the bulkhead window, it was photographed at London Bridge loading up for a fast run to Bromley. *C F Klapper*

The remaining chassis, along with other STs whose bodies were subsequently also removed for scrap, formed the basis for a batch of 20 armoured cars supplied to the Home Guard under General Sir Sirgisson Brookes in December 1940 and January 1941.

The impressive and massively strong steel-clad bodies were constructed for them at Chiswick and it is thought that they were fitted out internally in the Royal Army Ordnance Corps workshops at Bittacy Hill. With ½ inch thick armoured plating they would presumably have been quite slow and cumbersome when on the move. Nineteen of the armoured cars were based on former Tilling chassis (ST 853, 876, 889, 892, 898, 901, 902, 911, 924, 943, 948, 952, 954, 958, 978, 997, 1004, 1019), the odd man out being ex-Chariot ST 1028. It is doubtful if any of these impressive looking war machines were ever seriously used in action, and though the ultimate fate of most remains unknown, a few were returned to Chiswick during the summer of 1943 where their chassis were stripped for spares.

Two more Tilling STs also left the fleet during 1940 though it is not known whether their release was voluntary or if they were impressed by the military authorities. The latter was probably the case with ST 886 which passed to the Superintendent of Naval Stores at Devonport dockyard on 14th September, but the reason why ST 930 was acquired by the Ministry of Supply on 12th July is unknown. Under Blitz conditions sales were no longer on the agenda, especially after a direct bomb hit on the old Tilling premises at Bull Yard, Peckham on the evening of Saturday 7th September 1940 resulting in no fewer than 51 stored vehicles being destroyed, the bulk of which were STs, 24 in all (the remainder being 11 LTs, 11 TF private hire coaches, 1 CR and 1 T single decker and three miscellaneous vehicles). The STs destroyed included the first six LGOC type to be written off (ST 24, 247, 500, 526, 600, 788) as well as 16 Tillings (ST 890, 927, 938, 965, 967, 973, 974, 980, 990-992, 1003, 1007, 1008, 1010, 1021) and two ex-independents (ST 1030, 1031). After as much had been salvaged from the remains as possible, the casualties were all officially written off books on 22nd October. Nearly two months after the major catastrophe at Bull Yard, in the early hours of Friday 1st November 1940, ST 739 was destroyed along with three STLs when a series of fires took hold in Camberwell garage as a result of a bomb strike. The bodies of five more STs were fatally damaged in this same incident and replacing them made a heavy inroad into Chiswick's float of spare bodies.

With the relative peace of the pre-Blitz lull shattered, London Transport embarked on a hectic phase of activity to keep London moving. STs began to be brought out of storage from 13th September 1940 onwards and dispatched to a host of garages, 19 of which received STs in September alone with more to follow later. In addition to all its scheduled requirements, the Central Bus department needed to hold a float of 125 double deckers licensed ready for service to replace buses damaged by enemy action, as well as providing cover for the Underground during air raid alerts when the tunnels under the Thames were closed, or any other emergencies that might arise. The pressure on the fleet was further intensified on 20th October when 142 buses were restored to the schedules, whilst from the 24th of that month ten peak hour limited stop operations commenced covering services which paralleled surface railway lines deemed vulnerable to disruption, followed by a further ten on 4th November. Such was the pressure on the fleet that the famous and well recorded hiring

of provincial buses began on 22nd October to augment the Board's own resources after London Transport had appealed through the Minister of War Transport for help while its own vehicles were being repaired. Despite all this pressure, London Transport managed to find nine STs to double deck the bulk of route 247 (the section between Collier Row and Harold Wood) on 20th November 1940, leaving just two single-deck LTs to cover the rural eastern leg to Brentwood. The outward spread of STs during the autumn months of 1940 was so great that only three garages out of 52 in the Central area failed to receive any. These were Alperton, Clay Hall and Shepherds Bush; even unlikely locations from which STs hardly ever ran, such as Loughton and Twickenham, enjoyed small allocations for a short time.

The intense pressure on vehicle resources meant that even Tilling STs – which London Transport hoped it had finally discarded – had to be returned to passenger service. On 17th September a lone example, ST 937, was relicensed for service at Merton, and though their reappearance was slow at first with just four more coming into use at Croydon on the 27th of the same month, a spirited revival followed from 7th November through to 10th December. This was partly made possible by a decision taken on 29th October to reinstate for service all 34 Tilling STs then being used by the Home Guard, alternative arrangements having to be made at garages to accommodate their personnel. By the end of 1940 107 Tilling STs were back in service with Central Buses. The pre-war policy of segregating them from the LGOC type was abandoned and they were widely distributed among 21 garages. In many instances it had not been a straightforward case of putting them straight back on the road after a cursory mechanical inspection. Many had been omitted from the scheme to adjust their lighting systems to meet ARP requirements and this had to be done through the fitting of internal and platform cowls and headlamp masks, whilst on some which still retained side lights mounted at canopy level, these were moved downwards to make them more suitable in the blackout. In many cases steering column locking devices also had to be provided.

Perhaps the most interesting of all additions to the Central Bus fleet at this time, albeit temporarily, were four green STs, two of the ex-National type and two with square cabs ex-East Surrey, which were licensed on 17th September at Leyton (ST 106, 1101), Hackney (ST 107) and Dalston (ST 1095). This was the first time that any green STs had ever been deployed on Central Bus service, and they remained at work until 7th October when they were required for work 'back home' at Dunton Green.

In the Country Bus department, too, pressure of demand for additional rolling stock resulted in STs being returned to service in increasing numbers to meet normal service demands, to serve as reliefs on Green Line operations and to provide transport for strategic locations such as the London Aircraft Production works at Leavesden. The relicensing of STs really got under way on 23rd September 1940 and continued weekly up to 12th October, with a large number of consequent STL movements to allow the STs to be concentrated initially on a small number of garages with Dunton Green and Watford High Street being the main recipients. A new dimension was added to the picture on 12th October when the first twelve of many standard red STs were transferred into the Country area direct from Central Bus garages, the first recipients being Amersham with five and Watford High Street with seven.

The September and October relicensings saw the return to service at Watford High Street of most of the Bluebirds. The six Lewis vehicles were also made operational once again, and although three of these now carried standard LGOC bodies, the unusual and instantly recognisable Shorts' features could still be found on ST 1138, which was relicensed at Dunton Green on 23rd September, ST 1133 which started work at Hemel Hempstead on 7th October, and finally on ST 1134 which was licensed a week later at Amersham. All of this was overshadowed, however, by an event which occurred on 18th October when no fewer than 26 Tilling STs made a spectacular return to Country service, every one of them at Watford High Street which was under tremendous pressure at the time with 13 vehicles being required daily to transport LMS Railway staff to and from their temporary wartime headquarters alongside all its other commitments. Its staff must have wondered what they had done to deserve the imposition of such a sizeable fleet of outmoded, outside staircase vehicles. In the week prior to their appearance at Watford, 21 of the Tillings had been under preparation at various Country garages, even at such unlikely locations as Chelsham – which never ran STs of its own during the war – and the small Green Line base in Tunbridge Wells.

Further relicensing of STs for Country service took place on 1st and 11th November 1940 with many more in December, including 21 more red ones which were this time widely distributed to garages at Guildford, Hemel Hempstead, Northfleet, Staines, Tring and Windsor. Two of the fleet's oddities were relicensed in December. On the 10th, ST 1139 returned to service, this time at Windsor, and on the same day the last remaining 'pirate' ST, ex Empire ST 1029, was placed into service at Guildford, making its way to join ST 1139 at Windsor ten days later.

Shortly before Christmas 1940, on 18th December, the Bluebird STs were involved in an allocation reshuffle. For a few months the bulk of the batch – 17 in all – had been concentrated on Watford High Street garage, the remainder being scattered around the fleet with three at Windsor and one each at Amersham, Dunton Green and Hertford. Now all were brought together in three locations in roughly equal numbers – eight each at High Wycombe and Amersham and seven at Luton, a neat arrangement that did not last long.

By now it was becoming quite common to see vehicles in service with anti-shatter netting glued to their windows using a special heavy-bodied varnish. The use of netting had first been tried on an experimental basis from 10th September 1940 with an initial trial of 100 vehicles each on the bus, tram, trolleybus and Underground networks where it was applied to windows not fitted with safety glass. This was followed by a subsequent decision to extend it to all vehicles. Despite its undoubted usefulness, the window mesh proved very unpopular with passengers because it badly hampered visibility, and despite friendly exhortations not to vandalise it, it was not until 1942 when formalised peepholes edged by diamond shaped wooden frames were introduced that it began to be more generally respected. From the late summer of 1940 trials had also taken place with various types of wooden and metal boards to replace window glass which was being lost in large quantities because of bomb blast and was becoming increasingly hard to replace through supply shortages, and it quickly became commonplace to see buses operating in service with boarded up windows.

During 1941 another wartime measure became evident in the form of restricted blind displays with the aim of reducing the use of blind material by 50 per cent, although this impacted less on the STs than on other double deckers because in most cases their displays were already by no means over generous. In fact former Tilling, National and East Surrey buses were not affected at all and nor was the small fleet of lowbridge STs. The ex-LGOC camel backs, too, were unaffected except that, if any of these were still carrying their front intermediate point board listings, they eventually ceased to do so. Standard ex-LGOC STs had the bottom part of their front destination box masked out in black, and it was only the Bluebirds that really required very much masking. On these – and unlike the Bluebird LTs on Central Buses – the roof number box remained in use, but the front and back destination screens were masked out as were the top and bottom sections of all three 'via' boxes, the remaining space on which was now used to show the destination and a reduced list of intermediate points. The process of masking, and the manufacturing of blinds of the revised type, was by no means instantaneous and more than two years elapsed before the whole fleet had been dealt with.

The anti-shatter window netting which made its appearance in September 1940 was far from popular with passengers despite the protection that it offered, and the gloominess that it caused inside the bus can be seen on the upper deck of ST 159. Overhauled into green and white livery at Reigate in February 1941, this East Grinstead based bus now carries Country Bus-type thin, curved moulding around its driver's canopy and it has also lost its opening front windows. ST 159 was not one of the East Grinstead buses with low ratio rear axle and it was presumably restricted to localised short workings on route 409. *Andrew N Porter*

The hazards of the Blitz continued unabated into 1941 and the newly invigorated ST class continued to play a full role in keeping London moving. At the start of the year no fewer than 42 out of 52 Central Bus garages had an allocation of STs. Vehicles of the Tilling type continued to be allocated indiscriminately amongst these, and 28 garages had at least one and often many more Tillings on their books. However the position with regard to these was regularised during the third week of February when all were concentrated into five locations, their natural Tilling home bases of Bromley, Catford and Croydon, plus Chelverton Road and Plumstead. By dint of their age and versatility, the STs had become maids of all work within the fleet, covering for other classes when these were unavailable and handy for meeting emergency situations when these arose. At the summer Central Bus programme of 2nd April 1941 only 392 STs were actually scheduled for service from 21 garages whereas, in reality, a vastly greater number than this was licensed from double the number of garages and they could be expected to turn up on almost any route at any time.

Starting in March 1941 a slight easement in the vehicle availability position occurred with the relicensing for service of some of the temporarily withdrawn RTs, a process which continued through to the autumn as supplies of equipment for their modification gradually filtered through. Subsequent reallocations resulted in the withdrawal of STs from various locations; in fact ten Central Bus garages had lost their STs by the end of the year. A huge setback occurred, however, on the night of Saturday 10th May when Croydon garage was totally burnt out by bombing, causing the total loss of no fewer than 58 double deckers. Most of those destroyed were STLs but two Crossleys on loan from Manchester Corporation were amongst the casualties as were two Tilling STs (ST 893, 895). A third, ST 883, was also badly damaged but its chassis was salvageable and within five days it had been fitted at Chiswick with a replacement body and returned to service. With equally incredible efficiency, near normal operation was achieved at Croydon on the very next day after the bombing by transferring vehicles in overnight from all over the fleet with STs – 41 of them – in the majority.

Croydon garage presents a scene of almost complete destruction after the bombing of 10th May 1941. Comparatively unscathed compared with the burnt out wrecks behind, Tilling ST 883 shares the front row with three different types of STL. Almost miraculously, ST 883 was put back into service just five days later after receiving a replacement body at Chiswick. *L T Museum*

The diamond shaped apertures later inserted into the window mesh made it marginally more acceptable to passengers and less prone to wilful damage. It is carried in this instance by ST 1059, a Leavesden Road based vehicle seen coping with a shift break at Apsley Mills. Still carrying the 1939 livery at this stage in its career, it was repainted green and white in February 1942. *L T Museum*

The Croydon bombing virtually put an end to plans first mooted in February 1941 to convert 13 Tilling ST chassis into lorries for use within the miscellaneous vehicle fleet. The demands on this fleet had spiralled since the start of the war and an already existing shortage of lorries had been exacerbated by the military authorities impressing units of it for war related use. The Board had approved the purchase of up to 29 second hand lorries if these could be found, and the 13 ST conversions would have been in addition to this. Because of fluctuating war conditions, the whole project became quite a saga. After approving 13 conversions on 4th February, the policy was totally reversed on the 25th of the same month subject to a review two months later. On 30th April the scheme became active again, but this time with the number of conversions reduced to seven. Even this was put on hold after the Croydon bombing subject to yet another review after two months. Finally just one conversion took place, with the former ST 937 joining the miscellaneous vehicle fleet – in which it was mainly used as a breakdown tender – in January 1942 with fleet number 625J.

The Country Bus fleet was by no means immune to changes in 1941, the biggest in scale being a revision of work in Watford on 24th February which resulted in no fewer than 22 Tilling STs being transferred overnight from the High Street garage to the smaller premises at Leavesden Road, the first occasion on which the latter had ever had an allocation of STs. Nine went back to Watford High Street during April and May, but between 14th and 19th June all of this garage's Tillings were sent back to the Central area, mostly to Chelverton Road but the odd one to Catford, followed by all of Leavesden Road's which had departed to the same destinations by the 25th. A variety of standard Central and Country STs took their place. The Bluebirds, too, were on the move once again. By 2nd April this seemingly unloved class was concentrated almost entirely at Windsor, allocations of odd ones to Watford High Street and Leatherhead having proved very brief, whilst those not already at Windsor by 2nd April (two at St Albans and one at Reigate) finally reached there on 1st July. This influx of Bluebirds meant that Windsor lost many other STs including, in due course, its two oddities. ST 1029 returned to Central Buses at Croydon on 18th June and ST 1139 was lost to Addlestone on 15th November. At the end of 1941, 134 STs (excluding the lowbridge type) could be found at 16 Country Bus garages. This included 17 red STs which were distributed between Reigate and St Albans (4 each), Watford High Street and Addlestone (3 each), Hertford (2) and Windsor (1).

Relief from the worst horrors of the Blitz came in July 1941 as the German war machine turned its sights on Russia, and though the danger still lurked in the skies over London it was on a much reduced scale allowing a period of relative stability to return. London Transport was able to make a sizeable reduction in its licensed fleet as well as making a concerted effort to return the remaining hired provincial buses to their owners. As early as 1st August 1941 and again on 1st September and 1st October, big inroads were made into the ranks of the active ST fleet. More notable, however,

was a day of major service revisions on 29th October when the entire remaining fleet of Tilling STs was delicensed. Chelverton Road's final 24 had already departed on 1st October as a result of many more new and relicensed RTs being available, whilst the other four garages with Tilling STs had also seen their quantities reduced in recent weeks. However 97 of them were still active to the end (55 at Croydon, 18 at Bromley, 16 at Catford and 8 at Plumstead). The massive influx of standard LGOC STs from all over the fleet on 29th October also brought the demise of ex-Empire ST 1029 which, though it remained in the fleet, was destined never again to run in service in London.

Soon after the Blitz had ended a major event occurred which impacted upon the lowbridge fleet in an unusual way. For many years London Transport and its predecessors had not much favoured the use of this specialised type of double decker, the Board's half-hearted attitude toward their use being undoubtedly influenced by the hostility towards such vehicles shown by the Metropolitan Police. Apart from route 336 on which the eight lowbridge STs were employed, the only other such service was the 410 worked from Godstone garage by a fleet of 12 front entrance crash gearbox STLs. From 26th May the 410 had been unable to run right through between Reigate and Bromley due to closure of the road past the RAF's Fighter Command base at Biggin Hill for security reasons, and shuttle services had been worked at each end. In the Central area, which had never previously operated lowbridge buses, route 245 (Morden–South Wimbledon) had been converted to this type of vehicle in February 1941 (and renumbered 127) using Crossleys and Leylands hired from Manchester Corporation. Their return home posed a problem over double-deck availability which was solved indirectly by redeploying surplus Godstone STLs to route 336, thereby freeing up five STs for the 127. Although this was not enough to cover all of the nine scheduled workings it was better than nothing, the balance being covered by a return of single deckers in the form of LT type Scooters. The release of the

Morden station, and passengers are queuing to board Merton's lowbridge ST 163 on route 127. Judging by its fairly careworn condition quite a lengthy time has elapsed, and much hard work has been done, since ST 163 was repainted red in August 1941.
W J Haynes

Working from Dunton Green garage on the eastern section of the temporarily truncated route 410, ST 1138 remains little changed structurally from the days when it was the most modern member of the Lewis fleet. Ultimately becoming the penultimate ex-Lewis ST to retain its original Short Bros body, ST 1138 finally lost this in favour of a standard LGOC one in March 1942. *Frank Willis*

Godstone STLs had been made possible because the northern end of the truncated route 410, now cut off from Godstone garage and temporarily worked by Dunton Green between Bromley and Leaves Green, did not need lowbridge vehicles.

Five STLs were earmarked to provide Watford High Street's share of route 336 which they took over on 5th August 1941. The deposed STs were sent away to be quickly repainted into red livery, with ST 136, 140 starting work on route 127 from Sutton garage four days later on the 9th, followed by ST 141, 163, 1089 on the 12th. They were quite a mixed bunch having all been rebuilt to various degrees, with ST 141 and 1089 most notable in being the only ones of their type still to retain their original piano front profile. For the time being, Amersham's share of route 336 continued to employ STs using ST 157, 162, 1090 which remained in green livery. The five red lowbridge STs were destined to stay only a short time at Sutton. The major schedule revisions on 29th October which made possible the withdrawal of all the Tilling STs had other ramifications too, one of which was the re-allocation of route 127 to Merton garage which then remained synonymous with this route and its special fleet of lowbridge buses for many years to come.

From a position of acute vehicle shortage a year earlier, London Transport now found itself with a sizeable fleet of double deckers surplus to requirements. At the same time many provincial operators were experiencing severe rolling stock shortages brought about by the need to serve rapidly expanding industrial developments vital to the war effort as well as catering for the transport needs of military bases and airfields, all of this at a time when the supply of new rolling stock had virtually dried up. In London the first of the new 'utility' buses, STD 101, was not received until 24th October 1941 with a meaningful intake of further new utilities not commencing until the first of the Guy Arabs came into service

in December 1942, and a similar pattern was repeated throughout the provinces. It was now time for London Transport to reciprocate the earlier generous assistance received during the Blitz by lending its own surplus buses to other needy operators under arrangements organised by the Regional Transport Commissioners. Most needed double deckers for maximum carrying capacity, so it was inevitable that the vast majority of vehicles sent away on loan would be the same STs that were now lying redundant at various locations around London, and the only exceptions to this were a few Leyland Cub 20-seaters whose small capacity suited them for specific work in country districts. The first vehicles to depart on loan were five Tilling STs which were sent to Coventry Corporation on 30th November 1941, and 286 more STs followed them to various parts of the provinces during the next three years as described in chapter 19. This massive programme, which resulted in every single serviceable Tilling ST being sent away on loan as well as many standard LGOC type vehicles, saw the versatile ST class successfully undertaking a diversity of operations on a scale never achieved by any other London bus class before or after.

Despite all the autumn 1941 withdrawals, 1942 dawned with STs still operating from 33 Central and 16 Country garages, albeit only in ones and twos in several instances. However this picture was destined to change substantially during the year, encouraged by the resumption of new vehicle deliveries, albeit on a modest scale. The Central Bus department received the remainder of its new STDs during May 1942 and took in, at the same time, a small batch of B class Bristols, whilst near the year's end, on 1st December, the first of a steady inflow of new G class Guy Arabs came on books. The Country Bus department benefited from the receipt of new vehicles too, in the form of a batch of 'unfrozen' STLs, the first of which arrived during the closing month of 1941.

Following upon the conversion of the bulk of route 247 from single- to double-deck operation in 1940, further much needed upgradings took place during 1941 using STs as replacement vehicles. The first small move came on 14th May when the Kingston–West Molesey section of route 214 was dealt with, followed by a full scale double decking of the whole service through to Walton-on-Thames resulting in the final removal of all its LT single deckers and a renumbering to 131 on 29th October. Before this, on 9th July 1941, St Albans garage replaced Q types with STs on route 354 (St Albans–Marshalswick) and on 13th August LT single deckers were displaced from route 312 (Watford, Chilcott Road–Little Bushey) at Watford High Street and from route 204 (Lower Edmonton–Chase Farm) at Enfield, the latter being renumbered 128 at the same time. Continuing into 1942, on 25th February Uxbridge garage received four STs to convert route 220 (Uxbridge–Pinner), giving a big increase in seating capacity over the T class that had worked it previously, and on this occasion the same route number was retained, marking the abandonment of the former Central Bus policy of renumbering converted services below two hundred. On 4th March 1942 route 416 (Esher–Leatherhead) was changed over to STs, and on 12th May 1942 route 235 (South Croydon–Selsdon) was absorbed into route 64 worked by Croydon garage on which STs predominated.

During March and April 1942, as STL and LT availability improved, STs were removed from a whole host of Central Bus garages – Battersea, Chalk Farm, Enfield, Merton, Mortlake, Norwood, Nunhead, Palmers Green, Plumstead, Potters Bar, Sidcup, Upton Park and Willesden – though the position remained, as ever, fluid. Chalk Farm and Upton Park received some more later in the year whilst new allocations went to Muswell Hill and Putney Bridge, neither of which had had STs when the year began. This constant toing and froing of STs was to remain the enduring pattern throughout the remainder of the war and for the years that followed. Attempts were also made in 1942 to break up the two big remaining ST monopolies at Hounslow and Turnham Green, presumably to give each garage a proportion of newer and more modern vehicles and to inject higher seating capacity into some of their operations. A plan to exchange 28 petrol STLs between Bromley and Hounslow on 7th March appears to have been abandoned at the last moment, but a similar exchange – this time involving 39 vehicles – went ahead between Middle Row and Turnham Green on 27th May. Up to May 1940 Middle Row had been a formidable user of STs though latterly only a handful had been present and these were not officially scheduled; now it resumed its position as a major user of the class alongside a much reduced holding of petrol STLs.

A well documented feature of the wartime bus scene was the arrangement for assembling lines of double deckers at various parking places in the Central area between peaks to save wasting fuel and rubber on non-essential journeys. The Embankment on 15th July 1942 finds a line-up of STs and STLs from route 1 with Catford's ST 323 at the rear. The STL third from the back still retains its grey roof, all the others having been repainted brown.

STs in the Country area enjoyed a fair degree of stability during the first half of 1942 although outside staircase ST 1139 was taken out of service at Addlestone on 1st February and subsequently went on loan to the provinces. As recorded in chapter 20, Grays garage began to receive producer gas STs on 1st July although entry into service took place later than this, but on 30th September a major upheaval occurred that affected the whole Country ST fleet. Resulting from a further restriction in fuel supplies, the entire Green Line network was withdrawn on this date for the duration of the war together with the closure for the duration of garages at Romford and Tunbridge Wells. The result was that large numbers of STLs were made surplus, which, inevitably, took over ST duties. The latter disappeared entirely from nine garages – Dunton Green, Dorking, East Grinstead, Godstone, Leatherhead, Amersham, St Albans, Swanley and Leavesden Road – leaving a mere 25 (excluding lowbridge vehicles) at Addlestone (8), Reigate (7), Windsor (6), Watford High Street (2) and Hertford (2). In addition there were now red gas producer STs at Grays which numbered nine at the time with more due into service imminently (see chapter 20). Surprisingly, despite the mass delicensing of green STs that took place on 30th September, three red ones remained (excluding the Grays contingent), one each at Hertford, Reigate and Watford High Street.

Most notable of the 30th September events was the withdrawal of the previously sacrosanct STs at Godstone and East Grinstead. Suitable replacements had at last been found in the 'unfrozen' STLs which, with their crash gearbox transmissions, could cope adequately on routes 409 and 411, so eliminating the need to retain a fleet of specially equipped STs. The STLs came from Amersham, High Wycombe and Watford High Street, and the displaced STs were delicensed and subsequently converted in most cases to standard format for wider operation within the Country fleet.

The eight STs at Addlestone were of special note in that they were in camouflage livery of all-over light grey. This had been deemed necessary for all buses serving the militarily strategic Vickers Armstrong works at Weybridge and had been applied to the whole fleet at Addlestone. Repainting of the STs took place between 14th August and 3rd September, bringing a common livery to formerly red ST 26, 115, 144, 146, 590 and green ST 107, 1100, 1132.

By the summer of 1942 the whole question of paint supplies had become problematical. Even earlier than this, in December 1941, a decision had been taken to repaint bus roofs in bauxite (a shade of brown achieved by mixing red oxide with a carbon black tint) to conserve dwindling supplies of grey pigment, and the sight of brown roofs quickly spread throughout the fleet. By the beginning of August 1942 the future availability of sufficient supplies of Lincoln green was becoming doubtful and it was accepted that other shades may have to be used. Fortunately this never became necessary, but shortage of pigment for red paint resulted in a September trial of an STL painted Indian Red (which was actually a shade of brown and resulted from mixing bauxite with standard red) with cream rather than off-white reliefs. The subsequent supply of red paint deteriorated to the extent that all full repaints (as distinct from touch-up-and-varnish jobs) were done in brown and cream from 10th December 1942 up to and including 6th February 1943. Inevitably many Central Bus STs appeared in brown livery some of which – including Tillings – carried this when on loan to the provinces.

October 28th 1942 witnessed a resurgence of STs at two Country locations one of which, Epping, had never previously operated this class of vehicle. The other was Hertford, and the buses displaced in both cases were STLs. The Country Bus department had been considering for some time the redeployment of STLs to ease capacity problems in various areas and this was part of that process. At Hertford certainly, and possibly also at Epping, there was a reciprocal benefit in that the STs, with their greater speed and agility, were more suited to fast running on trunk services such as Hertford's 310/A (Enfield–Hertford/Rye House). Those old enough to remember them will recall their spirited performance on country sections of route. This principle was extended further in 1943, and it is significant that none of the routes reconverted to ST for operational purposes ever went back to STLs but remained in the hands of the ever-ageing petrol double deckers until new RTs arrived on the scene in 1948.

On 6th July 1942 lowbridge ST 162 was transferred from Amersham to join the Godstone STLs at Watford High Street. This was the last lowbridge ST ever to operate from there, for a schedule revision of 16th December 1942 saw the whole allocation on route 336 concentrated at Amersham to overcome driver shortages in the Watford area. The two lowbridge STs that had remained at Amersham were now rejoined by ST 162 along with three Godstone STLs and the first of a new batch of wartime lowbridge STLs created by combining new Chiswick-built bodies with old chassis. STL 2148 had been in service at Watford High Street since 1st August and was unique in being the only preselector bus on the 336.

Late in 1942 the size of the ST fleet diminished by two, one withdrawal being on a planned basis and the other through unforeseen circumstances. ST 40, which had been delicensed at Hertford as one of the mass withdrawals of 30th September, was stripped of its body at Chiswick Works later in the year and fitted, instead, with the cut-down Short Bros body from ex-Lewis ST 1138 which, repainted in khaki, was fitted out as a tree lopper. In this form it began work in January 1943 still carrying fleet number ST 40, which it continued to do until the end of the war even though, by June 1943, it had been officially renumbered 646J. The other two ex-Lewis bodies were also surplus by this time. Their rather light and flimsy construction probably meant that they had now come to the end of the road as far as passenger service was concerned and the pre-war policy of replacing them with standard ex-LGOC bodies was revived towards the end of 1941. The first to go was ST 1134, latterly at St Albans, which last ran with its Lewis body on 30th December 1941. Next was ST 1138 at Dunton Green whose last day was 5th March 1942, and finally ST 1133 at Leavesden Road on 18th March. After overhaul, all three returned to the same garages with their 'new' LGOC bodies. In a repetition of what had occurred with ST 1136 in 1939, the replacement bodies were unmodified to suit ex-Lewis chassis in that they still retained their nearside fuelling arrangements, making it highly likely that standard LGOC chassis had in fact been procured from the now defunct overhaul float and that the Lewis ones were dismantled for spares. This trio could be easily differentiated from the three 1939 rebodyings in retaining their large front indicator boxes, suitably masked, and also their rear boxes although these were not used in Country service.

The other two surplus Lewis bodies did not go to waste, for in July 1943 it was decided that these should also be used as tree loppers. As in the case of ST 40, the original plan was that they would be mounted on ex-LGOC chassis. Two standard LGOC bodies would thus be thrown up as surplus, usefully replenishing the stock of serviceable spare bodies which had now almost all been used up. However almost at the last minute the plan was changed and Tilling chassis were used instead, possibly because this involved considerably less modification to the Short Bros bodywork. ST 985 and ST 1001 had recently been returned off hire to Bournemouth Corporation from whom ST 1001, and perhaps also ST 985, had returned to London in damaged condition. They emerged as 5¾ ton tree loppers 647J and 648J respectively in the late summer of 1943, the conversion of ST 985 being completed on 20th August and ST 1001 on 29th September. Unlike ST 40, they were painted dark grey and carried their new fleet numbers from the start.

The second of the 1942 withdrawals mentioned earlier was ST 777. This had ceased running from Hammersmith garage on 22nd April 1942 and, after a period in storage, it had proceeded in August to Chiswick for overhaul. Whilst there, its sale was arranged to the Admiralty under the aegis of its Director of Stores at Bath, and the body was converted at Chiswick (as described in chapter 23) to suit its new role. Its sale to the Admiralty actually took place on 18th December. A few months later the same Admiralty department came back for two more identical purchases, and newly overhauled STs 337 and 798 were selected for sale to them. Both had previously been stored for several months on concrete blocks in the Forest Road yard at Walthamstow along with many other surplus STs; they were handed over to the Admiralty on 19th June 1943. Miraculously ST 798 survives to this day, but far away from Britain, as also detailed in chapter 23.

The fleet remained relatively unscarred by war during 1943 except for the loss of ST 657 on Friday 12th March. Working from Seven Kings garage, it was machine gunned from the air during the rush hour in High Road, Ilford, and tragically the driver and conductor were both burned to death in the fire that quickly ensued. As the months wore on STs came and went from various garages, the more notable losses being from Tottenham starting in January and Sutton from June, both of them as a result of an influx of new Guys received under the Acquisition and Disposal of Motor Vehicles Order 1942. Tottenham received its Guys direct, but Sutton's STs left when STLs arrived from Hanwell after the latter had become the second recipient of the new vehicles. In a re-run similar to the RT fiasco of 1940, Tottenham's Guys were all withdrawn for modification on 1st March giving STs a new boost there, but by May the situation had returned to normal and, for a while, STs ceased to be a force to be reckoned with at Tottenham. Later in 1943, mostly between October and December, there was a resurgence of ST usage by Central Buses to the extent that, whereas the class had been present at 24 garages at the start of 1943, it could be found at 35 at the year's end. Often these were only present in small numbers, with as few as one apiece at Elmers End, Harrow Weald, Hendon, Potters Bar and Victoria. They remained commonplace deputising for STLs and LTs, and they were also useful in freeing-up garages' regular fleets from learner duties (there being no specific training bus fleet in those days as there was in post-war years). STs also found their niche on the many supplementary schedules introduced.

Despite the pressures of war, with its resultant material and manpower shortages, the fleet had to be kept going and this this often required extensive timber replacement on bodies that would, in normal circumstances, have been scrapped. The extent of the work undertaken in Chiswick tram depot can be seen on Croydon's ST 17 which was off the road between 12th January and 1st February 1943.

In the Country area 1943 started off with a reshuffle on the first day of the year when – presumably having noted the success of the reintroduction of STs on route 310/A – trunk routes 301 (Watford Junction–Aylesbury) and 302 (Watford Heath–Hemel Hempstead) were converted from STL in the same way. For scheduling convenience Apsley Mills works services 301A/B/C were converted too as well as sections of works routes 377/A/B over which double deckers were approved to operate. Hemel Hempstead was the garage mostly affected and 20 STs were required there, while Tring needed 9 for its share of route 301. The latter were readily discernible as they were all Bluebirds as distinct from the standard Country types at Hemel Hempstead. The shuffling-around of STLs that ensued brought the withdrawal – temporarily at least – of the last STs and Reigate and Windsor.

The pattern established on the main road between Watford and Aylesbury by the 1st January 1943 injection of STs was destined to undergo yet another drastic change from 1st June when gas propulsion was introduced. As related in chapter 20, Tring was the garage most heavily affected by this and its Bluebird fleet disappeared overnight to be replaced by red LGOC-type STs. Epping had already seen the introduction of gas producers in May or June, whilst Addlestone also received them, although in this case the seven vehicles concerned (ST 47, 192, 324, 335, 648, 730, 801) were in grey livery into which they had been repainted in readiness for their new venture during April and May. Perhaps because of a last minute change of plan, two more were painted grey than were eventually needed (ST 29, 259), so they were painted red again without entry into service at Addlestone.

The Country Bus department was not alone in employing gas producer STs. A small supplementary schedule began running from Camberwell garage from 3rd March 1943, though no further inroads were made into the Central area until 1944 when Croydon and Catford garages joined the ranks using gas producers.

A few more double deckings took place during 1943 making use of the plentiful availability of STs. Most notable was a network of changes in the Addlestone area on 1st June where STs replaced Q-types on 461A (Walton–Ottershaw) and also on the Addlestone to Woking and Walton sections of routes 436 and 461 respectively. These services went straight over to gas bus operation on the day of their double decking. Minor in comparison was the 1st June conversion of works service 378 (Apsley Mills–Boxmoor) and the 22nd December conversion of the Hertford–Watton shorts on route 390.

As on Central Buses, a more widespread use of STs began to occur towards the end of the year, but the most interesting event of note was the reintroduction of Bluebirds at Watford High Street on 6th November. Only three arrived at first, but it soon became evident that a policy decision had been taken to create a permanent and long lasting base in Watford for these 23 vehicles, perhaps in a final acknowledgement that variations from standard in their mechanical specification made them best suited to be concentrated at one location. Some of the first to arrive had been out of service since September 1942 and still had no blind box maskings, which gave rise to some interesting displays until the appropriate masking was attached. By the end of 1943 eleven Bluebirds had arrived at Watford High Street and by June 1944 all were present, except ST 1034 which was involved in the gas producer programme and did not come until February 1945.

The Bluebird STs led a varied existence until they were all gathered together at Watford High Street towards the end of 1943. From January 1941 through to July 1942 ST 1073 was allocated to Reigate garage and was the only vehicle of its type then operating into the Country Bus southernmost territory. *Mick Webber collection*

By the end of 1943 it had become evident that the tide of war was turning in the allies' favour, giving London Transport the confidence to respond favourably to a request received from the Regional Traffic Commissioner on 5th November to recommence operation of the Inter Station service on a daily basis between 7pm and 3am. In pre-war days the Inter Station operation had been notable for its fleet of eight little half-deck 20-seat petrol engine Leyland Cubs. The early war years had found the Cubs used on a variety of occupations including working as lorries for London Aircraft Production and even, in one case, as a Home Guard changing room at Luton garage, but by October 1943 the Department of National Service Entertainment had shown an interest in borrowing the vehicles which went on loan in December to the Entertainment National Service Association (ENSA). They proved useful in carrying artistes, plus their scenery and props, to entertain troops and factory workers at locations all over Britain, but as the need for them declined four were returned to Chiswick where they were prepared for the resumption of their role on the Inter Station run. Six vehicles marked the minimum necessary to maintain the service, allowing for one spare, so the balance had to be made up with STs. In order to provide enough baggage space the rearmost two rows of transverse seats in the lower deck were removed and racks installed, with vertical bars against the windows to stop them getting broken. This reduced the total seating capacity to 40. In order to get the service started on 15th December ST 613 was converted first with ST 164 joining it as the spare bus by the 28th of the month. The traditional Inter Station livery was a very attractive pale blue and cream and ST 613 was turned out in this colour scheme. This added a fifth colour to those in which STs could now be found: red, green, brown, grey and now blue. However ST 164 remained red and in the initial days of the revived Inter Station operation it remained very much as the fall back option for use only when nothing else was available.

As in pre-war times the Inter Station service was worked from Old Kent Road garage and a proposal to allocate it more conveniently to Victoria was never proceeded with. Towards the end of 1944 the availability of Cubs diminished by one in November and another in December when they were hired to Railway Air Services Ltd to ferry airline passengers from the Company's office in Lower Belgrave Street to Croydon Airport. Whilst on this work the Cubs were housed in the basement of Victoria garage. Two replacement STs were needed and ST 454, 757 were converted and painted blue in November 1944. This situation then remained basically static through to the end of the war except that, in April 1945, yet another Cub was dispatched to Railway Air Services leaving just one still in use on the Inter Station run. On this occasion ST 771 received blue livery. Four STs were now in this eye-catching livery and could be widely seen out and about in central London, even in daylight during long summer evenings. A little oddly, despite being one of the two pioneer STs on the service, ST 164 continued to be in standard red.

As 1943 turned into 1944 a visible modification was in the process of being made to the great majority of STs, and also to many LT class vehicles, in a programme covering 2,019 buses in all. For a long time staff had been pressing for the large fare board container incorporated into the front bulkhead to be re-sited at the back of the vehicle on the platform wall. This, they rightly claimed, would make it much more convenient for conductors' use, and they cited the problem as having become more acute since so many women conductors were now employed who were unfamiliar with fares and found it hard to squeeze past standing passengers to consult the fare board. After resisting the request on the grounds of wartime economy, London Transport eventually agreed in August 1943 that the modification should be carried out, a sample vehicle having been inspected and approved, but the expenditure of £500 necessary to carry out the work was not finally authorised until December.

ST 613 at Old Kent Road garage in blue and cream livery. *Alan B Cross*

With many Tilling STs making their way back to London at the end of their provincial hires, the opportunity was taken to start relicensing some of them beginning with an initial batch of eleven on 1st January 1944. Although theoretically available for service use, they were normally to be found carrying passengers only in cases of emergency and were more commonly used on 'learner' duties. Their use was fleetwide and by April 1944 they were working as trainers from at least 29 Central Bus garages, although as they sometimes displayed CS (Chiswick) identification plates or, on occasions, nothing at all, their garage of origin was not always obvious. From 14th August they permeated the Country area too, also as learners. The first known case of Tillings returning to passenger service occurred on 1st January itself when at least five are known to have worked from Catford garage on route 75, but this seems to have been a one-off incident. A further case came on 28th February when five more (ST 837, 966, 979, 986, 1011) were hurriedly retrieved from the Forest Road storage site and sent to Fulwell trolleybus depot to cover a major breakdown in service on route 657 (Hounslow–Shepherds Bush) on which they were driven by trolleybus staff trained as a wartime measure to drive motorbuses but carrying HW (Hanwell) garage plates, which was presumably the garage at which they were fuelled. Similarly five green ex-East Surrey STs were relicensed at the same time (ST 1049, 1050, 1104, 1117, 1125) also for route 657, but these were crewed from Hounslow trolleybus depot. As a wartime measure, trolleybus depots had a nucleus of drivers trained on motorbuses to meet just such an emergency which, in this case, lasted only two days and the vehicles were delicensed again on 1st March. However a rather longer lasting emergency occurred later in March which again called for the relicensing of Tilling and Country Bus STs. A railway replacement service linking the Piccadilly Line station at Holloway Road with the Northern Line at Archway was co-ordinated from Palmers Green garage using

three vehicles temporarily allocated to it and four borrowed ones. Two Tillings were used on this occasion (ST 957, 989) and the green vehicles were former National ST 116, 132, 143, 152 and Lewis ST 1133. There were further examples of where Country vehicles were placed in Central garages for emergency work, an interesting one being the use of ST 1117, 1122, 1127, 1137 at Hornchurch in March and April 1944 to assist in the preparations for D-Day by transporting troops from Warley barracks to the rifle ranges at Rainham. Looking back, it seems surprising that Country vehicles were called upon when there were a large number of red STs in storage and theoretically available, but in all probability the green ones were more readily easy to extricate from storage and to make serviceable than many of their red counterparts.

Towards the end of March 1944 ST 687, an Upton Park vehicle that had been away for overhaul, returned to work fitted with a complete new set of seats on which the conventional upholstery had been replaced by wooden slats. Passengers in some parts of London were already getting used to wooden seats on newly built Guys, and London Transport had decided to experiment with converting existing vehicles to help eke out dwindling supplies of upholstery. ST 687 was one of a pair of converted double deckers examined at Chiswick by the Board's directors on 23rd March when the decision was taken to convert three to four vehicles per week upon overhaul. However only those with seat frames suitable for easy conversion were included within this plan and this specifically excluded the vast majority of STs (in fact all except the Bluebirds). ST 687 remained unique until its next overhaul in September 1947 when conventional seating was reinstalled. Although wooden seats were not destined to become a feature of the ST fleet, difficulty in procuring moquette meant that a substitute had to be found which materialised as a plain, dowdy and sometimes ill-fitting looking leathercloth, and several STs received this treatment either on one or both decks.

The bombing of Elmers End garage on 18th July 1944 brought a quantity of Tilling STs back into public service, albeit in many cases temporarily. ST 860, seen working on route 194, looked smarter than most having emerged from overhaul only as recently as 12th July following a spell with Red & White Services at Chepstow. It would have contrasted strongly with the great majority of those that helped out at Elmers End which were in poor condition and never ran in public service again. *Charles F Klapper*

With the introduction of the Central Bus summer programme on 19th April 1944, scheduled ST usage rose to its highest level since the start of the war. As many as 511 STs were now scheduled to work on 54 services, plus the Inter Station operation, from 31 garages. A sense of relative normality had returned on the home front, but this was not destined to last, for in June the first of the V1 flying bombs – commonly known as doodlebugs – fell unexpectedly from the sky to herald in a new era of indiscriminate destruction which impacted heavily on London Transport and its diverse infrastructure. The greatest blow of all as far as the bus fleet was concerned came when a flying bomb scored a direct hit on Elmers End garage on the evening of 18th July 1944. Elmers End was not only an operational garage but also one of the Board's four body overhauling shops so the 32 buses (including one single decker converted into an ambulance) that were completely destroyed belonged not only to Elmers End but to other garages too. Elmers End's own fleet consisted almost entirely of LTs, both double- and single-deck, so the number of STs completely written off was limited to a mere four. LGOC-type ST 545, 570, 637 had been part of Elmers End's own operational fleet and Tilling ST 879 had been its learner bus although delicensed at the time of its destruction. Within two days, 27 Tilling STs and one of the LGOC type had been hurriedly relicensed to provide the backbone of a replacement fleet. Ten of the Tillings had only just been rapidly patched up after suffering blast damage from a doodlebug strike close to where they had been stored at a dispersal point in Snaresbrook Road, Wanstead, along with some green STs on 5th July. On 22nd July the Elmers End intake was augmented by six green STs, although these were released back to the Country area after a few days. Subsequently, when the worst of the upheaval had subsided, the Tilling vehicles were replaced by standard STs as soon as practicable, 16 on 1st September and the remainder exactly a month later on 1st October. The great majority of these Tilling vehicles were destined never to run again. By now plenty of LGOC-type STs were making their way back from the provinces and no fewer than eleven of those received at Elmers End had come virtually direct from other operators with only a short intermediate halt at Chiswick to ascertain and perhaps rectify their mechanical condition.

Just before the era of the flying bombs arrived, London Transport began receiving the first of many new utility buses from a further manufacturer to supplement those being supplied by Guy. The first six new Daimlers were built to lowbridge specification and were ideal for route 127 at Merton, as this was the garage where it had been decided that all Daimler deliveries under the current programme would be concentrated. Between 3rd May and 1st June 1944 all five lowbridge STs were rendered surplus, which was fortuitous as it enabled three of the displaced vehicles (ST 136, 163, 1089) to release STLs from Amersham which were now needed back on route 410. This left ST 140 and 141 surplus to requirements and a new home was found for them far away from their former spheres of operation. Their new base was Addlestone where they augmented the fleet of wartime rebodied lowbridge STLs that had prevailed since June 1943.

A couple of double deckings took place on Country Bus routes in 1944 making use of the ample ST availability that now existed. On 5th April route 316 (Chesham–Hemel Hempstead via Bovingdon), which London Transport had long shared with Jesse Dell's Rover Bus Service, was time-tabled jointly with Rover for the first time and London Transport's share was double decked using two STs from Hemel Hempstead garage. Due to the operating terrain these had to be good hill climbers with 7:1 rear axle ratios, and fortunately some of these still existed from Godstone days and were readily available. On 16th August Hertford's route 327 (Hertford–Nazeing Gate) was also double decked with STs replacing the former T-types. Late in the year, on 18th December, an exchange of rolling stock between Northfleet and Addlestone took place resulting in a re-emergence of STs at the former and an influx of STLs at the latter.

Before the Northfleet/Addlestone swap occurred, a start had been made in repainting Addlestone's grey vehicles into Country area green starting with ST 144 on 26th October. However four were still grey when they migrated to Northfleet, and so were a couple that had been rendered surplus at Addlestone before this, on 1st September, and dispatched to Windsor. The last grey one of all, ST 324 at Addlestone, is recorded as having been repainted green on 14th February 1945. Even earlier than this a leisurely start had been made on repainting all the red STs in Country service, and likely to stay there, into the appropriate green livery as and when they became due for overhaul. The first had been gas producer ST 656 at Grays on 28th April 1944 and, in total, 22 had been dealt with by the time war ended, 11 at Grays, 6 at Epping and 5 at Tring. In most cases their rear indicator boxes were either plated over or completely removed at the same time, having never been used whilst in Country service. Reverting to green livery during the same era were the five lowbridge STs that had been painted red for route 127, the last being ST 136 at Amersham on 22nd March 1945.

The July 1944 bombing of Elmers End garage, which temporarily put the body overhaul shop out of action, inevitably resulted in a backlog of essential work that needed to be carried out but could not be accommodated at the other three locations. Arrangements were quickly made to send a number of vehicles to repairers in the provinces for their bodies to be overhauled and three of these were STs which were dispatched as follows:

ST 449 to Halifax Corporation on 15th August 1944

ST 222 to Coventry Corporation on 16th August 1944

ST 610 to Bolton Corporation on 16th August 1944

All three needed repair work as a result of bomb blast and this was attended to while they were away. Prompt attention was given to them and they had all been received back at Chiswick by 29th September. ST 449 was the most distinctive of them in Halifax's own version of London colours which were crimson and cream with black lining below the windows, in which it stood out noticeably from the rest when it re-entered service at Epping on 1st November. It also saw a spell of service in these colours at Hendon, but they were short lived and ST 449 was repainted into standard red livery in December 1945.

With the petrol supply situation easing by the summer of 1944, the use of producer gas was wound down and had totally ceased by 13th September. Not long afterwards, however, came the V2 rockets whose silent and unpredictable arrival threatened London with indiscriminate destruction far more deadly than the doodlebugs. The V2s quickly showed their potential for creating havoc to transport services and it was only through sheer luck that no major items of transport infrastructure were destroyed by them.

With 1944 drawing towards a close and the end of the war in sight, ST 1129 joins other vehicles on the forecourt of St Albans garage. It awaits its next trip on a local circular service, although the blind box has been partly masked and the full route number 334 cannot be seen. Before too many more months have elapsed, the masking will have come off the lamps and the white markings will have gone as will the netting and boards from the windows. ST 1129 stayed at St Albans until new RTs came along at the end of 1948. *D W K Jones*

1945 dawned, and despite the ongoing hazard from V2 rockets it was clear that a successful outcome to the war, in Europe at least, was now assured. On 1st March a rocket fell near Upton Park garage causing blast damage to 15 unlicensed Tilling STs parked in open storage close to West Ham football ground, and with the end of the war in sight it was decided not to repair them. They were dispersed to various garages where engines and other useful material was removed, the remains being earmarked for scrap. Unfortunately one of these was ST 839, the vehicle with an STL lower deck which, ironically, was probably the most structurally sound of all Tilling STs. Inevitably the rocket attacks diminished, the last to have a direct impact on the ST class being on 7th March in East India Dock Road when Barking's ST 188, along with three LTs, two STLs and two trolleybuses, all had their windows blown out.

New utility double deckers were now being received from the manufacturers in reasonable numbers, making it possible once again to reduce the number of garages at which STs were to be found. As the blackout was eased and anti-splinter mesh began to disappear from bus windows, the last two double deckings of the wartime era took place. STs took over from LT Scooters on Holloway's route 239 (Tufnell Park–King's Cross) on 7th March and, finally, STs replaced Qs from Northfleet's 497 (Gravesend–Northfleet) on the last day of that same month. On 1st April 1945 a scrapping programme began, the first for many years. The principal victims were Tilling STs, including those damaged at Upton Park and since stripped for spares. The bodies were removed at Chiswick and sold to the Steel Breaking & Demolition Company of Edgware, which had been London Transport's favoured scrap contractor in late pre-war years and had scrapped many one-time LPTB buses which had been taken by rail to the Company's yard at Chesterfield. The chassis were dismantled at Chiswick. Nine Tilling STs had perished in this way by the time the war ended and the programme continued thereafter.

Victory in Europe was declared on Tuesday 8th May 1945. On VE Day a grand total of 861 STs were licensed for service with London Transport, almost exactly three-quarters of its original fleet of 1,138. Of these 46 were Tilling type and mostly used as learners, 41 in the Central area and 5 in the Country. Central Buses had 632 ex-LGOC vehicles distributed among 38 garages, whilst 15 Country Bus garages were home for 151 green and 32 red STs of various enclosed staircase types. On the same date 66 STs were still at work with various provincial operators, comprising 38 Tillings and 26 LGOC plus ex-Empire ST 1029 and the oldest in the fleet, ST 1139. Every one of these vehicles was well beyond its originally allotted life span and many were clearly suffering from almost six years of make-do-and-mend maintenance. Ahead lay the hard road to recovery in which the STs – London Transport's maids of all work – were to play a major part.

CHAPTER 19
WARTIME LOANS

The war years found members of the ST class operating far beyond their normal London base with no fewer than 291 being loaned to provincial operators desperate for rolling stock to meet travel demands which had risen far in excess of peace time levels at a time when the manufacturing of new buses had almost entirely ceased. The setting up of many large military and air force bases placed a new burden on bus operators, but even more pressing was the need to provide transportation to cope with a huge surge in manufacturing, mostly war related, for which large new factories were established where none had existed before in areas chosen as being the least vulnerable to bombing. In the autumn of 1941 Lord Ashfield accompanied by Ernest Bevin, the Minister of Labour and National Service, toured provincial bus operators to assess their problems and decreed that spare vehicles from London Transport should be sent to help out, especially in districts where munitions factories had been established. As a result, from November 1941 onwards STs began to appear in cities and towns as far removed from London as Glasgow and Plymouth, and they subsequently augmented the fleets of no fewer than 48 different provincial operators.

This was, of course, a total reversal of the position that applied earlier in the war when, with the Blitz on London at its height, London Transport had been forced to appeal through the Minister of War Transport for buses to be loaned to it for a few months while its own ones were repaired. The huge and instantaneous response during a few days in late October 1940 is now part of London's wartime folklore, but all of the more than 450 buses sent to London had ceased running in the capital by August 1941. Almost all had been returned either to their owner or to other operators desperate for rolling stock, and only three of the hired buses remained on London Transport premises when the first outward loans of STs commenced. All three were owned by Glasgow Corporation and had been mechanically unserviceable for many months. They were towed one by one into Chiswick for repair and the last one, Albion Venturer YS 2087, finally returned home on 18th February 1942.

Before reviewing in detail the extensive catalogue of ST loans to other operators, it is appropriate to record briefly eleven vehicles borrowed in 1940/41 which had a particularly close relationship to the STs and – unlike most of the buses borrowed from provincial operators – did not look totally out of place running in the capital. Seven had arrived between the 27th and 29th October 1940 by courtesy of the Brighton, Hove & District Omnibus Company and were one-time Thomas Tilling vehicles identical when new to the Tilling STs in London. Unlike London Transport, the Brighton company pursued a policy during the second half of the 1930s of upgrading its ex-Tilling STs, in some cases with new and more modern bodies and, in many other instances, by fitting AEC or Gardner diesel engines, but the vehicles loaned to

London Transport included none of these. They remained identical in all major respects except livery to London Transport's own Tilling STs and they still retained their original Thomas Tilling fleet numbers. They operated from London Transport garages as follows:

6199	GK 6299	Nunhead, Old Kent Road, Norwood
6206	GN 6206	Potters Bar, Cricklewood
6231	GP 6231	Battersea, Norwood
6242	GP 6242	Streatham
6287	GW 6287	Tottenham
6292	GW 6292	Hanwell, Mortlake
6294	GW 6294	Nunhead, Old Kent Road

All ceased running in London service between 22nd and 25th July 1941 and all but one were returned to Brighton on the 28th. They were not needed in Brighton and were all subsequently loaned to other operators, with 6287 suffering a premature demise in June 1942 when it was destroyed by enemy action whilst working for Bristol Tramways. The one that did not go back to Brighton was 6199. This was impressed by the Admiralty for war service on 25th July whilst waiting at Chiswick for its return home which, in the circumstances, never took place.

Four other vehicles of interest were sent to London during October 1940. On the 23rd VO 3877/78 arrived from West Bridgford Urban District Council in whose fleet they were Nos. 18 and 19, whilst on the 27th FJ 7827/28 came from Exeter Corporation who numbered them 29 and 30. All four were ST lookalikes with LGOC-designed bodies built by Ransomes, Sims & Jefferies to the same style as those supplied to East Surrey and Autocar as described in chapter 10. Despite their fairly exotic liveries, they would have not have looked too much out of place on route 68 from Norwood garage which was the best place to find them.

West Bridgford	VO 3877	Norwood
West Bridgford	VO 3878	Norwood
Exeter	FJ 7827	Upton Park, Palmers Green
Exeter	FJ 7828	Streatham, Norwood

All four were taken out of service at about the same time as the Brighton Tillings, the Exeter pair returning home on 27th July 1941 followed by the West Bridgford duo on 10th August. It is a great pity that no photographs appear to have been taken of any of the eleven provincial STs during their nine months' spell of wartime service in London.

After the initial contingent of five Tilling STs went to Coventry Corporation in November 1941, the next to be loaned to a provincial operator was ST 998 which was sent to South Shields Corporation on 10th December. Its own battered look, with several windows missing, is matched by the sheer scene of war-inflicted dereliction against which it awaits the next departure to Marsden Road. *South Tyneside Council*

On Sunday 30th November 1941 the first five Tilling STs left Chiswick for service in the provinces. Their host was to be Coventry Corporation whose need for rolling stock had been dire ever since its tramway system had been bombed into uselessness on 24th December 1940. The loan was open-ended, as no-one could foresee in such difficult times when or how the need for these vehicles in Coventry would cease. London Transport had decided that all outward loans of double deckers to other operators would involve Tilling STs none of which were now required for service on their home territory, and to meet the needs of provincial operators as co-ordinated through the Regional Transport Commissioners, vehicles began to leave London on an almost daily basis from 10th December 1941 onwards to a host of different destinations. By the end of 1941 70 Tilling STs had gone to 18 operators, and the process continued into 1942. It is thought that a standard hire charge of £25 per vehicle per month was levied wherever they went. The recipient operators varied widely in size from the massive Midland Red down to the very modest 'Gloria de Luxe' fleet of Harper Brothers at Heath Hayes near Cannock, but all were established operators of stage carriage services on which the Tilling STs were often employed as well as on contract work. All sectors of industry borrowed STs from London including the main groupings – BET, Tilling, Red & White and SMT – plus municipals and independents.

Against a typical South Wales colliery back-drop, ST 873 on loan to the Rhondda Transport Company loads up with miners at the end of a shift, their faces still blackened with coal dust. ST 873 was on its second provincial assignment having previously worked in the Kilmarnock area with Western SMT. After returning from Rhondda, it never again worked for London Transport.

By July 1942 the great majority of Tilling STs had been placed on loan and the remaining stragglers followed on soon afterwards. Starting on the 23rd July standard ex-LGOC STs began being dispatched to the provinces too. On 1st August the only remaining ex-independent, ST 1029, was also sent as was London Transport's oldest vehicle, ST 1139, on 23rd December. Whilst, in theory, there should have been no Tilling STs remaining in London, this was never actually quite the case. For much of the time vehicles were coming and going as old loans expired and new ones started, and in several instances individual buses found themselves loaned out to as many as three different operators. In most cases they returned to Chiswick between loans and were sometimes even put through the overhaul regime whilst there, with the result that several returned to the provinces carrying wartime brown and cream livery. Sometimes vehicles came back to Chiswick for repairs that the company to which they were loaned was unable to carry out, prime examples of this being ST 854 which returned from Red & White in April 1942 minus its roof, ST 993 likewise and from the same operator in February 1944, and ST 944 from Hants & Sussex in June 1944 with its staircase smashed in. All were repaired and sent back.

By the end of 1942 the main clamour for the loan of London buses had died away and only four 'new' operators obtained STs in 1943, the last being Cardiff Corporation in the August of that year where they were only needed for a short, four month period anyway. One of the new names for 1943 was Northern Roadways Ltd of Glasgow which, unlike all the others, had not been an existing stage carriage operator and whose mere existence was the cause of some suspicion and

debate, even leading to a question in Parliament. This revealed that the company had been set up in June 1941, apparently by two Scottish businessmen seeking to profit through obtaining military and other transportation contracts, sometimes at the expense of other operators, which it appears to have succeeded in doing.

Two provincial operators of London STs are known to have converted some to producer gas operation for at least part of their stay. West Yorkshire is recorded as having had five at work on its trunk York–Harrogate run, but the identities of the individual vehicles are not known. In Coventry, the Corporation's transport department converted seven of its substantial holding of London buses to gas, these being ST 61, 153, 334, 385, 430, 806, 926. The last of these is the only known instance when one of London's Tilling STs was converted to run on gas, a process quickly reversed when passengers began complaining of fumes entering the bus through the open doorway apertures at the rear end.

The following table shows operators in the chronological order in which they borrowed STs, listing all vehicles in their care together with the date on which each one arrived (normally direct from Chiswick unless otherwise stated) and the date on which the hire contract officially finished. The latter is sometimes also the date on which the vehicle returned to Chiswick, though more often than not they came back a day or two after the hire had ceased. Some operators gave the STs a temporary fleet number in their own series, which is shown in the last column where known. A number in parenthesis, eg (2) or (3) against the London Transport fleet number, indicates that the vehicle was on its second or third assignment, having been with other operator(s) earlier.

Coventry Corporation

926	30/11/41	16/11/45
964	30/11/41	12/9/44
971	30/11/41	12/9/44
972	30/11/41	6/11/45
977	30/11/41	12/9/44
844	26/7/42	2/8/42 (direct to Walsall Corporation)
847	26/7/42	2/8/42 (direct to Walsall Corporation)
19	26/7/42	25/10/45
53	26/7/42	18/1/45
334	26/7/42	9/10/44
703	26/7/42	12/9/44
96	9/8/42	16/8/44
153	9/8/42	2/11/44
240	9/8/42	18/1/45
367	9/8/42	16/8/44
459	9/8/42	11/8/44
826	9/8/42	12/9/44
61	2/12/42	11/11/44
481	2/12/42	16/8/44
806	2/12/42	6/12/44
385	8/12/42	23/11/44
430	8/12/42	16/11/44
711	8/12/42	12/9/44
156	9/12/42	13/2/45
275	9/12/42	11/8/44
774	9/12/42	11/8/44
877 (2)	23/12/42	31/10/45
1139	23/12/42	28/11/45

South Shields Corporation

998	10/12/41	29/12/43
986	29/1/42	22/9/43
291	18/11/42	29/8/44
572	18/11/42	16/8/44

Venture Transport, Basingstoke

913	11/12/41	27/2/46	53
916	11/12/41	28/2/46	54
934	11/12/41	1/1/47	55
939	11/12/41	1/1/46	56
942	11/12/41	3/10/46	57
955	11/12/41	2/10/46	58

1005	11/12/41	2/1/47	59
953	16/1/42	1/3/46	46
963	16/1/42	2/1/46	47
395	23/7/42	28/8/44	48
408	23/7/42	28/8/44	49
800	24/7/42	28/8/44	50
101	29/1/43	29/8/44	51
256	29/1/43	29/8/44	52

Yelloway Motor Services, Rochdale

923	11/12/41	14/10/43
147	23/7/42	17/5/44

W L Silcox, Pembroke Dock

910	12/12/41	21/2/43
921	12/12/41	25/2/43
933	12/12/41	15/2/43

Birmingham & Midland Motor Omnibus Co (Midland Red)

920	12/12/41	2/10/44
922	12/12/41	1/11/44
935	12/12/41	13/10/44
936	12/12/41	6/10/44
941	12/12/41	13/10/44
951	12/12/41	1/11/44
905	14/12/41	2/10/44
931	14/12/41	30/10/44
959	14/12/41	3/11/44
124	30/7/42	23/8/44
128	30/7/42	25/8/44
211	30/7/42	1/2/45
422	30/7/42	23/8/44
175	23/11/42	30/8/44
366	23/11/42	30/10/44
724	23/11/42	25/8/44
419	7/12/42	23/8/44
595	7/12/42	23/8/44
757	7/12/42	4/10/44
803	7/12/42	1/2/45
244	8/12/42	28/8/44
466	8/12/42	23/8/44
755	8/12/42	3/8/44

Basingstoke based Venture Transport, a Red & White group company, amassed a small fleet of nine Tilling STs, none of which returned to London until well after the war had ended. ST 916 was one of a batch of seven received in December 1941, all of which carried the Venture fleet name and a local fleet number, in this case 54, which is shown in the driver's window. *Omnibus Society collection*

Western SMT Company

873	16/12/41	18/12/42
880	16/12/41	15/12/42
883	16/12/41	18/12/42
900	16/12/41	23/12/42
940	16/12/41	23/12/42
962	16/12/41	9/2/43 (direct to Paton Bros)

Rhondda Transport Company

899	18/12/41	22/1/43 (back 24/3/43 – see below)
903	18/12/41	1/2/44 (direct to Pontypridd UDC)
915	18/12/41	1/2/44 (direct to Pontypridd UDC)
872	1/1/42	13/9/43
1011	23/7/42	20/12/43
149	30/11/42	11/8/44
365	30/11/42	11/8/44
940 (2)	22/1/43	3/1/44
873 (2)	24/3/43	29/9/45
874 (2)	24/3/43	29/9/45
899 (2)	24/3/43	1/2/44 (direct to Pontypridd UDC)
910 (2)	29/3/43	1/2/44 (direct to Pontypridd UDC)
933 (2)	29/3/43	29/9/45
1029 (2)	17/9/43	30/9/45
844 (3)	10/11/44	30/9/45
964 (2)	10/11/44	30/9/45
977 (2)	10/11/44	30/9/45

Merthyr Tydfil Corporation

912	18/12/41	16/11/43
1022	18/12/41	31/8/44
877	15/1/42	5/9/42
1006	15/1/42	5/9/42
949	20/5/42	5/9/42
960	20/5/42	17/12/43
996	20/5/42	16/11/43
880 (2)	1/2/43	23/8/44
900 (2)	1/2/43	17/12/43

Hants & Sussex Motor Services, Emsworth

874	19/12/41	10/2/43
883 (2)	9/12/43	14/8/44 (direct to City of Oxford)
944 (2)	9/12/43	14/8/44 (direct to City of Oxford)

Trent Motor Traction Company

845	21/12/41	6/3/44
855	21/12/41	30/4/44
862	21/12/41	8/3/44
888	21/12/41	30/4/44
904	21/12/41	20/4/44
914	21/12/41	6/3/44
918	21/12/41	8/3/44
994	23/12/41	30/4/44
427	9/8/42	10/5/45
612	9/8/42	10/5/45
631	9/8/42	29/4/44

781	9/8/42	30/4/44
327	11/8/42	30/4/44
339	11/8/42	7/5/45
1009	11/8/42	6/3/44
476	14/8/42	7/5/45

Gosport & Fareham Omnibus Company (Provincial)

906	22/12/41	27/10/43	17
919	22/12/41	20/10/43	18

Harper Brothers (Gloria de Luxe), Heath Hayes

850	23/12/41	30/9/44
917	23/12/41	7/10/44

Sunderland Corporation

851	23/12/41	26/8/42
879	16/4/42	26/8/42
966	16/4/42	26/8/42

Red & White Services, Chepstow

961	24/12/41	17/12/43	
854	26/12/41	17/12/43	950
861	26/12/41	30/4/44	955
864	26/12/41	14/12/43	952
869	26/12/41	14/12/43	953
884	26/12/41	30/4/44	954
982	3/3/42	21/12/43	956
993	11/5/42	11/2/44	959
1000	11/5/42	21/12/43	961
1023	11/5/42	11/12/44	960
837	13/5/42	30/12/43	
987	13/5/42	2/7/45	
999	13/5/42	1/7/45	
860	8/6/42	3/5/44	
987	8/6/42	2/7/45	
867	12/6/42	15/11/44	

Sheffield Transport Department

885	28/12/41	25/2/44
891	28/12/41	25/2/44
897	28/12/41	28/9/43
907	28/12/41	25/2/44
908	28/12/41	28/9/43
925	28/12/41	25/2/44
947	28/12/41	28/9/43

There is no mistaking which operator ST 631 is working for. Although the destination screens are blacked out, a three-track route number box can just be discerned in the bulkhead window, and the brackets mounted on the front canopy by Trent appear to have been installed to take a destination board. *J G S Smith*

Birkenhead Corporation

866	30/12/41	27/4/44
878	30/12/41	27/4/44
881	30/12/41	28/1/44
944	30/12/41	3/11/43
957	30/12/41	28/1/44
981	30/12/41	3/11/43

Stockton Corporation

856	1/1/42	6/5/44
887	1/1/42	6/5/44
894	1/1/42	2/5/44
870	6/1/42	6/5/44
208	4/8/42	4/7/44
295	4/8/42	2/5/44
378	4/8/42	4/7/44
650	4/8/42	2/5/44

Crosville Motor Services

846	4/1/42	19/8/44	L 846
852	4/1/42	19/8/44	L 852
858	4/1/42	30/10/46	L 858
859	4/1/42	4/12/46	L 859
863	4/1/42	7/3/46	L 863
868	4/1/42	16/4/44	L 868
976	4/1/42	19/8/44	L 976
1016	4/1/42	4/12/46	L 1016
88	25/1/43	27/8/44	
304	25/1/43	27/8/44	
733	25/1/43	27/8/44	
846 (2)	27/8/44	15/1/46	L 846
852 (2)	27/8/44	13/11/46	L 852
976 (2)	27/8/44	11/10/46	L 976

Swindon Corporation

945	6/1/42	16/7/42

Devon General Omnibus & Touring Company

932	14/1/42	26/10/43
950	14/1/42	5/10/43

Aberdare Urban District Council

968	12/2/42	1/2/44	L 1
989	23/7/42	1/2/44	L 2
1002	23/7/42	3/9/43	L 3
851 (3)	30/8/43	1/2/44	

City of Oxford Motor Services

975	20/2/42	13/12/46	
983	20/2/42	17/12/46	
205	31/3/43	21/8/44	
767	31/3/43	21/8/44	
921 (2)	31/3/43	18/12/46	
883 (3)	14/8/44	16/12/46	(direct from
944 (3)	14/8/44	17/12/46	Hants & Sussex)

Central SMT Company

970	17/3/42	7/6/43 (direct to Northern Roadways)
1020	17/3/42	7/6/43 (direct to Northern Roadways)
1026	17/3/42	7/6/43 (direct to Northern Roadways)
928	23/3/42	7/6/43 (direct to Northern Roadways)
530	5/8/42	7/6/43 (direct to Northern Roadways)
670	5/8/42	7/6/43 (direct to Northern Roadways)

Cheltenham District Traction Company

838	12/7/42	28/10/44
843	12/7/42	30/12/43
857	12/7/42	21/11/43
871	12/7/42	30/12/43
882	12/7/42	21/11/43
929	12/7/42	21/11/43
946	12/7/42	27/9/44
956	12/7/42	21/11/43
969	12/7/42	25/10/44
988	12/7/42	26/9/44
995	12/7/42	21/11/43
1024	12/7/42	25/9/44

Walsall Corporation

842	20/7/42	27/9/44
1017	20/7/42	25/9/44
844 (2) (a)	2/8/42	25/9/44
847 (2) (a)	2/8/42	27/9/44

(a) Received direct from Coventry Corporation

Bournemouth Corporation

839	22/7/42	30/4/43
979	22/7/42	29/7/43
984	22/7/42	30/4/43
985	22/7/42	29/7/43
1001	22/7/42	29/7/43
1025	22/7/42	29/7/43

Pontypridd Urban District Council

310	28/7/42	3/9/44	P 1
369	28/7/42	3/9/44	P 2
949 (3) (a)	7/12/42	4/11/45	P 3
1006 (3) (a)	7/12/42	17/3/45	P 4
899 (3)	1/2/44	4/11/45	
903 (2)	1/2/44	12/4/44	
910 (3)	1/2/44	12/4/44	
915 (2)	1/2/44	17/3/45	

(a) Received direct from Bryn Motor Company

West Monmouthshire Omnibus Board

1029	1/8/42	5/8/43

West Yorkshire Road Car Company

182	2/8/42	16/9/45
249	2/8/42	16/9/45
311 (a)	2/8/42	30/9/45
409	2/8/42	28/12/44
566 (a)	2/8/42	29/8/44
592 (a)	2/8/42	1/9/44
747 (a)	2/8/42	24/8/44
565	6/8/42	18/8/44

(a) Operated by York-West Yorkshire Joint Committee.
ST 409 may also have been.

Cumberland Motor Services

62	5/8/42	16/8/44
204	"	16/8/44
223	"	17/11/43
332	12/8/42	17/11/43
342	"	16/8/44

Caledonian Omnibus Company		
398	12/8/42	8/2/45
778	12/8/42	8/2/45
239	19/8/42	8/2/45
605	19/8/42	8/2/45
763	19/8/42	8/2/45
380	25/11/42	3/10/44
387	25/11/42	13/6/45
421	25/11/42	13/6/45
424	25/11/42	13/9/45
454	25/11/42	3/10/44
501	25/11/42	12/9/45
585	25/11/42	12/9/45

Lancashire United Transport & Power Company			
74	16/8/42	24/8/44	L 1
243	16/8/42	24/8/44	L 2
314	16/8/42	17/8/44	L 3
351	16/8/42	22/8/44	L 5
357	16/8/42	22/8/44	L 6
531	16/8/42	17/8/44	L 4
675	16/8/42	24/8/44	L 7
749	15/12/42	28/9/44	L 13
5	18/12/42	29/8/44	L 8
581	18/12/42	29/8/44	L 9
737	18/12/42	26/9/44	L 10
374	28/12/42	26/9/44	L 11
490	28/12/42	28/9/44	L 12

Youngs Bus Services, Glasgow		
279	24/8/42	7/6/43 (direct to Northern Roadways)
512	24/8/42	7/6/43 (direct to Northern Roadways)
760	24/8/42	7/6/43 (direct to Northern Roadways)

Derby Corporation			
848	29/9/42	29/2/44	17
865	29/9/42	1/4/44	18
945 (2)	29/9/42	20/6/44	19
1015	29/9/42	31/3/44	20

Bradford City Transport		
851 (2)	5/10/42	30/6/43
879 (2)	5/10/42	30/6/43
966 (2)	5/10/42	30/6/43
362	9/10/42	23/8/44
505	9/10/42	23/8/44
726	9/10/42	23/8/44

Lincolnshire Road Car Company		
6	26/10/42	31/3/44
849	26/10/42	28/10/43
1018	26/10/42	28/10/43
1027	26/10/42	28/11/44
55	28/10/42	29/1/45
237	28/10/42	29/1/45
468	28/10/42	28/11/44
772	28/10/42	30/9/46
907 (2)	31/3/44	27/3/47

Bryn Motor Company, Pontllanfraith		
949 (2)	21/11/42	7/12/42 (direct to Pontypridd UDC)
1006 (2)	21/11/42	7/12/42 (direct to Pontypridd UDC)

County Borough of West Bromwich		
554	29/11/42	31/8/44
562	29/11/42	30/12/44
787	29/11/42	31/8/44

West Yorkshire chose to employ ST 182 on one of its key services, Leeds to Harrogate, with specially printed notices to this effect posted in the blind box apertures. A smiling lady passenger is lucky enough to sit next to the only window free of anti-shatter mesh. *R F Mack*

The Glasgow area was as far north as the STs penetrated and ST 512 was one of a trio sent to the large independent operator Young's Bus Service. After less than a year with Young's, the three STs passed to Northern Roadways for contract work in June 1943. *BCVM*

Enterprise & Silver Dawn Motor Company, Scunthorpe

420	3/12/42	1/10/45
532	3/12/42	1/10/45
753	3/12/42	1/10/45

Bristol Tramways & Carriage Company

524	13/12/42	19/2/46	3701
538	13/12/42	19/2/46	3702
587	13/12/42	19/2/46	3703
616	13/12/42	26/2/46	3704
617	13/12/42	26/2/46	3705
629	13/12/42	26/2/46	3706

Bath Electric Tramways/Bath Tramways Motor Company

268	13/12/42	5/2/46	3830
292	13/12/42	5/2/46	3831
348	13/12/42	12/2/46	3832
377	13/12/42	12/2/46	3834
463	13/12/42	12/2/46	3835
499	13/12/42	5/2/46	3833

Wilts & Dorset Motor Services

31	16/12/42	17/5/44	501
44	16/12/42	17/5/44	504
89	16/12/42	17/5/44	503
744	16/12/42	17/5/44	502
839 (2)	15/10/43	31/1/44	505
966 (3)	15/10/43	31/1/44	506
979 (2)	15/10/43	31/1/44	507
986 (2)	15/10/43	31/1/44	508

United Counties Omnibus Company

511	28/12/42	13/11/44
525	28/12/42	29/1/45
621	28/12/42	27/4/45

Hants & Dorset Motor Services

201	12/1/43	30/9/43
210	12/1/43	1/7/43
218	12/1/43	30/9/43
439	12/1/43	1/7/43
661	12/1/43	30/9/43
740	12/1/43	30/9/43
845 (2)	4/5/44	27/2/48
885 (2)	4/5/44	27/2/48
918 (2)	4/5/44	11/9/44
925 (2)	4/5/44	11/9/44

Paton Brothers, Renfrew

962 (2)	9/2/43	28/5/43

Northern Roadways, Glasgow

279 (2)	(a)		7/6/43	27/7/44
512 (2) (a)	(a)		3/8/44	
530 (2) (b)	(a)		9/9/44	
670 (2) (b)	(a)		29/9/44	
760 (2) (a)	(a)		10/8/44	
928 (2) (b)	(a)		20/7/44	
970 (2) (b)	(a)		3/8/44	
1020 (2) (b)			3/8/44	27/7/44
1026 (2) (b)			3/8/44	20/7/44

(a) Received direct from Youngs Bus Services
(b) Received direct from Central SMT

Cardiff Corporation

879 (3)	5/8/43	8/11/43
962 (3)	5/8/43	8/11/43
984 (2)	5/8/43	25/11/43

Not recorded in the company listings is ST 879 which set out for Central SMT on 17th March 1942 but broke down in Doncaster and failed to make it to Central's headquarters at Motherwell, being replaced a few days later by ST 928. ST 879 made its way back to Chiswick by the 27th and went off again, with its health presumably suitably restored, to Sunderland Corporation in April.

The great majority of operators kept the STs in London Transport livery throughout the period of their loans although, as noted earlier, some applied new fleet numbers for their own internal convenience. A few others, such as Trent and Venture, replaced the London Transport fleet names with their own. In fact Venture went one stage further and even installed internal clocks in line with the policy for their own fleet. After having STs on loan for a year, Lincolnshire repainted most if not all of its contingent in the dark grey that it employed during wartime for its own vehicles, and in some cases obliterated all signs of London Transport ownership to the extent of even showing itself as the legal owner. Also repainted grey were Gosport & Fareham's pair of Tilling STs although these were in a lighter shade than the Lincolnshire STs. For the benefit of its drivers, Crosville fitted full height doors to the cabs of its standard STs and added windows to the top half of the doors on its Tilling vehicles, all of which were promptly removed upon arrival back at Chiswick.

The London vehicles played an important role whilst in their temporary homes from which they were gradually released as war demands lessened or as new 'utility' Guys and Daimlers finally began to arrive. In some locations they had been particularly prominent, a prime example being in Carlisle where Caledonian based at least eight out of its twelve strong contingent of STs and Cumberland garaged four out of its five. Another good spot to find them was Nottingham into which Trent and Lincolnshire both ran STs regularly.

When the time came for them to be returned to Chiswick, the condition in which they came back varied considerably, perhaps reflecting the attitudes of the various managements to other operators' vehicles. Almost all of the STs returning from South Wales operators (with the exception of Cardiff) came back in deplorably dirty and dented condition, as did those from Stockton. ST 147 arrived back from Yelloway with both decks and even the driver's cab inexplicably littered with grass, hay and other vegetation. Some operators did not even trouble to clean the vehicles out after their last day of use, as witnessed by ST 31 and ST 744 from Wilts & Dorset which arrived at Chiswick on 18th May 1944 strewn inside with Salisbury area TIM tickets issued on the 16th, and STs 374 and 737 from Lancashire United which were received back on 26th September 1944, still littered with tickets dated for the 25th. When ST 866 and ST 878 returned from Birkenhead on 27th April 1944 one of them was found to carry a wooden window fitted by London Transport back in 1941 to which had been attached a signed notice from the Corporation saying "This window was missing when received". Presumably someone at Birkenhead feared that they might otherwise get charged for breaking it!

At the top end of the scale was Coventry Coporation which overhauled and fully repainted many of the STs that it had borrowed (green ST 1139 was not one of these) immediately before sending them back to London. They could be easily distinguished because a slightly lighter red than usual had been used and the window areas showed a yellowish tinge. Radiator guards were purple, the undersides of canopies were pale grey, the interior ceilings were white and standard Coventry transfers had been used for the USED TICKETS and other notices. Almost as thorough was Caledonian at Dumfries which also repainted its STs prior to their return, albeit not quite so thoroughly as fleet names and numbers were painted around, leaving them glaringly apparent on their faded paint in contrast to the rest of the panelling.

No photographs are known to exist of ST 530 working for Northern Roadways, but these two views illustrate clearly the new top deck with its angular 'utility' domes. Taken in post-war times, they record the bus in service at Southfields and in a scrapyard scene at Feltham. *Fred Ivey*

Two standard STs came back minus their original roofs. Lincolnshire sent ST 6 back in full wartime grey livery but totally topless, and no attempt was made at Chiswick to repair it. Instead the body removed from ST 40 when the latter was converted into a tree lopper was installed which, unusually, continued to display the fleet number ST 40 on the back platform for some time to come. ST 530 was in a different category altogether. Upon arrival back from Northern Roadways in September 1944 it was found to be carrying a new and completely non-standard top deck from the waistrail upwards. Constructed to full 'utility' specification complete with 'lobster' domes, the circumstances surrounding its fitting are not known. However in its general styling including the type of sliding windows used, it appears likely to have been a product of the Croft Bodybuilding & Engineering Company of Glasgow which built utility double deck bodies on reconditioned chassis for Scottish operators. Inside the upper saloon of ST 530 all the original LGOC seats were retained, but externally a more prominent indicator box than usual had been fitted at the front somewhat reminiscent of those used on the DL class of Dennis Lances, and the outside panels of the upper deck were painted in a darker shade of red than usual. ST 530 re-entered London Transport service at Grays on 1st November 1944 and from then onwards it became known as a very distinctive and instantly recognisable member of the ST class.

The final loans went out to the Rhondda Transport Company on 10th November 1944, but by this time the great majority of loaned vehicles had already returned to London Transport whose own escalating needs for rolling stock dictated that the programme should come to a close. At the end of the war in Europe on 8th May 1945 only 66 out of the original 291 STs still remained officially on loan to 15 operators: 38 Tillings and 26 standard types plus STs 1029 and 1139. All except three of these had come 'home' by the end of 1946 but the last returnees of all, ST 845 and ST 885, did not make it back from a prolonged spell as driver training buses with Hants & Dorset until February 1948.

CHAPTER 20
THE GAS PRODUCERS

In the middle of 1939 when war preparations were at their height, London Transport received a communication from the Ministry of Mines. The Ministry wished to examine the question of using producer gas as an alternative fuel for road vehicles and the Board agreed to join a committee to look into the matter. It was decided that tests using heavy vehicles including buses should begin as soon as possible, and on the assurance that no costs would be incurred by London Transport if it participated, the Ministry was offered "every facility" for carrying out its trials.

In truth, the Board would hardly have been surprised that such moves were being proposed. It was common knowledge that the use of producer gas for vehicle propulsion was already being widely practised in parts of continental Europe where nations saw the value of reducing reliance on imported oil, supplies of which could become severely disrupted in times of war, whilst there were also the ancillary benefits of cutting shipping costs and husbanding foreign exchange resources to be taken into consideration. The most prominent user of producer gas was Germany with many thousands of vehicles so equipped, but major strides had also been taken by Sweden, France, Denmark and Italy. All of these countries had either given subsidies or tax exemptions to encourage the development of producer gas as a viable means of propulsion. The picture was different in Britain where its use had been deliberately suppressed to protect the financial interests of oil producers, and notably the Anglo-Persian Oil Company in which the government itself had a very extensive holding, to the extent that a tax penalty had been placed on gas producer vehicles in order to put them at a financial disadvantage.

The principle on which gas producers work is that a limited supply of air is allowed to pass over a hot carbon bed and the oxygen in the air unites with the carbon to form, first, carbon dioxide which is then broken down into the carbon monoxide which is the main constituent in the combustible part of the gas, although hydrogen and methane are also present in much smaller proportions. The big advantage of producer gas, apart from being a home produced fuel, was that it could be made as the vehicle went along. In this way it was much more practical than the town gas used on vehicles in the First World War, which usually had to be carried in huge sacks on the roof, as well as being about one third of the cost. However the problem in 1939 was that, because of the government's previously negative attitude, there was little British expertise to fall back on and the experiments now hastily being carried out relied on foreign designs and patents. True, the government had set up in 1937 a committee under the chairmanship of Sir Harold Hartley to go into the question of producer gas propulsion, but this worked at a snail's pace and it was not until 1940 that it finally published designs for a British patented Government Emergency Producer (GEP) developed in liaison with the Department of Scientific & Industrial Research's fuel research station at Greenwich.

London Transport's wartime experience with gas producers occupied two distinct phases the first of which covered the initial experiments carried out at the behest of the Ministry of Mines. A factor common to both was that ST type vehicles were used. These were chosen because, being petrol engined, their conversion was simpler to carry out whilst promising a saving of almost twice as much liquid fuel as an equivalent sized diesel engine. A petrol engined double decker could, in theory, save as much as 6,000 gallons of fuel per year.

It was accepted from the start that, whatever system was used, a loss of power was inevitable because of the gas from a producer being of much lower value than petrol vapour. This meant that adjustments had to be made to the engine to compensate, principally by altering the compression ratio from 5:1 to 8:1 (which was reckoned to be as much as the structure of the engine could stand) by using specially shaped pistons. Cylinders were bored out from their original 100mm to 110mm. The induction manifold had to be modified to accommodate the air mixing valve which took the place of the carburettor when operating on gas. Ignition timing needed to be advanced considerably, while the jets on the Solex carburettor, which was now used only for starting up, were reduced in size. With all these modifications in place the original loss of efficiency estimated at between 40% and 50% when utilising gas was brought down to 25% to 30%, but this still marked a significant loss of engine power making it necessary to select the flattest possible routes for operation. Experience showed that it could be beneficial to re-site stops to avoid drivers having to pull away on adverse gradients, and a minute or two added into the schedule could also help.

Two buses had been earmarked to inaugurate the first trial, both of them recently overhauled vehicles removed from Watford High Street garage into Chiswick where the conversion work took place. One was former National ST 132 and the other was one-time East Surrey ST 1100. Two very different types of conversion were planned, only one of which destined to point the way forward to future developments, the other proving to be a dead end. The plan for ST 132 was that it would be modified to pull a trailer carrying a gas producer plant. This two-wheeled trailer was based on work that the Tilling group had been carrying out since 1938 as an initiative of its own based on French Gohin Poulenc patents, the manufacturing rights for which had been acquired by the Bristol Tramways & Carriage Company. It combined four basic units for the production of gas located on the trailer chassis which were, looking from the back forwards, a hopper to contain the fuel with the fire below it, a cooler, a filter and a separator, all of them quite bulky items. A perfect seal was needed along the tubes which led from the gas producer to the engine on which the very sensitive gas mixing valve was located. A towing attachment from the chassis was installed 2ft 6ins above the ground to tow the trailer which weighed approximately 15cwt.

ST 132 was photographed at
Chiswick Works in November 1939
– probably just before it entered
service for the first time – attached
to its trailer which is being loaded
with anthracite. This trailer differed
in many respects from the version
adopted as standard in 1942.
L T Museum

A side view of ST 1100 illustrates how comparatively compactly the producer gas unit fitted against the back of the bodywork, and shows the chassis extension upon which it was mounted. The unit has its protective cage in place around which was painted a wide white blackout marking.

In contrast, ST 1100 was fitted with an on-board gas producing unit fixed to the back of the bus itself on a chassis extension approximately 1ft 6ins in length. In comparison with the trailer on ST 132 this was a very compact unit which stood vertically without actually being attached to the bodywork. This unit, too, was based on a French design, the Bellay system, favoured by AEC who were associated with a new company, Gas Producers (Bellay) Ltd, formed to promote it in this country. The Bellay system comprised three large vertical tanks, the outer ones being the hopper and filter with a cylindrical central one between them which was a water cooler. The fire was located at the bottom nearside corner below the hopper, and the weight of the plant, at about 8cwt fully loaded with fuel and water, was almost half that of the gas producer trailer. When the vehicle was operational the Bellay unit was surrounded by a protective cage which gave it a box-like but much neater and more acceptable appearance than the trailer attached to ST 132.

Records of the sequence of events are sketchy and may not be completely accurate, but as far as can be ascertained ST 1100 was completed first ready to be road tested on 24th September 1939, with ST 132 being tested four days later. Both were unlicensed at the time. Resulting from the tests,

ST 1100 required strengthening of its springs to prevent grounding due the increased weight at the rear, whilst ST 132 needed adjustments to its brakes to cope with the extra weight of the trailer. In both cases the complete unit exceeded the 26ft maximum permitted length for a two-axle double decker, albeit in the case of ST 1100 by only about 5ins, and existing length of overhang and laden weight regulations were also contravened. The Ministry of Transport refused to grant a general dispensation at the time but, after negotiation, permission was given for gas producer vehicles to run experimentally on the Kingston to Epsom Downs section of route 406. The two buses were delivered to Leatherhead garage ready to be licensed on 1st November 1939 with the intention of running them as extras to the main service, at least in the initial stages while any problems were ironed out. It is thought that ST 1100 may have actually worked briefly in service on 1st November, but at the request of the Ministry of Mines it was quickly returned to the garage, and sustained operation of the pair did not finally begin until the 8th or the 15th (accounts differ on this). On neither vehicle could the hopper contain enough solid fuel to provide a full day's operation, and arrangements had to be made for this to be replenished when necessary at Kingston garage.

Without the protective cage in place, the various components comprising the Bellay system can be clearly identified. The hopper for the anthracite fuel is on the left with the fire box below it; to their right are the filters and coolers. *AEC*

Not long after the two gas buses entered experimental service on the 406, a third vehicle joined them. ST 1119 had been one of the large number of Country STs taken out of service on 30th September 1939, but instead of being de-licensed at Luton, where it had last run, it was removed to Chiswick ready for conversion work to begin. Like the other two, it had been overhauled as recently as July and was probably selected because it was still in very good mechanical order. As far as is known its conversion was identical or at least very similar to the work carried out on ST 132. It hauled a trailer, and it is probable that even as this early stage a decision had already been taken not to pursue any further the Bellay system as used on ST 1100. ST 1119 was ready for its first trial run under gas propulsion on 11th November, and on 16th December 1939 it joined the others at Leatherhead.

Details of the operational performance of the three gas STs have not survived, but it is clear that hill climbing proved a problem from the start. Only a few weeks into the trial, the Country Bus management decided to cut the operation back to Epsom town, eliminating the section up to the Downs and thereby cutting out Downs Hill. Later, the operation was expanded modestly to allow the vehicles to carry passengers on garage runs between Epsom and Leatherhead under the banner of route 408.

The final expansion of the initial gas producer fleet took place in February 1940 when two more one-time East Surrey STs arrived at Leatherhead on the 7th of that month. ST 1105 and ST 1125 had only come out of overhaul a few days before the mass withdrawals on 30th September 1939 and were almost certainly selected for that reason. They were taken out of storage on 21st November and 21st October respectively, after which their conversion to gas at Chiswick and subsequent testing would have begun. Their subsequent arrival at Leatherhead only brought the size of the gas producer fleet to four and not five as was probably intended, for on the same day ST 132 was returned to Chiswick with engine trouble, after which it was converted back to petrol and subsequently reallocated to Dartford for normal service.

Theory and practice do not always coincide, and this seems to have been the case with the Bellay system on ST 1100. It might have been expected that, by mounting the gas producer equipment on the vehicle itself, the consequent weight saving and the greater ease of providing leak-free pipe connections to the engine would have worked greatly in its favour. Further advantages were that frequent hitching and de-hitching was avoided, and there was the big added bonus that far less space was needed in garages where room did not have to be provided for parking the trailers. However, on the road, the Bellay system clearly proved less effective and reliable than the alternative, and the mere fact that the producer was attached to the vehicle proved a hindrance whenever the gas system was not working well because, instead of attaching a replacement trailer, the bus itself had to be taken out of service. During the spring of 1940 the experiment with ST 1100 was discontinued. Its last date in use is not known; all that is certain is that the vehicle is recorded as having been sent to Chiswick on 1st May after which it was converted back to conventional petrol operation.

The three gas producer STs with trailers fared better, and it has been recorded that they ran, probably somewhat intermittently, until at least 3rd April 1941. Only in the case of ST 1119 was a record made of the date on which the gas producing equipment was removed which was 24th May, although it may well have fallen out of use well before then. London Transport's first phase of gas producer operation was at an end, in common with many other operators of both buses and lorries who were similarly abandoning their gas producers.

The final demise of the initial gas producer trials in London can be ascribed in large measure to lack of interest by the Country Bus operating department, but the end was undoubtedly hastened by a widely perceived apathy on the part of the government. The latter, having promulgated a raft of useful new rules and regulations in 1940, now appeared to have lost interest. Aimed at encouraging the use of gas propulsion, the new regulations had included the Gas and Steam Vehicles Act 1940 which made taxation less onerous, and the Motor Vehicles (Gas Container) Provisional Regulations which regulated and helped to ease the use of such vehicles. Special regulations to enable buses to pull trailers and to stand at termini with their engines running (to avoid having to switch over to petrol to re-start) had been specifically aimed at encouraging bus operators to use gas producers.

Despite the discouraging results at Leatherhead, and in face of government inertia, London Transport's senior management still retained a firm interest in the use of producer gas as an insurance against the very real threat of a serious deterioration in the supply of liquid fuel, and early in 1942 the Board authorised a trial at Grays garage of 20 gas producer buses for which 32 trailers would be purchased. Grays was selected because the territory around it was flat, and because there was ample space on the garage premises for the construction of a gas service station and solid fuel store. Plenty of room was also needed for storing and cleaning the trailers, each of which required some 180 square feet of floor space for adequate manoeuvrability. Grays was also an appropriate choice because it was the nearest garage to Eastern National's headquarters at Chelmsford where much of the pioneering work on gas producers had been carried out on behalf of the Tilling group. Eastern National's experience already extended to having converted one of its garages – Maldon – entirely to producer gas operation. The Tilling group had produced a trailer of its own which was an improvement over an earlier government design in employing a water rather than a sisal filter. This was known as the Morison filter after Eastern National's chief engineer, W J Morison who had designed it, and it significantly reduced cylinder wear caused by incomplete filtration. Eastern National's training and maintenance expertise was close at hand, and was freely given.

It was originally intended that 20 of the trailers for the original scheme would be of the Tilling type, augmented by 12 others for comparison purposes. Four of these would be of the 'Ravenhill' design developed in Swansea by another bus operator, the South Wales Transport Company in conjunction with Amalgamated Anthracite Collieries; four would be of a type developed by the British Coal Utilisation Research Association primarily for use with Bedford lorries, and a further four would be experimental 21 inch government GEP type producers, the 21 referring to the diameter of the hopper which was greater than the normal 18 inches. As things turned out, none of these three 'odd' types were immediately available and it is thought that, in the end, the only ones obtained were two Ravenhills and possibly two of the 21 inch type. Conversion of the 20 STs was estimated to cost £250 per bus and the total scheme, including all work on the premises and purchase of trailers, was budgeted at around £8,000.

Barely had London Transport's scheme for Grays got off the ground when the government did a U-turn and suddenly started favouring producer gas vehicles once again, this time with a vengeance. A June 1942 announcement proclaimed that 10,000 vehicles were to be converted nationwide of which 2,500 would be public service vehicles, in a programme to be completed within an unbelievably short deadline of July 1943. Many bus operators were scheduled to take part in the scheme on the basis of converting 10% of their licensed fleet, which in London Transport's case meant the conversion of no fewer than 548 buses, completely swamping its own plan to convert a mere 20. The only type of gas producer plant immediately capable of being put into volume production was the Tilling model, and arrangements were immediately put in hand for these to be manufactured in large numbers by Bristol Tramways mounted on triangular shaped chassis built at West Bromwich by the large engineering conglomerate J Brockhouse & Son. The new gas producer trailers began to arrive in London from Bristol at a prodigious rate and were delivered direct to various Underground depots by train, where they were unloaded and stored until required for use. The earliest deliveries were known by Bristol Tramways as type 3T3 but the majority were of an improved 3T4 model.

For fuel, London Transport used anthracite which was purchased in bulk from Amalgamated Anthracite Collieries. Anthracite was considered preferable to coke in containing relatively pure carbon and burning with little flame or smoke. It was also readily available from the South Wales anthracite coalfield which, up to then, had been on short time working. The anthracite was loaded from sacks into the top of the hoppers on the gas producer trailers, each of which took about 400lbs. Once a hopper was loaded the fire was ready for lighting. Before this occurred the engine was started up on petrol after which a fire was lit at the foot of the hopper using a coal-gas jet. The gas given off passed through cooling chambers to the water filter and from there through a separator on the trailer to another on the bulkhead of the bus, and finally through a mixing valve to the engine. It was then necessary to gently coax the engine to run on gas, and once it was doing so satisfactorily the petrol could be turned off and the vehicle handed over to its scheduled driver.

It was decided to use standard red STs for the gas producer scheme, large quantities of which were lying idle and unlicensed. Four were chosen to start with, all fresh from overhaul, and during May 1942 these were converted to gas beginning with ST 656 and followed by ST 745, ST 335 and ST 720 in that sequence. Official records show all four as being converted to gas on the same day, 2nd June, but like many wartime records this is inaccurate. In fact, on that very day, ST 656 undertook a series of well photographed press runs with a simulated full load of 48 passengers and 12 standees, included within which was an ascent of the hill in Hanger Lane, Ealing which it is recorded as having mounted satisfactorily in bottom gear. The vehicle was unlicensed at the time and running on trade plates, as was the case when a further press run was arranged at Grays a few days later. On 1st July 1942 STs 656 and 745 were licensed at Grays, followed by ST 335 on the 16th, but some time elapsed before any of them were ready to enter passenger service.

The first positive recording of gas operation was on 16th August when ST 656 and ST 745 were both at work on route 372 between Grays War Memorial and Purfleet LMS Station, although there may have been other instances in the days before this. A big increase in the operation was foreseen in the Country Bus department's Allocation Book dated 8th July which stated that "from 30th September 1942 routes 370, 371, 372 and 375 will be gas bus operated". In fact this was not achieved, although six further gas STs, ST 401, 535, 594, 684, 720, 791 were licensed at Grays on 1st September. Neither was route 372 destined to remain a gas bus domain as it was withdrawn on 30th September as part of a reorganisation consequent upon the discontinuation of Green Line operations, with the sphere of operation of gas STs henceforth comprising routes 370 (Romford-Grays-Purfleet), 371 (Grays-Rainham via Chandler's Corner) and 371A (Grays-Rainham via Aveley). Route 375, mentioned in the Allocation Book, was a Rainham local operated by a single decker for which T 273 was converted to gas in October. However it soon proved impractical to operate a gas producer at such a distance from the refuelling point at Grays, and T 273 was subsequently removed to join eight other converted T types at Leatherhead and Addlestone.

Further STs were licensed on the 1st of each month – 4 in October, 2 in November and 4 in December, bringing the number of gas buses operated at Grays up to the planned total of 20 by the end of 1942 (19 STs plus T 273). The replacement of modern preselector STLs by highly temperamental and much older crash gearbox gas-powered STs did not go down well at first with the driving staff and many problems arose, but the introduction of daily joint meetings to discuss the previous day's delays gradually brought the drivers round to stoically accepting the gas producers as a wartime necessity.

Although 19 red STs were sent to Grays, a 20th was converted to gas in August 1942 which was ST 171. Confirmed in photographs as being fully equipped and attached to a gas trailer, it never ran in service in its intended form, being the first of very many STs whose engines were converted to run on gas and were equipped with tow bars but which never

ST 171 is parked outside Grays garage and ostensibly plated-up for service as GY4 although, in fact, it never actually carried passengers in producer gas form and was probably used purely for experimental work. The inlet arrangement to the engine compartment and the consequent repositioning of the autovac tank are clearly seen in this view. *L T Museum*

159

actually ran with gas producers attached. In ordinary service these could be easily recognised, not just by their extraordinary turn of speed thanks to the very high compression of their engines, but also by the range of pops and bangs that came from them in even greater quantity than a normal ST was apt to produce.

The mandatory nature of the government's 10% gas producer directive made it inevitable that the scope of operation would have to be widened beyond the Country Bus fleet, and in October 1942 investigations began into the feasibility of acquiring bombed land adjacent to Camberwell garage for the construction of a gas producer servicing plant. Things moved forward in February 1943 when no fewer than five former Grays STs moved into Camberwell for training purposes, followed by the licensing there of four gas producer vehicles on 1st March. The route selected for their operation was the lengthy 36 (West Kilburn–Hither Green), and a very modest start was made on 3rd March with three vehicles running supplementary to the main service and towing gas units incorporating modified flame traps to meet London County Council regulations. Photographic evidence shows that two of these were ST 174 and ST 725 and the third would have been another of the quartet licensed on 1st March, either ST 434 or ST 588. If it had not already become obvious at Grays, peak hour operation on route 36 would have fully established the fact that the Tilling gas producer unit was too small for heavily loaded double deckers, suffering excessive temperatures and general overheating, but with new trailers of this type now pouring off the production line, there was nothing that could be done about it.

Invaluable experience was rapidly being built up in the operation of gas producer units and their weaknesses were vividly exposed. Apart from the inherently dirty and messy business of handling the trailers, plus the care that had to be taken when unhooking them to avoid hot spots and to stop them running away (they had no brakes), there were repercussions on the petrol engine that put additional pressure on the garage staff. Rapid cylinder wear was mentioned earlier, but engines needed decarbonising and the sumps needed draining much more often than usual, whilst spark plugs had to be removed and cleaned after every 300 miles of operation.

Drivers had to learn new techniques to cope with vehicles which were decidedly more sluggish than normal. Even the slightest gradient required a rush to be made at it, and starting from rest on hills was almost impossible. They were instructed to change gears at maximum revolutions and not to hang on to high gears as this could cause suction through the fire to drop so that, by the time the lower gear was activated, there was insufficient gas available to take it up. Starting had to be in first gear, and at any hint of an upward gradient a prompt change down from 4th to 3rd had to be made. On the driver's right was an Extra Air Lever which had to be adjusted into position for about the first half hour's running until smooth running was achieved. The frequent pops and bangs that emanated from the bus could often be attributed to faulty ignition or insufficient gas, and on stands a high idling speed had to be maintained to keep the fire going in the hopper, which was done by adjusting the hand throttle. At termini it was the driver's job to poke the fire to reduce clinker (each trailer carried a poker), though often the conductors helped out with this work.

Conductors and others travelling on a gas powered ST may have been aware that it was running a little quieter than usual and with a gentle hiss above the sound of the engine. The conductor was expected to take an occasional glance at the trailer to make sure that it was not becoming red hot or that the cooling tank was not boiling. Sometimes, if red hot patches were showing, it was prudent to poke the fire briskly to clear excessive clinker that had formed or to eliminate an air pocket. Trailers gave off a really noxious sulphurous smell which could easily cause nausea, though mostly the fumes did not enter the bus or cause any problems except, occasionally, if a vehicle was stationary and the wind was blowing in the wrong direction.

After a while crews grew to recognise problems when they occurred. A badly pulling engine could be a result of air leaks, an overheated hopper or, at the other extreme, a fire that had died down too much. Irregular running, or engines that began to die when slowing down, could often be corrected by carefully adjusting the Extra Air Lever while the vehicle was in third gear. All in all, driving a preselector diesel STL – as all the drivers had done before the arrival of gas producers – was child's play compared with what they were now expected to do.

Meanwhile plans were in hand to widen the scope of the operation considerably, and in March 1943 gas producer STs went to Leyton, Willesden, Tring, Hemel Hempstead, Addlestone and Epping to commence training, followed by Hertford in May, Croydon in June and Catford in August. Eventually Leyton, Willesden and Hertford dropped out as, subsequently, did Clay Hall in the spring of 1944, and it was at Epping that the next successful operation began with the licensing of six vehicles on 1st May 1943. The exact starting date of the operation is uncertain (Traffic Circulars state 2nd June but it was almost certainly earlier than this and quite probably 5th May), and the routes operated were 392 (Epping–Ongar) and 396 (Epping–Bishops Stortford). Conventional operation was retained on route 339 (Ongar–Warley), albeit now with petrol STs instead of diesel STLs, as this was considered too remote from Epping garage for refuelling purposes.

More Country garages followed. Gas STs were licensed at Tring, Hemel Hempstead and Addlestone from 1st June 1943 though it is doubtful if actual service operation commenced quite as early as this at any of the three locations. Tring and Hemel Hempstead were partners in the operation of trunk routes 301 (Watford Junction–Aylesbury) and 302 (Watford Heath–Hemel Hempstead), the first instance of two garages running gas producer STs in unison. An unusual unit of the Hemel Hempstead gas fleet was ST 1034, the only Bluebird ever converted. This was, of course, in green livery unlike the main gas producer fleet which continued to be taken from Central Bus stock, the only other exceptions being ST 1062 and ST 1067, one-time East Surrey vehicles, which had joined the gas fleet at Grays on 3rd April 1943. At about this time the gas buses were given chassis classifications of their own, the bulk of them becoming 4ST whilst STs 1062 and 1067 were coded 5ST and the Bluebird 6ST.

Right ST 656 makes a halt in Acton during its well-publicised trial run on 2nd June 1942. The gentlemen standing by it may have been part of the press contingent invited along for the ride. Another two months were to elapse before London Transport felt confident enough to place gas producer STs into passenger service.

A grand total of 240 STs were modified at Chiswick for gas propulsion and 149 of these ran in service as gas buses at the garages shown:

1 (TC), 2 (TC), 9 (GY), 15 (Q), 18 (TL), 20 (TC,TL), 21 (Q), 26 (TC), 27 (TC), 29 (TL,TC), 33 (TC), 35 (Q), 37 (GY,Q,TC), 41 (TL), 43 (TG), 45 (TL), 46 (GY), 47 (WY), 56 (Q), 63 (GY,Q), 66 (HH), 67 (Q), 68 (Q), 69 (GY), 75 (Q), 82 (GY,Q), 90 (TG), 91 (GY), 94 (Q), 95 (EP), 99 (GY), 102 (Q), 108 (TG), 109 (TC), 118 (GY), 130 (Q), 155 (TL), 158 (Q), 160 (GY), 165 (GY), 166 (Q), 167 (TL,GY), 174 (Q), 176 (HH,Q), 177 (GY), 189 (TC), 192 (WY), 199 (Q), 213 (TC), 218 (TC), 221 (TL), 225 (TC, TL), 236 (EP), 245 (TL), 248 (Q), 253 (GY), 254 (EP), 259 (TL, TC), 262 (GY,Q,EP), 270 (TG), 276 (EP), 277 (HH), 278 (TC), 293 (TC,TL), 299 (Q), 303 (Q), 313 (TL), 316 (TC, TL), 324 (WY), 326 (TC), 329 (Q), 335 (GY,WY), 340 (TG), 345 (GY), 352 (HH), 354 (TL), 355 (GY), 356 (EP), 360 (TG), 384 (TC,TL), 390 (WY,TG), 394 (Q), 401 (GY,TL), 403 (GY), 410 (TL), 412 (TL), 425, (TL), 429 (TG,Q), 434 (Q,GY), 443 (Q), 461 (EP), 462 (GY,WY,TG), 463 (GY), 472 (TL), 477 (Q), 479 (TC), 480 (GY,TG), 483 (TC), 491 (TG), 495 (TL), 508 (GY), 521 (EP), 534 (TG), 535 (GY), 540 (Q), 546 (TC), 558 (TL), 571 (Q), 573 (TC, TL), 588 (Q), 594 (GY, Q), 608 (Q), 618 (GY,TG), 634 (GY,EP), 639 (GY), 648 (WY), 651 (TC,TL), 656 (GY), 661 (TL), 663 (Q,TL), 667 (TC), 669 (EP), 671 (EP,TC), 684 (GY,Q,TC), 701 (GY,TC), 710 (TC), 714 (TC), 717 (TL), 720 (GY), 722 (Q), 725 (Q), 728 (Q), 730 (WY), 745 (GY), 751 (HH,TG), 752 (Q), 761 (Q), 764 (TC,GY), 791 (GY,TC), 792 (Q), 801 (WY), 802 (GY,EP), 807 (TG), 808 (GY), 832 (TL), 1034 (HH), 1062 (GY), 1067 (GY).

The following vehicles were converted for gas propulsion but never operated as such and were probably never linked to a trailer:

ST 16, 23, 28, 48, 133, 151, 173, 184, 188, 191, 194, 196, 201, 206, 207, 216, 228, 229, 230, 242, 258, 264, 274, 286, 315, 330, 331, 333, 338, 341, 346, 349, 370, 392, 393, 402, 404, 413, 416, 426, 431, 444, 445, 446, 452, 456, 485, 492, 509, 513, 515, 550, 555, 557, 560, 561, 578, 598, 606, 609, 622, 625, 630, 637, 643, 645, 646, 662, 664, 674, 680, 683, 689, 693, 694, 695, 713, 740, 741, 756, 765, 776, 814, 815, 823, 830

Five vehicles ran under gas propulsion but not in service:

ST 14	Trainer at Clay Hall
ST 76	Trainer at Leyton and Clay Hall
ST 171	Use unknown
ST 494	Loaned to Experimental Fuel Research Station, Greenwich, September 1943 to November 1944
ST 748	Trainer at Clay Hall

The seven gas STs licensed at Addlestone on 1st June were for routes 461 (Walton–Chertsey) and 461A (Walton–Ottershaw). Addlestone had, in fact, a mixed allocation of double and single deck gas producers as it shared with Leatherhead garage the operation of T types on route 462 (Leatherhead–Staines). In common with all vehicles at Addlestone, the gas producers were in plain grey livery, those concerned being ST 47, 192, 324, 335, 648, 730, 801. With the exception of ST 335 all were on their first assignment as gas producers; ST 335 had been one of the four original conversions for Grays a year earlier and had been repainted grey at a recent routine overhaul.

On 9th June 1943 a one-bus experiment began at Grays when ST 160 was licensed for service towing its own special trailer. The earlier plan to try out the South Wales Transport Company's 'Ravenhill' type trailer had been put into action and two of these had been purchased as the minimum necessary to keep ST 160 fully employed. Whereas most trailers were identified by a single series numbered from 1 upwards, the two Ravenhills could be identified, not just by their distinctive shape, but also by their stock numbers RT 1 and RT 2. In service operation, ST 160 quickly proved its superiority with a road performance that did not appear to fall very far short of that achieved from a normal petrol engine, but whilst the experiment no doubt produced much useful data it had come too late to influence the current conversion programme.

It was now July 1943 and the government's deadline for 10% of the fleet to be running on gas producers had arrived. By the end of July Chiswick had managed to convert only 134 STs plus 9 Ts against its target of 548. Many of the converted STs had yet to enter service as gas producers, and some never did so. It became commonplace to see converted STs complete with towing bar attachment running in service minus trailers as purely petrol driven vehicles. New trailers were in the process of delivery from Bristol in quantities far greater than were immediately required, and many of these were destined

With its clippie standing on the platform watching proceedings, ST 535 leaves Grays garage ready to take up service on route 371A. As very often happened, someone has forgotten to attach the registration plate to the trailer. *Alan B Cross collection*

Inside Grays garage specially trained staff carry out the messy task of servicing the gas producer equipment between spells of use. The bus in the centre of the picture will be ST 160 with its very different-looking Ravenhill trailer. *L T Museum*

never to be used. In common with bus operators all over the country, London Transport found that the government's target was completely unachievable. Chiswick Works did not have the capacity to carry out engine conversions at the necessary rate and, even if it had done, many of the manufacturers responsible for supplying modification kits would have been unable to keep up. On top of all this, it was proving difficult to locate sites suitable for erecting gas producer servicing plants and to get them constructed once approved. Only a minority of routes were suited to the reduced performance of the vehicles, and negotiations with police and local authorities to obtain revised terminal arrangements to suit the trailers and amended stopping places to take account of inclines could prove very protracted.

Pressing ahead, it was now time to introduce gas operation into the Central area on a more intensive scale than just the three STs on route 36. Croydon garage was in the lead with an allocation of 20 buses to route 197 (Caterham Valley–Norwood Junction). Although the first training bus had arrived there in June 1943, operation did not commence until the first week of January 1944 and even then it was confined only to weekdays; the Central Bus department never scheduled gas producers to run on Sundays anywhere within its system. Catford garage came next, building up during April and May to a 28 vehicle operation on Mondays to Fridays divided between route 36 and route 124 (Forest Hill–Eltham), although on Saturdays an increased requirement on route 124 meant that none were employed on the 36. Catford was, in fact, the last 'new' garage to receive gas producers, although its build-up coincided with a similar expansion at Camberwell. Here the pioneering three bus supplementary schedule on route 36 was transformed into a full-blown operation requiring 16 buses augmented, from May, by a further seven on route 42 (Camberwell Green–Aldgate). Requiring a maximum of 67 buses from the three garages, this peak of Central Bus gas operation had been partly made possible by abandoning the earlier principle of always refuelling as vehicles passed their garages in favour of stationing tipper lorries laden with anthracite at strategic terminal points such as Hither Green and Norwood Junction. The very last gas buses placed into service were ST 21, 75, 571 and 761 at Camberwell on 9th May 1944.

With the tide of war now turning inexorably in the allies' favour, and with fuel imports remaining steady, the writing was now on the wall for the gas producers. Clearly sensing how events were likely to proceed, the Board gave authority on 21st March 1944 to scrap 22 unserviceable 3T3 type trailers and to break up 50 unused 3T4s for spare parts. On 4th April matters went one stage further when 300 more gas producer units were declared surplus. Although their days as gas buses were now clearly numbered, a start was made on repainting the Country area STs in green delivery and five were dealt with before the end of gas operation came. These were ST 656, 720, 745 at Grays and ST 95, 254 at Epping. The beginning of the end arrived on 9th August 1944 when the Board's Engineering Committee was advised that the Ministry of War Transport had given provisional authority for withdrawal of the gas producer fleet ahead of the official announcement. No time was lost in putting this into practice, and although the officially preferred option was for Central bus garages to be dealt with ahead of the Country ones, in fact most removed their trailers simultaneously between 14th and 29th August 1944. Only Grays and Camberwell were still operating gas producers into September, and if records are to

Photographs of gas producer STs in Central Bus service are rare. With the paintwork sparkling after its recent overhaul, Camberwell's ST 725 makes its way to Hither Green on the first day of the supplementary gas-bus schedule on route 36. *Alan B Cross collection*

be believed, the final gas producers were removed from ST 167, 639, 1067 at Grays on 8th September and ST 299, 477, 728 at Camberwell four days later. By the time the Minister belatedly summoned representatives of the PSV industry on 12th September to inform them that they could revert to the use of liquid fuel on all their vehicles, gas producer operation had already come to an end, not just in London but almost everywhere else too.

This may not, in fact, have been quite the end of the story so far as gas producer operation in London goes. According to official records, ST 160 at Grays did not lose its gas producer trailer until as late as 16th November 1944. This may merely be an inaccuracy in recording, but ST 160 was the vehicle linked with experiments using the two 'Ravenhill' trailers which were showing so much greater promise than all the others, and the possibility exists that London Transport perpetuated their use for a little longer in order to continue gaining operational data from them. It is known that a residual interest in gas producer operation survived to the extent that London Transport became involved in a trial conducted with the Ministry of Fuel & Power as late as December 1952 using STL 2676.

While arrangements were made to demolish or find alternative uses for the gas producer service stations (including one at Leyton which had never been brought into regular use), it was now a case of removing the engine conversion kits and tow bars from the numerous STs that were fitted with them. The de-conversion programme commenced on 30th October and was completed in January 1945.

CHAPTER 21
THE POST-WAR YEARS

The post-war history of the STs is unlike that of other double-deck classes in the London Transport fleet. Time expired and of limited seating capacity, and expensive to run because of their thirsty petrol engines, they were the least valued members of the fleet and a tendency to move them about frequently between garages to meet fluctuations in schedule requirements and vehicle availability gave them an air of impermanence. Time after time they were used as a fall back option when nothing else was available, and whereas other classes adhered fairly rigidly to their scheduled spheres of operation, STs could be found running almost anywhere. On Central Buses only three out of 52 garages counted STs as their sole, permanent double deck allocation – Hounslow, Uxbridge and Kingston – and the last two of these operated predominantly single deckers and consequently only had a small double-deck requirement. In addition to the routes operated from these three garages, on which the presence of STs could always be guaranteed, there were a number of others designated as exclusive ST territory. Some, such as routes 5A and 67, were among the less heavily loaded and were obvious territory on which to work STs with their low seating capacity. Other STs were working 'Supplementary Schedules' – extras introduced to cover all or part of existing services normally worked by other types and introduced under a wartime authorisation issued by the Regional Transport Commissioner back in October 1943. In yet another category were STs scheduled as make-weights in the absence of sufficient vehicles of the right type, such as on route 11 where Dalston's allocation of 4 STs was dwarfed by its 41 STLs, whilst over and above these were STs based at various garages where none were actually scheduled but which needed them to make up for shortages of other types of vehicle.

The pattern described above did not apply to the eight lowbridge STs which led a comparatively static existence post-war, and which outlasted the rest of the fleet, latterly in diesel powered form. These are dealt with in chapter 22.

The very first post-war allocation of buses in the Central area, which was actually introduced with the summer programme on 2nd May 1945 just a few days before the war in Europe ended, envisaged a maximum Monday to Friday allocation of 477 STs from 28 garages. In fact 632 STs were dispersed amongst 38 garages, a big discrepancy illustrating how widespread the use of these vehicles actually was compared with the official version of events. Naturally the largest holding of STs was at Hounslow (which had 73 on its books to cover 64 scheduled workings), but quite substantial fleets could also be found at Croydon (53), Catford (50), Camberwell (47), Turnham Green (41), Cricklewood (40) and Middle Row (38). At the other end of the scale were odd ones, twos and threes at Plumstead, Harrow Weald, Hanwell, Sidcup, Sutton and West Green.

The situation on Central Buses on 2nd May 1945 was as shown opposite:

In the early post-war period Hounslow was London's pre-eminent centre for ST operation and Kingsley Road echoed constantly to the sound of STs coming and going on the host of services listed in the timetable panels on the wall of the old garage. With its driver in his white summer coat and hat, Hounslow's Short Bros bodied ST 219 is about to depart on the 55 minute run on route 98 to Ruislip worked jointly with STs from Uxbridge garage. *Alan B Cross*

Routes with a full ST allocation

		Garage	No. of vehicles (Mon-Fri)
1	Willesden–Lewisham	Catford	17
		Cricklewood	11
5A	North Cheam–Clapham Common	Camberwell	8
7	Liverpool Street–Kew Green/Acton Vale	Middle Row	34
25A	Ilford–Lambourne End	Seven Kings	17
33	Brook Green–Hounslow	Hammersmith	12
		Hounslow	6
42	Camberwell–Aldgate	Camberwell	7
59	Thornton Heath–Chipstead Valley Road	Croydon	7
59B	Thornton Heath–Old Coulsdon	Croydon	7
67	Stoke Newington–Waterloo	Tottenham	7
81	Hounslow–Slough	Hounslow)	
81A	Hounslow–Langley	Hounslow)	33
91	Wandsworth Bridge–Cranford	Turnham Green	32
98	Hounslow–Ruislip	Hounslow	6
		Uxbridge	12
110	Hounslow–Twickenham	Hounslow	5
111	Hounslow–Hanworth	Hounslow	7
116	Hounslow–Staines	Hounslow	9
117	Hounslow–Egham	Hounslow	18
121	Ponders End–Chingford	Enfield	3
131	Kingston–Walton-upon-Thames	Kingston	7
143	Archway–Hendon Central	Holloway	8
187	South Harrow–Hampstead Heath	Alperton	8
		Cricklewood	11
197	Caterham Valley–Norwood Junction	Croydon	20
220	Uxbridge–Pinner	Uxbridge	5
239	Tufnell Park–King's Cross	Holloway	3
247 *double deck section*	Collier Row–Harold Wood	Hornchurch	9

Routes with a partial ST allocation

Inter Station	Waterloo Circular	Old Kent Road	4
11	Liverpool Street–Shepherds Bush	Dalston	4
12	Oxford Circus–South Croydon (*section*)	Croydon	4
16	Victoria–Sudbury Town	Cricklewood	10
		Victoria	9
28	Wandsworth Plain–Golders Green	Battersea	7
36	Hither Green–West Kilburn	Camberwell	18
47	Shoreditch–Farnborough	Bromley	7
54	South Croydon–Selsdon	Croydon	10
55	Chiswick–Hayes	Turnham Green	6
59A	Camden Town–Addiscombe	Camberwell	6
65	Ealing–Leatherhead	Kingston	6
113	Oxford Circus–Edgware	Hendon	6
175	Chase Cross–Poplar	Upton Park	3
194	Forest Hill–Croydon	Elmers End	2

STs working Supplementary Schedules over the sections of routes shown

2	Arnos Grove–Crystal Palace	Cricklewood	2
		Norwood	5
4A	Finsbury Park–Angel, Islington	Holloway	2
9	Aldwych–Hammersmith	Mortlake	8
12	Charing Cross–Dulwich	Catford	2
		Nunhead	2
47	Lewisham–Farnborough	Bromley	3
65	Ealing–Kingston	Turnham Green	4
68	Chalk Farm–Upper Norwood	Chalk Farm	6
77A	Charing Cross–Raynes Park	Victoria	7
175	Chase Cross–Dagenham	Upton Park	3
194	Shirley–Croydon	Elmers End	2

No night services were scheduled for ST operation.

Inevitably this situation did not remain unchanged for very long. Starting on 8th December 1945 Willesden garage, which had not featured in the above list, became the focus for a major influx when a start was made in putting some of the many until now disused STs back on the road. A majority had been in storage awaiting mechanical or body rectification work whilst others had come back after working in the provinces. Even more came Willesden's way in February 1946 when a clear out of now surplus STs from Country Buses resulted in 14 being sent there from nine country locations. These, together with other ST arrivals, indirectly enabled many STLs from all over the fleet to be released for major body overhauls, resulting in STs appearing on all of Willesden's operations but most notably on the 18B (Brent Station–London Bridge) which was officially demoted to full ST status.

Within a few months two scheduled ST routes were handed over to newly delivered Guy Arabs, the 247 during August and September 1945 and the 121 in October. On the plus side, Peckham circular service 243 operated by Old Kent Road garage was double decked using STs on 12th September 1945 followed by Uxbridge's 225 (Eastcote Lane–Northwood) on 17th April 1946. On the same day further STs based at Uxbridge took over the short, peak hour only 90A (Hayes End-Hayes Station) formerly worked by STLs from Twickenham, but vanished from it again just over a couple of years later, on 18th August 1948, when it was absorbed into existing route 98. Earlier, a new ST route created on 9th October 1946 was the 7A which was, in effect, the Acton Vale leg of Middle Row's route 7 diverted in the City of London to terminate at London Bridge.

The summer programme for 1945 on Country Buses commenced on 4th July on which date the department was operating 192 STs distributed amongst 15 out of its 30 garages. Some garages, such as Hatfield, no longer possessed petrol-fuelling facilities and thus never ran STs in the post-war era. The official Allocation Book is not totally precise on exactly how many were scheduled for service (inclusive of regular duplicates and staff buses), but the Monday to Friday maximum figure was probably in the region of 147. Interestingly, the majority of these were in the Northern Division, garages in the south having been modernised to a much greater degree with a higher proportion of STLs. The Monday to Friday allocation on 4th July is shown opposite.

Two former gas producer buses share the forecourt of the modern garage at Epping whose complete double-deck fleet consisted of STs. ST 462, in the foreground, and ST 521 are both now in green livery and, like all red to green repaints at the time, have lost their rear indicator boxes. *Alan B Cross*

Routes entirely ST worked

301	Watford Junction–Aylesbury	)	Hemel Hempstead	5
301C	Hemel Hempstead–Tring	)	Tring	10
302	Watford Heath–Hemel Hempstead		Hemel Hempstead	7
310	Enfield–Hertford North	)	Hertford	18
310A	Enfield–Rye House	)		
314	Hemel Hempstead–Fleetville		St Albans	1
			Hemel Hempstead	2
316	Chesham–Berkhamsted		Hemel Hempstead	4 (including works journeys on other services)
324	Watford Bypass–Croxley Green		Watford High Street	7
327	Hertford–Nazeing Gate		Hertford	4
339	Coxtie Green–Warley		Epping	3
345	Oxhey Hall Farm–Kingswood	)	Watford High Street	8
346	Oxhey Hall Farm–Maytree Cres.	)		
370	Grays–Romford		Grays	4
371	Grays–Rainham	)	Grays	21
371A	Grays–Purfleet	)		
392	Epping–Ongar		Epping	9 (10 Thursdays) (includes route 396)
395	Hertford–Ware	)	Hertford	2
395A	Hertford–Musley Hill	)		
396	Epping–Bishops Stortford		Epping	see route 392
416	Leatherhead–Esher		Leatherhead	1
497	Gravesend–Northfleet		Northfleet	2

Routes worked partly by STs in conjunction with other vehicle types

331	Hertford–Buntingford	Hertford	1 ST 3 STL
353	Windsor–Berkhamsted	Amersham	5 ST 4 STL
390	Hertford–Stevenage (note a)	Hertford	1 ST 1 T
408	Warlingham–Guildford	Leatherhead	10 buses in total, both ST and STL
429	Dorking–Newdigate circular (note b)	Reigate	1 ST (plus Dorking 6 STL)
436	Staines–Woking (note c)	Addlestone	1 ST (plus 4 STL lowbridge & 1 ST lowbridge)

(a) ST to work Hertford–Watton section only
(b) ST also works Newdigate–Redhill section of route 439
(c) ST not allowed on Staines–Chertsey section

Works and other services with ST workings (usually alongside other double or single deckers)

301A	Watford Junction–Ovaltine Works	Hemel Hempstead
301B	Watford Junction–Aylesbury	Hemel Hempstead
307/A	Cupid Green–Hemel Hempstead (*section only*)	Hemel Hempstead
311	Radlett–Shenley Hospital (*section only*)	Watford High Street (Wednesdays only)
315	Watford–Garston (*section only*)	Watford High Street (not Wednesdays)
321A	Sundridge–St Albans Abbey Station	St Albans
377A/B	Cupid Green–Apsley Mills (*section only*)	Hemel Hempstead
378	Boxmoor–Apsley Mills	Hemel Hempstead
399A	Epping–Theydon Mount	Epping
	Supplementary schedule & school private hire	St Albans
	Fairfield Aviation Company private hire	Watford High Street

Although Dorking had no scheduled Monday to Friday ST workings it had a solitary Saturday one on route 470 (Dorking–Warlingham).

STs were also scheduled to work odd journeys over parts of route 341 (St Albans–Hertford) from Hertford garage and routes 362/A (High Wycombe–Ley Hill) from Amersham, but in practice spare vehicles could be found working on almost any STL service at one time or another. A restriction, which was rigidly applied, was that only those with 7:1 rear axle ratios were allowed on routes 316 and 362/A.

The very essence of Country Bus operation just after the war is captured by this scene of two STs and a Q at Watford Junction. Square cab ST 1094, a Hemel Hempstead based bus on route 301, stands at the front ahead of Leavesden Road's Q 99. A one-time LGOC ST, also on route 301, is at the back. *Alan B Cross*

At four Country garages the entire double-deck rolling stock consisted of STs; these were Epping, Grays, Hemel Hempstead and Tring, although their domination at Hemel Hempstead ceased in December 1946 when decrepit but higher capacity Tilling STLs were transferred in from the Central area for works services, and similarly at Grays in April 1947 when Gardner engine Bluebird LTs made their appearance. As mentioned in an earlier chapter, STs held unique sway on very heavily used and tightly timed trunk operations 301, 302 and 310/A, while Leatherhead's similarly busy 418 (Kingston–Little Bookham) was double decked on 15th January 1946 using newly relicensed red STs.

Although country towns such as Grays and Hertford were buzzing with ST activity in the early post-war years, the best place to go to see them was undoubtedly Watford where those from Tring, Hemel Hempstead and from the local High Street garage could all be found. This was almost the only place to go to be sure of seeing Bluebird STs which had now all been gathered together at Watford High Street garage and, whilst normally kept busy working on Watford locals, they could quite often be seen as far afield as Uxbridge or Luton on the

officially STL worked 321. In January and February 1946 this long trunk service was the first in the Country area to receive post-war double deckers in the form of 20 new STLs; in fact the new vehicles were strictly confined to the 321 at first. Their impact on the ST fleet was very minor as it was mostly standard STLs that were deposed, but the situation at Watford was very fluid and was made more so by big changes on 29th May 1946 which saw the withdrawal of routes 315 and 324. STs now made their way on to the new 334 (Croxley Green–North Watford) and 334A (Watford Met Station–North Watford), but they continued as regular performers on the now strengthened 321 and gradually took over almost completely the linked routes 311 (Watford–Shenley) and 312 (Watford–Little Bushey). Not far away, in St Albans, withdrawal of the St Albans to Sandridge section of route 314 left this route entirely in the hands of Hemel Hempstead's STs, but reintroduction of seasonal daily route 368 (Sandridge–Whipsnade Zoo) saw four STs from St Albans fully employed on this until the 1946 season ended on 2nd October. Down south, new route 468 (Great Bookham–Chessington Zoo) gave employment to two STs from Leatherhead.

Looking more down at heel than usual and desperately in need of a fresh coat of paint, ST 582 was amongst the influx into Willesden in December 1945 that resulted in the total takeover of route 18B by STs. This was one of the few STs rebuilt with flush lower side panels in 1938, a feature much more associated with the LT class. *Alan B Cross*

With the return of peacetime conditions route 368 to Whipsnade Zoo became a popular summer operation. Seen on a crew change opposite St Albans garage, ST 588 spent three years in the country area but was never repainted green. In the background a new STL departs away from the photographer on route 321 heading for Luton.
Alan B Cross

Despite several having been lost during the war and the existence of an ongoing scrapping programme for others, the Tilling STs were once again very much in evidence at the end of the war and were used, for the most part, as driver trainers. Although licensed and theoretically available for passenger service, they were seldom used on these duties except to cover emergencies. With a pressing need to give refresher training to ex-servicemen arriving back and to train new staff to replace those who could not or chose not to return, they were kept busy, and in May 1945 46 Tillings were employed in this role at 18 Central and 5 Country garages. Others joined them as they returned from hire in the provinces. Their outside staircases and generally decrepit condition made them very unpopular with staff to the extent that an agreement was in force with the Transport & General Workers' Union that they would only be used in a passenger carrying capacity to cover in emergencies and were not to be used for normal service. However by the autumn of 1946 the backlog of maintenance inherited from the wartime era was becoming ever more apparent, and the resultant rolling stock shortage was becoming ever more serious because of an upsurge in activity by Ministry of Transport vehicle examiners. Faced with this escalating problem, the Union agreed to lift its restriction on the use of Tilling STs. From October 1946 vehicles of this type began covering shortages at a whole range of garages. With their sagging waist lines and a frequent lack of proper route and destination displays, many of them would undoubtedly have created a very unfavourable impression of London Transport on the travelling public, most of whom were totally unaware of the critical rolling stock situation that the Board was faced with at the time.

Operation of the summer supplementary schedule on route 74 between Marylebone Station and London Zoo fluctuated yearly between garages according to staff availability. In 1945 Middle Row ran it, but when Holloway took over in 1946 it presented an early opportunity to find Tilling STs back in passenger service. This was the last full year of existence for ST 946; it was scrapped in September 1947.

ST 993 must have been photographed on a Sunday on newly double decked route 243 as the shutters are firmly down on the famous Jones & Higgins store in Peckham. This vehicle was quite a rarity after the war in retaining the original two-section destination and route number display. Most Tilling STs, if they used the destination box at all, were fitted with a single blind. *Omnibus Society collection*

Not long after the war ended the two real oddities remaining within the ST class arrived back from the provinces. ST 1029 was returned by the Rhondda Transport Company on 30th September 1945 and ST 1139 came back from Coventry Corporation a couple of months later on 28th November. Both were examined at Chiswick on their return, where the one-time Empire vehicle was found to be unfit for further use and was dispatched to the Walthamstow yard for storage until arrangements could be made for it to be scrapped in June 1946. ST 1139 was more fortunate. Possibly as a result of its body being strengthened shortly before the war, it was deemed fit for further use despite being of an obsolete, outside staircase design. Its fate seemed to be destined as a driver trainer for which purpose it was licensed at Guildford on 12th January 1946. However on 2nd July of the same year it moved to Windsor garage where, incredibly, it subsequently resumed a public role shuttling to and fro between Windsor and Datchet Common on route 445. Seldom straying on to any other service, ST 1139 became a well known sight in Windsor and, right to the end, it managed to retain its grey roof from earlier days which, somehow or other, no-one had ever got around to repainting brown. On 19th May 1948 route 445 was reduced to single-deck operation using T types, but ST 1139 soldiered on at Windsor for a little longer on miscellaneous jobs. It was finally delicensed on 23rd September 1948 and sent to Chiswick where it was recorded as being dismantled on 19th October.

The condition of many buses within the fleet in the early post-war era was undoubtedly dire and it was for this reason that London Transport took the decision that the ST and LT classes, along with all petrol STLs, must be replaced before scrapping of the remaining trams could be resumed. Many of the latter were far older, with some dating back to the first decade of the century, but they were inherently stronger and could be made to soldier on for a little longer even though the cost of continuing to run them was becoming prohibitive. Fortunately for the bus engineering department, much of the fleet continued initially to be exempted from Certificate of Fitness regulations and was running under wartime Defence Permits, thereby escaping the full rigours of current requirements as to safety and roadworthiness. However the Board's own Bodywork Inspection Committee ensured that the very worst vehicles were kept off the road and the Ministry of Transport's roving vehicle examiners continued issuing 'PSV 71' certificates which virtually ensured that a bus would never run in public service again. London Transport had agreed with the trade unions that, once delivery of the new RT class commenced, the first 500 would be used to replace all remaining outside staircase vehicles, then all other petrol engined LTs, and finally 231 standard STs. This agreement fell by the wayside as vehicles outside these categories were deemed permanently unfit in ever increasing numbers. The inevitable result was that outside staircase buses, including some Tilling STs, remained in service through to 1949, a full ten years longer than ever foreseen in pre-war days.

Although ST bodies were only very infrequently changed between chassis after the war, they continued to be lifted at Chiswick as part of the overhauling process. In this instance only the chassis of ST 112 is being overhauled, quite a regular practice at the time as facilities did not exist to overhaul every body that came into the works. As sometimes happened, the overhauling of the chassis proved to be a futile exercise because, a month later in December 1947, the body was condemned and ST 112 was sent for scrap.
L T Museum

After being deposed from its regular haunt on route 445, ST 1139 continued to see occasional service from Windsor garage, often on routes 417 and 484. With the appropriate route number posted in the bulkhead window, it was photographed in Windsor shortly before withdrawal in September 1948. *V C Jones*

The authorised scrapping of 27 Tilling STs, nine of which had gone before the war ended, continued up to October 1945 by which time all 27 had been disposed of. This was followed between February and May 1946 by the scrapping of ten redundant ST bodies which had been placed in storage at Chiswick at various times between 1938 and 1944. Nine were standard LGOC style bodies, some of which were complete but structurally weakened after half a decade of open storage, though others were war damaged beyond repair including the camel back body from ST 244 fire damaged at Camberwell and the body from ST 6 which had come back from the Lincolnshire Road Car Company minus its roof. The tenth, and only green one, was a Ransomes body finally on ST 1112 which had become redundant since the 'float' for these vehicles was abandoned in September 1939. Immediately after this, between May and September 1946, five more Tillings were scrapped along with ST 1029, but after these departed no further forward programme was authorised for the scrapping of STs. Instead it was left to fate to decree when vehicles would be earmarked for disposal, generally as a result of vehicles being diagnosed at Chiswick as being totally beyond redemption either through general deterioration or because of serious accident damage. The first in this category was ST 365 which had been out of service after being de-licensed at Camberwell garage on 1st October 1945, the first green one being ST 1102 taken out of service at Watford High Street exactly a month later. Both were burnt and their chassis scrapped in November 1946. Others inevitably followed, spasmodically at first but gaining in momentum from June 1947 onwards as the initial supply of new RTs came on stream.

In July 1945 two more STs were sent to Chiswick to be converted to tree loppers, but unlike the earlier conversions these retained their own bodies. Tilling ST 865 had last been used as a temporary replacement at Elmers End after the bombing incident and ST 870 had spent a few months as a trainer after returning from the provinces. The conversion of both and repainting into lorry green had been completed by 10th August 1945 whereupon they were numbered 650J and 651J respectively in service vehicle stock. However their passenger carrying days were not quite over and both enjoyed a further day of glory in 1946. In May of that year they returned to Chiswick for conversion into grandstands for the forthcoming Derby Day on 6th June. Transverse wooden seats were installed on the upper deck in five rows, each about 6 inches higher than the one in front to give a good view of the racing from all of them. Downstairs, upholstered longitudinal seats were provided along each side with a table in the middle, presumably for beer bottles and betting slips. The upstairs seating was constructed with heavy timber and there must have been some doubt about the ability of the upper saloon floor to support the weight of these plus spectators totally unaided, as three 3 inch steel tubes were inserted from the lower deck floor, through the table, to support the upper deck. At a time of extreme austerity and shortage of materials it is understandable that the venture received no publicity, but it no doubt provided a good day out for members of the Board, very senior officials and their guests. It is rumoured that the same conversions may have been carried out for Derby Day in 1947 but no confirmation has been found for this.

Faced with a seemingly intractable vehicle shortage, the Board had to look beyond its own resources to keep as much of the fleet as possible on the road. Whilst mechanically basi-

cally sound if in some cases a little tired, the real point of weakness with almost all STs lay in the condition of their timber framed bodywork which, in the majority of cases, had worn loose allowing water ingress, especially around the windows, with subsequent rotting. Far too often the passenger could hear creaking bodywork and, in wet weather, could see the rain coming in. The loss of the Chiswick body shops to aircraft production and the consequent dispersal of body overhauling to decentralised units had, along with shortages of materials and skilled staff, resulted in half a decade of managed neglect to the extent that extreme levels of remedial work were now necessary to make good the shortfall. Towards the end of 1944 a small amount of body overhauling recommenced at Chiswick, and after the end of the war a certain amount of quite major work such as replacing complete pillars using pre-prepared units was done on vehicles at their home garages, but much more drastic action was also needed. On 8th September 1945 an agreement was made with Mann Egerton & Co Ltd to overhaul five bodies a week at their works in Aylsham Road, Norwich, a converted World War I aircraft hangar, and the first two vehicles were sent there six days later. The first to go to Norwich were LTs, which were deemed to be the higher priority, though STs also began to be sent there from 24th May 1946. In all 31 STs were dealt with by Mann Egerton between then and 21st November 1946 when the final one arrived back in London, considerably fewer than the 259 LTs overhauled up to the end of 1946 at which time the programme switched to more strategically important STLs. When newly arrived back from Norwich the overhauled vehicles looked immaculate and internally they were refreshed by the latest new brown décor capped by a light green moulding which had now been adopted for all ST and LT overhauls in place of the drab grey used previously. When Country area STs were repainted these, too, were given the brown interior colour scheme which saw the gradual phasing out of the rather cheerful light green which had previously distinguished them from the Central Bus fleet.

Although facilities did not exist to maintain any semblance of a regular overhaul programme on the STs in post-war years, it was quite common for them to be called into Chiswick for what was termed a 'chassis overhaul' when all the mechanical components would be dealt with. This did not mean that the appearance of the bodywork was neglected; in fact repaints were commonly carried out both at Chiswick and in garages to keep them looking superficially smart however creaky and leaky the structure had become beneath the surface. However this was a completely uncoordinated process to the extent that some STs were repainted twice within a year or eighteen months whereas others, which had last been repainted during the war, began to take on a very neglected appearance. Fortunately the latter were in a minority. Even Tilling STs sometimes appeared newly repainted. The most notable of these was ST 910 which, having received wartime brown and cream livery in February 1943, continued to carry it years after all the others had reverted to red and was still doing so in service at Tottenham until as late as July 1948, the month in which it finally achieved fleet colours. Somewhat before this, in early June 1947, the last two STs to carry Inter Station blue and cream – ST 164, 470 – were painted back into standard red. Meanwhile red STs in the Country area continued to appear in green after being repainted, continuing a process which had started towards the end of the war and had continued on an 'as and when' basis thereafter. The post-war months of

1945 had seen 18 dealt with followed by 16 more in 1946 and 12 in 1947, continuing into 1948. One notable odd-man-out amongst these was ST 9 at Grays which was the only one with a camel back style of body to receive green livery.

The final conversions of STs into service vehicles took place during this period starting with the rebuilding of six Tilling vehicles into 7 ton mobile staff canteens between September 1946 and April 1947. Painted in quite a striking all-red colour scheme and retaining their original body outline apart from the removal of their projecting indicator boxes, they became a familiar sight at various outlying locations for a number of years. Numbered 688-693J in the service vehicle fleet, they were formerly ST 888, 969, 867, 917, 951, 922. Three further conversions to service vehicle status took place after this, though in a rather unusual way. In October 1947 ST 6, whose body had been condemned some months earlier, appeared at Palmers Green garage with a towing eye attached at the rear specifically for use as a towing bus. This was a new departure for London Transport which had never previously adapted a double decker specifically for this purpose, and it was followed by ST 523 similarly equipped at Plumstead in November 1947 and ST 44 at Potters Bar in December. The use of a standard double decker as a towing vehicle clearly had its limitations and it may well have been the intention all along to fit a lorry body capable of carrying a full supply of equipment and spare wheels when factory capacity permitted. This omission was rectified in January and February 1948 when all three returned to Chiswick to be fitted with neat looking lorry bodies at which time they were officially transferred into service vehicle stock as 719-721J.

A new phenomenon evident from early in 1947 was the 8-seater ST, a condition to which STs of various types were converted from about February onwards. These were vehicles deemed by the Bodywork Inspection Committee to be unfit for further passenger service but in good enough mechanical condition to serve as permanent driver trainers. Previously the usual practice had been to use vehicles from the licensed fleet as 'learners', but a dedicated training fleet was now built up licensed at private car rate and with an appropriate reduction in seating capacity, four seats being retained on each deck.

On Saturday 10th May 1947 the first of London Transport's long awaited and well overdue fleet of standardised post-war double deckers took the road, marking the start of a process that was to transform the face of the capital's transport system within seven years. Operated from Leyton garage, RT 402 and others that soon joined it marked a total break from the obsolete and generally decrepit vehicles that they replaced. They were a huge novelty at first and their gradual spreading out across the fleet caused much excitement in the early days. It was only in later years, as vehicles of the RT family conquered more and more of the network, driving one after another of the older and not so old classes out of existence, that the full effect of London Transport's policy of achieving maximum standardisation finally dawned. Bold and foresighted as the policy was, it ultimately left little of interest in its wake from a bus scene that had once been so varied and fascinating.

Peering into the lower deck of Bluebird ST 1076, the absence of seats is immediately obvious. Unfit for further passenger service but still mechanically sound, this was a conversion into an 8-seat 'learner' bus in November 1947. Allocated to Grays and seen in the garage yard alongside one of the native TFs, it was an unusual sight in a corner of London Transport's territory where this type of ST had never previously been found. At some time in its career ST 1076 had been given a new roof with narrow mouldings, but it never gained the built-in route number holder that it was meant to receive.
S A Newman

The first RT deliveries had no impact on the STs. Leyton garage was soon joined by Croydon as an early recipient, but Leyton had no STs on its books at that time and the first arrivals at Croydon were sent for the purpose of replacing nearly new STDs which were needed at Loughton to oust outside staircase LTs. Quite rightly, the first targets for replacement were the remaining scheduled outposts of outside staircase LT operation, but this began to change in November and December 1947 when the continued intake of new RTs at Croydon ousted the 22 STs scheduled to operate on route 197. Their introduction followed hot on the heels of a massive rescheduling throughout the fleet on Wednesday 12th November 1947 in connection with the introduction of a 44 hour week for bus workers. This was a major exercise involving new schedules for every service which, in some cases, had to be reallocated between garages to produce workable schedules, often resulting in types of vehicle appearing on routes where they had never been seen previ-ously. The impact of this on the STs was not particularly great because, unlike other classes, they had a habit of turning up anywhere to cover shortages so there was seldom any novelty in seeing them on a 'new' service. However Hammersmith lost its scheduled ST allocations on routes 33 and 47, the vehicles being transferred to route 72 (East Acton–Esher) although, perhaps for capacity reasons, their stay there was short lived and they were soon replaced by LTs.

For the next two years STs were involved in almost every RT conversion that took place on Central Buses irrespective of whether they were officially allocated to the routes being converted or not. An unofficial policy appears to have been adopted of removing STLs and LTs from their scheduled operations during the weeks or even months prior to the conversion of a route to RTs, allowing STs to flood in to take their place as a sure indication that the arrival of new buses was not far away.

Route 14 was typical of so many STL routes temporarily swamped with STs to proclaim that the arrival of new RTs was imminent, at least as far as the Holloway allocation was concerned. Putney Bridge had operated RT2s on the 14 for the best part of a decade. At the Putney terminus is Holloway's ST 231 with Putney Bridge's RT 12, also on route 14, standing some distance behind. *Allen T Smith*

The first conversion of 1948, in January and February, was centred on Middle Row's routes 15 and 28, both of which were scheduled for petrol STLs but on which STs could commonly be found. The displaced STLs were moved across to routes 7/A, the sudden release of STs from which allowed a scrapping programme to begin which, though slow at first, gradually built up in momentum. It also allowed the release of LTs from route 102 (Chingford–Golders Green) at Palmers Green to meet a commitment to the union who were happy to receive STs for a few weeks until STLs became available. In February the straight conversion of Turnham Green's route 91 from ST to RT released 36 more STs for use elsewhere, and in February and March it was the turn of Cricklewood garage where a mass of new RTs took over routes 1, 13 and 240. The first of these had been a scheduled ST operation, but the 13 and 240 were early cases of STLs being released beforehand leaving only STs to be displaced. Similarly at Upton Park in March and April, routes 15 and 100 had accumulated more than 20 STs instead of the usual LTs prior to conversion.

London Transport had now entered the era of being a nationalised entity, the new London Transport Executive being but one of the many offshoots of the British Transport Commission activated on Thursday 1st January 1948. Not long after this, on 27th February, the last two wartime loans returned to London Transport from Hants & Dorset. ST 885 was found to be in good enough condition to start work as a driver trainer less than a week after arriving back, but ST 845 was condemned and quickly dismantled. Apart from the new legal name now carried on the buses, nationalisation did not appear to change very much on the ground, and the introduction of new RTs continued unabated. From January an inflow of STs to Holloway was sufficient to ensure that the whole 26 bus allocation of route 14, when converted to RT in April and May, saw not a single STL displaced. Catford, in June and July, witnessed the end of its scheduled ST operation on route 1 but further STs were lost when routes 89 and 160, theoretically both STL operated, were modernised at the same time. Coinciding with this was an influx of RTs at Willesden where the ST-worked 18B was converted along with route 46, more than half of whose STLs had recently given way to STs. Back in April and May a straight RT for ST swap had taken place at Seven Kings on route 25A and now, at last, it was time for Country Buses to receive RTs.

The Country Bus department was allocated 227 new RTs, far more than enough to complete the replacement of all its STs. The first of them entered service at one of the most far flung outposts, Tring, on 21st July 1948. Next day half of Tring's eight STs departed to bolster numbers at other Country garages, and the remaining four left on 5th August. Petrol vehicles never ran from Tring again. The obvious next choice for new RTs was Hemel Hempstead, not just for the trunk 302 but also for route 314. Here the clear-out of STs was only partial; 32 departed in August and September but some remained for route 316 and various works journeys, which meant that they could still be glimpsed covering sections of route 302 as well as irregular and mainly peak hour routes such as 307, 377 and 378. Once again the deposed STs were assimilated elsewhere on Country Buses with the exception of a single red one which was sent to Croydon. Even more red STs were still present at Leatherhead whose route 418 was next on the conversion list in August and September, no fewer than twelve being returned to Central Buses, leaving Leatherhead with an all-green ST fleet destined to last a few months longer for its other operations.

had focused on quite lengthy services, the 345 and 346 were strictly local operations but by far the busiest of their type in the Watford area. Now greatly diminished as a part of the Watford scene, only eight out of the 23 Bluebirds remained in service after the 345 and 346 received RTs. This was a reflection of the poor structural condition of these vehicles, seven of which – almost one third of the total – had been amongst the earliest withdrawals in 1947.

The last really major, lengthy Country service to be changed over from ST to RT operation was the 310/A at Hertford on which new vehicles were installed from the end of September and into October 1948. The outlet for redundant green STs to other garages within the Country area had now been exhausted so a new home for them on Central Buses had to be found. The quiet, outer suburban route 32 (St Helier–Worcester Park) worked from Merton garage was selected as a suitable backwater to put them on, and between 2nd and 13th October ten one-time LGOC STs now in green livery made their way to Merton to oust utility Daimlers from it. This was more than was actually needed to cover the eight scheduled workings, but the quantity had to be inflated to compensate for two of the earliest arrivals being condemned as unfit for service after less than a week at Merton. In the annals of London Transport history this must have been one of the shortest lived allocations ever recorded. Presumably as a result of staff displeasure, the policy was abruptly changed and a totally different arrangement was rapidly formulated for reallocating surplus green STs to Central Buses. Henceforth, instead of being allocated in pockets as originally intended, they would be distributed as widely as possible with only small numbers going to each garage. Merton's green STs quickly drifted away to Tottenham, West Green, Camberwell and Middle Row, but very many other garages also received green STs in the weeks and months to come.

Pursuing a policy of modernising trunk services first, route 370 at Grays was next in September 1948. Only a minority of Grays' STs was lost on this occasion, most being retained a little longer for the more heavily bussed 371/A. Next came the first inroad into the big ST fleet at Watford High Street, also in September. Its remaining red ones had departed a month earlier when green replacements had arrived from Tring and Hemel Hempstead and only green ones were lost on this occasion. In contrast to the conversions at Tring, Hemel Hempstead, Leatherhead and Grays which

Above Few Bluebirds remained in regular passenger service at the time Watford High Street's busy 345 and 346 succumbed to new RTs. Their arrival marked the end of its public service career for ST 1073, but it was converted into a staff bus and subsequently outlasted all the other Bluebirds by a fair margin. It retained its original thick roof moulding to the end.
V C Jones

The last really intense Country bus service with a full ST allocation was Hertford's 310/A. Shortly before new RTs came on the scene one-time East Surrey ST 1060 was photographed under the trolleybus wires at Enfield. Despite a mass exodus of STs from Hertford, ST 1060 lingered on there through to March 1949 when it finally departed for scrap.
D A Thompson

Typifying the short lived influx of green STs to Merton for route 32 in October 1948 is ST 91 formerly based at Hertford. Looking very smart, having been repainted as recently as July 1948, it was repainted yet again, but now red, in November less than a month after being transferred to Tottenham. *Alan B Cross*

Some did not remain green for long after returning to the Central area. The first two to be repainted back into red livery were ST 182 at Catford and ST 511 at Middle Row on 5th November 1948 and many more followed. This resulted in some extreme cases of STs being repainted from red to green, and then back from green to red, all within the same year. A prime example of this was ST 392 which became green at Watford High Street in June 1948 and reverted to red at Old Kent Road in December. Financial considerations may have played a part in a sudden reversal of this policy, and after ST 592 at Edgware was repainted red on 25th February 1949 no more were dealt with, the remainder being allowed to stay green for the rest of their time with Central Buses.

Before taking the story of RT introduction to Country Buses on to the concluding months of 1948 and into 1949, it is opportune to pause at this point to look back at other happenings affecting the ST family. Of particular interest was the setting up in April 1948 of a 'Special Events' fleet of double deckers consisting of vehicles which were no longer considered fit for regular use but which could, at a pinch, cope with occasional low-mileage work at events, such as major race meetings at Epsom and Ascot or the annual tennis tournament at Wimbledon. Additionally, in 1948, there were the

Olympic Games which were staged in London between 29th July and 21st August. STs in the 'almost time expired' category were obvious candidates for the Special Events fleet along with similarly aged LTs and slightly newer petrol STLs, and ten STs were amongst the vehicles initially selected. The majority were red LGOC types (ST 430, 467, 517, 536, 579, 632, 790) augmented by three Country Bus vehicles, ex-East Surrey ST 1050 and Bluebirds ST 1037, 1081. They were divided equally between Reigate and the long-closed garage at Slough which had been specially re-opened to house part of the Special Events fleet. The two Bluebirds quickly expired, ST 1081 as early as 24th April and ST 1037 in mid-June, when ST 517 was also condemned, but the remainder soldiered on throughout the summer of 1948 after which they drifted away for scrap between August and October. However three more STs were required as Special Events stand-bys at Camberwell and Old Kent Road throughout the winter months of 1948/49, leading to ST 79 joining the Special Events fleet in July followed by ST 723 in October and, finally, Tilling ST 945 in December.

Although divided into many sub-types each with its own special features, the ST class never contained many true oddities which, at a quick glance, could be identified as being a specific vehicle. Of the few oddities that lasted in service into the post-war era, all three main ones met their demise during 1948. The withdrawal of ST 1139 at Windsor on 23rd September has already been noted. Prior to this 'all-metal' bodied ST 150, easily recognised by its flat panelling and generally 'different' appearance, departed from the scene at

The unmistakable 'all metal' ST 150 as it frequently appeared in post-war times, running from Tottenham garage on route 73 and looking a little battered. It finally met its end at Reigate garage, along with various Special Events vehicles, in June 1948.
Alan B Cross

Another instantly recognisable vehicle was ST 530 with its 'utility' top deck and roof. Officially withdrawn from service in June 1948 and transferred to 'learner' duties, it looked very much as though it was running into Camberwell garage off service when photographed on 3rd February 1949. *Alan B Cross*

the end of May. Principally remembered for several years' service from Tottenham garage, whence it could often be found on trunk route 73, ST 150 had latterly worked for a short spell at Old Kent Road and, from 1st May, at Reigate. In its latter capacity it was possibly a Special Events bus although not specifically shown as such on surviving records, and its ultimate demise before the summer's events had been concluded probably resulting from an unhappy encounter with one of the Ministry vehicle examiners who were prone to turn up at Derby Day and other similar events to study the vehicles on offer, not only from London Transport but from

the myriad of small coach companies who attended on these occasions. ST 530, with its utility upper deck, officially ceased public service on 23rd June 1948 when it became a driver trainer. Latterly at Chalk Farm, it had worked previously from a variety of garages, enjoying none of the permanency that ST 150 had experienced at Tottenham. A mystery surrounds its later days because a photo exists purporting to show it running in service from Camberwell during the period when it was officially allocated there only as a 'learner' from October 1948 onwards. ST 530 finally went for scrap in March 1949.

Not immediately obvious as a 'one-off', ST 195 carried the very last ST body to be built for the LGOC which was notable for the revised positioning of its staircase. The main tell-tale feature from outside is the blanking-off of the fifth window rather than the usual fourth one. *S A Newman*

For most of the post-war period right up to March 1949 when it joined the Special Events fleet, ST 492 could be spotted running from Cricklewood garage, usually on routes 16 and 60. Viewed from the front, the white section of the driver's canopy was fairly obviously deeper than usual, but the main difference lay in the non-standard Y-style emergency window at the back. It is not known why or when these alterations were made. *Fred Ivey/Alan B Cross*

Once Aldenham opened as a body repair shop, a sizeable number of buses, including several STs, quickly accumulated there awaiting attention. Prominent in this late 1948 view is ST 1126 which has undergone repairs to the cab and various side panels and mouldings and is now ready for repainting before resuming service at Reigate on 22nd December. *D A Jones*

The unrelenting influx of new RTs throughout 1948 gave, from the public perspective, an appearance of buoyancy and confidence to the London Transport fleet which masked the fact that, throughout the year, the vehicle availability position continued to be dire. The use of hired coaches on peak hour operations helped to alleviate the problem and from December 1948 a large influx of brand new ECW bodied Bristols diverted from twelve companies within the now nationalised Tilling group provided further much needed relief, but urgent action had to be taken internally to keep as many older vehicles such as STs on the road as possible. The loss of Mann Egerton's input in renovating STs and LTs was keenly felt, and by the latter part of 1947 efforts were being made to find alternative outside contractors willing and able to work on these vehicles.

Meanwhile, however, part of the large factory at Aldenham built shortly before the war as a depot for the proposed Northern Line extension and latterly used for aircraft production was converted for use as a centre for the heavy repair of bus bodies. Not yet in London Transport ownership, the premises had been hired by the latter since July 1947 for the storage of new RT chassis pending their dispatch to the coachbuilders, the first vehicles for repair – two LTs and two RTs – being sent there on 24th March 1948. Starting with green ST 359 on 5th April, many STs were subsequently handled too, sometimes emerging to display a speciality of the works which was the fitment of heavy steel straps to support body pillars that were no longer adequate to cope on their own.

A speciality of the Aldenham body shop was the fitment of heavy steel straps to give strength to lower deck pillars that were no longer fully self supporting. This was a time saving process compared with the installation of completely new pillars and was perfectly adequate for vehicles with only a limited life span ahead of them. An example of this work is shown in this May 1948 view of ST 624. *L T Museum*

Despite their now advanced age and obvious obsolescence, STs still managed to look quite resplendent when newly returned from Berkeley's repair and paint shops at Biggleswade. Catford's ST 231 cuts quite a dash in Woolwich in December 1948 when compared with the vastly more dowdy Bluebird LT standing behind. *Alan B Cross*

Two outside contractors were duly identified to undertake body overhauls on STs and LTs. Their task was to completely repaint the vehicles inside and out after repanelling as necessary, but structural work was limited to the bare essentials needed to secure a minimum of twelve months' further operational life. This was based on the premise, ultimately very nearly achieved, that none of these buses would be required for operational duties beyond the end of 1949. One of the two contractors, Marshall's Flying School Ltd of Cambridge, concentrated almost entirely on LTs and only enters the ST story because ST 275 and 518 were dispatched there on 23rd March 1948, returning for service on 21st and 28th May respectively. On the other hand Berkeley Caravans Ltd of Biggleswade played a very important role and handled far more STs than LTs. Starting with ST 466, 561 on 12th January 1948, no fewer than 102 STs went to Berkeley's (which was renamed Berkeley Coachworks Ltd during the course of the contract), although in six cases work was discontinued when the body structure was found to have deteriorated too badly. In three instances vehicles were returned after a few months for further overhauling, one of which was rejected by Berkeley on its second visit. The last ST of all to travel to Biggleswade was ST 636 on 5th January 1949, returning back on 8th February.

ST 275 was one of just two STs reconditioned by Marshall's in Cambridge. Newly allocated to Potters Bar in May 1948, it takes second place on the stand at Arnos Grove to Tilling ST 905, the latter displaying the barest minimum of route information but probably scheduled to run through the Hertfordshire countryside to the 84's far terminus at St Albans. Both STs are operating in place of petrol STLs which were fading fast at the time. *D A Thompson*

Although 1948 marked a string of minuses for the STs as their spheres of operation gradually dwindled away, they managed to participate in the introduction of a few new route numbers in both Central and Country districts. On the far eastern extremity, new off-peak route 374 was introduced between Grays and Uplands Estate on 4th February using STs from other services. It was accompanied, for positioning purposes, by odd journeys on another new route, 371B (Rainham–Uplands–Grays). On Central Buses, new route 162 (Staines–Stanwell) displaced single-deck route 224 from Stanwell on 5th May 1948 using a single ST from Hounslow, doubled up to two at weekends. STs were also the staple diet from Croydon garage on routes 166 and 166A from 7th April 1948, though these were merely a renumbering of the former 59 and 59B.

Reverting now to the new vehicle programme on Country Buses, the Hertford conversion was followed by Northfleet which had amassed a fleet of STs for inter related and nominally STL operated 487 and 488 (Swanscombe–Gravesend but with different termini at each end). Further STs had gathered in place of STLs at Windsor on routes 457/A (Windsor–Uxbridge) and at St Albans on route 330 (St Albans–Welwyn Garden City), and these were deposed next. In November 1948 it was the turn of Epping to receive new

RTs. This had been the last Country garage with a one hundred per cent double-deck fleet of STs, all of which had moved out by 2nd December after which Epping never again had any STs on its allocation. Now covered by RTs were routes 339 and 396, the former having been a linking up of the old 339 and the former 392 in November 1947 to form a through Epping–Warley service. After Epping, it was mostly a case of Country garages receiving a second allocation of RTs to eliminate STs from their remaining scheduled workings and also to make a concerted start on displacing STLs. Watford High Street's 334/A lost STs in November and December as did Leatherhead's route 468. The single ST on route 416 had by now been replaced by an STL but the busy 406 (Kingston–Redhill) had latterly been allocated a substantial number of STs instead of STLs from both Reigate and Leatherhead garages, and both received new RTs for it in December 1948 and January 1949. At about the same time Grays lost STs from the 371/A/B and 374, whilst in January and February Hertford's remaining ST workings on routes such as 327, 331 and 395/A gave way to RTs. Finally, with new Cravens bodied RTs now being centralised on Watford High Street garage, the last ST enclave of any significance in the Country area, routes 311 and 312, finally fell in February and early March 1949.

The exodus of STs from the Country Bus fleet had been prodigious. By January 1949 every one of the one-time LGOC STs still operational had been returned to the Central Bus fleet, and between the 17th of that month and 7th February 24 STs which had always been Country vehicles were also sent to work at Central area garages. Eighteen of these were Ransomes bodied ex-East Surrey (and in one case ex-Autocar) vehicles which appeared as real oddities on Central area services, not just because of their green livery but also because of their square cabs and back destination boxes.

Two, in fact, no longer had square cabs, ST 1118 at Merton being the single vehicle in the batch with a standard LGOC float body, and ST 1119 at Victoria having been converted to round-cab configuration at some time in its career. Making less of an impact in the Central Bus fleet were five Short Bros bodied STs from the second East Surrey batch and a single ex-Lewis vehicle now carrying an LGOC body. Square cab ST 1108 at Dalston took on a certain notoriety in March 1949 in being the only one of the 24 transferred-in green STs to be repainted red.

The biggest surprise of all came when Ransomes bodied ST 1108 was, uniquely, repainted in red livery. At the same time repair work was carried out on the front canopy which unusually gained a thick, flat black moulding in place of the narrow, rounded sort normally associated with the Ransomes bodies. ST 1108 was photographed at Victoria on 14th May 1949 working from Dalston garage.
Fred Ivey

Opposite By the start of 1949 one-time East Surrey and National STs were beginning to appear at Central Bus garages, bringing added variety to the central fleet. Of particular interest was Victoria's ST 1119 which, as its PG registration mark shows in the photograph at Hyde Park Corner, should have had a square cab. The view of the rear, taken on another day at Vauxhall, confirms that a Ransomes body is still carried.
Alan B Cross

After most scheduled ST workings on Country Buses had been converted to RT and attention had turned to replacing STLs, a few STs were left at garages to serve as spares when required. Reigate retained ST 1138 for this purpose through to July 1949. The metal strip projecting from the top section of the driver's doorway aperture has been provided with the aim of reducing draughts. These were added, in either full or half-height form, to several Country area STs.

A by-product of the clearing-out of STs from their normal country operations was that, for the first and last time since the war, a few green ones were based at Leavesden Road between August 1948 and March 1949 to work on the LMS contract (a joint operation with Watford High Street and still using its old title despite the LMS Railway having now disappeared with nationalisation) and on various factory duplicates. Before this a couple of Tilling STs had done similar work at Leavesden Road but had now become time expired. By the 1949 summer programme on 18th May 1949 the only scheduled ST operations still remaining were:

316	Chesham–Adeyfield	HH	2 ST daily	(a)
377	Markyate–Boxmoor	HH)		
377A/B	Markyate–Apsley Mills	HH)	3 ST Mon-Fri	(b)
410	Bletchingley–Reigate	RG	2 ST Saturdays	(c)

(a) Joint with Rover Bus between Chesham and Hemel Hempstead. Journeys also worked on 302, 307/A, 378

(b) Works services. Journeys also worked on 301A, 302, 378. Also covered by one STL from Leavesden Road

(c) Section of main Bromley–Reigate route mostly worked by Godstone garage with lowbridge buses

The summer programme brought the extension of route 316 from its old terminus in Hemel Hempstead to the new suburb of Adeyfield, the first planned neighbourhood to be built as part of the massive New Town development. Although London Transport's oldest buses were hardly in keeping with the ethos of the brave New Town, the 316 could be extended out of layover time at no additional cost and, besides, Adeyfield was still sparsely inhabited at the time and it was expected that newer vehicles would have taken over before the bulk of residents moved in.

Even quite late in their lives it was not totally unknown for STs to deputise on Green Line relief work, inappropriate as they were for this type of duty. An example of this was ST 821 which was photographed at Victoria on a 704 relief working from Windsor on 24th August 1948. Fate treated ST 821 kindly, and when it was finally withdrawn in May 1949 it was set aside as a museum bus. This was one of many green STs to have the original moulding around the cab canopy replaced by a narrower one. *Alan B Cross*

A few other Country garages still kept STs at this time as spares, notably Northfleet and Watford High Street which both had six, with smaller numbers at Hertford, which retained two, plus one each at Grays, St Albans and Staines. Soon after this date, on 26th May, one of the Watford contingent – ST 821 – was removed to Chiswick and subsequently retained as a museum vehicle. Absent from Watford now were the Bluebirds the last of which, ST 1074, had been withdrawn from service on 14th March 1949, although a couple which had ceased regular service earlier survived to eke out a spasmodic existence in the 1949 Special Events fleet. Outlived by even a few of the notoriously flimsy and undeniably obsolescent Tilling STs, the Bluebirds had never lived up to their early promise but it was ironic that – with the exception of a few oddities such as the one-time 'pirate' buses and the pioneer ST 1139 – the newest type of ST was the first to cease public service.

Although not in public service there was, in fact, one Bluebird ST that outlived most of the class. ST 1073 was one of nine STs selected for conversion into staff buses to be used principally for conveying employees from various outposts to the new bus works at Aldenham. Starting with ST 1057 in September 1948 and carried out at Aldenham itself, these were unusual conversions which effectively turned the vehicles into single deckers whilst still retaining their top decks. Having ensured that all the upstairs windows were fully closed, the staircases were removed and the staircase apertures panelled over. Seats were then installed where the staircase had been and also on a raised section built on to the back platform to produce fairly cosy 33-seaters. The doorway was left open but a canvas cover was provided for cold or rainy days. Most of the conversions were done during the final three months of 1948 and embraced a variety of ST types. In addition to Bluebird ST 1073, the other conversions comprised ex-East Surrey ST 1040, 1057, and LGOC standards ST 160, 354, 355, 737, 795, 829. Under the regulations prevailing at the time staff buses were allowed to operate unlicensed using trade plates, and the nine were distributed amongst a number of garages – Putney Bridge, Leyton, Hounslow, Hammersmith and Turnham Green – with some being allocated to Aldenham itself. By March 1950 deterioration in the bodywork had begun to cause withdrawals and by 1st May, five which were still surviving as staff buses were diverted for use as driver trainers with their registration numbers restored, Bluebird ST 1073 being one.

Putney Bridge garage was where ST 1073 could usually be found between spells of duty as a staff bus, a role upon which it embarked in November 1948 after its top deck had been sealed off and the staircase removed. The raised section permitting five seats to be installed on the platform of the staff bus, and the furled canvas sheet in case of rain, are demonstrated on green ST 160 which was a February 1949 addition to the staff bus fleet. *Alan B Cross/ D A Jones*

Looking now at Central Bus RT conversions from July 1948 onwards, there was not a single one up to the end of the year on which a substantial number of STs was not released even though these usually did not comprise the official allocation. Dalston saw only STs depart from route 9 and not a single STL, and the same applied for route 9 at Dalston in August and September. Mortlake's conversion of route 9 at the same time saw more STs go than LTs whilst Elmers End – which had not run STs since March 1946 – began to receive them from March 1948 onwards in preparation for the RT conversion of route 194 in August and September. After Elmers End came a 'real' ST conversion, and a major one at that, when their monopoly at Hounslow garage was finally broken with the arrival between September and November of sufficient new RTs to cover the 45 ST workings on routes 81/A, 116 and 117. The unusual sight of brand new buses at last flooding the streets of Hounslow was rendered even more of a novelty because, among their number, were the very first RTs without roof boxes, an aesthetic modification which was by no means universally popular at first.

By May 1948 route 21 (Moorgate–Farningham) had been officially allocated STs from both Sidcup and Old Kent Road garages in place of its former LT contingent, and these were scheduled to go next. Old Kent Road began to receive RTs in November 1948 for this and also for route 243, with Sidcup following in December with the first production RTLs. Also in December the modernisation of route 29 at West Green (with RTLs) and Potters Bar (RTs) saw many STs displaced.

At the start of 1949 STs could still be found in use at no fewer than 33 Central Bus garages and they were still a commonplace sight throughout much of the operating territory, continuing to appear unexpectedly on services to which they were not officially allocated as well as on their own steadily diminishing scheduled workings. The latter now included route 4A (Finsbury Park–Clapham Common) worked from Camberwell and Holloway garages, but conversely STLs from Camberwell had now moved the other way to displace STs from the 5A, whilst at Holloway route 143 was now STL operated. 1949 was destined to be a remarkable year in which no fewer than 1,592 new double deckers entered service, a feat which can barely be imagined these days.

With new vehicles coming on stream at such a phenomenal rate a means had to be found of disposing of the old ones efficiently. A strict embargo by the British Transport Commission on its subsidiaries selling redundant buses for further use as public service vehicles, even if they were still fit to be used as such, meant that there was little demand for London Transport's surplus buses and it depressed their value purely to that of scrap. In truth this is all that most of the bodies were fit for, but the early post-war demand for serviceable chassis suitable for rebodying could not be tapped because of the embargo. In the immediate aftermath of the war unwanted chassis were dismantled at Chiswick where essential units could be retained for re-use, and the pre-war practice of selling bodies to the Steel Breaking & Dismantling

Company was resumed. However contact with the latter soon ceased and for a while bodies had to be broken up at Chiswick which quickly became overwhelmed with the task. Soon the storage of redundant buses became a problem and was only partly solved by stockpiling them in non-operational premises such as the old AEC works at Walthamstow and Bull Yard, Peckham. Respite came through a contract with Cox & Danks Ltd who were paid to dismantle bodies at a large yard on the Faggs Road trading estate at Feltham where withdrawn vehicles arrived in large numbers from 25th October 1948 onwards.

The Cox & Danks operation was very impressive in its scale, but it still left the problem of dismantling and disposing of the chassis once these had been returned to Chiswick. What was really needed was someone who would relieve London Transport of its burden by buying and scrapping complete vehicles. A contractor prepared to do this was sought and the company finally selected was R L Daniels Ltd who possessed a large yard in Ferry Lane, Rainham. For the princely sum of £16 1s 3d per bus Daniels agreed to purchase all surplus vehicles, although this did not include drivers' mirrors, batteries and tyres which were salvaged at Rainham by London Transport's own staff. In the event of a body only being scrapped the agreed price was £1 10s 0d per body delivered to Rainham. When vehicles arrived at the scrap yard carrying major mechanical units with a potential operating life of more than 7 to 9 months, these items were removed and returned to London Transport who replaced them with similar scrap units. Certain non-ferrous pieces such as floor plates, ventilators and tie rods could be repurchased by London Transport at £80 per ton and ferrous items like springs and wheel hubs at £3 per ton. In the event of Daniels finding a purchaser for a complete vehicle (other than for use as a psv, of course) any profit would be divided equally between both parties.

The first bus arrived at the Rainham yard on 19th April 1949 and the contract worked remarkably smoothly with no fewer than 1,157 vehicles (1,078 double-deck and 57 single-deck) having been sent there by the end of the year. London Transport's storage problems became a thing of the past because in the great majority of cases vehicles were delicensed and driven by the Executive's staff under trade plates to Rainham on the very same day. With acres of once familiar London buses to be seen in various states of dereliction, Rainham quickly replaced Feltham as a Mecca for enthusiasts wishing to view London buses in their final days and perhaps to collect a few souvenirs.

April 4th 1949, and two newcomers have just arrived in Cox & Danks' yard under trade plates from a rendezvous point at Chiswick Works. Demolition of their bodywork will take place within a few days and the chassis will be returned to Chiswick for dismantling. Right up to the previous day ST 1085 had been licensed for service at Enfield, and it was noteworthy in being one of a handful of Ransomes STs to have its registration number built into the back panel. Accompanying ST 1085 is LT 1, the historic precursor to the whole family of LGOC double deckers then rapidly approaching the end of their days. *Fred Ivey*

Top On the last day that Tilling STs ran in normal service, 27th March 1949, the garage with the largest contingent in stock was Alperton. One of its three was ST 880 which, now minus its cab door, was photographed proceeding through Ealing. ST 880 was destined to spend a further eight months in the training fleet.

Centre A day of reckoning at Uxbridge garage. Some brand new RTs have just arrived and await entry into service next day. About to move on were ST 289, on the left, destined to enjoy a further six months of work at Willesden, and ST 515 whose less happy fate was a trip to Cox & Danks's yard at Feltham. ST 515 was, in fact, a Hounslow based bus sent to cover a shortage of Uxbridge's own STs during their final days. *Fred Ivey*

Bottom The last long, busy route on which STs predominated was the 65, and evidence of bunching is provided by ST 77 and ST 474 running nose to tail in Kingston. Still looking quite fresh after a visit to Berkeley's, Turnham Green's ST 77 later moved on to become the last camel back ST in the fleet. Representing the small Kingston garage allocation on route 65 and running its final days of service, ST 474 is notable at this late stage in still displaying an offside route number stencil. *Denis Battams*

On the very first day of 1949 all the STs still remaining in service that had been reclassified from 49 to 48 seaters nearly ten years earlier were now once again deemed to be 49 seaters. In practice, quite apart from amending notices on the vehicles, nothing changed physically. The year opened with just 19 Tilling STs still licensed for passenger service at eleven garages. However their days were now numbered and, unable to resist trade union pressure to withdraw them any longer, the final nine were theoretically made available for service for the very last time on 27th March. Shared between six garages, these comprised ST 880, 979, 1022 at Alperton, ST 993 at Dalston, ST 850, 1024 at Middle Row, ST 914 at Old Kent Road, ST 910 at Tottenham and ST 1011 at Willesden. All was not quite finished, however, for four of them joined four previously withdrawn Tillings in the 1949 Special Events fleet.

The list of Central Bus routes handed over to new vehicles during 1949 on which STs had been drafted in shortly beforehand to replace the scheduled type, either totally or partially, is too long to enumerate here, but highlights include the officially STL operated 34 at Palmers Green and 35 at Camberwell when the first SRTs came on the scene in April and May 1949. From May onwards an ST exodus began, together with LTs, from Tottenham after the first RTWs took the road on route 41, although in this case the concurrent receipt of new RTLs for route 73 was also a factor. Scheduled ST operations replaced by new vehicles were Croydon's 166/A in February and March, the whole of Uxbridge's double-deck operation on routes 98, 220 and 225 in March and April, along with Hounslow's share of route 98 in the latter month, all of which were replaced by RTs, plus Alperton's route 187 which gave way to RTWs in August and September. Also in September route 42 at Camberwell was taken over by SRTs and Hounslow's final ST clearance came with the arrival of RTs on routes 33, 110, 111 and 162. In the same month routes 7 and 7A at Middle Row and 84 at Potters Bar, having become almost entirely ST operated by default upon withdrawal of their scheduled petrol STLs, were also handed over to new RTs. Another route to become predominantly ST worked as its petrol STLs went for scrap was the 65. Kingston's minority share on it had, of course, long been STs but by 1949 Turnham Green's STLs were fading fast and ST operation became the norm. As a token modernisation a few oil engined STLs were drafted into both garages, but new RTs at Kingston and RTLs at Turnham Green had begun sweeping the old order away by October. In the same month Kingston's route 131 also lost its STs.

At the start of the winter programme on 26th October the only scheduled ST workings remaining on Central Buses were:

Route	Garage	Mon-Fri	Saturday	Sunday
4A	Camberwell	7	-	-
	Holloway	18	15	
40	Upton Park	9 (a)	-	-
55	Turnham Green	8 (b)	11	-
67	Tottenham	7	6	-
133	Croydon	6 (c)	-	-
239	Holloway	3	3	-
	Totals	**58**	**35**	**-**

(a) Plus 9 LT from Upton Park and 18 STL from Camberwell
(b) Plus 24 STL from Hanwell
(c) Plus 26 STL from Croydon and 21 STL from Streatham

A long time resident at Croydon garage since gas producer days, ST 479 stayed on right through to November 1949 to cover the minority ST working on route 133, moving on 9th November to Old Kent Road and then, in quick succession, to Holloway and Dalston, such was the instability in the ST fleet in its final weeks. In the Brixton Road, a Wolseley car bumps along the tram tracks in an effort to overtake. *Fred Ivey*

By now it was becoming very evident to the casual observer that STs – and LTs too – were becoming heavily depleted in numbers as, one by one, their spheres of operation were lost. Such was the pace of enforced withdrawals because of poor structural condition that a shortage of LTs was developing, and though as many as 158 STs were still licensed for Central Bus service, their numbers were dwindling fast too. At the start of the winter programme, when STs were scheduled to run from six garages, they could in fact be found at 19 as follows:

Holloway (J)	24	Plumstead (AM)	5
Turnham Green (V)	22	Alperton (ON)	5
Willesden (AC)	18	Old Kent Road (P)	5
Upton Park (U)	16	Bromley (TB)	5
Camberwell (Q)	13	Palmers Green (AD)	3
Chalk Farm (CF)	8	Victoria (GM)	3
Tottenham (AR)	8	Catford (TL)	2
Croydon (TC)	7	Potters Bar (PB)	1
Norwood (N)	6	Cricklewood (W)	1
Barking (BK)	6		

Included among the above were five still in green livery: ST 333, 648 at Holloway, ST 335, 462 at Old Kent Road, and square cab ST 1129 at Camberwell.

With the end of the road imminent for both types, Upton Park's STs were all replaced in December 1949 by a large influx of LTs. By the northern portal of Blackwall Tunnel, ST 199 heads off on a peak hour run to Ford Works. It left Upton Park for Tottenham on 16th December but was condemned a few days later. *Alan B Cross*

The situation was one of total flux. Not long beforehand, garages which had seldom run STs in post-war years had done so for a few months in 1949 and had lost them only as recently as July (Clay Hall) and August (Edgware and Enfield). On the winter programme day, 26th October, Turnham Green was actively in the throes of losing the final STs from its once large batch on route 65, with route 55 due to follow on as more new RTLs arrived, the last STs moving out of Turnham Green on 9th November. On the other hand the small numbers of STs at Old Kent Road, Plumstead and Palmers Green marked the start of a new build-up which gathered further momentum in November to permit the release of LTs from route 53A (Plumstead and Old Kent Road) and STLs from route 112 (Palmers Green) ahead of the arrival of new RTLs at Plumstead, RTs at Old Kent Road and RTWs at Palmers Green. When new vehicles duly arrived for route 53A they displaced not only the recently acquired STs but many LTs too, the latter leaving in batches on 1st and 14th December to eliminate the remaining STs from Upton Park.

Before this, in early November, Croydon's ST workings had been taken over by STLs, and by the middle of December the only routes still with STs officially allocated to them were 4A, 67 and 239. However, even at this really late stage, STs made one final come back on 14th December when augmentations were made on three services, and STs had to be used as these were the only vehicles available at the time. Thus Norwood was allocated three for the otherwise STL worked route 3 (Camden Town–Crystal Palace), Tottenham also gained three to join utility Guys on linked routes 76 (Victoria–Edmonton with journeys to Brimsdown) and 34B (Walthamstow–Brimsdown), and Sutton gained four to run alongside Daimlers on route 93 (Putney Bridge–Epsom). On the same day single deck route 226 (Golders Green–Cricklewood) was double decked, and with insufficient STLs initially available, Cricklewood garage received eight ST rejects from Upton Park to meet its rolling stock requirements. Interestingly, all the STs required to implement the 14th December schedule changes were distributed to the various garages a fortnight beforehand, possibly to allow plenty of time to ensure that they really were roadworthy. Further garages to receive STs in the closing months of 1949 were Chelverton Road, Hounslow, Leyton and Mortlake; these were only in small numbers and were probably to cover short term shortages of other types, but it is indicative of the unsettled nature of the ST fleet even in its final days of service that such moves were still being made. Most vehicles remaining were in very poor structural condition and their continued presence was a source of irritation to the majority of staff. As 1949 closed a concerted effort was made to draft STLs into Holloway from 19th December onwards and its last STs ran on routes 4A and 239 on Saturday the 31st.

The Country Bus winter programme for 1949 came into effect on 5th October by which time only three STs were scheduled for service, all at Hemel Hempstead on route 316 and various works services. During the course of the summer programme the STs held at several garages as spares had come to the end of the road with Staines losing its last one in June, Grays in August, Hertford in September and Windsor at the start of October. This left only four garages apart from Hemel Hempstead still able to put STs into service, Northfleet being the most prolific with four. Reigate still retained two as did Watford High Street and St Albans. An odd man out was ST 1108 at Reigate. This had been the only square cab ST to

Route 67 gained minor renown in being the last in the fleet served completely by STs. One of those working on it from Tottenham garage right up to the very last day – and the last ST with rebuilt sides to remain in use – was ST 582. Its last day of operation was 17th January 1950; promptly on the next morning it left for Daniels' scrapyard at Rainham. *Fred Ivey*

All through 1949 the engineers at Northfleet seemed to think nothing of putting the odd ST out on their major 480 service where it inevitably invoked adverse comment from both passengers and crews when compared with the regular fare of new RTs. ST 1130 was one of the ST survivors. It arrived at Northfleet from Reigate on the first day of 1949 and managed to last through to 12th December when it made its ultimate journey to Daniels' scrapyard. *Alan B Cross*

be repainted red for central area service and it retained this livery after returning to Country work in June 1949. One by one, more of the remaining Country STs fell by the wayside leaving just seven active at the close of 1949, two each at Northfleet (ST 1059, 1126) and Watford High Street (ST 1062, 1092) and one at St Albans (ST 1055), while Hemel Hempstead was now reduced to just two (ST 818, 1136) to cover its three scheduled workings.

Coverage at Hemel Hempstead had been a problem throughout the summer, partly due to its specific requirement for vehicles with hill climbing ability. None of the STs with which it started the year had proved sufficiently robust to stay the full course and the ever present likelihood of 'PSV 71' failures made forward planning difficult. Suitable replacement STs were drafted in from other garages, but from July onwards until the end of ST operations Hemel Hempstead never had more than two STs on its books, just the bare necessity for covering the full daily timetable on route 316.

Above STs were still scheduled to run on route 4A into 1950, albeit only on the Camberwell garage allocation. Holloway's contribution, typified by ST 165, ceased at the very end of 1949 when STLs became available. Repainted from green to red in February 1949, this Holloway based bus was photographed heading down Goswell Road at the Angel Islington.

Two STs remained at Hemel Hempstead to cover Country Bus's last scheduled ST operation. One of these was one-time Lewis ST 1136 which had been an early example of the type to receive a standard LGOC body a decade earlier. Behind it at Chesham is one of the blue Bedford OBs typifying the Rover Bus contribution to route 316. *Alan B Cross*

189

The Special Events fleet turned out in force for the main 1949 race meeting at Ascot where more than a dozen of them – probably mostly STs – shared the yard with 10T10 coaches on Green Line 701. Leading the queue ready for the exodus were Tilling ST 1011 and Bluebird ST 1083, both types then extinct in normal service. ST 1011's time in the Special Events fleet came to an abrupt end in Reigate garage on 29th June when it was proclaimed a 'PSV71' failure. A similar fate befell ST 1083 at the same location on 8th July.

Below ST 1091's canopy had been propped up on the nearside by a curved strengthening extension from the bulkhead, but otherwise it looked comparatively healthy for a Special Events bus when photographed on Derby Day 1949. In fact ST 1091 lasted until the Special Events fleet was terminated on 27th February 1950, and during the latter part of 1949 it could sometimes be seen after dark, quite remarkably, covering for Leyland Cubs on the Inter Station service. *Fred Ivey*

An unusual episode which may have been connected with Hemel Hempstead's troubles over ST serviceability occurred on 9th June when no fewer than nine of the type currently licensed within the Special Events fleet were stationed there, having formerly been kept at Reigate. The main Epsom race season had now finished and, with no other work immediately in prospect for them, it is tempting to think that they might have been intended for use, sparingly of course and only on occasional factory runs in view of their fragile condition, to bulk up the main Hemel Hempstead ST fleet. They were a mixed bag: red ST 396, 776, green ST 594, and standard Country STs 1041, 1047, 1056, 1086, 1091, 1098. On 6th July disaster struck when a Ministry inspection team paid a visit and slapped 'PSV 71' notices on every one of them except STs 1041 and 1091 (which may have been out on the road at the time). This was by far the most severe 'PSV 71' incident ever recorded at a London Transport garage in a single day, and it was made worse by the fact that one of Hemel Hempstead's own regular allocation of STs – ST 1054 – was also declared a 'PSV 71' failure and it took a couple of days before a suitable replacement could be rustled up from elsewhere. The two remaining Special Events STs stayed on at Hemel Hempstead until they were sent back to Reigate on 10th August.

ST 1129 became renowned in its later days as the last green ST in Central Bus service and, of course, the last with a square cab. Retained at Camberwell to work route 4A, right to the end it remained capable of turning up anywhere and in this instance had just passed the well known "Dirty Dick's" pub in Bishopsgate. *Fred Ivey*

The 66-strong 1949 Special Events fleet contained a very similar mixture to that of 1948, comprising many STs, LTs and petrol STLs. The most notable feature was that, with eight of them in stock, Tilling STs now had a major presence in the Special Events fleet in which they carried paying passengers for the very last time. At least four of the eight, and possibly more, ended up with 'PSV 71' stops which were an ever present hazard for the fragile Special Events fleet. By London Transport's own reckoning the vehicles within it were no longer structurally fit for regular service, so it was hardly likely that any would emerge unscathed if unfortunate enough to encounter the very strict scrutiny of a Ministry of Transport examiner. Three Bluebird STs were also in the 1949 Special Events fleet, presenting yet another opportunity to travel on a type of vehicle no longer in regular service. At least one and possibly two of these suffered Ministry 'stops' and the last Bluebird that could theoretically have carried passengers was ST 1034 which went for scrap on 25th July. Much of the Special Events fleet was sent to the scrapyard at the end of the summer but just five STs remained licensed within it for the remainder of 1949. Based at Old Kent Road garage were three former East Surreys still in green livery, ST 1041 and square cab STs 1091 and 1095. Two

of these were survivors from the Ministry blitz at Hemel Hempstead in July, and while for most of the time they remained idle, quite remarkably they were observed making occasional forays on to the Inter Station service in place of the usual Cubs. Kept in a corner of Camberwell garage, and not actually used for any recorded specific purpose, were ST 15 and – amazingly – Tilling ST 887. Just why one of these decrepit and much derided outside staircase vehicles should have been retained right through to the end of 1949 when so many theoretically more suitable STs would have been available will probably always be a mystery.

As recorded earlier, the last day of 1949, Saturday 31st December, marked the official end of STs from Holloway on the 4A and 239, their replacements being STLs released by the arrival of RTs on route 19. A day earlier, the STs newly scheduled only a fortnight beforehand at Sutton (for route 93) and Tottenham (routes 34B/76) ran for the last time; there was no requirement for them at the weekend and more appropriate vehicles were available from Monday 2nd January 1950 onwards. In a similar vein, the last remaining camel back ST ran for the final time on 30th December; this was ST 77 at Palmers Green which was delicensed on 2nd January. On 4th January route 316 at Hemel Hempstead – which had

The STs' capacity to surprise lasted right to the very end, and even as late as 1st January 1950 ST 189 arrived for service at Dalston. Instead of being hidden away, it was put to work on one of London's most high profile services, on which it was seen at Victoria contrasting with one of the 'regulars' on route 11, Hammersmith's RTL 345.

latterly been the only operation within the entire fleet to include a Sunday ST allocation – was officially taken over by STLs. Normal STLs were not permitted to operate on this route but the 'unfrozen' crash gearbox vehicles were an exception to this, and two of these were brought in from Godstone to enable the conversion to take place. This was not quite the end of STs at Hemel Hempstead as the deposed STs remained licensed for a little while longer which probably meant that route 316 and the various works services had still not quite seen the last of them.

Even as late as 1st January 1950, when it could be confidently predicted that the STs were now in their last month of

service, the old habit of employing them as an expedient for covering last minute shortages had still not completely died, with the result that three were reintroduced at Dalston and two at Clay Hall, neither of which had had any since the midsummer of 1949. After this, though, it was downhill all the way for the vehicles that remained. The route 316 conversion and a bout of delicensings on 5th January left a total of 71 STs still licensed, 64 of them split amongst 14 Central Bus garages and 7 at four locations on Country Buses. From now onwards delicensings were carried out in batches every few days but the most notable came on 18th January. On the previous day, Tuesday the 17th, the few remaining scheduled

A Country survivor right up to the very last day of operation on 26th January 1950 was ST 1055. Based at St Albans, where it was photographed on 17th December 1949, it remained in regular use right to the end and could normally be found working alongside STLs on route 369.
Alan B Cross

ST 354, ekeing out its last days on training duties, was a one-time 33-seater staff bus as can be seen by the absence of a staircase. Many years earlier it had participated in the vehicle recording trials at Holloway garage, the residue of which is still visible on the bus roof. In the distance, on the far right, a new RT with full blinds indicates that the first tram conversion has taken place on 1st October 1950, no full blind sets having been in use on Central Buses before that date. Tram 1402, a 40-year old E1 rehabilitated in May 1936, was taken out of use soon afterwards following a collision, a couple of months prior to the final demise of ST 354 which came on 7th December 1950. *Fred Ivey*

ST operations ran for the last time. Camberwell's share of route 4A and Norwood's odd workings on route 3 now succumbed to STLs but, historically, the most significant loss was route 67 which had been the last full bastion for the ST class. Its demise was brought about by the introduction of new RTLs on Enfield's only STL route, 128, the whole stock of which was moved the short distance to Tottenham overnight ready for operation on route 67 on the 18th.

Fortunately examples of most major sub-types and of all the main bodybuilders lasted to the end. The final Strachans bodied vehicles, ST 533 at Barking and ST 750 at Cricklewood, were withdrawn on 16th January. The last ex-National (ST 818) and the last ex-Lewis (ST 1136) were both delicensed at Hemel Hempstead on the 25th. This also happened to be the final day of operation for STs on Central Buses when the last five in service were all LGOC bodied vehicles; delicensed on the 26th were ST 102 at Barking, ST 148, 707 at Norwood and ST 410, 692 at Camberwell. Country Bus operation survived just one day longer, the final quartet being Short's bodied ST 1055 at St Albans, ST 1062 at Watford High Street and ST 1059 at Northfleet, the latter being accompanied at its Kentish base by the last remaining Ransomes vehicle, ST 1126.

For the fare paying passenger, an era was now at an end. True the lowbridge STs remained in service as related in the next chapter, but these were now oil engined and lacked the performance, not to mention the sounds, smells and constant backfiring so typical and indelibly associated with the STs after two decades of service. The five Special Events STs were still licensed and theoretically could put in an emergency appearance, but it is doubtful if any of them were used at all in 1950. With the rolling stock position much improved, the decision was taken to disband the Special Events fleet. On 9th February ST 15 and ST 887 at Camberwell were delicensed and immediately dispatched for scrap, and the same fate overtook ST 1041, 1091, 1095 at Old Kent Road on the 27th of the same month.

The story was not yet quite at an end. A few of the 33-seater staff buses continued in this role up to April 1950 after which five of them joined a fleet of driver trainers which was visibly still active, with examples likely to turn up unexpectedly almost anywhere as a final rather sad reminder of better days. None of these were the former 8-seater learners all of which had long since fallen by the wayside; in fact most had only been drafted into the training fleet fairly recently. As the months wore on certain of them fell by the wayside because of mechanical failure, but from July through to October 1950 the ST trainer fleet remained fairly static in size at 21. Right to the last they were a mixed bag with standard LGOC types in the majority but including two of the Ransomes square cabs, three of the ex-East Surrey Short Bros batch and a single Bluebird. Inevitably the decision was finally taken to cease the use of petrol engined vehicles with the end of 1950 as a deadline, and from October onwards the ST trainers were gradually phased out.

The very last petrol engined double decker to be used by London Transport was green ST 1062 which was finally delicensed on 2nd January 1951. Although carrying Addlestone (WY) garage plates, it was actually allocated to Windsor garage throughout its spell of trainer duties, outside which it was photographed in the company of a pair of Cravens bodied RTs. ST 1062 was an oddity is having acquired at some time in its long career an LGOC-type front indicator box, and it was the only one of its batch ever to have been modified in this way. *Denis Battams*

CHAPTER 22
THE LOWBRIDGE FLEET – 1945-1953

Because of their huge difference in design and shape, and the specialised but restricted nature of their spheres of operation, the small lowbridge fleet always seemed to be set apart from the mainstream ST class. This was especially perceived to be so after the war by the growing and ever more knowledgeable band of enthusiasts capable of recognising individual vehicles and closely following their movements, through the era of dieselisation and into a working life that took them three years beyond that of ordinary STs.

When the war ended the established pattern was that six out of the eight lowbridge STs would be based at Amersham to cover five scheduled workings on route 336 whilst Addlestone had the remaining two, one of which was officially scheduled to work alongside STLs on the 436 leaving the other as a spare. Amersham's post-war contingent started off with ST 136, 157, 162, 163, 1089, 1090 leaving Addlestone with ST 140, 141. For a short time, between November 1945 and June 1946, an extra vehicle was needed at Amersham and ST 141 was sent there for that purpose; in June 1946 ST 1089 moved south to Addlestone and this is how the situation then remained throughout the remainder of the nineteen-forties. While the fortunes of the main ST fleet were turbulent throughout the second half of the decade, the lowbridge STs remained a picture of stability.

Shortly before the war ended a start was made on upgrading the braking systems on all eight by installing triple servos, a task also undertaken on many standard STs in the Country fleet. This been completed by March 1946, and thereafter no other mechanical changes were envisaged for a while. The bodies, however, needed a great deal of attention despite having had much reconstruction work carried out on them in pre-war years. No replacement vehicles were then in the offing and the official view was that they would be needed for service until at least 1953, well beyond the anticipated lifespan for the main ST fleet. In March 1947 a programme of heavy overhauling commenced which lasted through to June 1949 and resulted in vehicles being out of service for anything from two to six months at a time in a variety of overhaul shops. Three were dealt with at Chiswick Works, ST 140 and ST 1089 were handled at Chiswick tram depot and ST 163 at Reigate, whilst the last two, ST 136 and ST 157, underwent major body rebuilds at Aldenham. The length of time that some vehicles spent in overhaul caused problems at Amersham where difficulty in covering the schedule reached crisis level between April and June 1948 with three STs away at the same time. Unfortunately the overhauling process could not be staggered better as vehicles had to be dealt with as and when they became seriously unfit, and their temporary replacement by single deckers inevitably led to problems over lack of capacity.

The lowbridge STs formed one of London's most fascinating double-deck classes because of the many small variations that could be found within such a small batch of vehicles. An early post-war scene finds ST 136 at Croxley Green station heading for its Watford terminus at Leavesden Road garage. It was instantly recognisable in retaining the original 1930 style of lower deck panelling even though the equivalent panels on the upper deck and the whole of the front profile had been modernised before the war. The rounded tops to the opening windows were another feature unique to this bus.

The only one in the class never to appear on route 336 after the war was ST 140 which stayed at Addlestone until the first RLHs arrived and was revived there later. Photographed at Staines GWR station (renamed Staines West in September 1949 and closed in March 1965) in the company of Hounslow's ST 785 and a Kingston 14T12, it demonstrates one of the various styles of panelling used to cover the strengthening bracket projecting from the nearside bulkhead to the upper deck overhang which was inserted on most of these vehicles upon rebuilding. The autovac tank was removed when a diesel engine was fitted in October 1949. *Alan B Cross*

ST 1090 bears almost no resemblance to its original appearance as the only Strachans bodied one out of the eight lowbridge STs. Restructuring of the front has swept away the square cab as well as providing a now modernised upper structure, whilst the side panels and mouldings are now of the conventional ST type. The thick band above the windows was unique to ST 1090 at the time, and at some stage in its career the vehicle has received a Short Bros-style oval staircase window which it did not have originally. The bus standing behind is ST 162. *D A Thompson*

In general the post-war bodywork rehabilitation led to vehicles retaining the same shape and general features that they had gained before the war. Surprisingly, despite heavy re-pillaring at Aldenham between August and December 1948, ST 136 even managed to keep its sub-standard platform cut-away and its original Short Bros curvaceous rear window. The big exception was ST 141 which was overhauled at Chiswick Works between February and June 1948. This was one of only two (the other being ST 1089) which had retained the original style of piano front. The body shop plans for the rebuildings carried out in pre-war years must have been dusted off and re-used, for ST 141 emerged from overhaul with the revised frontal profile long since familiar on the other six lowbridge STs, and it now carried the same ST-style body mouldings as these (ST 136 excepted). After this, ST 1089 was left as the only one of the eight still carrying its original Short Bros front end, which it continued to do for the rest of its operating career.

At overhaul all eight were reupholstered in the current RT style moquette, a luxury not afforded to other STs, and they were allowed to retain the light green painted décor which was thoroughly renewed and looked very smart. Possibly it had been thought that the brown paintwork which was now standard for other older vehicles in the fleet might have looked too dark and claustrophobic in the cramped interiors of the lowbridge STs. The last two overhauls emerged from Aldenham carrying a version of the green and cream external livery now standard for all newer type vehicles but never normally used on anything as old as STs. On the first of them, ST 136 whose overhaul was completed on 8th December 1948, the cream relief extended only around the upper deck windows, there being no suitable moulding lower down on which to apply it. However the result transformed the overall appearance of the vehicle and certainly gave it, as intended, a more modern air. The second from Aldenham and the last ST of all to be overhauled, ST 157, emerged on 27th June

1949 carrying the complete green and cream livery, having been given a fairly substantial amidships moulding on which to paint the central cream band. From then onwards, right to the end of their active days, there was no chance of mistaking these two lowbridge STs for any of the more conventionally liveried vehicles in the batch.

After leaving Aldenham, ST 157 proceeded direct to Chiswick where its petrol engine was removed and an AEC 7.7 litre diesel unit fitted instead. This was done on 30th June in anticipation of the acceptance of a recommendation made on the very same day by the Chief Mechanical Engineer, A A M Durrant, that all eight of the lowbridge STs should be converted to oil. It was part of a wider programme to convert 163 of the remaining petrol vehicles (the others being 99 LT single deckers, 37 T type and 24 LTC private hire coaches), using in most cases overhauled engines taken from scrapped STLs. The only exceptions were to be the LTCs whose engines would be 8.8 litre units removed from LT double deckers. At the time it was stated that the STs would be required for a further four years, and though the conversion of each of them was expected to cost £65, the saving in fuel and maintenance costs per annum per vehicle was reckoned to be £430, giving an estimated total saving over four years of no less than £13,760. Needless to say, on the clear evidence of the figures submitted, approval of the conversion programme proved a mere formality, and one by one the other seven lowbridge STs were dealt with starting with ST 1089 on 2nd November 1949 and ending with ST 163 on 1st February 1950. Externally no change was made to the appearance of them as a result of the dieselisation except for removal of the now redundant autovac tank, but the observer only had to listen to the transformed sound and witness their muted performance to know that something major had taken place.

The arrival of hired Bristol K6As transformed the rolling stock availability position for route 336, and Amersham garage at last found itself with a surfeit of lowbridge vehicles. Even so, it was most unusual to find ST 163 on loan to Hemel Hempstead garage to work on route 316 as happened on this occasion, which would have been strictly unofficial as the rules clearly specified that "Only ST type with 7 to 1 diff. or 17STL with 6¼ to 1 diff. may operate on this route". *F G Reynolds*

At ST 136's Aldenham overhaul in December 1948 no further structural changes were made but its appearance was transformed by its new green and cream livery. It was carrying this, albeit now a little faded, when it made its surprise appearance on the meandering route 127 from Merton garage eighteen months later. The autovac tank had been removed as a result of ST 136's conversion to diesel in January 1950. *Alan B Cross*

Belated relief to the vehicle availability crisis on route 336 came in the form of a brand new double decker on 17th December 1948, but by that time the very worst of the pressures caused by the vehicle overhaul programme had abated. This new bus was Bristol K6A HLJ 25, numbered TD 876 in the Hants & Dorset fleet, from which it had been diverted direct to London Transport from the manufacturers, one of the earliest of many Tilling group Bristols to help out in London during the next 1½ years. Three more arrived at Amersham in February 1949 when, at last, plenty of vehicles were available for route 336 for the first time in many years.

Just about the time that conversion of the lowbridge STs to diesel was being approved, events which could not have been foreseen threw up the unexpected opportunity to acquire 20 brand new low height double deckers. The Road Passenger Executive of the British Transport Commission had recently taken control of the road passenger transport assets of the Midland Counties Electricity Supply Company, a former Balfour Beatty subsidiary which had been nationalised along with the rest of the electricity supply industry in 1948. One of its subsidiaries was the Midland General Omnibus Company which, once it was placed under the scrutiny of the Tilling Group Management Board, was found to have orders in hand for 20 Weymann bodied AEC Regent IIIs which the new management regarded as unnecessary. London Transport was asked if it would be interested in taking these, in lowbridge form if desired, which in August 1949 the Executive decided to do. Thus was the RLH class born. Constructed to Midland General specification but with modifications to suit London Transport requirements such as destination screens and upholstery, they were purchased from the Road Passenger Executive as soon as they were built with the first five being made available for service at Amersham on 25th May 1950.

For a few days RLHs and STs ran together on the 336, but four STs were transferred out on 31st May and the last to remain, ST 157, was delicensed on 23rd June. STs never again returned to the 336 but now, in the twilight of their lives, they were destined to appear in places where they had never been seen before. First, however, came the question of what to do with the two at Addlestone where nine new RLHs were due on 22nd June; the Executive's response was to delicense the pair on the very next day.

Perhaps not really knowing what to do as a long term measure with the recently oil-engined STs, three of the Amersham contingent were dispersed on 31st May to garages that did not really need lowbridge STs and where they were observed to have been employed principally as trainers: ST 141 and 1090 at Watford High Street and ST 163 at Reigate. Only ST 162 went to work immediately on a regular lowbridge service by joining the fleet at Addlestone, where it became surplus on 27th June and was delicensed, as were the trio at Watford and Reigate. All eight STs would now have been out of use had ST 136 not been relicensed on 28th at Merton to join the Daimler utilities on route 127, a service on which it had last worked in red livery back in May 1944. Further revivals followed later in 1950. On 27th September ST 162 went back to Addlestone whilst ST 157 broke into new territory for the class by joining a miscellany of new RLHs and wartime-bodied lowbridge STLs on route 410 (Bromley–Reigate) working from Godstone garage. Even more surprising new territory greeted ST 141 when it was relicensed at Harrow Weald on Central Bus route 230 (Rayners Lane–Northwick Park).

Lowbridge STs were now working at a wider spread of locations than ever before, covering every sphere – other than their 'own' route 336 – of London Transport's very limited range of lowbridge operations. With twenty new RLHs now in stock, and another much larger batch newly ordered for delivery starting in October 1952, it was now inevitable that the STs would be released from service earlier than their previously anticipated date of 1953. In fact when 1951 started out with just four of them in service, it marked the beginning of the last full year of lowbridge ST operation. Many comings and goings took place during the year and for a brief period, between 1st and 9th July 1951, usage of the class reached its nineteen-fifties maximum with seven out of the eight in service, the exception being ST 1089 – the most authentic looking one of all – which had remained idle since it ceased running at Addlestone in June 1950. On 10th July ST 136 at Merton became the first of the type to be permanently withdrawn from service although it may have stopped running somewhat earlier than this, ST 162 having been relicensed for the 127 on 15th June. On 17th September the latter was transferred to Harrow Weald as a replacement for ST 1090 which had run there since July and was finally delicensed with its career ended on the next day. The so-far unused ST 1089 finally came back into service at Godstone on 1st October as a replacement for ST 157 which was temporarily off the road. The year 1952 began with five still going strong at Addlestone (ST 140, 163), Godstone (ST 1089) and Harrow Weald (ST 141, 162)

Five remained the number in use through to October which was destined to be their very last month of service. On

1st February ST 1089 at Godstone was withdrawn in favour of the much more robust and now relicensed ST 157. Then, on 2nd April, came the last big surprise when ST 157 was transferred to East Grinstead, a garage never previously associated with lowbridge double deckers of any sort. Working alongside single deckers from both East Grinstead and Crawley garages, mostly 4Q4s, it took up residence regularly on route 424 (Reigate–East Grinstead).

Spread out over less than three weeks in October 1952, the end came at last. First to go were ST 141 and ST 162 at Harrow Weald which departed on 9th October, just six weeks ahead of the first new RLHs going into service on route 230. Addlestone's pair, ST 140 and ST 163, shared service with the latest RLHs on routes 436 and 461 for five days before being delicensed on 15th October. Last of all was ST 157, delicensed at East Grinstead on 27th October just ahead of the arrival of new RLHs on 1st November. Apart from oddments ekeing their lives out in the service vehicle fleet, the ST days in London were now over, 22 years after they began.

All that was left now was to dispose of them. The glory days of the huge dismantling yard in Ferry Lane, Rainham were but a memory and London Transport now sought to dispose of its surplus stock on a wider basis. ST 141 went first, in December 1952, to C J Green & Company, a dealer in Tooting Bec Road, and the remainder were taken between February and April 1953 by W North of Leeds Ltd, the famous dealer and scrap merchant under whose auspices huge numbers of old London buses met their fate in the nineteen fifties. The last to go to North's huge yard at Sherburn in Elmet was ST 163 on 16th April 1953.

Top right Until it went for overhaul and rebuilding in February 1948 ST 141 also retained its original front end and side mouldings, but these were then lost although the oval window was allowed to remain. This view of the rear shows the revised emergency window and platform arrangement installed before the war. In the case of ST 141 (even in its 1948 rebuilt form) and also STs 162 and 1089, the emergency window divider had a plain central bar; on all the others a typical London Transport Y-style window was fitted.

Centre right On loan to Harrow Weald from Merton, ST 136 presents an opportunity at Rayners Lane to note the rear end's unusual mixture of styles. At the top, the generally rounded contour and the STL type emergency window give a fair impersonation of mid-1930s styling. Down below the original contour of the Short Bros body, including the typically rounded platform window, miraculously survive, but even more surprising is the retention of the narrow platform cut-away many years after this was eliminated from other vehicles in the fleet. *Peter Mitchell*

Bottom right Differing from ST 136 in many respects, but sharing with it a new green and cream livery, is ST 157, the last lowbridge ST ever to receive an overhaul. The provision of a substantial moulding above the lower deck windows has enabled a cream band to be provided which was absent from ST 136, but at the same time the oval staircase window was removed. The scene is Bromley North station soon after ST 157 began its spell at Godstone on route 410 in September 1950.

The withdrawal of Addlestone's STs left ST 157 as the sole survivor of the class in public service with London Transport, but only for twelve more days. During its six final months based at East Grinstead ST 157 could usually be found on route 424, as in this scene at Reigate, but it was also known to make occasional forays on to parts of route 409. *Ken Blacker*

CHAPTER 23
AFTERLIFE

The postscript to the story of the STs is, like that of the LTs in the companion volume, inevitably brief because so many of them met their fate in the yards of Cox & Danks at Feltham and R L Daniels at Rainham which, in their time, both presented a mass spectacle of once familiar London buses in various stages of dismantling before finally going up in smoke.

Had the war not intervened the story might have been different. Scheduled withdrawals of STs had commenced in August 1939, and had the vehicles concerned not been held back from disposal in case of war emergencies, their still fairly new and quite modern chassis might well, in some cases, have found new owners as occurred with many T-type AEC Regals. In fact only 29 STs passed out of London Transport ownership during the six years of war (excluding, of course, those destroyed by enemy action), and 20 of these went in a single deal to the Home Guard in December 1940 and January 1941. As recorded in chapter 18 the nineteen Tilling and one 'pirate' chassis involved had mostly suffered war damage resulting in their bodies being scrapped and leaving the chassis to be converted into armoured cars, a role which they undertook for little more than two years. Prior disposals of complete vehicles had been four Tillings (ST 841, 901, 1013, 1014) which were sold to the British Broadcasting Corporation in May 1940. In July 1940 a single Tilling, ST 930, passed to the Ministry of Supply and in September of the same year a similar vehicle, ST 886, went to the Admiralty at Devonport. The first and only wartime sales of LGOC type STs were also to the Admiralty, with ST 777 going in December 1942 followed by ST 337, 798 in June 1943.

Pile them high! A sad ending after nearly two decades of service is this funeral pyre of bodies at Feltham awaiting the final torch. The only one clearly identifiable is ST 53 which was withdrawn from service at Hounslow in March 1949, but the Tilling ST below it retains its final route number and destination right to the final bonfire indicating that its last duty had been in the Special Events fleet. *Fred Ivey*

The fate of most STs was sealed by the condition of their bodywork, but all the clues with ST 606 point in a different direction. The freshly painted front wheel, mudguards, dumbirons and radiator top indicate that it was undergoing a major docking when it was condemned, as does the freshly cleaned up paintwork. The contrasting back wheel and axle are probably a pointer to the problem area which brought the process to a an abrupt halt. ST 606 was withdrawn at Palmers Green on 24th February 1949, depriving the Daily Mail of its full benefit from the recently applied front posters advertising the Ideal Home Exhibition which was not due to open until 1st March. *Fred Ivey*

Not immediately obvious as an ST, this unworldly-looking contraption with only the tiniest of windscreens was one of the twenty armoured cars constructed in Chiswick Works where the photograph was taken. The chassis has been cut short just behind the rear axle to accommodate the strange new bodywork. It can be identified by the fleet number ST 901 and chassis number 661624 which are painted on top of the camouflage just ahead of the front wheel. The chassis was later returned to London Transport who sold it to Steel Breakers for scrapping in October 1945. *L T Museum*

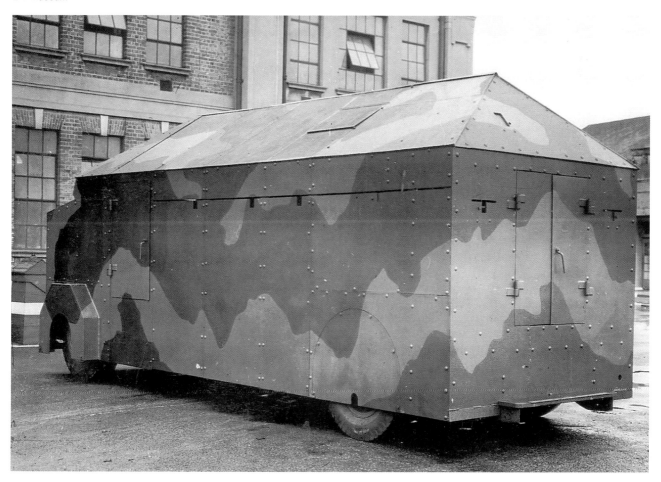

The very first STs to pass to new owners for continued use as public service vehicles came not from London Transport but from the BBC which, with the war ended and their services no longer required, withdrew ST 841, 1013, 1014 in August 1946 and sold them to Ellen Wright, the owner of Grey Saloon Coaches, for contract work in the Southend-on-Sea area. This was short lived and is believed to have ceased by December of the same year, and at least one ended up as a lorry. The fourth BBC vehicle, ST 909, was more fortunate and could be found masquerading as a coach for Sharpe's of Grays until the end of the decade.

With very few exceptions, such as ST 675 which went in January 1948 to the Westinghouse Brake & Signal Company for use as a mobile test bed for braking apparatus, London Transport sold very few STs direct to new owners for further use in the post-war period. Neither did R L Daniels although the latter had permission to do so provided that the vehicles concerned were not used on stage carriage work. Some of the few that 'got away' are illustrated here. More readily on view to the casual observer were the 15 STs which, between 1942 and 1947, were converted into service vehicles, all of which outlasted the main ST fleet and were operational into the early nineteen-fifties and, in one case, well beyond this. They were:

New and former No.			*Conv*	*Wdn*
625J	ST 937	5 ton breakdown tender	1/41	(b)
646J (a)	ST 40	5¾ ton tree lopper	1/43	10/52
647J	ST 985	5¾ ton tree lopper	9/43	5/53
648J	ST 1001	5¾ ton tree lopper	8/43	3/53
650J	ST 865	5¾ ton tree lopper	9/45	1/53
651J	ST 870	5¾ ton tree lopper	9/45	6/53
688J	ST 888	7 ton mobile canteen	9/46	3/52
689J	ST 969	7 ton mobile canteen	12/46	10/51
690J	ST 867	7 ton mobile canteen	12/46	5/53
691J	ST 917	7 ton mobile canteen	1/47	6/52
692J	ST 951	7 ton mobile canteen	3/47	10/51
693J	ST 922	7 ton mobile canteen	4/47	11/54
719J	ST 6	5½ ton towing lorry	1/48	5/55
720J	ST 523	5½ ton towing lorry	2/48	(c)
721J	ST 44	5½ ton towing lorry	2/48	6/55

(a) Ran as ST 40 until July 1945
(b) Withdrawal date not known. Sold October 1963
(c) Withdrawal date not known. Sold August 1955

Though not part of the service vehicle fleet, and not quite an ST either but looking very much like one, was a very special training bus that, from March 1947 onwards, could be found at garages shortly before new RTs were due. Carrying

The now-preserved ST 922 served as mobile canteen 693J from April 1947 onwards, its official base being Merton garage although it seldom returned there unless mechanical rectification was required. The kitchen and a small eating area were situated downstairs, with much more leisure space available on the upper deck for those willing to carry their food up the open staircase, which was not an inviting prospect in wet weather. With no supply of running water, the ST mobile canteens fell far short of today's far more stringent hygiene regulations. *Peter Mitchell*

the fleet number O961079 – which was in fact its chassis number – it was the incongruous combination of a Tilling ST body and a new RT chassis. Very smartly painted in two-tone Green Line livery with gold lettering, it carried the inscription 'Mobile Training Unit', indicating its intended use for training fitters in the intricacies of maintaining and repairing RTs. It was fitted out on the lower deck with an assortment of benches, tables, cupboards and stands. Both decks were sealed by doors and the upper one, which retained most of its seats, was used as a lecture room. Most of the Tilling bodywork remained intact but the front bulkhead had been moved forward by about 3 inches to suit the longer wheelbase and the whole cab structure was, of course, new. At the rear a temporary chassis extension provided support for the platform. The old Tilling body (No. 13922) had come from ST 977 and had not seen service in London since returning from the Rhondda Transport Company in September 1945. In this hybrid form, Tilling O961079 served for no fewer than seven years, and when no longer required for training the chassis emerged with a brand new Weymann body as RT 4761. The old Tilling body was scrapped in May 1954.

Another much lesser known ST to continue working beyond 1950 but not included within the service vehicle fleet was ST 314. This had been withdrawn from service at Mortlake in March 1948 and most of its body was removed and burnt two months later. The section of the vehicle that remained was employed as a towing lorry principally for use within Chiswick Works. It survived through to 1954 and was dismantled in May of that year.

Viewed from the back, O961079 could quite easily be mistaken for a standard Tilling ST, although the rear wheel embellishment looked somewhat incongruous as did the Green Line-style livery. At the front, the design of the cab, fully maximising the benefit of the RT's unusually low bonnet line, was far neater than the arrangement applied several years earlier to ST 1140. *Peter Mitchell/A D Packer*

For some unknown reason ST 314 was never included as part of the service vehicle fleet even though the work it performed made it a wholly appropriate candidate. Adapted in March 1948 with cut down bodywork and permanently attached starting handle, it proved handy for towing defective buses within Chiswick Works and to the scrap yards. See here at Chiswick in the company of a redundant CR and 4Q4, it was not finally dismantled until July 1954 and was thus the last ST officially remaining within the London Transport fleet. *London Tramways Trust*

One of the few STs not sold direct to a breaker after the war was ST 962 which was withdrawn from service at Old Kent Road in May 1948. With the top deck removed at Chiswick, it was presented to the British Legion jointly by London Transport and the Ministry of Pensions and could be seen in this form in and around London for a number of years. *Allen T Smith*

A sad consequence of war was the massive surge in the number of unfortunate people requiring prosthetic limbs. Body 10621, removed from ST 319 in September 1939, was donated to Roehampton Hospital in December 1944 where the severed rear end was used for giving amputees confidence in boarding buses and climbing stairs. This photograph was taken long after the war's end, in January 1951. *Denis Battams*

A Tilling ST which adopted a totally new guise was ST 909, and very few of those who saw it at Derby Day in 1948 could have known that it was once a London double decker. ST 909 was one of those that had spent the war carrying staff for the British Broadcasting Corporation. Henry Sharpe of Grays snapped it up from Mountnessing Auto Spares but the origin of the coach body is not known. *Alan B Cross*

205

The lowbridge STs that enjoyed a brief renaissance on Isle of Grain contract work were amongst the oldest double deckers in the mainly Leyland fleet of Wilberjim Coaches. The thick moulding above the lower deck windows identifies this one as being the former ST 157.
John C Gillham

Of greater potential for sale to third parties for further passenger use when they finally came off service were the eight lowbridge STs with their much sought after 7.7 diesel engines, and in fact W North of Leeds, who purchased seven of them, promptly found a new home for four with J H W Watson of Strood, better known as Wilberjim Coaches. ST 140, 157, 162 and 1089 all arrived at their new home in Kent in April 1953 and were promptly repainted into Wilberjim's brown and cream colours for workers' services to the Isle of Grain oil refinery. However, as in the case of the Grey Saloon Coaches on the other side of the Thames estuary a few years earlier, the requirement for them was brief and appears to have ended by April 1954.

Of only two STs still in existence in this country, the longest in continuous preservation is ST 821 which was last licensed for passenger service at Watford High Street on 26th May 1949. On the next day it was taken to Chiswick for assessment and was duly selected as the bus that would be preserved by London Transport to represent the ST class whose days were then rapidly drawing to an end. It appears that physical condition rather than any historical considera-tion was the deciding factor in choosing ST 821 in preference to a vehicle more typical of the class as a whole, and the fact

that it had been overhauled as comparatively recently as December 1947 would undoubtedly have been taken into consideration. It was one of the batch of four supplied to National in February and March 1931 and, having never run in the Central area, it was still in green livery and typical of Country STs in still retaining the small front indicator box accessed from within the upper saloon, with no destination display at all at the rear. A plus point in its favour, however, was that it still retained its original body and chassis which would not have been the case had a more typical ST been chosen. On 11th January 1950 ST 821 was officially trans-ferred to the museum fleet and two months later it moved to Reigate where, in the old East Surrey annex, most of London Transport's museum fleet was then housed. Whilst at Reigate and out of public view ST 821 was given a fresh coat of paint which, unfortunately, was Central Bus red, a livery which it had never carried in London Transport days. A move to the splendid Museum of British Transport at Clapham in February 1960 heralded more than four decades of public display. The Clapham museum closed in 1971 but ST 821 moved, along with the London Transport elements of the former collection to temporary exhibition premises at Syon Park in 1973, and in March 1980 to the much bigger and better premises at Covent Garden by which time it was back in authentic green livery. At the time of writing ST 821 remains in the London Transport Museum collection but is back in store at its offsite premises at Acton and is only on occasional public view.

Having run at Hounslow until December 1948, ST 309 was another rarity that did not pass direct from London Transport to a breaker. The buyer on this occasion was a Mr. J Lever of Cottenham, Cambridgeshire, and ST 309 ended its life as a store shed in nearby Sutton. Photographed in April 1961 it was still largely complete albeit dilapidated, but the few preservationists existing at that time did not have the funds to save it. *G R Mills*

ST 346 ended its working days at Kingston in August 1949, departing from there on the 18th to Daniels' yard at Rainham. The only ST known to have emerged from there in one piece, it was subsequently used by the renowned Ballet Montmartre for its British tour with the back modified, presumably to accommodate stage props and scenery, and a neat protective doorway for the driver. After the tour was over, ST 346 returned to Rainham and was scrapped. *D C Fisk*

A miscellany of vehicles in St Albans garage typifies the fascinating and mixed scene to be found in 1949 with, on the right, tree lopper 646J – alias ST 40 – carrying the ex-Lewis Short Bros body formerly on ST 1138. Also present are 6Q6 Q 236, green ST 158 from the training fleet, and 4Q4 Q46. *D A Jones*

A much more dramatic preservation success, which can be attributed almost entirely to the foresight and forcefulness of the late Prince Marshall, is that of Tilling ST 922. This had almost certainly not carried fare paying passengers since working for Midland Red during the war, but from May 1945 it undertook a spell of 'learner' duties from various garages until being delicensed on 1st December 1946. Then came conversion into mobile canteen 693J in which role it outlived its fellow canteen conversions to end its working days for London Transport in November 1954. In its latter years it had been based at Sutton garage and was a familiar sight on the bus stand at Belmont. Its withdrawal did not quite mark the end of its career, however, for British Road Services needed a canteen for construction workers building a new site at Tufnell Park and purchased 693J in May 1955. About two years later it was surplus to requirements and passed to Rush Green Motors where it remained, towering prominently over a sea of used cars and gradually deteriorating, until rescued by Prince Marshall in about December 1966.

The complete restoration that followed, and its subsequent relicensing as a psv in April 1972, was a considerable achievement and a tribute to those who helped to supply the funds for this remarkable work to be carried out. ST 922's return to passenger service on special route 100 under the auspices of Prince Marshall's Obsolete Fleet has gone down in the annals of London bus history. After Mr Marshall's death in 1981 ST 922 remained in the custody of Obsolete Fleet until its ownership passed to the London Bus Preservation Trust in January 1984. ST 922 was based at the Trust's museum in Cobham for many years, but since 2011 it has featured prominently in the new London Bus Museum at Brooklands and, being in much better structural condition than ST 821, it still carries passengers from time to time.

One other ST is known to remain in existence as a static museum piece and, though nowadays much altered from its original condition, it is the sole surviving representative of the many hundreds of standard LGOC STs once so familiar to Londoners. As recorded earlier in this chapter, ST 798 was one of a pair sold in June 1943 to the Royal Navy who repainted it from the brown livery, which it then wore, to grey and converted it into an anti-submarine warfare simulator. Based latterly at Chatham and carrying naval registration number 81RN81, it was included in a 1953 sale to the fledgling Israeli navy of various naval craft including second-hand submarines and destroyers. At the time of writing it is an exhibit at the Clandestine Immigration and Naval Museum in Allenby Street, Haifa, where it is regarded as an important part of Israeli naval history. For this reason, entreaties to allow its return to the UK have proved unsuccessful.

ST 922's renaissance as a London bus on special service 100 on 29th March 1980, reviving London Transport's attractive livery of the nineteen-thirties, was a remarkable achievement by Obsolete Fleet. Its operational base at the time was the old London Transport (and former National Steam Car Company) garage at Nunhead which had itself been no stranger to STs in earlier days. The Cenotaph is in the background as ST 922 glides from Whitehall into Parliament Street.

Having now been in preservation for more than half a century without any major work having been carried out on it, London Transport Museum's ST 821 is now a valuable if somewhat frail historic gem. Now in correct green livery after an earlier spell of inappropriate red, ST 821 is a nostalgic reminder of the ST class as it appeared in its final years. Unfortunately, unlike ST 922, it is no longer on regular public display, but can be viewed intermittently at the Museum's premises in Acton. *Neil Chilvers*